Promotional Practices and Perspectives from Emerging Markets

This volume explores the dynamic nature of emerging markets, which constitute a major share of global GDP, with a focus on the opportunities for growth and the challenges for businesses in meeting the needs of a diverse set of consumers.

With the objective to ensure sustainable growth, there is a need for multinationals belonging to and working in emerging economies to learn best practices and continuously evolve. To conduct business in both urban and rural areas, marketing and promotions are potent tools when applied correctly to portray the right brand image. The book studies recent trends and developments in promotional practices as business strategy, sustainability, and innovation across businesses, including retail, textile, and digital technology. It highlights the path that managers should take in order to better understand the potential of distinct market segments and take marketing managerial decisions accordingly.

This book will be useful to scholars and researchers of marketing, management studies, business management, financial management, business economics, international business, finance, digital technologies, development studies, and economics. It will also interest policymakers and practitioners in the field.

Sudhir Rana is Associate Professor in College of Healthcare Management and Economics at the Gulf Medical University, Ajman, UAE.

Avinash K Shrivastava is Assistant Professor at International Management Institute, Kolkata, West Bengal, India.

Sachin Kumar Raut is a full-time doctoral scholar in the Department of Marketing at Fortune Institute of International Business, New Delhi, India, and Cotutelle Doctoral Scholar in the Department of Business and Law at the University of Agder, Norway.

Advances in Emerging Markets and Business Operations

Series Editors:

Avinash K Shrivastava
International Management Institute, Kolkata, West Bengal, India

Sudhir Rana
College of Healthcare Management and Economics, Gulf Medical University, Ajman, UAE

This series hosts key debates on themes, issues and advancements taking place in emerging markets and new ways of handling challenges in operating businesses in emerging markets. It explores doing business in emerging markets from multidisciplinary and multinational geographic perspectives based on fresh theoretical and empirical research, qualitative and quantitative reviews, data and case studies. The series aims to cover a wide range of aspects in business and operations, including opportunities and progress, with a focus on emerging markets and economies:

- *Comparison of Traditional versus Modern Business Models* used by firms from developed economies and emerging economies; entrepreneurial innovations; digitalization; technology and businesses strategies for sustainable development; service innovation and management; mergers and acquisitions.

- *Advancement in Business Practices* including general practices within finance; human resource management; marketing; international business; information technology; operations; and specific practices such as product & service development; investments; governance and policies; role of government.

- *Doing Business* in sectors such as manufacturing; services; retail; B2B; supply chain and distribution; transportation; cross-culture; consumer and market behaviour; automation and technology; retail and luxury; human capital; emerging brands; selecting and investing in emerging markets; benefits and challenges; foreign direct investment; growing business sectors.

- *Operational Aspects* in supply and demand chain management and logistics; manufacturing processes optimization; project management and scheduling; total quality management; transportation and logistics management.

- *Methodological Progress in Research and Business Education* such as industry disruptions and role of analytics; impact of analytics on culture and business environment; decision sciences; operations research; business intelligence tools and applications; multi-criteria decision-making; scientific and software-based research (big data, soft computing, artificial intelligence, neural networks, fuzzy logic, evolutionary algorithms); and business curriculum, pedagogy, and accreditations of business schools.

The series offers a comprehensive understanding of management and its allied domains within the context of emerging markets and economies, especially international business, economics, marketing, finance, operations and supply chain management, human resources and governance. It will be useful to both scholars and practitioners interested in interdisciplinary research on emerging markets, business analytics, business models, consultancy and policy.

Doing Business in Emerging Markets
Progress and Promises
Edited by Sudhir Rana and Avinash K Shrivastava

Emerging Trends in Decision Sciences and Business Operations
Edited by Avinash K Shrivastava and Sudhir Rana

Promotional Practices and Perspectives from Emerging Markets
Edited by Sudhir Rana, Avinash K Shrivastava and Sachin Kumar Raut

For more information about this Series, please visit: www.routledge.com/ Advances-in-Emerging-Markets-and-Business-Operations/book-series/ AEMBO

Promotional Practices and Perspectives from Emerging Markets

Edited by Sudhir Rana, Avinash K Shrivastava and Sachin Kumar Raut

LONDON AND NEW YORK

First published 2023
by Routledge
4 Park Square, Milton Park, Abingdon, Oxon OX14 4RN

and by Routledge
605 Third Avenue, New York, NY 10158

Routledge is an imprint of the Taylor & Francis Group, an informa business

British Library Cataloguing-in-Publication Data
A catalogue record for this book is available from the British Library

Library of Congress Cataloging-in-Publication Data
A catalog record for this book has been requested

ISBN: 978-1-032-26914-6 (hbk)
ISBN: 978-1-032-32549-1 (pbk)
ISBN: 978-1-003-31558-2 (ebk)

DOI: 10.4324/9781003315582

Typeset in Sabon
by Apex CoVantage, LLC

Contents

Figures

Tables

Contributors

Manpreet Arora teaches in the School of Commerce and Management at Central University of Himachal Pradesh, India. Besides 4 co-edited books, she has more than 40 research papers and book chapters to her credit. Her interest areas include Accounting and Finance, Strategic Management, Communication, and Qualitative and Interdisciplinary Research.

Søren Askegaard is Professor of Marketing, Researcher in Glocal Consumer Cultures and current President of the International Consumer Culture Theory Consortium.

Arpan Bumb is Graduate Student at Birla Institute of Technology and Science, Pilani, Rajasthan, India.

Surajit Ghosh Dastidar (Ph.D. IIT Kharagpur) is Associate Professor and HOD – Marketing at EIILM-Kolkata.

Aurelia Ilies is a Ph.D. student in Economics and International Business at Alexandru Ioan Cuza University of Iasi, Romania.

Gauri Joshi is Assistant Professor at Symbiosis Centre of Management and Human Resource Development, a constituent of the Symbiosis International University, Pune, India. Her research interest is in Consumer Behaviour towards Sustainability.

Kanupriya is Doctoral Scholar at Indian Institute of Foreign Trade, New Delhi, India.

Ravi Kulkarni did his Ph.D. in Mathematics from Pune University, Pune, India. His research interests include Multivariate Analysis and Text Analysis.

Piotr Kwiatek is Associate Professor of Marketing at Kozminski University, in Warsaw, Poland, focusing on Customer Relationship Management.

Madhuri Mahato is Engineering Graduate and holds a dual Master's degree in the area of Human Resource Management to her credit. She is also a Ph.D., UGC NET holder, and an Internationally Certified trainer with around 12 years of experience. She is currently associated with Amity University Jharkhand, India, as Assistant Professor and Program Coordinator (Management and Allied Division).

Junaid Mohammed is Bachelor of Management Studies at the School of Management and Entrepreneurship at Shiv Nadar University, Greater Noida, Uttar Pradesh, India, a recognised institute of eminence.

Rajesh Panda is Professor at Xavier Institute of Management, XIM University, Bhubaneswar, India. His research interests are in Online Shopper Behaviour, Retailing, International Trade, etc.

Stavros Papakonstantinidis is Associate Professor of Communication Studies at Central College, Pella, IA, USA, focusing on Strategic Communication.

Bikramjit Rishi is Associate Professor of Marketing at the Institute of Management Technology (IMT), Ghaziabad, India.

Gerardo del Cerro Santamarîa served as Visiting Scholar at the London School of Economics in Political Science.

Aditi Sharma is pursuing her Ph.D. in Marketing Capabilities from the Department of Commerce, University of Jammu, India. She has participated in several conferences, seminars, workshops, and webinars.

Bodh Raj Sharma is Profound Researcher in the field of Marketing. His areas of interest are Consumer Behaviour, Marketing Capabilities, and retailing ethics and digital retailing. He has published research papers in the journals of national and international repute.

Roshan Lal Sharma teaches English in Central University of Himachal Pradesh, India. Besides having 17 books to his credit, he has published more than 60 research papers and book chapters in journals and books of repute. His interest areas include Indian Writing in English, Literary and Cultural Theory, Mystical Poetry, Comparative Literature, Business Communication, and Qualitative and Interdisciplinary Research.

Sangeeta Sharma is Associate Professor at Department of Humanities and Social Sciences, Birla Institute of Technology and Science, Pilani, Rajasthan, India.

Pratima Sheorey is Director and Professor at the Symbiosis Centre for Management and Human Resource Development, a constituent of the Symbiosis International University, Pune, India. Her research interest is in Consumer Behaviour and Consumer Engagement and Loyalty.

Kira Strandby is interested in Consumer Culture in general and Digitalization in the global South in particular.

Julie Vardhan is Academician with more than 17 years of experience, encompassing both academics and industry. She was associated for around a decade with Manipal University in Dubai prior to joining Amity University Jharkhand.

Promotion Perspectives and Practices in Emerging Markets

*Sudhir Rana, Avinash K Shrivastava
and Sachin Kumar Raut*

The times when world's economy was powered by Western Europe, the United States, and Japan are old gone. With the fast-paced growth of the emerging economies, now the 59 percent of the total global GDP (on the basis of purchasing parity) is being shared by the emerging markets (Muller, 2018). With the saturation of developed economies and markets, the multinationals have increased their set-up in the new and emerging markets to capture new and wider range of customer base. The global downturn in the economy has spurred these multinationals to explore prospects around the globe. A number of multinationals based in developed world are using local strategies to wield their way in the economy. Emerging markets are sharing the global economy at differential pace which created heterogeneity among these economies (Buckley & Ghauri, 2004). They include markets as diverse as Peru, China, Ghana, and India (to name a few). These countries have diverse segments of customers ranging from high income to low income, with majority being low income (Prahalad, 2010). Addressing the needs of each segment with niche promotional and marketing strategies is important consideration the companies need to keep in mind before entering in new emerging markets (Dalgic & Leeuw, 1994). Large population in these markets is also a unique advantage in the emerging markets (Wilson & Purushothaman, 2003). This helps a company to develop a promotional strategy niche to that large segment of the population. For example, food brands like Dunkin Donuts have differently flavoured donuts according to the market they are serving to; similarly, when Dominos entered Asian market, it had sea food toppings for most of the Asian countries while for India it uses curry. Therefore, understanding the cultural differences and tying up with local partners can help the firms in ensuring best promotional and marketing strategies and enable the global entrant to attain market leadership at much sooner pace (Rao-Nicholson & Khan, 2017).

Business in emerging economies are continuously responding to the changes taking place in the dynamic business environment. The past two

DOI: 10.4324/9781003315582-1

decades have enabled them (emerging economies) gather steam around their high-potential and a high-market share. Modernization, government initiatives, shifts in education management, and the revolution brought in by the young and the millennial have helped to bring about this change. The businesses and firms in the developed economies are cashing in on the opportunities from emerging markets, and they, in turn, find advantages that can be garnered from the rest of the world. Rana et al. (2020) found out that the pace of growth has slowed in the developed economies and increased in the emerging markets which are low-income countries. Multinational enterprises like TCS, Huawei, AirAsia, and Embraer in emerging economies like China, India, Malaysia, Vietnam, Turkey, and Brazil are reaping benefits of market share across industries all over the world through innovation and technology (Rana et al., 2020). In order to ensure sustainable growth, the need to learn best practices from each other and continuously evolve becomes even more relevant for the multinationals in emerging economies to climb up the ladder. The best strategy for an emerging market player would be to understand the needs of the local consumers and evolve with them. To reach the countryside or dwellers in the towns, marketing and promotions are potent tools when applied rightly to portray the right brand image and include most of the market. Through this book, the managers will be able to better understand the potential of the distinct market segment and accordingly take marketing managerial decisions to form promotional strategies. Competitive advantage can be built by understanding what new can be bought to customers and drive it into a need for them.

Chapter 1: Hybrid Forms of Governance: The Franchise System is contributed by Aureliea Ilies. Franchising is widely associated with well established, profitable companies that seek to develop by imposing their business model on a national or international level through franchisees. The franchisor's decision to franchise instead of keeping his business is based on his desire to grow his business as much as possible, for which purpose he needs capital, and to be present in as many markets as possible even if it involves losing control of the business. From the franchisee's point of view, the decision is mainly based on the fact that he has access to scarce resources that he could not procure under different conditions. This chapter analyses the theory behind the choice between different types of hybrid organizations with a focus on the franchise system.

Chapter 2: Why Consumers Respond to Deals is contributed by Surajit Ghosh Dastidar. Consumer sales promotion deal is increasingly being used by the marketers as a powerful component of the marketing mix. The primary objective is to differentiate the brand and augur its utility, with the aim to stimulate its demand. However, to ensure the effectiveness of sales promotion campaigns, marketers need to identify their target audience and understand why they respond to specific deals. This shall enable marketers to ensure that the deals appeal to the target consumers, and they perceive it as a value addition. This chapter aims to present a framework of the various correlates of consumers' deal-responsive behaviour based on review of extant literature. These have been discussed from both consumer and marketing perspectives.

Chapter 3: Entrepreneurship in Emerging Markets: An Empirical Study on Digital Natives in Kuwait is contributed by Stavros Papakonstantinidis and Piotr Kwiatek. This chapter decodes the entrepreneurial mindset of the Digital Natives living in the Middle East, particularly in Kuwait. It answers what needs to be done in an emerging market and in a wealthy state such as Kuwait to enhance entrepreneurship. This empirical study investigates Digital Natives' entrepreneurial capacity (EC) and entrepreneurial intention (EI) using the scales adopted from the Entrepreneurial Intention Question-naire (EIQ). The study offers evidence showing the role of technology as a driving force for increasing Digital Natives' entrepreneurial capacity. Also, it discusses the practical implications of encouraging entrepreneurship and reducing anxiety. This study contributes to the literature being the first to explore the entrepreneurial mindset of the Digital Natives living in Kuwait.

Chapter 4: Early Bird Catches the Worm: Exploring Promotional Capa-bility of retailers is contributed by Bodh Raj Sharma and Aditi Sharma. Promotion represents the most crucial element of the marketing mix for acquiring and retaining customers. However, the promotion strategy needs to be carefully formulated and implemented as various promotional cam-paigns have varying outcomes ranging from the creation of awareness about the product, attracting customers to retail outlets, and demonstration of the products by the salespeople. The study empirically explores the promotional capability of retailers on the basis of the data obtained from customers and retailers through the questionnaires. With the dyadic approach and cross-validation, there can be more lucidity about the nature and extent of the promotional capability of retailers. The findings indicate that retailers apply advertising and sales promotion to present their brands and attract custom-ers by offering huge discounts, coupons, gifts, vouchers, and extra benefits for increasing their sales and margins. The findings of the study provide implications for retailers, customers, researchers, and decision-makers.

Chapter 5: The First is Free: Promoting Facebook in Emerging Markets is contributed by Kira Strandby and Søren Askegaard. While the Internet has effectively conquered the minds and lives of consumers in large parts of the world, it remains to some an elusive and valuable resource. In an apparent quest to close the digital divide, companies such as Facebook engage in tech philanthropy – offering variations of their services for free in low-income markets. This practice has been contested by advocates of net-neutrality, who believe that such practices create an unequal playing field for smaller actors in the marketplace, ultimately leading to less competition and inno-vation. This study explores how Facebook uses zero-rating as a promotion tool, not only a standard process in an extensive number of emerging mar-kets but also a contested practice, subject to interdiction in countries like India or Brazil. This study focuses on the context of Uganda. Concluding thoughts reflect on notions of power and exploitation in the 'Realpolitik' of developing contexts.

Chapter 6: Globalization and Innovation Districts: R+D, Knowledge Exchanges, and Assemblages is contributed by Gerardo del Cerro Santamaría. This chapter addresses the recent development of innovation districts as a distinct spatial formation aimed simultaneously at economic development and urban regeneration. Innovation districts initially obey the logic of the market and the location decisions of specific companies. To meet this demand, many metropolitan governments have decided to plan and create innovation districts as a tool for development, regeneration, and the global promotion of their cities. The chapter also explores the knowledge environment that is typical of innovation districts, where high density and high frequency interactions among experts and practitioners contribute to fostering innovative outputs. Knowledge exchanges are based on social learning, collective intelligence, and the specific epistemic culture in any given innovation district. They are best explained with a metaphor of assemblages, which highlights the hybrid character of knowledge and innovation production. The chapter ends by exploring some promising research directions: socio-materiality, complexity and holism and trans-disciplinarity.

Chapter 7: Impact of Creativity in Advertising on Customer's Recall Value: A Perspective from Emerging Markets is contributed by Sangeeta Sharma and Arpan Bumb. Globalization has substantially bolstered international competition, requiring marketers to come out with innovative strategies in designing the advertisements. If the advertisement is brimming with creativity, it can create an indelible impact on the mind of the viewers. There are different techniques used by advertisers to break the clutter, thus making the advertisement conspicuous. Through this chapter an attempt is made to study the parameters which are included in creative advertisements such as fluency, flexibility, emotional connect, and linking unrelated details. The study also presents the parameters in form of a model using exploratory and confirmatory factor analysis and utilizes structural equation modelling statistical techniques to unravel the role of creative parameters on recall value. The study finds that creativity leads to an increase in unaided recall value of the advertisements hence providing advertisers a tool in their arsenal to design creative advertisements, in turn, increasing the recall value.

Chapter 8: Energy Star Labels in Promoting Energy: Efficient Appliances in India is contributed by Gauri Joshi, Pratima Sheorey, Rajesh Panda, and Ravi Kulkarni. Sustainable consumption refers to the act of purchasing products which are environmentally friendly, reduce waste, and use relatively lesser natural resources as compared to conventional products. These sustainable products are identified by the product labels which differ from the conventional labels and are termed as eco-labels. Eco-labels are used to award and promote environmentally enhanced goods and services and offer information on quality and performance with respect to consumer health, resource consumption, and so on. This chapter focuses on reviewing the various appliance-based energy star labels in the BRIC nations and analyses the barriers to their popularity in a tier 1 city of India. The study checks for the consumer's perceptions of energy stars ratings on the appliances and identifies the barriers hindering consumers from purchase eco-labelled appliance. It uses the mixed method approach along with PLSPM for quantitative analysis. It checks the mediating impact of the barriers between consumer's green purchase intentions and behaviour. The chapter has policy-related recommendations for the promotion of energy-star-labelled appliances in emerging economy like India.

Chapter 9: Cultural Marketing in the Indian Textiles Industry: A comprehensive Perspective is contributed by Kanupriya. This study seeks to locate the Indian textiles industry in the cultural marketing milieu. The chapter discusses the theme through an extensive review of literature and examples from contemporary textiles advertising in India of Jack and Jones and Myntra brands. The study explains some of the desirable and undesirable characteristics in cultural marketing, the challenges, and future prospects of the same for the Indian textiles industry. In sum, the Indian textiles industry holds tremendous promise for the strategists of cultural marketing both in the present and future times if they look beyond the traditional norms and focus on emerging areas such as environment, gender, and labour sensitivities. All in all, the study succeeds in building a comprehensive conceptual framework on the topic that could serve as important groundwork for any future research on the same.

Chapter 10: Religion and Strategic Marketing Communication: Perspectivizing Key Facets of Consumption is contributed by Manpreet Arora and Roshan Lal Sharma. Religion has always occupied a place of prominence in people's lives the world over. At one point, its practice would serve as a means of salvation/self-actualization; but it would never be viewed as a way of making money. In recent years, there has been a shift in the perception of religion as a commodity/product/brand that can be produced, packaged, advertised, and sold by business concerns to the masses. People remain oblivious about the capital investment involved in marketizing religion and the profit that eventually accrues to the coffers of business houses. This chapter deals with the communicative dimension of marketing of religion to demonstrate how business concerns today benefit enormously from religious practices that require whole range of products/materials. After surveying available literature concerning religion and its consumption, the research questions will be formulated related to diverse dimensions of the consumption of religion, communicative dimension of its marketing/advertising, and future potential of its consumption across the world. The chapter will also highlight how marketing and commoditization of religion after a point start regulating even value-registers, belief system, and buying behaviour of the consumers. Consumption of religion today has become an industry with huge marketing potential and never-plummeting demand for products used in religious practices.

Chapter 11: Design, Execute, and Manage Promotions: Study on Social Media Platforms is contributed by Bikramjit Rishi and Junaid Mohammed. The advent of social media and the applications that followed continue to hold significant influence in today's market landscape. An ever-evolving area, social media has gone from being solely a source of information delivery to an agent of change which bought about a revolutionary shift in methods of marketing, ways of perceiving consumer behaviour, predictive analyses, and more. Citing to the increasing ability of Internet access, the usage of social media has only strengthened its stronghold at every corner of the world. Synchronously, companies and businesses found it imperative to be present in social media circles to amplify their marketing initiatives. With a large of businesses being active on social media, the urgency of having a strategic approach to performing on the social media surfaced. So the chapter proposes a framework of social media strategy, which would further inspire social media goals and objectives, identifying target audiences and social media channels and designing an experience. The chapter explains how the effectiveness of these strategies is constantly put to test and scrutiny through metrics indicative of how adroitly the strategy materialized on-ground. In the end, the chapter concludes that social media and its dynamicity bring challenges in strategy implementation and its outcomes.

Chapter 12: Prosocial Behaviour and Impact of Influencers During Crisis: A Study Based on Sentiment Analysis is contributed by Julie Vardhan and Madhuri Mahato. As organizations, products, and individuals identify relevant social media platforms to engage with communities, there are a group of individuals who have gained a wide follower base by branding themselves as experts in areas like fashion, nutrition, style, social ideas, or political viewpoints. Considered as micro-celebrities or social media influencers or influencers, these individuals are gaining a wider audience among the youth and millennial generation than the traditional celebrities. The chapter proposes to understand the role of influencers in bringing out the prosocial behaviours during the recent pandemic.

References

Buckley, P. J., & Ghauri, P. N. (2004). Globalisation, economic geography and the strategy of multinational enterprises. *Journal of International Business Studies*, 35, 81–98.

Dalgic, T., & Leeuw, M. (1994). Niche marketing revisited: Concept, applications and some European cases. *European Journal of Marketing*, 28(4), 39–55.

Muller, D. (2018). *Emerging Markets Powerhouse of Global Growth*. Ashmore. Retrieved from: www.ashmoregroup.com/sites/default/files/article-docs/MC_10%20May18_2.pdf.

Prahalad, C. K. (2010). *Fortune at the Bottom of the Pyramid: Eradicating Poverty Through Profits* (5th ed.). New Delhi: Pearson Education.

Rao-Nicholson, R., & Khan, Z. (2017). Standardization versus adaptation of global marketing strategies in emerging market cross-border acquisitions. *International Marketing Review*, 34(1), 138–158.

Rana, S., Prashar, S., Barai, M. K., & Hamid, A. B. A. (2020). Determinants of international marketing strategy for emerging market multinationals. *International Journal of Emerging Markets*, https://doi.org/10.1108/IJOEM-09-2019-0742.

Wilson, D., & Purushothaman, R. (2003). *Dreaming with BRICs: The Path to 2050. Global Economics*. Paper No. 99. Goldman Sachs, New York.

1 Hybrid Forms of Governance

The Franchise System

Aurelia Ilies

Introduction

The present study aims at a brief appraisal of governance structures focusing on hybrid institutional arrangements, identified and analysed from different angles by many authors during the last century. We note, however, the major contributions of the authors who outlined the theory of governance structures with a starting point in the work of R. Coase, *The Nature of the Firm* (1937), and continuing with O. Williamson in *Markets and Hierarchies* (1975). It is also necessary in this context to mention C. Ménard because he was the one who provided the image and content of the different types of hybrid arrangements in *The Economics of Hybrid Organisations* (2004) and especially in a previous article, *On Clusters, Hybrids and Other Strange Forms: The Case of French Poultry Industry* (1996).

Franchising as a form of organization of economic activity had been registered as being one of the fastest developments in the world. This way of doing business is widespread in most areas of activity because it presents much lower risks compared to other hybrid arrangements and at the same time brings considerable benefits to the partners involved. This form of organisation requires continuous collaboration and a common system of rules of conduct to follow.

The chapter is based on the key concepts outlined on hybrid governance structures, with an emphasis on organisation through the franchise contract. This way of organising best meets the needs identified by both the franchisor and the franchisee due to the mutual benefits arising from this agreement. Proof of the efficiency of the organisation mode is the spread of this type of business worldwide and in all areas of activity. The franchise implies a form of common planning, the emphasis being on the continuity of cooperation between partners.

The chapter is structured on five parts, namely: *Introduction, Governance structures, The size of the franchise system, Franchise decision,* and *Conclusions.*

DOI: 10.4324/9781003315582-2

Governance structures

Introduction to governance structures

The governance structure, as defined by Oliver Williamson, is 'the institutional matrix within which the whole of a transaction is decided' (Williamson, 2005). In the issue of governance structures, Oliver Williamson is both a consecrated, cited and controversial authority. His work on governance structures is strongly inspired by Ronald Coase who 'linked the efficiency of human efforts to the choice between two major forms of organising economic activities – market or firm – and offered an explanation of this choice in terms of transaction costs' (Pohoață, 2009, pp. 176–177). In this context, governance structures become institutional arrangements, as the author defined them earlier.

The article *The Economics of Governance* written by Oliver Williamson gives us a starting point in understanding governance structures in terms of transaction costs (Williamson, 2005). In defining transaction costs, it identifies ex ante costs, such as those related to negotiations, and ex post, related to the execution part of a contract. In this approach are also revealed the causes of these costs related to the limited rationality of individuals, uncertainty, opportunism, and information asymmetry.

Transactions take place in an uncertain environment and between individuals with limited rationality. Limited rationality does not allow for clairvoyance and the strength of 100 per cent anticipation of the future. At the same time, it is not synonymous with myopia and naivety. Economic agents have sufficient capacity to allow them an 'economising' behaviour; to undertake logical reasoning; to be aware that, objectively, they must enter into contractual relationships and manage their business with minimum costs, transaction, and production; that the transactions do not take place by chance but in a certain organisational environment, be it a market or a company; that, finally, the way in which a transaction is organised (even if the object of the transaction aims at the same good) is defining in the dimensioning of total costs, with different management methods corresponding to different levels of efficiency (Pohoață, 2009, p. 178).

Adherents of organisation theory have long been concerned with choosing how to govern the company because it is a decision of great strategic importance that the company must take and which has a major impact on business performance (Yin and Zajac, 2004; Rana et al., 2021). Therefore, the latest research examines why companies use different governance mechanisms, such as franchising, sales and distribution channels, make-or-buy decisions, or subcontracting, to explain the control over the value of these structures.

For the past 25 years or more, the dominant explanation for the choice of governance mechanism has been effective contracting (Williamson, 1984) which indicates that the choice of the form of governance of the organisation depends largely on the cost–benefit analysis of governance arrangements based on market, and those based on hierarchy. However, there are also researchers who argue that effective contracting would explain only in small proportion the choice of the governance structure of the organisation (Rana et al., 2018), perhaps for the simple reason that these theories do not take into account the dynamics of the governance structure of an organisation and also how this process influences the current decisions of the organisation (Koghut and Zander, 1992; Herrmann and Rana, 2020).

Before moving on to the analysis of hybrid governance structures, we consider it necessary to chronologically frame the two main governance structures: the market and the firm. It is very clear, as it appears from Coase's words, that in the beginning it was the market with determinants as demand, supply, and price system (Raut et al., 2022). As Ménard rightly points out, the market is nothing more than a subset of the various existing institutional arrangements that have been developed to make the transfer of property rights possible (Ménard, 2004).

An alternative to allocating resources through the market is through the firm or in other words, vertical integration. This situation is reached when the transaction costs recorded on the market exceed the benefits, and it is necessary to streamline by choosing a new form of organization (Bhandari and Raut, 2019). It is an alternative to market transactions as noted by Ronald Coase.

> Outside the firm, production is driven by price movements and coordinated through a series of exchange transactions on the market. Within the firm, these market transactions are eliminated, and instead of a complicated market structure, with exchange transactions, we will meet a coordinating entrepreneur who organises and directs the production.
>
> (Coase, 1937, p. 26)

It is therefore clear that these are two alternative methods of coordinating production.

While the market uses the price as a result of the supply–demand ratio, the firm uses hierarchical order as a coordination mechanism. When the cost of using the price mechanism is high, the organisation of activities through vertical integration, under the command of an authority, seems to be more advantageous.

Hybrid governance structures

In the 1991 article *Comparative Economic Organization: The Analysis of Discrete Structural Alternatives*, Oliver Williamson uses for the first time the term 'hybrids' referring to forms of organisation of economic activity that do not correspond to either the attributes of the market or the hierarchy (Williamson, 1991). Pohoață notes that

> the transition from the coasean diptych, market-firm, to the williamso-nian triptych market-firm-hybrid meant a process of factual individu-alisation and theoretical recognition of some transactional forms and governance structures that borrow from the features of the firm or mar-ket without being able to be identified with any of them.
>
> (Pohoață, 2009, p. 187)

In other words, we are talking about hybrid governance structures that encompass both the market relationship, the exchange relying on the price mechanism, and the structures of the hierarchy, thus proving that there is a middle ground here as well; one that combines the virtues of the polar forms leaving aside their minuses, without being, neither pure market forms nor integrated administrative structures one hundred percent. Hybrid institu-tional arrangements encompass the main attributes of the market, as well as of the firm by creating a new different structure.

Hybrid institutional arrangements have been the subject of numerous studies, especially on inter-firm contracts and on the dominant form of hybrid contracting and franchising (Rubin, 1978). In the mid-1980s, there was a growing interest in theorists to express their ideas about these new governance structures. Apparently unimportant is that many studies do not come from the sphere of economics but rather from that of marketing or management. In a 1995 study, Grandori and Soda reviewed more than 160 articles on cross-company networks, of which only 16 were published in business journals and of which a significant number were based on transac-tion cost theory (Grandori and Soda, 1995).

Initially calling them 'a collection of weirdos', Ménard identified six cat-egories of hybrid organisations (Ménard, 2004, pp. 345–376):

- Subcontracting networks: The subcontracting is a contract based on which a party assumes, by organising the necessary means and man-aging its own risk, the performance/execution of a work/service in exchange for a sum of money. An enterprise requires another or others to realise a part of its production or components necessary to complete the production, the conception, and the decision to realise the produc-tion belonging to the main company. The literature on subcontracting and how it operates is abundant, especially in the automotive and con-struction industries. Examples are provided by Aoki (1988), Sako and Helper (1998), Dyer (1997), and Eccles (1981).
- Business networks: Business networks consist of at least three compa-nies signing a joint collaboration agreement to start a pre-established activity, within a certain period of time, the object of activity being able to target both production and distribution.

- Franchising: It is the operation in the form of a contract by which a person called a franchisor grants to another person, called a beneficiary or franchisee, the right to exploit a set of industrial or intellectual property rights, for the purpose of producing or marketing certain types of products and/or services. In the literature, the franchise is given increased attention, perhaps because of the rapid development it has seen since the 1970s (Rubin, 1978; Klein et al., 1978; Dnes, 1996; Williamson, 1984; Lafontaine and Slade, 1997).
- Collective trademarks: Collective trademarks are generally owned by an association or cooperative organisation whose members may use that brand to market their products. Usually the association establishes a set of criteria for the use of the collective trademark and offers each company the possibility to use the trademark, subject to the fulfilment of these criteria. Collective trademarks can be an effective way of jointly marketing the products of a group of undertakings for which it would be more difficult to make their individual trademarks recognised by consumers and/or accepted for distribution by major distributors. Due to the large number of partners involved, the risk of opportunism is high, although difficulties also arise with regard to monitoring and control. This form of organisation has franchise-like features (Dwyer and Oh, 1988).
- Partnerships that associate, around a brand name (founder), several individuals to take advantage of the reputation of the initiator and, at the same time, to create the right ground for completing professional skills.
- Alliances such as those between airlines, domestic or international, that are forced, in an increasingly inclusive environment, to agree on issues regarding flight schedules, reservations, loyalty, fares, etc., while maintaining a competitive environment (Baker et al., 2008; Alberts et al., 2016).

Peculiarities of hybrid governance structures

Claude Ménard summarises the common features of hybrid governance structures by identifying three benchmarks: joint investment, contractuality, and the competitive environment.

Joint investment

All studies on hybrid forms of governance, regardless of their orientation, show that they tend to organise their activity through coordination and cooperation between companies, so that investment decisions are common. Hybrid organisations exist because the market is not able to attract the necessary resources and capabilities (Teece and Pisano, 1992), while integration would be a loss of flexibility and incentives, the latter being the motivation to choose these modes of governance. These forms of organising economic activity are selective in the choice of partners and involve joint planning. Developing an appropriate information system between partners is essential for them, but information asymmetry is a major challenge (Mathewson and Winter, 1985).

Attracting investment and resources does not make sense if there is no continuity of the relationship between partners. This continuity requires a certain level of cooperation so that the partners are freed from the autonomy encountered in the market, while at the same time giving up the benefits of the constraints that the hierarchy could offer.

Contractuality

Hybrid arrangements are always the subject of a contract. We are dealing with a contract whose dominant feature is sustainability. If the long term for which it ends does not give it this trait, automatic renewal remains a solution. The contract is usually incomplete, with the free spaces consciously left to serve, if necessary, adjustments and renegotiations. At the same time, the contract provides only the general framework for cooperation. Coordination mechanisms act on this field, which complete the contract and, at the same time, ensure the realisation of the conjunction of the partners' efforts.

Competitive environment

The third characteristic of hybrid arrangements is that, unlike integration through the firm, they maintain the central attribute of the market which is competition. The partners in an agreement compete against each other permanently to attract resources in a strong competitive environment whose dominant feature is uncertainty, which makes it difficult to survive. Also, if the specificity of the investment is moderate, the partners tend to focus on other forms of organising the activity, increasing the instability of these arrangements, which is why it is necessary to implement internal regulations.

In accordance with Williamson's (1991) model, according to which hybrid organisations are neither markets nor hierarchies, but have their own characteristics, a number of new concepts are emerging. The assets' specificity or investments, uncertainty, information asymmetry, moral hazard, and opportunism are just a few examples, which we will further develop in close connection with the size of transaction costs.

The role of transaction costs in choosing the governance structure

Among those who laid the foundations of the transaction cost theory are W. Commons, who identified in the transaction costs the 'basic unit of analysis', and R. Coase for whom 'transaction costs are a criterion of choice between market and firm' (Coase, 1983). Although not mentioned, transaction costs are the main topic discussed in Coase's paper, *The nature of the firm* (1937), considering that this is also the main reason why economic agents use the firm, at that time, as the only alternative to the market. In trying to identify how they operate the author has not been very successful, but in linking their existence to the environment in which they coexist and are determined, he uses the limited rationality of individuals and the uncertainty that manifests itself in the environment.

Transaction cost theory states that firms develop governance mechanisms in order to reduce transaction costs, thus becoming more efficient (Williamson, 1981). A distinction is made between two types of government contracts for which transactions are repeated: the market and bilateral contracts. Market-based governance is an effective solution when transactions are standardised, the parties are independent persons, and their identity is not relevant.

Concerned about the size of transaction costs, many authors contribute by trying to place them in various categories. Not only notable are Williamson's efforts to identify ex-ante and ex-post costs, but also those of other less acclaimed authors such as Dunning (1993) or Rosen (1997).

In general terms, transaction costs are those that occur in the case of a transfer of ownership when the persons concerned try to impose their exclusive rights. Matthews (1986) provides the following definition: 'Transaction costs 'consist of the costs of arranging a contract ex-ante and monitoring and enforcing it ex-post, as opposed to production costs, which are the costs of executing the contract' (p. 906). Transaction costs are occasional expenses, with both fixed and variable transaction costs. Until recently, most economic theories assumed the completeness of information, with transaction costs being introduced late. The latter were associated with the costs of obtaining information in connection with the exchange.

Eggertsson (1990) identifies a number of activities, related to the exchange of property rights between individuals, which can lead to transaction costs:

(1) Searching for information about the distribution of prices, the quality of products and work performed, looking for potential buyers or sellers, as well as information about their behavior and external circumstances;

(2) Negotiations needed to find out the true position of buyers and sellers when prices are endogenous;

(3) Drawing up contracts;

(4) Monitoring the contractual partners to see if the terms of the contract are respected;

(5) Enforcement of a contract and payment of damages when the partners do not comply with their obligations;

(6) Protecting property rights against third-party intrusion.

(Eggertsson, 1990, p. 30)

Other authors have expressed concerns about the extent to which transaction costs can contribute to the realisation of national income. Undoubtedly, D. North is the one who starts the analysis in this direction by providing statistical evidence on the US economy between 1870 and 1970. In the same direction are the contributions of those who continued the analysis of the size of the transaction sector, mainly Wang (2003) and Polski (2001).

For a better understanding of transaction costs, we must highlight their determinants according to which the choice of a governance structure is more convenient for us. In the literature, the predominant role is attributed to uncertainty, asymmetric information, and limited rationality that lead to opportunistic behaviours on the part of economic agents. Limited rationality prevents economic agents from accurately predicting all situations that would lead to non-compliance with commitments. Opportunism acquires major significance because it manifests itself in a competitive environment where information is not always available at hand. This imposes costs that not all agencies are willing to pay or even afford. In this context, it is necessary to use incomplete contracts which involve leaving some gaps in case the unfavourable conditions encountered require additions.

Another criterion in choosing the governance structure is the degree of specificity of the investment or, in other words, of the assets used by different economic agents whose sole objective is to maximise profits. Specific assets are those resources that cannot be immediately reused for any purpose other than the present one so that their present value is always higher than if they were used in alternative ways (Klein et al., 1978). A specific asset requires some dependency relationship between the holder and the group to which it is addressed. When the degree of asset specificity is low, it is recommended to use the market to reduce production and transaction costs. As the degree of specificity increases, the solution to reduce transaction costs comes from the firm. Hybrid forms remain an alternative for situations where none of the aforementioned forms meets the preferences of economic operators in terms of benefits. In trying to understand the conditions under which some organisational arrangements tend to prevail, Ménard (2018) proposes a framework that combines transaction cost and relational contract models, analysing the agrifood industry.

Concerned about the choice of governance structure, Williamson's (1996) sees uncertainty as a determining factor of particular importance in relation to the degree of specificity of assets. The choice between the three forms of government seems to exclude the hybrid form when the degree of uncertainty is high, using the advantages offered through the market and the company. The same author analyses the frequency of transactions in relation to the specificity of assets, transactions that he categorises as being occasional and repetitive and according to which the choice process tends to be more difficult to perform. When dealing with non-specific assets, regardless of the frequency of transactions, the market is the solution. In other cases, either firm integration or hybrid governance structures are used.

Studies focusing on the influence of transaction frequency in making the decision of vertical integration, based on empirically obtained results, are insignificant, mainly due to the ambiguity of the effect of transaction frequency on the level of transaction costs. The characteristics of transactions are not the only variables that influence organisational choices, an important role being reserved for the institutional environment.

The size of the franchise system

Constituent elements of the franchise agreement

Franchising as a form of organising economic activity is one of the fastest growing in the world. The governance structure of a firm refers to the structure of decisions and property rights. At the franchise level, decision-making rights refer to the transfer of authority over the use of specific assets and those on the local market through the franchise agreement. Property rights are related to the number of stores owned and other residual income, such as royalties.

In commercial law, a franchise is a contract whereby a trader named a franchisor allows another trader named a franchisee or beneficiary to use the franchisor's brand and know-how to distribute a product or service or to manufacture a product in accordance with the standards of the franchisor, in exchange for a sum of money. The purpose of this contract is to gain access to the franchisor's marketing network and to capitalise on the goods or services produced or provided under the franchise.

Through the franchise agreement, the parties involved seek to obtain mutual benefits and at the same time undertake to comply with certain regulations. The franchisor has the interest to expand its franchise network and collect its royalties, while the beneficiary seeks to exploit the franchisor's business concept in order to make a profit.

The franchise contract is a consensual, synallagmatic contract with successive execution, intuitu personae, and adhesion. Consensus refers to the fact that the parties do not have to give a certain form, not even in writing, for it to be validly concluded. It is a synallagmatic because the parties seek to obtain mutual benefits.

The franchise contract is in successive execution because the exploitation of the products or services that are transmitted by contract takes place for a certain period of time in which the beneficiary has the possibility to amortise his investment. The character intuitu personae refers in the case of the beneficiary, to the creditworthiness and managerial skills he proves, and in the case of the franchisor, the object of the franchise, the field in which it operates, the success of the business, market image, etc. The adhesion character consists in the fact that the beneficiary, once he has consented to the conclusion of the contract, is obliged to obey the rules imposed by the franchisor.

Typically, a contract highlights the roles and responsibilities of the parties involved, the allocation of decisions and control rights, the planning of the various contingencies, how the parties will communicate, and how they will be able to resolve their disputes. We can say that a contract is complete when all the relevant terms and clauses are specified and when we take into account not only the occurrence of events whose anticipation was not possible but also the concrete way in which they can be resolved. If the parties want to reduce the risk of opportunistic behaviour, the number of contractual guarantees will be higher which will turn the incomplete contract into an almost complete one (Oxley, 1997 and Rana, 2018).

In practice, all contracts are incomplete due to the costs of drafting the contract, the limited rationality of the parties involved, which make it impossible to anticipate all events that could affect the transaction, the inability to verify all relevant variables (Grossman and Hurt, 1986). Even if the parties involved in the contract could anticipate all the events and could verify all the behaviours, which is practically impossible, they may not be interested in the full contract, precisely because of the drafting costs.

Franchise agreements can be considered a special type of bilateral contracts, being the main tool in the relationship between franchisor and franchisees. It is an essential mechanism for regulating, controlling, and resolving conflicts of interest, blurring the opportunistic behaviour of the parties involved. The constituent elements of the franchise agreement are the franchisor, the franchisee or the beneficiary of the franchise, and the franchise network (which is made available to the beneficiary).

A franchisor is a person or a firm governed by private law, with full capacity to exercise, financially independent, who grants under a contract the right to operate or develop his own business, product or service, and the know-how, assistance and techniques necessary for the business, in successive services, in exchange for which he is entitled to a royalty.

The franchisor uses human resources and financial means to promote its brand, research, and innovation, ensuring the promotion and viability of the product, and undertakes to provide the beneficiary with initial training for the operation of its brand (Rana et al., 2020). He has both the quality of trader and the quality of owner of some commercial attributes as the brand, trade name, and emblem.

The franchisee or the beneficiary is the merchant selected by the franchisor following the manifestation of his will to adhere to the principle of homogeneity of the franchise network. It is characterized by legal independence from the franchisor and carries out its own activity in accordance with the laws of the place.

The beneficiary is most often selected by the franchisor following exchanges of mutual information through which, on the one hand, the franchisor informs the beneficiary on the content and conditions of the franchise, and, on the other hand, the beneficiary provides the franchisor with information on its financial capacity and its ability to operate the franchise in good conditions. In order to join the franchise network, the beneficiary must have an initial capital that involves the payment of network entry fees, the endowment with the necessary equipment, as well as for the training of the staff.

We can define the franchise network as that complex and unitary system, created by the franchisor exactly and subordinated to it through advertising, consisting of an economic (practical) side that is characterised by the sale of goods and/or services in order to obtain profit and a legal side consisting of the rights and obligations of the parties to the franchise agreement having as main nexus between them the brand (franchisable concept) given in use by the franchisor to all beneficiaries symmetrically, a system with ramifications over a certain geographical area, independent of the other but homogeneous.

The key features of the franchise network are the homogeneity of the network and advertising. The first relates more to the practical side and implies equal treatment between the beneficiaries, on the part of the franchisor, and the second feature relates to the franchisor's competence and the degree of his control over the beneficiaries. It follows that the network is a perfect unit in which the franchisor's brand, a symbol of the network's identity and reputation, is the guarantee of the quality of services offered to consumers.

Different types of franchises

Over time, various types of franchises have emerged. The most used criterion for classifying franchises is the field of activity in which they operate. According to this, the distribution franchise, the service franchise, and the production or industrial franchise are identified.

The distribution franchise has the widest coverage area among this type of contract and is materialised either in the distribution by the beneficiaries of the products manufactured by the franchisor or in the distribution of some products for which the franchisor is in turn a distributor. Some examples may be Yves Rocher, Paco Rabanenne, Penguin, Pronupția, or Bata.

The service franchise is experiencing a spectacular development due to the economic sector in which it operates. Service franchising is the means by which the franchisor covers certain markets with his own services through independent traders who offer them to consumers as if they were offered by the franchisor itself. In this category of contracts, the determining role belongs to the know-how, this being also the main way of attracting the clientele. The most well-known service franchises are those in the field of restaurants (McDonald's, KFC, Pizza Hut) and the hotel industry (Inter-Continental, Holiday Inn), but they have developed in most of the service areas we know today.

The production franchise, as its name suggests, means that the franchisee can not only sell but also produce certain products according to the franchisor's instructions. It is one of the important forms of technology transfer that involves the know-how created and tested by the franchisor, the use of patented inventions over which the franchisor has the right to operate, as well as specialised technical assistance provided to the beneficiary before and during production. It is the easiest way for the franchisor to enter new markets, but it involves high risks in terms of maintaining company standards and protecting the know-how transferred. Among the most well-known production franchises is, without a doubt, Coca-Cola.

A second classification of franchise agreements can be made according to the way the franchise is operated. Therefore, the following are distinguished:

- The *financial franchise* that emerged as a result of the diversification of the service franchise. It is found especially in large projects that require adequate capital in the first phase of the investment.
- The *stand franchise* developed due to the appearance of shopping centres and assumes that in a store, the franchisor allows the opening of a stand designed personally in which the beneficiary is to distribute his products.
- *Affiliate franchise* is that activity in which an independent merchant, who already has an activity, converts its own object of activity and enters a franchise network.
- *Zonal franchising* differs in that the franchisor allows the beneficiary to have several distribution points in the same geographical area.
- *Polydistribution* takes place when several franchisors cede the exploitation right to a single beneficiary.

Another classification of franchise types can be made depending on the degree of determination of the franchisable concept. On this criterion, we can differentiate between:

- *Business franchise*, which is also the most complex form of franchise, involves a complete transmission of information from the franchisor to the beneficiary.
- *Nice franchise* which is a special category of franchise because it only addresses reputable brands, with franchisees imposing high standards on potential beneficiaries who would like to join this franchise network.
- *Multi-conceptual franchise* which is characterised by changes to the franchisable concept, either by improvements or restructuring.
- *Reciprocal franchise agreement* which is an agreement between several franchisors or beneficiaries operating in a market with similar products.
- *Sub-franchise* which is a form of contract quite rare in practice that is achieved through intermediaries. The franchisor grants the master franchisor the right to set up a franchise network derived from the initial one or to contract various beneficiaries who are sub-beneficiaries to the main franchisor in a network controlled by the master franchisor.

Another type of franchise is the social franchising which is derived from social entrepreneurship. Social franchising differs greatly from the traditional form of franchising. The first difference is related to the entity's mission (its orientation towards social and not for profit) with different types of target groups, respectively, beneficiaries and customers. The second difference is that the franchise units involved in the social franchise contract differ from those involved in the commercial version (e.g., social enterprises are opposed by individual businessmen). Another difference is related to the values adhered to by the actors involved in social franchising: social entrepreneurs are more concerned with helping and showing others that they care than making money (Thompson, 2002).

Franchising can be an effective way to deal with the complexities imposed by social entrepreneurship. In addition to helping entrepreneurs with the support and structure needed to develop a sustainable business, they also have the means to implement it. Social franchising is an adaptation of the commercial franchise in which a developer of a successful social concept, the franchisor, allows franchisees to use his name and concept for social gain. Hybrid organisational forms as is the case of social enterprises offer a promising alternative to capitalist forms of business (Cornforth, 2020). Social franchising can be defined as a system of contractual relationships, which uses the structure of the commercial franchise to meet the proposed social objectives (Tracey and Jarvis, 2007). It is therefore a new institutional arrangement in the field of social entrepreneurship and a tool through which social objectives can be more easily achieved.

Franchise decision

A whole series of theoretical and empirical research tries to explain why companies choose to distribute products and services through franchise channels. The franchisor's decision to franchise instead of keeping his business is based on his desire to grow his business as much as possible and to be present in as many markets as possible even if it involves losing control of the business. From the franchisee's point of view, the decision is mainly based on the fact that he has access to scarce resources that he could not procure under other conditions. Franchising takes place when a franchisor sells to franchisees the right to use his trademark in order to market products or services under the franchisor's name, using his know-how. In terms of how it is organised, franchising is recognised as a model of rapid growth in companies mainly because through this form of organisation, customers from quiet dispersed geographical areas can be served.

When it comes to organising distribution networks, there are a variety of possible solutions that can be chosen by those who sell a product or service. The extreme positions of this spectrum are marked on the one hand by the distribution through an independent company, through the employed staff, and on the other hand by independent subjects. Franchising, being a business based on the cooperation between the owner of the business concept and its franchisees, occupies a middle position given that franchisees are different entities but at the same time are linked to the franchisor based on the franchise agreement. Moreover, franchisors usually operate through both independent companies and franchised units, often simultaneously.

From the perspective of agent–principal theory, the choice between independent companies and franchised units, and consequently the character of the entire distribution system, depend on the contractual approach of the specific solution, from the spectrum of possibilities, as well as on the franchisor's ability to monitor different variables of input or output. Three scenarios differ depending on the influence of the franchisor on these variables. As long as the agent's additional resource, such as personal effort, does not exert a major influence on the results of a franchise unit, principals will no longer have any interest in resorting to franchising, preferring instead to hire managers (Mintzberg, 1973). Even when the agent gains influence within the units through the resources he makes available, the principals will prefer to keep their units. The franchisor could just as easily control agencies by imposing high standards of performance. When it proves impossible and inefficient to monitor the agent's results, the franchisor will focus on distribution through the franchising system.

Classical literature on this subject, rooted in economics, can be grouped into two different theories that may explain the decision to franchise: the theory of resource scarcity (Oxenfeld and Kelly, 1969) and the theory of agency (Lafontaine and Kaufmann, 1994). Another theory, more recent, tries to explain the prevalence of the franchising system based on the organisational characteristics that differentiate it from other forms of ownership, the theory of multiple organisation (Bradach, 1997). Next, we will analyse these theories as they were developed by franchise theorists.

Resource scarcity theory

As mentioned, franchising is a quick way to grow a business because franchising provides the franchisor with one of the basic resources to grow his business, namely capital. The franchisor is in the situation of wanting to grow his business by obtaining economies of scale or by increasing market share, a goal for which he needs financial resources that are not exactly at hand, and the intervention of the franchisee at this stage helps him overcome this obstacle which stands in the way of its growth. The franchisee not only contributes with royalties but also finances the investment in the unit that the franchisor has decided to franchise by providing capital for the entire period of operation. So, franchising seems to be the best solution when a business needs to grow fast and its owner needs financial and human resources at a low price. Caves and Murphy (1976) state that the franchisee is for the franchisor the cheapest source of financial resources that could be found to finance his growth and that there is no economic substitute for the financial resources provided by the franchisee. The theory of resource scarcity developed by Oxenfeld and Kelly (1969) is based on the explanation that the reason why the franchisor uses the franchise system is to gain access to resources that the franchisee possesses and that he can make available to the franchisor in order to grow its business.

Reviewing the theory of resource scarcity, Rubin (1978) discovers that the franchisor could find other financial resources besides those that could be provided by the franchisee. Although franchising may not be the best source of capital for the franchisor, Lafontaine and Kaufmann (1994) consider that given the fact that the parties put together management skills and financial resources, franchising has a greater advantage than when a franchisee sells shares, thus maintaining the control rights. The sale of shares by companies to potential external investors implies a loss of control from a strategic point of view because they usually become partners in the company and gain the right to influence the strategic decisions of the company. In the case of franchising, the partners are independent persons who contribute to the development of the franchise network and do not own shares in the company as in the previous case, which makes the franchisor maintain absolute strategic control over the company he owns.

The theory of resource scarcity is based on the idea that the franchisor uses the franchise system because otherwise he would not have access to the financial resources he needs. In other words, if the franchisor identified other sources of financing for his business, he would no longer resort to franchising, preferring to grow his business using his own configuration. As a consequence, franchising would be a temporary resource for the organisation to cope with the difficulty of accessing the resources needed for development and growth, and, once the franchisor has obtained the resources he needs, he will change his development strategy. According to the hypothesis of redirection of property rights developed by Oxenfeld and Kelly (1969), once the franchisor has obtained the necessary resources to finance his growth, he will no longer opt for franchising but, on the contrary, will buy units from franchisees.

The hypothesis of redirection of property rights predicts that in the long run most franchise networks will be transformed into sole proprietorships (the original franchisor), and only a part of the franchised units will be left to certain franchisees (it is the franchise units in geographical areas that are not easily accessible or that register very poor performance). Subsequent studies, however, show that there is no empirical evidence to support this hypothesis. In many of the industries analysed, franchise networks do not change their strategy even if they have access to financial resources. Other empirical evidence suggests that franchise networks tend to adopt dual structures, owning both stand-alone enterprises and franchise units. There are also cases when franchisors provide financial support to franchisees, who contribute only in terms of managerial skills.

Agency theory

It is highlighted in the previous subchapter that the theory of resource scarcity explains only to a certain extent the reason for resorting to franchising. The main reason why the theory of resource scarcity is questioned is due to the fact that empirical evidence shows that many franchise networks continue to franchise new units even when they have a multitude of resources. Therefore, when these companies decide to franchise, they do so not because they encounter difficulties in procuring resources, but because franchising brings an additional advantage to the franchisor, which cannot be explained by the theory of resource scarcity.

Contrary to the theory of resource scarcity, some researchers have pointed out the idea that the franchise system would highlight aspects much more important than those related to the procurement of financial resources by the franchisor, namely, the motivation of the franchisee. Franchisees risk their own money when they decide to join the franchise network, and they are the owners of the business, which is why they have every interest in making the business as profitable as possible. The motivation of franchisees is superior to that of company managers even when company managers would have variable salaries depending on their performance.

Brickley and Dark (1991) developed the idea that the franchise system is an immediate answer to the classic principal–agent problem studied in agency theory. Agency theory explains that when there is a separation between the principal (owner of property rights) and the agent (manager), there is a problem with the agency, and that the principal is always unsure of the agent's behaviour. The issue facing the principal is whether the agent makes every effort to achieve all the objectives defined by the principal, and whether the agent's behaviour is in the principal's best interest or self-interest. In conditions of uncertainty and information asymmetry regarding the efforts of the agent, the main one introduces in the landscape the costs of monitoring the activity of the agent. The only way to reduce these costs is to give the agent residual rights that can align his personal interests with the interests of the principal. The franchise agreement highlights precisely these aspects.

The agency theory explains that through the franchise system, the main agent problem is reduced because the franchise contract aligns the interests of the parties involved in the contract and sets a common goal shared by both the franchisor and the franchisee. Franchisees are not employees of the franchisor but the owners of their own business, so it is in the interest of franchisees to make every effort to achieve good financial results. Therefore, franchising is a strong motivator for franchisees and reduces the problem of monitoring that the franchisor would have if he wanted to hire a manager.

Following the logic behind the agency theory and the way in which it explains why companies make the decision to franchise, it could be concluded that in the end, franchising companies will own 100% of the franchised units. In this context, all companies will want to take advantage of franchise marketing by taking advantage of the low agency costs associated with franchise systems. It is the exact opposite of what the resource scarcity theory indicates about the distribution of franchised units. As Martin (1988) points out and the agency theory supports it, franchise networks that combine a mix of companies and franchise units will evolve until they become companies made up only of franchise units. In reality, this prediction has the same results as in the case of the redirection of property rights. There is no empirical evidence to indicate that the franchise units will become 100% franchised, as there is no evidence that they would become 100% owned by the company. What can be observed is that they maintain a stable mix of own companies and franchised units.

Multiple organisation theory

Hybrid company structures are a combination of distinct parameters within company organisation. Today, the phenomenon of hybrid companies occupies a fairly widespread area in business. Combining organisational methods such as price and hierarchy with organisational institutions such as the market or the firm, the result is a broad spectrum of organisational constellations (Ouchi, 1980; Williamson, 1991). Within the multiple organisation theory, those who run a business decided to use separately both the price, specific to the market, and attributes of the hierarchy to obtain an identical result. Others have chosen to run their business through a mix of price and hierarchy. Even if both methods have the characteristics of hybrid forms of organisation, only the latter is a form of multiple organisation activity.

An example of multiple organisation activity is one in which a company has its own sales department and at the same time cooperates with independent sales agents to streamline its business. Other firms, such as those in the automotive industry, produce components or even an end product within the firm and purchase the same components from external suppliers (Walker and Weber, 1984). What is interesting is that franchise networks hire managers to run the stores they own and at the same time hire independent operators, namely franchisees. According to those mentioned earlier on the forms of organisation, the former seem to be under the influence of the hierarchy, while the latter are motivated by the price system.

Arguments for the parallel use of the pricing system and hierarchy within the same organisation are varied. First, Hennart (1993) argues that mixing the two methods will minimise the cost of organising the system, given that the cost of each form increases progressively when it tends to a pure form of organisation. Second, Brickley and Dark (1987) consider the multiple form of organisation to be the result of numerous decisions accordingly, each trying to find the perfect organisational solution for different individual environments. Finally, Bradach (1997) and Lewin-Solomons (1998) argue that multiple organisation theory will make it difficult for the principal to achieve synergies, and, thus, the generation of gains that exceed the costs could arise with the complexity of the organisation. Under such conditions, they presuppose a model of multiple organisation that exceeds the performance of the organisation in the form of franchise networks or independent companies, as long as the principals know how to exploit the full potential of multiple organisation theory.

From a broader perspective, these arguments differ only in the nature of the diverse understanding of the importance of the parameters that franchisors must take into account when setting the strategy for organising the enterprise. Hennart (1993) and other researchers around Brickley and Dark use cost, growth, and risk issues when trying to demonstrate the effectiveness of multiple forms of organisation. Bradach (1997) and Lewin-Solomons (1998), on the other hand, believe that the multiple forms of organisation improves trust and cooperation between the members of a system and, implicitly, increases the overall quality of the system.

The empirical evidence reported supports the idea that neither the theory of resource scarcity nor the theory of agency is able to fully explain the franchising decision. Based on the fact that the form of organisation in industries is based on mixed structures, Bradach (1997) formulates the theory of multiple organisation which explains that the mix of own companies and franchise units owned under the same brand is what gives a competitive advantage to a company. He also discovers that most franchise chains are made up of a mix of own companies and franchised units. One of the reasons he identified is that some units are more suitable for one form of ownership than others. Another reason is that the existence of one type of store has positive impacts on the other, and vice versa. According to this theory, the reason for resorting to franchising is the simultaneous access to the most important advantage held by the company, which is uniformity, and the most important advantage held by franchised companies, namely, adaptation.

Uniformity and adaptability are two major, often contradictory, goals that any type of business must aim for in order to survive. Uniformity means that each consumer must find a common image, design, and serving technique in any unit under the same brand, regardless of how it is owned. Adaptation means almost the opposite: the franchise network needs to adapt to everchanging markets in order to take advantage of new threats and opportunities identified in local markets. To do this, the units need constant innovation and a thorough knowledge of local markets. Even if uniformity and adaptation seem to be two contradictory objectives, using a mix of independent franchise units and own companies, these objectives can be achieved simultaneously.

Cost–benefit analysis

Franchise networks combine aspects of two ways of organising, price and hierarchy, within the same institution. Due to the personal risk arising from the structure of property rights, franchisees are connected to this network through the franchise agreement and, at the same time, are driven and motivated by the price constraints identified in the market. Regarding the model presented by Williamson (1991), franchise networks are located between the poles representing the market and the hierarchy, as forms of hybrid organisation. In order to survive, these networks must meet the efficiency criterion. As presented in Coase's 1937 paper, this criterion of efficiency was defined as generating minimal transaction costs (Williamson, 1975), a term later used in organisational cost economics (Hennart, 1993). Given the benefits of the hybrid form of organisation in relation to the costs involved, it should be sufficient to decide on the best form of network organisation.

Most attempts to explain the structure of property rights in a franchise were based on shortcomings in fixed-wage contracts. An important aspect of these contracts is how an agent's behaviour can be properly controlled before the contract is signed, an action that would have involved rather high costs for the principal. By sharing the store's profit with the agent, through residual property rights, harmful behaviours such as evading obligations or pursuing opportunistic actions are significantly reduced. The franchisee will simply share through these costs any shortcomings they may encounter. According to Rubin (1978, p. 226), franchising is supposed to be effective because it reduces the monitoring costs that would exist to replace the agent's opportunistic and excessive behaviour of a company's assets and resources. Minkler (1992, p. 243) extended this view by proposing that franchisors need specific local market information, such as consumer preferences, local suppliers, and infrastructure, whose acquisition costs increase with unfamiliarity, heterogeneity, and local market volatility. Although Minkler's assumption that franchisees know more than managers of a company unit is questioned, it is plausible that they are more willing to provide some information to the franchisor as they benefit both directly from the unit and indirectly from its brand to make a successful business. Following Mikler, franchising is supposed to be more efficient as the franchisor's spending on acquiring local information, which would otherwise have been directed to research centres or managers' bonuses, is substantially reduced.

Another prominent attempt to explain the existence of franchising considers that the lack of resources that makes it difficult for companies to grow rapidly is ameliorated by both the expansion of capital and the managerial talent with which each franchisee who joins the franchise network contributes. The rapid growth of the company is important for at least two reasons. First, the fixed costs for the development, standardisation, marketing, and control of the network of decentralised distribution units will be competitively acceptable, only if they are shared by a larger number of units (Caves and Murphy, 1976). Second, with each new point of sale, it will contribute to the increase of notoriety among the consumers and to the increase of the brand value of the entire franchise network.

A third explanation of franchising was presented by Martin (1988) and Chaudhuri et al. (2001) who proposed that franchisors behave like risk managers when choosing the form of organisation from a multitude of other options. The more risky the locations with volatile sales are and the more expensive they are to monitor, the more likely franchisors will be to leave them in the hands of franchisees. On the other hand, locations in more stable areas that do not require frequent monitoring are retained and managed through managers. Ultimately, the franchisor's risk aversion could motivate him to withdraw from any form of risk by choosing a pure arrangement to retain only general management duties.

Summarising these arguments, it is considered that franchising can overcome this obstacle related to the structure of property rights, as the costs of the franchisor's monitoring of the agent and those related to gathering information from the local market are reduced. Moreover, it is assumed that franchising is a form of organisation that aims to grow a business based on scarce resources, most often capital and management, and through which the risk of specific distribution of the franchisor is reduced by selecting the most favourable locations. However, it is shown that these benefits are accompanied by certain costs associated with this form of organisation.

Due to the different reward mechanism, hybrid forms of organisation, such as franchising, incur organisational costs that are different from those encountered in the hierarchy, for example. While managers employed in a company are rewarded with fixed salaries in exchange for a predetermined activity based on a contract and based on the achievement of certain objectives, franchisees are remunerated strictly based on the results obtained and personal efforts. Quoting Hennart (1993, p. 529), 'each form has its own prejudices'. Within the hierarchy, where individuals such as employees are paid according to orders, they are more likely to evade their obligations or simply to work less than they agreed through the contract. Using the price-based mechanism in franchising will translate into the opposite effect so that franchisees will want to reduce the franchisor's earnings and maximise their own earnings. The less supervised both parties are, the greater the tendency to abduct and deceive the partner.

Franchisees can cheat in at least two ways. First of all, by offering services or products of a lower quality than those provided by the franchisor's standards, which will result in a decrease in brand value and, implicitly, will affect all members of the network. As Norton (1988b) pointed out, this free riding behaviour is often found in areas where customers frequent only a small part of the total number of stores, as it is the case with units located on highways, train stations, or tourist areas.

Second, franchisees may be reluctant to follow the initiatives of franchisors that may be promising in some respects, but the outcome of such actions within each unit in the network may be uncertain or completely absent. Such resistance is often encountered in investments that generate effects on all members of a network. National promotion events, for example, funded by all franchisees benefit the entire network while the franchisor alone will recover only a part of the investment made. As for the strict uniformity of franchised units, both free riding behaviour and reluctance to pursue strategic conduct can be fatal for the franchisor, situations that can be dealt with through the regulations of the franchise agreement or even using third parties which can have the quality counsellors or, in the worst cases, through very long and very high cost litigations. The more customer satisfaction will decrease due to these behaviours of franchisees, the more it will suffer the reputation of the entire network, all units belonging to the same franchisor being equally affected.

Given the benefits and costs of hybrid forms of organisation, the determination of models for establishing property rights within distribution networks, and not alone it only, should be predictable. The franchisor must consider the costs of hybrid forms in relation to the benefits they bring, so that, quoting Carney and Gedajlovic (1991, p. 609), 'it is this compromise that urges the franchisor to own and operate the units in a distinct form', a fact also supported by the followers of the organisation theory.

Contrary to such a process are the results of researchers such as Oxenfeld and Kelly (1969) or Hunt (1973), who provided a model of the life cycle of a franchise network. The more the networks expand in terms of number of units, stabilise, form restrictions, objectives, and have capabilities and new opportunities, the more their shape is altered and structural changes will occur in the end. A franchisor who has reached market maturity, in an attempt to increase the number of units he owns in a specific local market, will eventually incur much lower costs of monitoring and gathering information. In addition, the growth of the network will make previously scarce resources, such as capital and management, more accessible and reduce the impact of owning locations in more risky areas. As for the trade-off in this situation, the net benefits of the hybrid form will continue to decline as the network matures, making franchising the least desirable option for mature networks. On the same level, Oxenfeld and Kelly (1969, p. 69) hypothesise the redirection of property rights:

> We will claim that the most successful franchise systems will become networks owned entirely by a single company; we will argue that franchising is advantageous for a successful franchisor especially during the start-up period of the company but also after that, for the exploitation of marginal locations.

As a consequence, hybrid forms such as franchising and multiple organisations should be less used during the growth period of a network, remaining to resort to arrangements within a simple company.

Conclusions

This chapter is based on the key concepts outlined on hybrid governance structures, with an emphasis on the franchise agreement. This way of organising economic activity best responds to the needs identified by both the franchisor and the franchisee due to the mutual benefits arising from this agreement. Proof of the efficiency of the organisation is the spread of this type of business worldwide and in all areas of activity present.

Contrary to organisation through the firm, franchising involves a common form of planning with an emphasis on continuity of cooperation between partners. As we are talking about a contract, its sustainability and the conditions under which it could be renewed are important.

From the franchisor's point of view, the decision to franchise meets the need of growing the business while at the same time expanding on new markets even if it means a loss of control on the business. The franchisee's decision to franchise best reflects the need to access scarce resources which will be difficult to procure under other conditions.

According to the theory of resource scarcity, the franchisor uses the franchise system because otherwise he would not have access to the financial resources he needs. In other words, if the franchisor identified other sources of financing for his business, he would no longer resort to franchising, preferring to grow his business using his own configuration. It is pointed out that the theory of resource scarcity explains only to a certain extent the reason for resorting to franchising. The main reason why the theory of resource scarcity is questioned is due to the fact that empirical evidence shows that many franchise networks continue to franchise new units even when they have a multitude of resources.

Franchise networks combine aspects of two ways of organising, price and hierarchy, within the same institution. Due to the personal risk arising from the structure of property rights, franchisees are connected to this network through the franchise agreement and, at the same time, are driven and motivated by the price constraints identified in the market. Franchising seems to be the best solution when a business needs to grow fast and its owner needs financial and human resources at a low price.

References

Alberts, S., Wohlgezogen, F., Zajac, E.J., *Strategic Alliance Structures. An Organisation Design Perspective*, Journal of Management, vol. 42, pp. 582–614, 2016.

Aoki, M., *Information, Incentives and Bargaining in the Japanese Economy*, Cambridge University Press, Cambridge, 1988.

Baker, G.P., Gibbons, R., Murphy, K.J., *Strategic Alliances: Bridges Between Islands of Conscious Power*, Journal of the Japanese and International Economies, vol. 22, pp. 146–163, 2008.

Bhandari, K.R., Raut, S.K., *9 Leveraging Tacit*, Advances in Management Research: Innovation and Technology, vol. 1, no. 1, pp 127–138, 2019.

Bradach, J.L., *Using the Plural Form in the Management of Restaurant Chains*, Administrative Science Quarterly, vol. 42, pp. 276–303, 1997.

Brickley, J.A., Dark, F.H., *The Choice of Organisational Form – The Case of Franchising*, Journal of Financial Economics, vol. 18, pp. 401–420, 1987.

Brickley, J.A., Dark, F.H., Weinbach, M.S., *An Agency Perspective on Franchising*, Financial Management, vol. 20, pp. 27–35, 1991.

Carney, M., Gedajlovic, E., *Vertical Integration in Franchise Systems – Agency Theory and Resource Explanations*, Strategic Management Journal, vol. 12, pp. 607–629, 1991.

Caves, P.E., Murphy, W.F., *Franchising: Firms, Markets and Intangible Assets*, Southern Economic Journal, vol. 42, pp. 572–586, 1976.

Chaudhuri, A., Ghosh, P., Spell, C., *A Location Based Theory of Franchising*, Journal of Business and Economics Studies, vol. 7, pp. 54–67, 2001.

Coase, R., *The Nature of the Firm*, Economica, vol. 4, no. 16, pp. 386–405, 1937.

Coase, R., *The New Institutional Economics*, Journal of Institutional and Theoretical Economics, pp. 229–31, 1983.

Cornforth, C., *The Governance of Hybrid Organisations*, in Handbook on Hybrid Organisations, Edward Elgar Publishing, Cheltenham, www.elgaronline.com, 2020.

Dnes, A., *The Economic Analysis of Franchise Contracts*, Journal of Institutional and Theoretical Economics, pp. 297–324, 1996.

Dwyer, F.R., Oh, S., *A Transaction Cost Perspective on Vertical Contractual Structure and Interchannel Competitive Strategies*, Journal of Marketing, vol. 52, no. 2, pp. 21–34, 1988.

Dyer, J.H., *Effective Interfirm Collaboration: How Firms Minimise Transaction Costs and Maximise Transaction Value*, Strategic Management Journal, pp. 535–556, 1997.

Eccles, R., *The Quasifirm in the Construction Industry*, Journal of Economic Behavior and Organization, pp. 335–357, 1981.

Eggertsson, T., *Economic Behaviour and Institutions*, Cambridge University Press, Cambridge, 1990.

Grandori, A., G. Soda, *Interfirm Networks: Antecedentes, Mechanisms and Forms*, Organization Studies, pp. 183–214, 1995.

Grossman, S.J., Hart, O.D., *The Costs and Benefits of Ownership: A Theory of Vertical and Lateral Integration*, Journal of Political Economy, vol. 94, no. 4, pp. 691–719, 1986.

Hennart, J., *Explaining the Swollen Middle – Why Most Transactions Are a Mix of "Market" and "Hierarchy"*, Organization Science, vol. 4, pp. 529–547, 1993.

Herrmann, H., Rana, S., *Which B2B Thinker Are You?* International Journal of Indian Culture and Business Management, vol. 21, no. 1, pp. 45–62, 2020.

Hunt, S., *The Trend Toward Company-Owned Units in Franchise Chains*, Journal of Retailing, vol. 49, pp. 3–12, 1973.

Klein, B., Crawford, R.G., Alchian, A.A., *Vertical Integration, Appropriable Rents and the Competitive Contracting Process*, Journal of Law and Economics, vol. 21, no. 2, pp. 297–326, 1978.

Koghut, B., Zander, U., *Knowledge of the Firm, Combinative Capabilities, and the Replication of Technologies*, Organization Science, pp. 383–397, 1992.

Lafontaine, F., Kaufmann, P.J., *The Evolution of Ownership Patterns in Franchise Systems*, Journal of Retailing, vol. 70, pp. 97–113, 1994.

Lafontaine, F., Slade, M., *Retail Contracting: Theory and Practice*, Journal of Industrial Economics, vol. 45, no. 1, pp. 1–25, 1997.

Lewin-Solomons, S., *The Plural Form in Franchising – A Synergism of Market and Hierarchy*, Working Paper, Iowa State University, 1998.

Martin, R., *Franchising and Risk Management*, American Economic Review, vol. 78, pp. 954–968, 1988.

Mathewson, G.F., Winter, R.A., *The Economics of Franchise Contracts*, Journal of Law & Economics, pp. 503–526, 1985.

Matthews, R.C.O., *The Economics of Institutions and the Sources of Growth*, The Economic Journal, vol. 96, no. 384, pp. 903–918, 1986.

Ménard, C., *On Clusters, Hybrids and Other Strange Forms: The Case of French Poultry Industry*, Journal of Institutional and Theoretical Economics, vol. 152, no. 1, pp. 154–183, 1996.

Ménard, C., *The Economics of Hybrid Organisations*, Journal of Institutional and Theoretical Economics, vol. 160, no. 3, pp. 345–376, 2004.

Ménard, C., *Organisation and Governance in the Agrifood Sector: How Can We Capture Their Variety?* Agribusiness, vol. 34, pp. 142–160, 2018.

Minkler, A., *Why Firms Franchise-A Search Cost Theory*, Journal of Institutional and Theoretical Economics, vol. 148, pp. 240–259, 1992.

Mintzberg, H., *The Nature of Managerial Work*, Harper and Row, New York, 1973.

Mitsubishi, H, Shane, S., Sine, W.D., *Organization Governance Form in Franchising: Efficient Contracting or Organizational Momentum?*, Strategic Management Journal, vol. 29, no. 10, pp. 1127–1136, 2008.

Norton, S., *Franchising, Brand Name Capital and the Entrepreneurial Capacity Problem*, Strategic Management Journal, vol. 9, pp. 105–114, 1988b.

Ouchi, W.G., *Markets, Bureaucracies, and Clans*, Administrative Science Quarterly, vol. 25, 1980.

Oxenfeld, A.R., Kelly, A.O., *Will Successful Franchise Systems Ultimately Become Wholly-Owned Chains?* Journal of Retailing, vol. 44, pp. 69–87, 1969.

Oxley, J.E., *Appropriability Hazards and Governance in Strategic Alliances: A Transaction Cost Approach*, The Journal of Law, Economics, and Organization, vol. 13, no. 2, pp. 387–409, 1997.

Pohoață, I., *Repere în economia instituțională*, Economic Press, București, 2009.

Rana, S., *Business Performance: Earlier Stage and Looking Forward*, FIIB Business Review, vol. 7, no. 3, pp. 153–155, 2018.

Rana, S., Prashar, S., Barai, M.K., Hamid, A.B.A., *Determinants of International Marketing Strategy for Emerging Market Multinationals*, International Journal of Emerging Markets, vol. 16, no. 2, pp. 154–178, 2021.

Rana, S., Raut, S.K., Prashar, S., Hamid, A.B.A., *Promoting through Consumer Nostalgia: A Conceptual Framework and Future Research Agenda*, Journal of Promotion Management, vol. 27, no. 2, pp. 211–249, 2020.

Rana, S., Saikia, P.P., Barai, M.K., *Globalization and Indian Manufacturing Enterprises*, FIIB Business Review, vol. 7, no. 3, pp. 167–175, 2018.

Raut, S.K., Sakpal, S., Soni, R., *Understanding the Service Quality Dimensions and Achieving Resilience in Service Retail*, edited by Yanamandra Ramakrishna, in Handbook of Research on Supply Chain Resiliency, Efficiency, and Visibility in the Post-Pandemic Era, pp. 136–156. IGI Global, UAE, 2022. https://doi.org/10.4018/978-1-7998-9506-0

Rubin, P.H., *The Theory of the Firm and the Structure of the Franchise Contract*, Journal of Law & Economics, pp. 223–233, 1978.

Sako, M., Helper, S., *Determinant of Trust in Supplier Relations: Evidence from Automotive Industry in Japan and the United States*, Journal of Economic Behavior and Organization, pp. 387–417, 1998.

Teece, D., Pisano, G.P., *The Dynamic Capabilities of Firms: An Introduction*, Journal of Economic Behavior and Organization, pp. 537–556, 1992.

Thompson, J.L., *The World of Social Entrepreneur*, The International Journal of Public Sector Management, vol. 15, no. 5, pp. 412–431, 2002.

Tracey, P., Jarvis, O., *Toward a Theory of Social Venture Franchising*, Entrepreneurship Theory and Practice, vol. 31, no. 5, pp. 667–685, 2007.

Walker, G., Weber, D., *A Transaction Cost Approach to Make-or-Buy Decisions*, Administrative Science Quarterly, vol. 29, pp. 373–391, 1984.

Williamson, O., *Markets and Hierarchies*, The Free Press, New York, 1975.

Williamson, O., *The Economics of Organization: The Transaction Cost Approach*, American Journal of Sociology, vol. 87, no. 3, pp. 548–577, 1981.

Williamson, O., *The Economics of Governance: Framework and Implications*, Zeitschrift Für Die Gesamte Staatswissenschaft/Journal of Institutional and Theoretical Economics, vol. 140, no. 1, pp. 195–223, 1984.

Williamson, O., *Comparative Economic Organization: The Analysis of Discrete Structural Alternatives*, Administrative Science Quarterly, vol. 36, no. 2, pp. 269–296, 1991.

Williamson, O., *The Mechanisms of Governance*, Oxford University Press, Oxford, 1996.

Williamson, O., *The Economics of Governance*, American Economic Review, pp. 1–18, 2005.

Yin, X., Zajac, E., *The Strategy/Governance Structure Fit Relationship: Theory and Evidence in Franchising Arrangements*, Strategic Management Journal, vol. 25, no. 4, pp. 365–383, 2004.

2 Why Consumers Respond to Deals

Surajit Ghosh Dastidar

Introduction

'Presently, marketers are using sales promotion as key marketing tools (Shah & D'Souza, 2009), as these can envisage competitive advantage and induce immediate consumer response towards their brands, leading to purchases (Pelsmacker, Geuens & Bergh, 2001). Sales promotion tools are short-term monetary or non-monetary incentives that augur the utility of a brand and thereby stimulate consumers to buy unfamiliar/new brands, switch brands or repeat-buy a brand (Pelsmacker, Geuens & Bergh, 2001; Rana et al., 2020a). The popularity of sales promotion is particularly evident because of high media costs, the urge to differentiate among immense competition clutter, high consumer expectations, and the desire of marketers to earn quick revenue to meet sales targets (Shah & D'Souza, 2009; Raut, Sakpal and Soni, 2022). Also, as there are no definitive practices to accurately measure advertising effectiveness in India, marketers are increasingly using deals over advertising in India (Shah & D'Souza, 2009). As this chapter focuses on sales promotions targeted at end consumers, the term 'sales promotion' relates to consumer-oriented sales promotion and is termed as 'deal'. Examples of deals include coupons, sales, price-offs, refunds or rebates, premiums (free gifts), buy-one-get-one free offers, shelf spacing, and contests, which are common in India (Jethwaney & Jain, 2006) as well as in the Western countries (Lichtenstein, Burton & Netemeyer, 1997). Multiple types of deals are used because all the deals may not work in the same way (Prendergast, Poon & Tsang, 2008), and the challenge before marketers is to choose the most appropriate deal out of many alternatives for best results (Raju, 1995). Each deal must appeal to the target audience and be perceived by them to add value (Hatton, 1998). For example, a 'money off' offer will have a limited appeal to a price-insensitive segment. Hatton (1998) has suggested that efficiency and effectiveness need a combination of good marketing and promotional strategies.

The Indian marketplace has seen a sea change in the last two decades with the opening up of economy and proliferation of brands and influx of a large number of foreign products into India. This has resulted in the shift

DOI: 10.4324/9781003315582-3

of bargaining power in the hands of consumers and an increase in competitiveness among marketers. Marketers are under severe pressure to show good bottom line results on a short-term basis (Shah & D'Souza, 2009) and keep consumers away from buying competitors' products (Stafford & Stafford, 2000). As in the West, advertising is increasingly losing Importance in India due to the proliferation of media costs and incessant clutter of advertisements (Shah & D'Souza, 2009). Cultural factors also create an environment conducive to deals in India. Festivities in the Indian context are accompanied by sales promotion offers as part of the celebrations as shopping is a part of the culture during such occasions. Consumers seem to be attracted to a variety of deals during 'puja' (worship) celebrations and new-year season (Kumar, 2009). Therefore, though no accurate statistics for sales promotion expenditure in Indian marketplace is available today (Shah & D'Souza, 2009), marketers in India are adopting sales promotions in a big way (Shah & D'Souza, 2009).

Most theories of sales promotion simply assume that monetary savings (Narasimhan, 1984; Bawa & Shoemaker, 1987; Blattberg & Neslin, 1990) are the only benefit that motivates consumers to respond to sales promotion (Belch & Belch, 1990; Gijsbrechts, Campo & Goossens, 2003). This is probably because promotions provide a feeling that money is getting saved and hence reduce the pain of paying. They may also grant access to higher-quality brands which could not be bought at their normal price (Kumar, 2009). However, Chandon, Wansink, and Laurent (2000) suggest that monetary savings cannot fully explain why and how consumers respond to sales promotions, because sales promotions provide consumers with benefits beyond monetary savings (Liu & Wang, 2008). For instance, it has been observed that some consumers switch brands because of a deal but then do not redeem it (Soman, 1998) or respond more to an on-shelf coupon than to a similarly advertised temporary price reduction that offers the same monetary incentive (Dhar & Hoch, 1996) or respond to insignificant price deals (Hoch et al., 1994). Martinez and Montaner (2006) found that consumers with more financial constraints do not seem to be more deal-prone than other consumers with a higher economic level. Several non-monetary motivators of consumers' proneness to deals were also assessed such as socio-demographic, hedonic, normative, and behavioural characteristics of consumers (Dastidar & Datta, 2008). Among the first studies which attempted to characterize the deal-prone consumer based on socio-demographic variables was the study by Webster (1965). He claimed to identify and distinguish the deal-prone consumer on the basis of his/her demographic, socio-economic, or purchasing characteristics from others in the market. However, empirical studies yielded a blurred demographic portrait of deal-prone consumers (Martinez & Montaner, 2006). In this respect, Blattberg et al. (1978) proposed that demographics correlate only indirectly, if at all, with deal-proneness, because shopping patterns exert a direct influence on overt deal-proneness (Ailawadi, Neslin & Gedenk, 2001). However,

Pechtl (2004), Carpenter and Moore (2008), and Liu and Wang (2008) found that the mediating effect of demographics on deal-proneness is not significant. Some authors have emphasized the hedonic benefits generated by the purchase of a promoted product (Shimp & Kavas, 1984; Rana et al., 2020b), both for price and non-price promotions. Hedonic benefits are tied to intangible attributes, and they are experiential and affective. Some outstanding hedonic benefits of promotional actions are entertainment and expression. For example for those consumers who enjoy shopping, some promotions may be amusing and increase this entertainment benefit provided by the product purchase. Thus, Ward and Hill (1991) explored consumer perceptions of games and sweepstakes, citing fun as one of the reasons for consumer participation in these types of promotions. However, as no conclusive results could be obtained from the studies assessing economic, demographic, hedonic, and behavioural characteristics as antecedents of deal proneness (Dastidar & Datta, 2006; Martinez & Montaner, 2006), it has been recommended to investigate psychological variables as potential antecedents of deal-proneness (Martinez & Montaner, 2006), as psychological traits are usually stable within one-self (Kassin, 2003). In this respect, psychographically, a somewhat more consistent picture of the deal-prone consumer has been found (Martinez & Montaner, 2006). The relative success of psychographic variables suggests that the real reasons for deal-proneness lie more deeply than the cold statistics of demographics or buying patterns (Gazquez-Abad & Sanchez-Perez, 2009). Schindler, Lala, and Corcoran (2008) suggested that more attention should be given to psychological factors that intrinsically influence an individual to develop into a deal-prone consumer.

Literature review

Consumers' deal proneness

Consumers' deal proneness is defined as *'a general proneness to respond to sales promotions because they are in deal form'* (Gazquez-Abad & Sanchez-Perez, 2009). According to this definition, deal proneness gives a measure of consumers' psychological propensity (intention) to buy goods that offer deals, rather than their overt behaviour (actual purchase) (Gazquez-Abad & Sanchez-Perez, 2009). Deal-prone consumers are those who modify their purchase behaviour so as to benefit from the temporary incentive offered by a deal (Wakefield & Barnes, 1996). Rothschild and Gaidis (1981) use behavioural learning theory or, specifically, Operant Conditioning theory to explain consumers' proneness to deals. According to this theory, deals serve as a reward that might generate immediate consumer response (Schultz, Robinson & Petrison, 1998) as they alter the price–value relationship that the products offer to the consumers (Schultz, Robinson & Petrison, 1998). However, Lichtenstein, Netemeyer, and

Burton (1990) argue that deal proneness should not be conceptualized as being isomorphic with actualized deal responsiveness purchasing behaviour, but should be conceptualized and measured at a psychological level as a construct that affects the actualized purchasing behaviour. Both marketing practitioners and researchers have strived to identify and understand the 'deal prone' consumer (e.g. Lichtenstein, Netemeyer & Burton, 1990; Lichtenstein, Burton & Netemeyer, 1997; Schneider & Currim, 1991) because characterization of the deal-prone consumer contributes to the understanding of consumer behaviour (Webster, 1965) and enables marketers to design better promotional campaigns (Shah & D'Souza, 2009). However, results of deal proneness studies have been modest and conflicting (Martinez & Montaner, 2006).

Lichtenstein, Burton, and Netemeyer (1997) who looked at various deals and consumers' deal proneness found that there are some common traits among deals that lead some consumers to be prone to deals in general. This view suggests that consumers favourably predisposed to one type of deal are, on average, more likely to be favourably predisposed to other deal types. Thus, this perspective also implies that there is sufficient similarity across types of deals to justify targeting a single deal-prone segment of consumers that would be more likely than others to respond to deals of all types (Lichtenstein, Burton & Netemeyer, 1997). However, other studies examining the 'domain specificity' of the deal proneness construct concluded that such a concept is best conceptualized at a deal-type specific level (e.g. coupon proneness, rebate proneness) as opposed to being conceptualized at a general level. Blattberg and Neslin (1990) contend that consumer behaviour may be related to differing response sensitivities across types of deals, thus suggesting a need to distinguish among consumer responses to the type of deal. Consistent with this perspective, Henderson (1987) opines that consumers' attitude and response to deals should be differentiated. Other empirical evidences too suggest that deal sensitivity differs across consumers and deal types (e.g. Schneider & Currim, 1991; Mayhew & Winer, 1992; Ailawadi, Neslin & Gedenk, 2001). These results would lead to the rationale that deal proneness is promotion-type specific. A third group of researchers has suggested a 'middle' position between these two perspectives. For example Schneider and Currim (1991) have dichotomized deal-prone consumers into 'active' and 'passive' deal prone. They view active deal-prone consumers to be more likely to engage in the relatively intensive search required to respond to deals like coupons or contests. In contrast, passive deal-prone consumers are more likely to respond to deals such as in-store displays, where there is minimal searching limited to the in-store environment. Schneider and Currim (1991) also claimed an overlap between active and passive deal proneness. According to these authors, the actively deal-prone household may behave as though it were passively deal prone on some occasions – that is, the shopper may not set aside time to look for a deal before the store trip. Yet, the shopper will react to a deal if a brand is displayed/featured. Overlap between active and passive deal proneness can also occur if shopping duties are shared by members of the same household (e.g. one shopper may be actively deal prone, the other passively deal prone). Ailawadi, Neslin, and Gedenk (2001) establish a similar differentiation between proneness to out-of-store deals and proneness to in-store deals. For these authors, the former deals are those which take place out of the shops and demand some effort from the consumer – they would be related to the active proneness as proposed by Schneider and Currim (1991). On the other hand, in-store deals are those which are developed inside the point of sales and discovered by the consumer when shopping. These types of deals require a reduced effort from the buyer and are related to passive proneness. Shimp (1990) classified deals as price- and non-price-oriented. Coupons, sales, rebates, and rupees-off deals, for example, result in lower purchase prices, while other deals (such as contests, free gifts with purchase, shelf displays, and buy-one-get-one-free offers) do not offer a lower purchase price. Chandon, Wansink, and Laurent (2000) pointed out that price-oriented deals provide more congruent benefit to utilitarian products, whereas non-price-oriented deals are more compatible for hedonic purchase. Thus, conflicting findings lead to an uncertainty about the domain specificity of deal proneness regarding

Table 2.1 Differentiating proneness to deals

Store-based (Ailawadi, Neslin & Gedenk, 2001)	Proneness to out-of-store promotions	It takes place out of the shops and demands some effort from the consumer.
	Proneness to in-store promotions	It is developed inside the point of sales and is discovered by the consumer during shopping.
Price-based (Price, Feick & Guskey-Federouch, 1988)	Price-oriented promotions	Result in lower purchase price (e.g. coupons, sales, rupees off labels, rebates).
	Non-price-oriented promotions	Do not result in lower purchase price (e.g. buy-one-get-one-free offers, gifts, contests/sweepstakes, displays).
Buyer's search-based (Schneider & Currim, 1991)	Active proneness	It refers to the consumers' sensitivity to store flyers and coupons. This proneness requires an intense search from the consumer to find interesting promotions.
	Passive proneness	It demands a limited search developed at the point of sales. Such proneness is reflected in the consumers' sensitivity to in-store displays.

Source: Author's own

deal type. Gazquez-Abad and Sanchez-Perez (2009) recommend that as the diversity of deals being used is rapidly increasing, to treat them as a homogenous set of tools that may elicit similar behavioural responses, or whose proneness may be predicted by similar predictor variables, is presumptuous. The various deals, therefore, need to be studied individually. While coupons in particular have received a great deal of attention from the literature, other deals have also been receiving unparalleled research attention (Gazquez-Abad & Sanchez-Perez, 2009).

Bawa, Srinivasan, and Srivastava (1997) studied coupons' use by considering the joint effects of coupon attractiveness and coupon proneness on redemption and estimated this at the product category level, taking varying coupon redemption behaviours across categories into account. Results underlined the importance of product category level estimation. These authors stated that non-category specific coupon proneness measures have low predictive power and perform poorly in explaining using coupons in a specific category. Regarding product category, Cunningham (1956) and Massy, Frank, and Lodahl (1968) found empirical support for product class specific deal proneness. Also, Swaminathan and Bawa (2005) in a study found that deal proneness differed in case of high-involvement and low-involvement product categories. Narasimhan, Neslin, and Sen (1996) also found difference in effectiveness of shelf display between high-priced and low-priced product categories. Ainslie and Rossi (1998), on the other hand, provided evidence of substantial correlations, validating, in part, the notion that sensitivity to marketing mix variables is a consumer trait and is not unique to specific product categories. So with respect to product category deal-proneness domain specificity, prior research has led to conflicting findings.

Pechtl (2004) distinguish between overt and intrinsic deal proneness. The former is based on those indicators used to measure how sensitively a consumer responds to deals – that is purchase time, brand choice, purchase quantity, category consumption, store choice, or search behaviour. It refers to consumers' overt behaviour towards deals (Dickson & Sawyer, 1990). The introduction of scanners in self-service outlets, particularly in the United States and Europe, has allowed retailers to easily measure how sensitively a consumer responds to promotions. In addition to previous studies focused on overt deal-proneness, another body of literature on deal-proneness has considered more intrinsic aspects of this concept. For example Hackleman and Duker (1980) emphasized the inability of deal-prone consumers to resist a bargain, and Henderson (1987) noted the commitment of deal-prone individuals to a deal (e.g. coupons). Lichtenstein, Netemeyer, and Burton (1990) specified deal-proneness using the concept of transaction utility and suggested a psychological interpretation of this construct. Intrinsic deal-proneness is based on emotional, motivational, and affective aspects of promotions in buying behaviour (Laroche et al., 2001).

Why do consumers respond to deals?

Characterizing deal-prone consumers

As consumers' deal proneness may be motivated by several factors, Aila-wadi, Neslin, and Gedenk (2001); Shah and D'Souza (2009); and others have argued that it is essential to identify deal-prone consumers and understand the underlying motivators of their deal-responsive behaviour. From extant literature, we find that deal-proneness has traditionally been related to *economic savings* and *price sensitivity* (Dastidar & Datta, 2008). Prominent studies in this area are discussed in the following paragraph.

Most research has concluded that more price-sensitive the consumer, the more positive will be his or her attitude towards sales promotions (Gijsbre-chts, Campo & Goossens, 2003; Miranda & Konya, 2007; and others), and they will respond well to promotional actions (Chen, Monroe & Lou, 1998). Price sensitivity implies individuals' price perception and their sensitivity to changes or differences in prices (Wakefiled & Inman, 2003). Related to this is the saving feeling and reduced pain of paying achieved from deal redemption. Deals also enable lower-end consumer segments' access to premium brands (Kumar, 2009). This is explained by the theory of economic utility (Dodson, Tybout & Sternthal, 1978). It states that deals serve as economic incentives that enhance the utility of a brand, thus inducing brand switching, and the extent of switching depends on the economic value of the deal (micro-economic theory) (Bawa & Shoemaker, 1987). Using utility theory, Thaler (1985) further explained that the total value of transaction to a consumer is the sum of transaction utility and acquisition utility. Deals increase the transaction utility as the price paid is lower than the internal reference price, which results in a saving feeling. Deals also increase the acquisition utility as reduced cost increases the product value (Thaler, 1985). However, some robust studies observed that some consumers switch brands because of a coupon but then do not redeem it (Dhar & Hoch, 1996; Soman, 1998). Some other robust studies found that some consumers respond more to an on-shelf coupon than to a similarly advertised temporary price reduction that offers the same monetary incentive (Schindler, 1992; Dhar & Hoch, 1996) or respond to insignificant price deals (Inman, McAlister & Hoyer, 1990; Hoch et al., 1994). These studies clearly suggest that monetary savings cannot fully explain why and how consumers respond to sales promotions (Chandon, Wansink & Laurent, 2000; Dastidar & Datta, 2008). According to Chandon, Wansink, and Laurent (2000), there may be failure to redeem the coupons responsible for the purchase decision because these consumers value the exploration benefits that coupons provide at the time of the decision but not the monetary savings they provide at the time of payment. This implies that sales promotions provide consumers with benefits beyond monetary savings (Liu & Wang, 2008). This argument is reiterated by Martinez and Montaner (2006) who found that consumers with more financial constraints do not seem to be more deal prone than other consumers with a higher economic level. Lichtenstein, Netemeyer, and Burton (1990) extend this argument stating that since deal-prone consumers would favourably evaluate a purchase offer because it is offered in deal form, it follows that consumers who are highly deal prone will be more likely to use deals irrespective of the magnitude of savings offered by the deal. On the other hand, consumers who use deals to purchase a brand only when the magnitude of savings offered by deal is high would be lesser prone to respond to deals (Janda, 1996).

On the basis of aforementioned argument that economic savings cannot fully explain the motivation to redeem deals, several studies were carried out assessing consumers' psychological characteristics and mechanisms; hedonic, behavioural, normative, household characteristics and demographic characteristics, as well as deal characteristics and brand equity as potential antecedents of deal-responsive behaviour (Dastidar & Datta, 2008). Prominent studies in this regard are discussed in the following paragraphs. A framework of the various correlates of consumers' response to deals is presented in Figure 2.1.

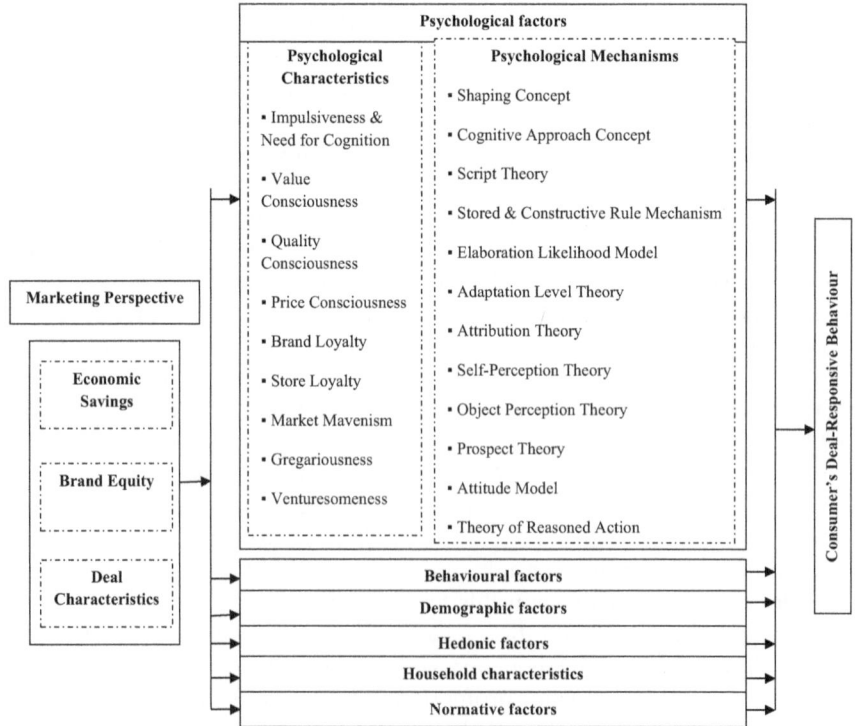

Figure 2.1 Correlates of consumers' response to deals

Apart from the studies focusing on economic utility, some authors emphasized the *hedonic benefits* generated by the purchase of a promoted product (Shimp & Kavas, 1984). Hedonic benefits imply experiential and affective benefits such as entertainment, exploration, and self-expression (Shimp & Kavas, 1984). For example, for those consumers who enjoy shopping, deals as well as information search on deal availability may be amusing (Beatty & Smith, 1997). Thus, hedonic benefits provide additional utility over economic benefit (Urbany, Dickson, & Kalapurakal, 1996). Ward and Hill (1991) assessed consumer perceptions of games and sweepstakes, citing fun as one of the reasons for consumer participation in these types of deals. Interestingly, Chandon, Wansink and Laurent (2000) combine both aspects of economic benefit and hedonic benefit stating that deals may provide both economic benefits as well as hedonic benefits at a time. They also point out that price promotions provide more economic benefit, whereas non-price promotions are more compatible for hedonic purchase.

Among the other studies investigating antecedents of consumers' deal-responsive behaviour, *normative factors* (motivation to conform to the subjective norms) have received attention (Shimp & Kavas, 1984). On the basis of 'Theory of Reasoned Action' (Fishbein & Ajzen, 1975), which states that consumers' response towards deals is influenced by their attitude towards their behaviour and perceptions of whether important others (e.g. peers, spouse) think one should or should not use deals for brand choice (Shimp & Kavas, 1984), Ailawadi, Neslin, and Gedenk (2001) found normative influencing factors in relation to reference groups to be significant in explaining consumers' response to deals. Related to this, Huff and Alden (1998) found the attitude of reference groups towards discounted products (offered on deal) and fear of embarrassment to influence response to deals. Interactions between attitude and subjective norm are more prominently manifested in collective cultures, for example in India (Yuna et al., 2008).

There are some compelling reasons to model the impact of *deal characteristics* on redemption intentions. It is argued that a person's coupon usage behaviour will depend not only on his or her inherent coupon proneness or desire to use coupons, but also on the attractiveness of the coupons encountered. For example a consumer may be inclined to use coupons but may exhibit low coupon usage if he or she fails to find coupons that are sufficiently attractive (i.e. coupons with high face values or for a preferred brand). Coupons for large-share brands and with higher face values tend to enjoy higher redemption rates (Bawa, Srinivasan & Srivastava, 1997). According to *Microeconomic Theory*, the deal redemption intention is likely to be higher in case of higher utility (e.g. face value of coupon) as compared to lower utility. Also, whether the coupon is for a preferred brand or for a brand the consumer occasionally purchases determines coupon redemption intention.

Consumer response to promotional offer was more positive when the premium (free gift with purchase) was direct than when it was delayed.

Also, consumer appreciation of a promotional offer was negatively associated with the quantity of the product one needed to buy to avail the offer. The price of a product had no impact on consumer reactions to a premium-based promotional offer. Consumers may be driven to purchase a product in which they have little interest if the premium is sufficiently attractive (D'Astons & Jacob, 2002).

As regards *brand equity*, Rao (1991) suggests that high-equity brands can offer deals to induce switch from low-equity brands. Blattberg and Wisniewski (1989) found that high-equity brands gain more from a price cut. They argue that non-monetary deals will be less effective in the case of low-equity hedonic brands, and monetary deals will be more effective for high-equity utilitarian brands. However, Bronnenberg and Wathieu (1997) report contrasting results.

In *behavioural terms*, Bawa and Shoemaker (1987) reported that active shoppers who are less loyal to brands and stores are more coupon prone than routinized shoppers who are more loyal to brands and stores. This is explained by the 'script' theory by Gardner and Strang (1984), which states that routinized response to deals is primarily through the use of stored scripts (according to Schank and Abelson (1977), a script is 'a structure that describes an appropriate sequence of events in a particular context') whereas non-routinized response to deals is primarily through an attitude formation process. Montgomery (1971) found that those who are more exposed to media are more likely to respond to deals. Ailawadi, Neslin, and Gedenk (2001) and Martinez and Montaner (2006) found that consumers who plan their shopping are likely to respond to deals. Consumers who plan their shopping are likely to consider out-of-store deal since these deals encourage and help them to plan the shopping (Ailawadi, Neslin & Gedenk, 2001). In addition, planning shoppers eventually learn the deal patterns of the establishments, and they adapt their decisions to these patterns acquired inside the store (Krishna, Currim & Shoemaker, 1991). Shoppers enjoy searching for deal-related information (Beatty and Smith, 1997) as well as obtain additional utility through discounts (Urbany, Dickson & Kalapurakal, 1996). Therefore, they redeem discount coupons and glance through store flyers (Kolodinsky, 1990).

Among studies assessing *demographic characteristics* as antecedents of deal proneness, Webster (1965) conducted one of the first studies in which he correlated deal proneness with families' demographic, socioeconomic, and purchasing characteristics. Webster, however, did not distinguish different types of deals and different product classes. Webster's pioneering work led to a number of studies dedicated to deal proneness. Montgomery (1971) examined possible relationships between a housewife's dealing activity in a product class and some social-psychological and purchasing characteristics. Blattberg et al. (1978) stated that it is possible to identify a deal-prone household by using demographic variables in case of several product categories. McAlister (1986) extended these segments and differentiated between those who stockpiled goods because of a deal and those who did not. However, empirical studies yield a blurred demographic portrait of deal-prone consumers (Ainslie & Rossi, 1998), and findings in literature are inconsistent regarding who is more deal prone (Kwon & Kwon, 2007). While some researchers such as Bawa and Shoemaker (1987), Lichtenstein, Burton, and Netemeyer (1997); and Ailawadi, Neslin, and Gedenk (2001) found positive relationship between age and deal proneness, Pechtl (2004) found insignificant relationship. Similarly while Kwon and Kwon (2007) and others found positive relationship between income and deal proneness, Jolson, Joshua, and Rosecky (1987) found negative relationship, and Carpenter and Moore (2008) found no relationship. While Ailawadi, Neslin, and Gedenk (2001) and others found a relationship between gender and deal proneness, Carpenter and Moore (2008) and others found no evidence of such relationship. Also, while Cho and Kang (1998); Kwon and Kwon (2007); and others found positive relationship between education and deal proneness, Jolson, Joshua and Rosecky (1987) found negative relationship, and Teel, Williams and Bearden (1980) found insignificant relationship. While Cotton and Babb (1978) found positive relationship between female employment and deal proneness, Blattberg et al. (1978) found a negative relationship, and Bawa and Shoemaker (1987) and others found insignificant relationship. Similarly, while Blattberg et al. (1978) found positive relationship between the presence of children and deal proneness, Narasimhan (1984) found negative relationship, and Bawa and Shoemaker (1987) found insignificant relationship. While Mittal (1994); Ailawadi, Neslin and Gedenk (2001); and others found positive relationship between family size and deal proneness, Cotton and Babb (1978) found negative relationship, and Webster (1965) found insignificant relationship. Also, while Webster (1965) found positive relationship between age of housewife and deal proneness, Teel, Williams, and Bearden (1980) found a negative relationship, and Bawa and Shoemaker (1987) found insignificant relationship. Thus, considerable inconsistency is found in demographic studies, which could be due to the use of different measures, methods, and study of different types of promotions. In this respect, Blattberg et al. (1978) demonstrated that demographics correlate only indirectly, if at all, with deal-proneness, because shopping patterns exert a direct influence on overt deal-proneness (Ailawadi, Neslin & Gedenk, 2001). However, Carpenter and Moore (2008) and Liu and Wang (2008) found that the mediating effect of demographics on deal-proneness is not significant. While demographic characteristics have been studied primarily with the objective of profiling consumers, the underlying reason for deal proneness has not been studied (Kwon & Kwon, 2007). Some studies suggested that psychographics are much better discriminators than demographics (Park & Gómez, 2004; Bhandari and Raut, 2019).

Among studies assessing *household characteristics* as being indicators of deal proneness, Blattberg et al. (1978) predicted that deal proneness would be lower for households with children under six, no car, higher income, working wives, and a rented home. A model of utility maximization was proposed, predicting that the intensity of coupon usage is related inversely to a household's opportunity cost of time. The coupon usage was expected to be lower for households that are more educated, have children under six, and in which both husband and wife are working. They found coupon usage higher for households with higher levels of education, and no children under eighteen. They also found that the number of purchases made with a coupon first increased and then decreased with household income. Bawa and Shoemaker (1987) reported that coupon-prone households are more educated, have higher income, are urban, less brand loyal, and store loyal.

Monetary as well as non-monetary motivators for consumers' proneness to deals such as consumers' demographic, hedonic, normative, and behavioural characteristics and deal characteristics have been studied. These have been studied in the context of U.S. market where consumer panel data are easily available, which provide extensive information on demographics and purchase behaviour (Lichtenstein, Burton & Netemeyer, 1997). However, no conclusive results could be obtained from these studies (Dastidar & Datta, 2006; Martinez & Montaner, 2006) as evident from the review of literature. This prompted many researchers (Park & Gómez, 2004; Martinez & Montaner, 2006 and others) to recommend assessing *psychological* variables as possible antecedents of deal proneness, primarily because psychological variables (individual traits) are considered to be stable within oneself (Kassin, 2003). In this respect, psychographically, a somewhat more consistent picture of the deal-prone consumer has been found (Martinez & Montaner, 2006). In an article, Gazquez-Abad and Sanchez-Perez (2009) opine that the relative success of psychographic variables suggests that the real reasons for deal proneness need to be assessed more deeply rather than simply profiling deal-prone consumers on the basis of their demographics or buying patterns or using only extrinsic factors to understand consumers' deal-responsive behaviour. This argument is congruent with the suggestion of Schindler, Lala, and Corcoran (2008) that more attention should be given to psychological factors that intrinsically influence an individual to develop into a deal-prone consumer. In this regard, a number of studies used psychological variables to identify the deal-prone consumer. Prominent studies among these are discussed in the following paragraphs.

Some studies assessed *value consciousness* as being antecedent of deal-responsive behaviour. Value is defined as the ratio of benefits to price (Martinez & Montaner, 2006). Wakefield and Barnes (1996), Ramaswamy and Srinivasan (1998), and others found that value-conscious consumers are more likely to respond to deal offers.

Other researchers assessing *quality consciousness* obtained mixed results. Quality is a utilitarian benefit associated with the purchase of a product (Martinez & Montaner, 2006). While Lichtenstein and Ridgway (1993) found a positive relationship between quality consciousness and deal response, Martinez and Montaner (2006) found negative relationship.

Pertaining to *price consciousness*, all studies, such as those of Wakefield and Bush (1998), Martinez and Montaner (2006), and others, found that price-conscious consumers are likely to respond to deals.

Except studies by Mittal (1994) and Wakefield and Bush (1998), who found positive relationship between *brand loyalty* and response to deals, most of the other studies such as those of Bawa and Shoemaker (1987), Wakefield and Barnes (1996), and others found that brand-loyal consumers are unlikely to respond to deal offers. Ailawadi, Neslin, and Gedenk (2001) and Grover and Srinivasan (1992) found that brand loyals may respond to that brand's deals but not to the competitors' deals. McCann (1974) found an insignificant relationship.

Pertaining to *store loyalty*, while Ailawadi, Neslin, and Gedenk (2001) and Martinez and Montaner (2006) found a positive relationship with response to deals, Bawa and Shoemaker (1987) found a negative relationship. McCann (1974) found an insignificant relationship. Sirohi, McLaughlin, and Wittink (1998) stated that store-loyal customers are satisfied with the deals offered by the store they are loyal to.

Raghubir and Corfman (1999) and Ailawadi, Neslin, and Gedenk (2001) found that those high on *market mavenism* are likely to respond to deals. Feick and Price (1987) define market mavens as 'individuals who have information about many kinds of products, places to shop, and other facets of markets and initiate discussions with consumers and respond to requests from consumers for market information'. They are heavy users of coupons (Price, Feick & Guskey-Federouch, 1988).

Lichtenstein, Burton, and Netemeyer (1997) and Ailawadi, Neslin, and Gedenk (2001) found that consumers who are high on *impulsiveness* and *need for cognition* are more likely to respond to deals. Impulsiveness is a trait which induces purchases 'on impulse' as an unplanned purchase (Blattberg & Neslin, 1990). Consumers with high need for cognition process information centrally, which is a diligent and active processing of the information (Lichtenstein, Burton & Netemeyer, 1997).

Webster (1965) and Montgomery (1971) stated that consumers high on *gregariousness* (implying extrovertness) and *venturesomeness* (implying innovativeness) are more likely to respond to deals.

Though the previous studies were able to identify a finite number of influential psychological factors, the review of literature as presented before shows conflicting results in many cases. Also, these studies did not attempt to investigate all the relevant factors at one time.

Some psychological mechanisms that explain consumer's response to promotions

A number of theories have been forwarded to explain the psychological mechanisms that underlie the consumer's deal responsive behaviour. Some of these are discussed next.

Shaping concept: Rothschild and Gaidis (1981) use behavioural learning theory to explain consumer response to deals. They put forth the concept of 'shaping', which suggests that a substantial deal offer, such as a free sample, can induce initial trial with subsequent smaller incentives inducing repeat purchases until the behaviour is learned after which the incentives can be retracted. If the incentive reward is greater than the regard associated with the product, then the repeat purchases are unlikely when the incentive is withdrawn. Also, if the deal is retracted before the behaviour is learned, then the consumer may switch to another brand. This theory further suggests that intermittent promotion schedules may be more effective than continuous schedules.

Cognitive approach concept: In contrast to 'shaping' concept, Raju and Hastak (1980) proposed a 'cognitive approach'. According to this approach, a deal is considered to be a cue at the point of purchase, which triggers certain psychological processes within the consumer. These psychological processes encode the deal and form beliefs leading to the evaluation of the brand and post-trial experience. In the pre-trial stage, Raju and Hastak (1980) draw on *social judgement theory* to suggest that a deal will not be considered unless the brand is already priced within the consumer's acceptable range or the deal is large enough to move the price within that range.

Script theory: A model by Gardner and Strang (1984) indicates that one way consumers may respond to promotions is primarily through the use of stored scripts. According to Schank and Abelson (1977), a script is a structure that describes an appropriate sequence of events in a particular context. Consumers may also respond to deals through an attitude formation process. This sequence is more likely to occur when the consumer's response is not routinized.

Stored and constructive rule mechanisms: Bettman and Zins (1977) differentiate between information processing leading to a choice that takes place prior to a store trip and one that takes place on site. The former follows a *stored* rule mechanism, while the latter takes the form of a *constructive* rule mechanism. These researchers suggest that information presented in the store may have more impact than that presented outside the store if the consumer is operating under a constructive rule mechanism.

Elaboration Likelihood Model: The Elaboration Likelihood Model of Petty and Cacioppo (1981) suggests that human information processing follows two distinct routes: the central route and the peripheral route. Inman, McAlister, and Hoyer (1990) propose the consumer's need for cognition as one possibility and find that the response to a promotion differs depending upon which route the promotional information was processed. Differences in effort and costs related to the use of different types of promotions, or differences in motivation for thinking about a purchase, may result in households generally favouring one type of promotion over another (Schneider & Currim, 1991).

Adaptation Level theory: According to this theory, consumers possess an adaptation level price or 'internal reference price' for a given product.

The internal reference price implies the price a consumer expects to pay for a product, which is formed on the basis of past prices paid/observed either for the same or similar products. The internal reference price is a benchmark against which price points are compared and judged as high, low, or medium. The existence of internal reference prices has been confirmed in several experimental studies (Gurumurthy & Winer, 1995). Researchers have proposed that consumers respond to a price deal after comparing the promotional price with their internal reference price (Kalwani & Yim, 1992). Sustained price promotional campaign is likely to lead consumers to lower their reference price for the promoted product. Lowered reference prices will lead to the unwillingness of consumers to pay the full price of a product once the deal is retracted.

Attribution Theory: Attribution theory describes how consumers explain the causes of events (Mizerski, Golden & Kernan, 1979). Different types of attribution can be distinguished on the basis of the object about which the attribution is being made. When a consumer attributes a purchase to self (the 'why-did-I-buy' question), it comes under the *self-perception theory*. However, when attribution is made about an object/brand (the 'why-is-brand-X-on-promotion'), it comes under *object perception theory*. An analysis of each in the context of promotion is discussed next.

Self-perception Theory: Researchers who have applied self-perception theory to price promotions (Dodson, Tybout & Sternthal, 1978) have stated that a purchase made through a promotion offer is likely to lead the consumer to attribute the purchase to an external reason (i.e. the promotion) rather than an internal reason (i.e. liking for the product). In such cases, the attitude towards the brand will be less favourable resulting into diminished repeat purchase probability. Basically, self-perception theory suggests that the result of sustained price promotional campaigns may not be positive on consumer attitudes and behaviour.

Object Perception Theory: Researchers who have applied object perception theory to price deals have stated that a brand offering a deal may be perceived to have compromised in quality due to which it is offering an incentive. However, whether a brand shall be perceived to be of lower quality or not depends on factors such as the consistency ('Is the brand always on promotion?') and the distinctiveness of the price promotion ('Is it the only brand on promotion?'). Although early researchers had suggested that the mere presence of a promotion would lead to perceptions of lower quality (Dodson, Tybout & Sternthal, 1978), results of later studies showed that a promotion's information value is context specific (Raghubir & Corfman, 1999). In a situation where deals are common, consumers are unlikely to make negative attributions about a brand just because it is offering a deal.

Prospect Theory: This theory proposes that people perceive outcomes of a choice as perceived 'losses' and 'gains' relative to a subjective reference point (Kahneman & Tversky, 1984). Researchers who have applied this theory to promotions (Diamond & Sanyal, 1990; Diamond & Campbell,

1990) have stated that consumer's perception of promotion as a 'loss' or 'gain' depends on the type of deal. They proposed that non-price deals such as premium offers, which segregate the promotional gain from the purchase price, will be viewed as gains. On the other hand, price deals such as price off, which integrate the promotional gain with the purchase price, will be viewed as reduced losses. Diamond and Sanyal (1990) used Prospect Theory to predict that non-price deals would be viewed as gains and would be more preferred than price deals that would be viewed as reduced losses.

Attitude Model: Multi-attribute models of attitude (Fishbein & Ajzen, 1975) depict the consumer's decision to perform a specific behaviour as being the logical consequence of beliefs, attitudes, and intentions with regard to the behaviour. As per this model, consumers' intention to buy a brand may be dependent on their positive/negative attitude towards the deal that the brand is offering.

Babakus, Tat, and Cunningham (1988) investigated how the three attitudinal factors – price consciousness, time value, and satisfaction/pride – affected consumers' decision to use coupons. A positive relationship between coupon usage and consumer price consciousness was found. It was found that the more a consumer valued his or her time, the lesser was the tendency to use coupons. The authors found that consumers use coupon more when they feel greater satisfaction and pride with coupon usage.

Theory of Reasoned Action: Shimp and Kavas (1984) applied the Theory of Reasoned Action to understand consumer's decision to use coupons. As per the model, consumers' response towards coupon offer would be influenced by their intention to use coupons. This would be determined by their attitude and subjective norms. Consumers' attitude formation would be a function of their beliefs in the rewards vis-à-vis the costs of using coupons, while subjective norms would be formed through consumers' perception of whether relevant others appreciate their effort to clip, save, and redeem coupons. The authors stated that beliefs regarding the rewards accrued from coupons had high positive correlation with attitude while inconveniences and encumbrances regarding coupon usage had weak negative correlation with attitude. The authors found that both attitudes and subjective norms had significant influence on the intention to use coupons.

Limitations of the theoretical approaches

The theoretical approaches used to explain consumers' response to deals had certain limitations. The price-perception-based studies fail to explain consumers' response to non-price deals such as free gift offers and premium offers. Attribution theory too fails to explain consumers' response to deals when all brands promote frequently.

Research regarding the prospect-theory-based prediction that consumers will prefer non-price deals (perceived as 'gains') over price deals (perceived as 'reduced losses') is not conclusive. Although attitude models strive to explain the consumer decision process, several studies have found a weak correlation between attitude and behaviour.

The Elaboration Likelihood Model uses an individual difference variable (need for cognition) to explain consumers' response to deals. Information regarding the relationship of this variable with other managerially action-able variables such as demographics is scant. A robust theoretical frame-work that can adequately explain consumers' response to different types of deals is required.

Research on promotions has primarily concentrated on factors related to price and their effects on consumers' judgements. For example studies per-taining to adaptation level theory have examined the impact of discounted promotional price on consumers' internal reference price. Researchers have used the concept of transaction utility to relate psychological pleasure with obtaining a price discount. Similarly, the assimilation contrast theory has been used to examine the optimum size and presentation format of price discounts in promotional advertisements. The focus on price has probably been due to the fact that majority of the promotion research has focused on price promotions, namely price-offs and coupons. These approaches, there-fore, have limited generalizability as the analyses of factors affecting promo-tion choice are mainly restricted to price.

Studies that focused on psychological antecedents to explain consum-ers' response to deals primarily involved a single product. For example, the theoretical models – adaptation level theory, transaction utility theory, assimilation contrast theory, attribution theory, attitude models – are based on single-product focus. These studies have assessed the impact of deals on price perceptions, quality perceptions, and savings. While research on retail price deals has found a positive cross-product impact of promotion, psychology-oriented studies have not systematically verified this aspect of promotional response (Dang, 2004).

Some guidelines for effective promotion campaigns

Are all deal types equally effective?

Empirical studies by Gupta (1988) and Dastidar (2016) have established that sales promotions predominantly stimulate brand switching and risk-taking/innovative purchase behaviour by providing stimulation to reach Optimum Stimulation Level (OSL). Marketers employing a variety of deals should note that consumers' deal proneness levels are higher for some deal types (e.g. shelf display, free gift, rupees off, sale, buy-one-get-one-free) than others (e.g. contests and coupons). A number of earlier studies (e.g. Bawa, Srinivasan & Srivastava, 1997; Martinez & Montaner, 2006; Dastidar, 2016) established that variety seeking (brand switching) and innovativeness positively influence consumers' response to deals. As deals partially act as source of stimulation (Kahn & Raju, 1991), they enable consumers to reach their OSL. OSL is a property that characterizes an individual in terms of his general tendency towards environmental stimuli. It can be expected that consumers with higher exploratory tendencies (tendency to obtain one's OSL) are more likely to respond positively to deal offers. Therefore, offering price reductions in the form of price-oriented deals rather than merely reduced prices can result into higher sales.

When should be promotion done?

According to Object Perception Theory, whether or not consumers will attribute lower quality to the brand owing to the fact that it is on promotion depends on two factors – (i) Consistency ('Is the brand always on promotion?') and (ii) Distinctiveness ('Is it the only brand on promotion?'). If consumers observe that a brand is on promotion when no other competitor brand is offering promotions and that a brand is always on promotion, they may assume that the brand may have compromised in quality. So, promotional campaigns should not be planned under the aforementioned circumstances. Consistency also lowers the internal reference price, as explained by Adaptation Level theory. When consumers are offered a lower price level (through promotional offers) for a product consistently for a long period, they adapt to the new lower price point and refuse to pay higher price when the product retracts the promotional offer.

What discount level should be offered?

Since discounts as promotional offers modify the price level, they involve changes in price perceptions. According to Assimilation Contrast Theory, price modifications should be done only within an acceptable range of price. If the reduction of price point is too large, consumers will relate it with reduction in quality as perceived quality is directly proportional to the price. Also, it needs to be remembered that if price modification is too small and it remains below the just noticeable difference (j.n.d.) level, consumers will not take note of the promotional offer. Therefore, though the company will incur investment, the impact of promotional campaign will not be there.

What form of promotion should be used?

According to Prospect Theory, consumers perceive outcomes of a choice as either 'losses' or 'gains'. Non-price promotions, such as premium offers, free samples, and buy-one-get-one-free offers which segregate the promotional gain from the purchase price, are typically perceived as 'gains'. On the other hand, price promotions such as price off and rebates which integrate the promotional gain with the purchase price are typically perceived as 'reduced losses'. Though technically, the face value of the promotional offer may be the same, the perception of gain is more intense than the perception of reduced loss, thereby rendering greater happiness among consumers regarding the promotional offer. So, marketers can use such promotional offers that are distinct from the purchased product for greater effectiveness.

How to alleviate negative perceptions regarding promotions?

It is typically found that consumers develop various negative perceptions about promotions such as – (a) There is greater competition in the market, (b) Companies get scared, (c) Companies want to get rid of old stock, (d) Companies want to attract customers *anyhow*, (e) Companies include the cost of deal in the purchase price itself, and (f) If Companies give more, they reduce the quality. It is suggested that justifying the promotions can alleviate price–quality perceptions. It will convince the consumers that the price reduction is only a temporary affair to increase the economic utility of the product. Also, a regular promotion with reason (e.g. semi-annual sales) may result into higher purchases as otherwise they have to wait for long to get promotional offers.

Is consumer sales promotion profitable?

While apparently sales promotions seem to be a profitable initiative, some pertinent factors should be noted while estimating the profitability accrued because of the sales promotion campaign. First, higher profitability is assumed to be achieved from incremental sales. Incremental sale implies the additional sales obtained because of promotions over and above the base sales that would be achieved even without the promotional campaign. The question is where does the incremental sale come from? It may be obtained from (i) greater purchase of existing customers, i.e. stockpiling and (ii) inducing switch of customers from other brands. It may be noted that in the first case, the incremental sale is actually achieved by stealing from the brand's own future potential sales. Due to stockpiling, the customers are not going to purchase the brand in the immediate future, resulting into a decline of sales. So, profitability calculated over a longer period may not really show any boost. Profitability will depend to a large extent on the number of customers who switch from other brands to avail the promotional offer. The profitability accrued from the promotional campaign should be calculated as thus:

Profit (from promotional campaign) = Incremental Sales × Margin – Total Sales × Discount.

Discount implies the per unit investment towards the promotional campaign. It should be noted here that while only the incremental sales are considered to estimate revenue, total sales are considered to estimate costs. Therefore, the profitability model will not be profitable unless the promotional campaign can ensure large sales, which can compensate for the profit deficiency in the model. Thus, two things should be ensured for gaining profitability – large sales from campaign and larger share of the sales obtained should be due to switching from other competitor brands.

Conclusions

A review of the extant literature based on the framework of correlates of deal responsive behaviour presented in this chapter points out that sales promotion campaign based on economic framework alone may not be appropriate. In order to be able to identify the deal-prone consumer and provide higher value through the deal offer, marketers also need to focus on consumer-related factors, for example psychological, behavioural, normative, hedonic, demographic factors as well as deal characteristics and brand equity from a marketing perspective.

A large number of studies aimed to understand the deal-responsive behaviour of consumers. While most of the studies focused on only one or few deals at a time and attempted to generalize their findings, other studies have found that response to deal offers varies across deal types. Therefore, marketers should devise deal-specific strategies for their promotional campaigns.

It is also evident that studies assessing demographic, behavioural, and socio-economic aspects as antecedents of deal proneness have obtained inconsistent results. On the other hand, studies pertaining to psychological variables were more fruitful. Deal characteristics have also been identified as significant correlates of deal-responsive behaviour. However, the marketing factors and behavioural factors are mediated by the psychological factors of consumers. This chapter has discussed consumers' response to deals under different promotion contexts.

Future research should focus on integrating the various correlates and provide simple feasible guidelines to the marketing practitioners. This chapter has strived to point out the various theoretical models and empirical findings that have contributed to a greater understanding of sales promotions.

References

Ailawadi, K. L., Neslin, S. A. & Gedenk, K. (2001). Pursuing the value-conscious consumer: Store brands versus national brand promotions. *Journal of Marketing*, 65(1), 71–89.

Ainslie, A. & Rossi, P. E. (1998). Similarities in choice behavior across product categories. *Marketing Science*, 17(2), 91–106.

Babakus, E., Tat, P. & Cunningham, W. (1988). Coupon redemption: A motivation perspective. *Journal of Consumer Marketing*, 5(2), 37–44.

Bawa, K. & Shoemaker, R. W. (1987). The coupon prone consumer: Some findings based on purchase behaviour across product classes. *Journal of Marketing*, 51(4), 99–110.

Bawa, K., Srinivasan, S. S. & Srivastava, R. K. (1997). Coupon attractiveness and coupon proneness: A framework for modeling coupon redemption. *Journal of Marketing Research*, 34(4), 517–525.

Beatty, S. E. & Smith, S. M. (1997). External search effort: An investigation across several product categories. *Journal of Consumer Research*, 14(1), 83–95.

Belch, G. E. & Belch, M. A. (1990). *Introduction to Advertising and Promotion: An Integrated Marketing Communications Perspectiv*, 3rd edn, New York, Richard D. Irwin, Inc.

Bettman, J. & Zins, M. A. (1977). Constructive processes in consumer choice. *Journal of Consumer Research*, 4(2), 75–85.

Bhandari, K. R. & Raut, S. K. (2019). 9 Leveraging tacit. *Advances in Management Research: Innovation and Technology*, 1(1), 127–138.

Blattberg, R. C. & Neslin, S. A. (1990). *Sales Promotion: Concepts, Methods, and Strategies*, Englewood Cliffs, NJ, Prentice Hall.

Blattberg, R. C., Buesing, T., Peacock, P. & Sen, S. K. (1978). Identifying the deal prone segment. *Journal of Marketing Research*, 15(3), 369–377.

Blattberg, R. C. & Wisniewski, K. J. (1989). Price-Induced patterns of competition. *Marketing Science*, 8(Fall), 291–309.

Bronnenberg, B. J. & Wathieu, L. (1997). Asymmetric promotion effects and brand positioning. *Marketing Science*, 15(4), 379–394.

Carpenter, J. & Moore, M. (2008). US consumers' perceptions of non-price retail promotions. *International Journal of Retail and Distribution Management*, 36(2), 111–123.

Chandon, P., Wansink, B. & Laurent, G. (2000). A benefit congruency framework of sales promotion effectiveness. *Journal of Marketing*, 64(4), 65–81.

Chen, S. F. S., Monroe, K. B. & Lou, Y. C. (1998). The effects of framing price promotion messages on consumers' perceptions and purchase intentions. *Journal of Retailing*, 74(3), 353–372.

Cho, J. & Kang, J. (1998). Consumers' attitudes toward clothing coupons. *Family & Consumer Sciences Research Journal*, 26(3), 328–345.

Cotton, B. C. & Babb, E. (1978). Consumer response to promotional deals. *Journal of Marketing*, 42(3), 109–113.

Cunningham, R. M. (1956). Brand loyalty – what, where and how much. *Harvard Business Review*, 34(1), 116–128.

Dang, P. J. & Koshy, A. (2004). An empirical view of the different types of consumer promotions in India. *Working Paper No-2004–03–03, IIM-Ahmedabad*.

Dastidar, S. G. (2016). An investigation of consumers' exploratory tendencies as motivators of their responsive behavior to deals. *IIMB Management Review*, 28(2), 72–87.

Dastidar, S. G. & Datta, B. (2006). Consumer exploratory behaviour and its implications on marketing. *The ICFAI Journal of Marketing Management*, 4(4), 31–49.

Dastidar, S. G. & Datta, B. (2008). A theoretical analysis of the critical factors governing consumer's deal responsive behaviour. *South Asian Journal of Management*, 15(1), 76–97.

D'Astons, A. & Jacob, I. (2002). Understanding consumer reactions to premium based promotional offers. *European Journal of Marketing*, 36(11/12), 1270–1286.

Dhar, S. K. & Hoch, S. J. (1996). Price discrimination using in-store merchandising. *Journal of Marketing*, 60(1), 17–30.

Diamond, W. D. & Campbell, L. (1990). Framing and sales promotion: The characteristics of a good deal. *Journal of Consumer Marketing*, 7(4), 25–31.

Diamond, W. D. & Sanyal, A. (1990). The effect of framing on choice of supermarket coupons. *Advances in Consumer Research*, 17, 494–500.

Dickson, P. R. & Sawyer, A. G. (1990). The price knowledge and search of supermarket shoppers. *Journal of Marketing*, 54(3), 42–53.

Dodson, J. A., Tybout, A. M. & Sternthal, B. (1978). Impact of deals and deal retraction on brand switching. *Journal of Marketing Research*, 15(1), 72–81.

Feick, L. F. & Price, L. (1987). The market maven: A diffuser of market place information. *Journal of Marketing*, 51(3), 83–97.

Fishbein, M. & Ajzen, I. (1975). *Beliefs, Attitude, Intention, and Behavior: An Introduction to Theory and Research*, Reading, MA, Addison-Wesley.

Gardner, M. P. & Strang, R. A. (1984). Consumer response to promotions: Some new perspectives. *Advances in Consumer Research*, 11, 420–442.

Gazquez-Abad, J. C. & Sanchez-Perez, M. (2009). Characterising the deal-proneness of consumers by analysis of price sensitivity and brand loyalty: An analysis in the retail environment. *The International Review of Retail, Distribution and Consumer Research*, 19(1), 1–28.

Gijsbrechts, E., Campo, K. & Goossens, T. (2003). The impact of store flyers on store traffic and store sales: A geo-marketing approach. *Journal of Retailing*, 79(1), 1–16.

Grover, R. & Srinivasan, V. (1992). Evaluating the multiple effect of retail promotions on brand loyal and brand switching segments. *Journal of Marketing Research*, 29(1), 76–89.

Gupta, S. (1988). Impact of sales promotions on when, what, and how much to buy. *Journal of Marketing Research*, 25(4), 342–355.

Gurumurthy, K. & Winer, R. S. (1995). Empirical generalizations from reference price research. *Marketing Science*, 14(3), 161–170.

Hackleman, C. & Duker, J. (1980). Deal-proneness and heavy usage: Merging two segmentation criteria. *Journal of the Academy of Marketing Science*, 8(3), 332–344.

Hatton, A. (1998). *Marketing Plans with a Winning Edge*, India, Macmillan Publishers.

Henderson, C. M. (1987). Sales promotion segmentation: Refining the deal-proneness construct. *Working Paper, Amos Tuck School of Business Administration, Dartmouth College, Hanover, NH 03755.*

Hoch, S. J., Kim, B., Montgomery, A. L. & Rossi, P. E. (1994). Determinants of store-level price elasticity. *Journal of Marketing Research*, 32(1), 17–29.

Huff, L. & Alden, D. L. (1998). An investigation of consumer response to sales promotion in developing markets: A three-country analysis. *Journal of Advertising Research*, 38(May–June), 47–57.

Inman, J. J., McAlister, L. & Hoyer, W. D. (1990). Promotion signal: Proxy for a price cut? *Journal of Consumer Research*, 17(1), 74–81.

Janda, S. (1996). Some psychological correlates of coupon proneness. www.sbaer.uca.edu/research/1996/pdf/02.pdf.

Jethwaney, J. & Jain, S. (2006). *Advertising Management*, New Delhi, Oxford University Press.

Jolson, M. A., Joshua, L. W. & Rosecky, R. B. (1987). Correlates of rebate proneness. *Journal of Advertising Research*, 27(1), 33–44.

Kahn, B. E. & Raju, J. S. (1991). Effects of price promotions on variety-seeking and reinforcement behaviour. *Marketing Science*, 10(4), 316–337.

Kahneman, D. & Tversky, A. (1984). Choices, values and frames. *American Psychologist*, 39(4), 341–350.

Kalwani, M. U. & Yim, C. H. (1992). Consumer price and promotion expectations. *Journal of Marketing Research*, 29(1), 90–100.

Kassin, S. (2003). *Psychology*, New Jersey, USA, Prentice-Hall Inc.

Kolodinsky, J. (1990). Time as a direct source of utility: The case of price information search for groceries. *The Journal of Consumer Affairs*, 24(1), 89–109.

Krishna, A., Currim, I. & Shoemaker, R. (1991). Consumer perceptions of promotional activity. *Journal of Marketing*, 55(2), 4–16.

Kumar, S. R. (2009). *Consumer Behaviour and Branding-Concepts, Readings and Cases: The Indian Context*, 1st edn, (India), Noida, Dorling Kindersley.

Kwon, K. N. & Kwon, Y. (2007). Demographics in sales promotion proneness: A socio-cultural approach. *Advances in Consumer Research*, 34, 288–294.

Laroche, M., Pons, F., Zgolly, N., Cervellon, M. C. & Kim, C. (2001). A model of consumer response to two retail sales promotions techniques. *Journal of Business Research*, 56(7), 513–522.

Lichtenstein, D. R., Burton, S. & Netemeyer, R. (1997). An examination of deal proneness across sales promotion types: A consumer segmentation perspective. *Journal of Retailing*, 73(2), 283–297.

Lichtenstein, D. R., Netemeyer, R. G. & Burton, S. (1990). Distinguishing coupon proneness from value consciousness: An acquisition-transaction utility theory perspective. *Journal of Marketing*, 54(3), 54–67.

Lichtenstein, D. R. & Ridgway, N. M. (1993). Price perceptions and consumer shopping behavior: A field study. *Journal of Marketing Research*, 30(2), 234–245.

Liu, T. C. & Wang, C. Y. (2008). Factors, affecting attitudes toward private labels and promoted brands. *Journal of Marketing Management*, 24(3–4), 283–298.

Martinez, E. & Montaner, T. (2006). The effect of consumer's psychographic variable on deal proneness. *Journal of Retailing and Consumer Services*, 13(3), 157–168.

Massy, W. F., Frank, R. E. & Lodahl, T. (1968). *Purchasing Behavior and Personal Attributes*, Philadelphia, University of Pennsylvania Press.

Mayhew, G. E. & Winer, R. S. (1992). An empirical analysis of internal and external reference prices using scanner data. *Journal of Consumer Research*, 19(1), 62–70.

McAlister, L. (1986). The impact of price promotions on a brand's market share, sales pattern and profitability. *Report no. 86–110*, Cambridge, Marketing Science Institute.

McCann, J. M. (1974). Market segment response to the marketing decision variables. *Journal of Marketing Research*, 11(4), 399–412.

Miranda, M. & Konya, L. (2007). Directing store flyers to the appropriate audience. *Journal of Retailing and Consumer Services*, 14(3), 175–181.

Mittal, B. (1994). An integrated framework for relating diverse consumer characteristics to supermarket coupon redemption. *Journal of Marketing Research*, 31(November), 533–544.

Mizerski, R. W., Golden, L. L. & Kernan, J. B. (1979). The attribution process in consumer decision making. *Journal of Consumer Research*, 6(2), 123–140.

Montgomery, D. B. (1971). Consumer characteristics associated with dealing: An empirical example. *Journal of Marketing Research*, 8(1), 118–120.

Narasimhan, C. (1984). A price discrimination theory of coupons. *Marketing Science*, 3(2), 128–146.

Narasimhan, C., Neslin, S. A. & Sen, S. K. (1996) Promotional elasticities and category characteristics. *Journal of Marketing*, 60(2), 17–30.

Park, K. & Gómez, M. (2004). The coupon reports: A study of coupon discount metho ds. http://aem.cornell.edu/research/researchpdf/rb0407.pdf.

Pechtl, H. (2004). Profiling intrinsic deal-proneness for HILO and EDLP price promotion strategies. *Journal of Retailing and Consumer Services*, 11(4), 223–233.

Pelsmacker, P. D., Geuens, M. & Bergh, J. V. D. (2001). *Marketing Communications*, England, Pearson Education Limited.

Petty, R. E. & Cacioppo, J. T. (1981). Issue involvement as a moderator of the effects on attitude of advertising content and context. *Advances in Consumer Research*, 8, 20–24.

Prendergast, G. P., Poon, D. T. Y. & Tsang, A. L. (2008). Predicting premium proneness. *Journal of Advertising Research*, 48(2), 287–296.

Price, L., Feick, L. & Guskey-Federouch, A. (1988). Couponing behaviors of the market maven: Profile of a super couponer. *Advances in Consumer Research*, 15, 354–359.

Raghubir, P. & Corfman, K. (1999). When do price promotions affect pre-trial brand evaluation? *Journal of Marketing Research*, 36(2), 211–222.

Raju, J. S. (1995). Theoretical models of sales promotions: Contributions, limitations, and a future research agenda. *European Journal of Operational Research*, 85(1), 1–17.

Raju, P. S. & Hastak, M. (1980). Consumer response to deals: A discussion of theoretical perspectives. *Advances in Consumer Research*, 7, 196–201.

Ramaswamy, V. V. & Srinivasan, S. S. (1998). Coupon characteristics and redemption intentions: A segment level analysis. *Psychology and Marketing*, 15(1), 59–80.

Rana, S., Raut, S. K., Prashar, S., & Hamid, A. B. A. (2020b). Promoting through Consumer Nostalgia: A conceptual framework and future research agenda. *Journal of Promotion Management*, 27(2), 211–249.

Rana, S., Raut, S. K., Prashar, S. & Quttainah, M. A. (2020a). The transversal of nostalgia from psychology to marketing: What does it portend for future research? *International Journal of Organizational Analysis*. Ahead-of-print No.

Rao, R. C. (1991). Pricing and promotions in asymmetric duopolies. *Marketing Science*, 10(2), 131–144.

Raut, S. K., Sakpal, S. & Soni, R. (2022). Understanding the service quality dimensions and achieving resilience in service retail, in *Handbook of Research on Supply Chain Resiliency, Efficiency, and Visibility in the Post-Pandemic Era*, edited by Ramakrishna Yanamandra (pp. 136–156). IGI Global, UAE. https://doi.org/10.4018/978-1-7998-9506-0

Rothschild, M. L. & Gaidis, W. (1981). Behavioral learning theory: Its relevance to marketing and promotions. *Journal of Marketing*, 45(1), 70–78.

Schank, C. & Abelson, P. (1977). *Scripts, Plans, Goals, and Understanding: An Inquiry into Human Knowledge Structures*, New York, Hillsdale.

Schindler, R. M. (1992). A Coupon is more than a low price: Evidences from a shopping simulation study. *Psychology and Marketing*, 9(6), 431–451.

Schindler, R. M., Lala, V. & Corcoran, C. G. (2008). Intergenerational influence in consumer deal proneness. *Advances in Consumer Research*, 35, 735–736.

Schneider, L. G. & Currim, I. S. (1991). Consumer purchase behaviour associated with active and passive deal proneness. *International Journal of Research in Marketing*, 8(4), 205–222.

Schultz, D. E., Robinson, W. A. & Petrison, L. A. (1998). *Sales promotion Essentials: The 10 Basic Sales Promotion Techniques . . . and How to Use Them*, 3 edn, New Orleans, NTC Publishing Group.

Shah, K. & D'Souza, A. (2009). *Advertising and Promotions: An IMC Perspective*, New Delhi, Tata McGraw Hill Publishing.

Shimp, T. A. (1990). *Promotion Management and Marketing Communications*, Dryden, IL, Hinsdale.

Shimp, T. A. & Kavas, A. (1984). The theory of reasoned action applied to coupon usage. *Journal of Consumer Research*, 11(4), 795–809.

Sirohi, N., McLaughlin, E. W. & Wittink, D. R. (1998). A model of consumer perceptions and store loyalty intentions for a supermarket retailer. *Journal of Retailing*, 74(2), 223–245.

Soman, D. (1998). The illusion of delayed incentives: Evaluating future effort-money transactions. *Journal of Marketing Research*, 25(4), 425–437.

Stafford, M. R. & Stafford, T. F. (2000). The effectiveness of tensile pricing tactics in the advertising of services. *Journal of Advertising*, 29(2), 45–56.

Swaminathan, S. & Bawa, K. (2005). Category-specific coupon proneness: The impact of individual characteristics and category-specific variables. *Journal of Retailing*, 81(3), 205–214.

Teel, J. E., Williams, R. H. & Bearden, W. O. (1980). Correlates of consumer susceptibility to coupons in new grocer product introductions. *Journal of Advertising*, 9(3), 31–46.

Thaler, R. (1985). Mental accounting and consumer choice. *Marketing Science*, 4(3), 199–214.

Urbany, J. E., Dickson, P. R. & Kalapurakal, R. (1996). Price search in the retail grocery market. *Journal of Marketing*, 60(2), 91–104.

Wakefield, K. L. & Barnes, J. H. (1996). Retailing hedonic consumption: A model of sales promotion of a leisure service. *Journal of Retailing*, 72(4), 409–427.

Wakefield, K. L. & Bush, V. D. (1998). Promotion leisure services: Economic and emotional aspects of consumer response. *Journal of Services Marketing*, 12(2/3), 209–223.

Wakefiled, K. L. & Inman, J. J. (2003). Situational price sensitivity: The role of consumption occasion, social context and income. *Journal of Retailing*, 79(4), 199–212.

Ward, J. R. & Hill, R. (1991). Designing effective promotional games: Opportunities and problems. *Journal of Advertising*, 20(3), 69–81.

Webster, F. E. (1965). The deal-prone consumer. *Journal of Marketing Research*, 2(May), 186–189.

Yuna, Z. S., Vermab, S., Pysarchika, D. T., Yuc, J. P. & Chowdhury, S. (2008). Cultural influences on new product adoption of affluent consumers in India. *The International Review of Retail, Distribution and Consumer Research*, 18(2), 203–220.

3 Entrepreneurship in Emerging Markets

An Empirical Study on Digital Natives in Kuwait

Stavros Papakonstantinidis and Piotr Kwiatek

Introduction

The term Digital Natives (DNs) was first coined by Marc Prensky in 2001 when the author explored an academic concern about the new generation of first-year students. Prensky (2001) identified in his millennial students a natural inclination or digital nativity to technology. According to Prensky (2001), DNs demonstrate fundamental differences from previous generations, coined as Digital Immigrants (DIs). DNs demonstrate an almost instinctive preference and understanding of how the technology works while feeling more comfortable within an online-based environment than the offline world (Palfrey & Gasser, 2010). In Prensky's words, they "spend their entire lives surrounded by and using computers, video games, digital music players, video cams, cell phones, and all the other toys and tools of the digital age" (Prensky, 2001, p. 1).

The millennials living in the Middle East and North Africa (MENA) region are the most disruptive consumers, learners, and citizens (Kandil, 2019). MENA's Digital Natives are proud of their heritage while being more open to exploring different cultures and adopting different lifestyles than the previous generations (Benni et al., 2016). The majority of MENA's millennials are online and active on social media; content generation savvy and continually getting informed of news, brands, promotions, and trends. MENA's millennials seem less optimistic and more concerned about rising living costs and unemployment than their parents (Ipsos, 2018).

Extensive scholarly literature explores how millennials or else Digital Natives (DNs) behave in the workplace and the classroom (Jarrahi & Eshraghi, 2019; Metallo & Agrifoglio, 2015; Ahn & Jung, 2014; Hoffmann et al., 2014; Mäntymäki & Riemer, 2014). Nevertheless, MENA's millennials remain a mystery regarding their beliefs for entrepreneurship and attitude toward accepting technology for business, self-efficacy, and anxiety for the future (Kesharwani, 2020; Bhandari and Raut, 2019; Al-Wugayan & Alshimmiri, 2010). This study puts the Digital Natives living in the Middle East, particularly in Kuwait, under the microscope. Specifically, this study aims to decode the entrepreneurial mindset of the DNs by investigating their

DOI: 10.4324/9781003315582-4

entrepreneurial capacity (EC) and entrepreneurial intention (EI) using the scales adopted from the Entrepreneurial Intention Questionnaire (EIQ).

This research examines what needs to be done in an emerging economy such as Kuwait to empower and support young entrepreneurship. The main question that this study aims to answer is to what extent digital natives living in Kuwait are open to accepting technology to start their business. Through a systematic exploration, the objective of this study is to answer a set of research sub-questions:

1. Who are the Digital Natives living in Kuwait (DNs)?
2. What are the factors that impact DNs' entrepreneurial mindset?
3. How do entrepreneurial intention (EI), entrepreneurial capacity (EC), and DNs' acceptance of technology correlate?
4. What is the role of anxiety and self-efficacy in DNs' decision to start a business?

Kuwait: An Emerging Market

On December 18, 2019, Kuwait Times reported that the leading index compiler MSCI Inc. has officially upgraded Kuwait to Emerging Market status, effective since May 2020 (Kuwait Times, 2019). Kuwait has been reclassified from its previous status as a 'Frontier Market' after the Arab state's market development reforms had been undertaken by the trilateral task force of Boursa Kuwait, the Capital Markets Authority (CMA), and Kuwait Clearing Company's (KCC). The 2019 Annual Market Classification Review held on June 25, 2019, upgraded Kuwait's status in the coveted index as compiled by MSCI Inc. Kuwait successfully addressed and implemented all MSCI's recommendations.

Kuwait makes the right research candidate for further exploration. A McKinsey report discusses that although the Middle East is taking giant steps into digital business disruption and governments encourage going digital, "only 6 percent of the Middle Eastern public lives under a digitized smart government" (Benni et al., 2016, p. 8). This makes an interesting oxymoron of public desire to do business online while recording low levels of adoption. Some Middle Eastern governments have begun implementing core digitized initiatives, with the UAE leading the Middle East in digital adoption. Research on technology adoption in Kuwait is scarce, mainly focusing on developing e-government applications (Rabaai et al., 2015). Also, Al-Wugayan and AlShimmiri (2010) discuss university students' views in Kuwait concerning their intentions to start their small businesses. Our study is the first to explore the relationship between entrepreneurship and technology acceptance of millennials living in Kuwait.

The recent COVID-19 crisis has accelerated a nationalization plan that calls for limiting hiring expats in selected sectors to replace these jobs with the local population (Kuwait Today, 2020; Raut, Sakpal and Soni, 2022).

As reported in Al Arabiya News, the nationalization plan could involve a number of the 40,000 Kuwaitis who got repatriated due to the COVID-19 crisis and want to remain in the country (Tuqa, 2020). The State of Kuwait is at an exciting crossroad of implementing an ambitious plan to employ Kuwaitis in the public sector and also to give incentives to its youth for starting their business. According to the United Nations Development Program (UNDP) report (2018), Kuwait's youth comprise 72% of the population. Children between ages 0 and 14 formulate around 37% of the people, and young adults between ages 15 and 34 represent 35% of the total population (United Nations Development Program, 2018). The UNDP report calls for severe challenges for the Government and society in exploring how youth in Kuwait could benefit from the development of education, life-long training, multiple forms of employment, health, and recreation activities. This study contributes to the understanding of how the Digital Natives living in Kuwait think of their entrepreneurial endeavors.

Literature Review

Defining Digital Natives

Digital Natives were born in the late 1990s early 2000s. They grew up experiencing technological advances such as the proliferation of the Internet, the evolution of multi-touch screen interaction, the penetration of social media, and the adoption of mobile and wearable devices. Their sociological profile demonstrates people who consider email communication as an old-fashioned communication method. Instead, millennials use social media to communicate, do business, and get entertained (Kandil, 2019). DNs are eager to experience first any new technological gadget in the market, for example, the new iPhone series or any other smartphone or wearable device (Jarrahi & Eshraghi, 2019).

For DNs, technology and information are everything. News that was reported an hour ago is already old and outdated. Privacy, multitasking, newsfeed, and communication are notions utterly different from that of the previous generations. They have no problem posting online their eating habits, checking in restaurants and events, uploading personal images, and broadcasting personal stories (Papakonstantinidis, 2014). Each generation varies in terms of shaping influences and values (Table 3.1). Broad conclusions are highlighted regarding each generation's work behavior. Compared to the previous generations of Boomers and Generation Xers, millennials (Gen Yers) demonstrate a distinct entrepreneurial intention (Iyer, 2018), reflecting their generational beliefs on work and success (Table 3.1).

A qualitative study by the Ipsos Group on MENA's millennials describes the quintessential youth as educated people with principles and ambitions. The same report writes that MENA's DNs are proud of their heritage and are eager to maintain "the entrepreneurial spirit of their millennial predecessors . . . as

Table 3.1 Comparing generational characteristics

Generation	Boomers	Generation X	Digital Natives (Gen Y)
When were they born?	The mid-1940s to late 1960s	The early 1970s to early 1990s	The late 1990s to early 2000s
What influences them?	Mass media, activist movements, the space race, immigration waves, and father-working family	School, general discussions (energy crisis, drugs, gangs, AIDS), technology's baby steps, working mothers, divorced families	The proliferation of technology (social media and smartphones), school shootings in the United States, multicultural societies, various family structures
Which major historical events shaped their reality?	The Post WW2, the Cold War, the Vietnam War	The fall of the Berlin Wall, the Gulf War	The 9/11 attack
How do they see work?	Boomers are collectivists who see themselves as being part of the whole to serve the community. Live to work.	Generation Xers are individualists who see themselves as being independent and self-reliant. They do not want to work in government/ public institutions. Instead, they aim for personal success through the private sector and entrepreneurial efforts. Work to live.	Millennials have blurred lines between collectivism and individualism with high self-confidence, openness, and a unique sense of privacy – work–life balance.
How do they get entertained?	B&W TV/ radio/cinema/ newspapers/ magazines	Colored TV/ VHS/ video games/ cinema	Social media/ smartphones/ streaming services
How do they define success?	Success will come only through education and hard work.	Success will come from flexibility and adaptability in changing careers.	Success will come through making our own business our way.

Source: Author's own

they strive to spearhead their businesses and create a platform that can let their voice be heard" (Ipsos, 2018, p. 4). DNs prefer online streaming services for entertainment such as Spotify, YouTube, Netflix, and Twitch. For DNs, the transition from college to the professional world goes through social media.

The Entrepreneurial Mindset in Emerging Market Economies

The entrepreneurial mindset includes extrovert competencies such as intention and open-mindedness, the necessary business capacity, and knowledge (Taipale-Erävala et al., 2019). We approach entrepreneurship as a mindset rather than a concept of people starting their businesses. According to the British Council (2017):

> *Technological developments are reshaping our workplaces and changing how businesses operate, while the global nature of business means more young people will have jobs crossing different continents and sectors. It is, therefore, important we equip future generations with the skills they need to navigate a world of work we cannot yet envisage.*

In an International Labor Organization report, it is argued that "development of core skills, awareness of workers' rights and an understanding of entrepreneurship are the building blocks for lifelong learning and capability to adapt to change" (Brewer, 2013, p. iii). For millennials, developing an entrepreneurial mindset allows them to acquire skills to strengthen their employability, create occupational opportunities, innovate, and build their socioeconomic status (Herrmann & Rana, 2020; Papakonstantinidis, 2019; Etemad & Keen, 2018). Evidence links entrepreneurship with the "push and pull" factors. Unemployment, redundancy, and job dissatisfaction are factors that could lead individuals to start a business (Mueller & Thomas, 2001). There is a debate about the factors that impact entrepreneurial intention (EI) and entrepreneurial capacity (EC). EI is more impacted by external contextual factors than people's characteristics (Scarborough & Cornwall, 2018). Nevertheless, personality traits, intention (EI), and capacity (EC) impact business decisions and opportunities (Engle et al., 2010).

Scholarly work has indicated an interest in examining how entrepreneurs in emerging economies compete and stand out internationally (Lee-Ross, 2017; Ratten et al., 2016; Ratten, 2014; Kiss et al., 2012; Rana, 2018; Rana, et al., 2021). Engle et al. (2010) explore the application of Ajzen's model of planned behavior to predict entrepreneurial intention (EI) in different countries. Also, network knowledge in emerging economies could encourage an individual to start a business more than developing an entrepreneurial culture (Ratten et al., 2016). A Bank of America report states that factors such as receiving approval from family and friends seem more significant than expert advice (Miller, 2016). The current study investigates which factors impact DNs' level of EI. It explores whether DNs' self-efficacy and technology acceptance are significant factors that shape their entrepreneurial mindset.

Social Media Acceptance and Digital Natives

Social media includes a wide range of individual social network sites. An online social networking site is defined as

> *a web-based service that allows individuals to (1) construct a public or semipublic profile within a bounded system, (2) articulate a list of other users with whom they share a connection, and (3) view and treasure their list of connections and those made by others within the system.*
>
> (Boyd & Ellison, 2007)

The main characteristic of a social networking site is the sense of community that traditional websites cannot develop. In social media, users are willing to share personal information while following a set of rules and norms that characterize the community (Brooks & Anumudu, 2015).

Millennials use social media to increase their popularity and reach (Mäntymäki & Riemer, 2014; Rana et al., 2020). Social media is a low-cost advertising and communication platform that furthers engagement with customers and users of the Internet (Altman, 2017). Companies and organizations have started using various social media applications (blogging, microblogging, video streaming, and podcasting) not only to announce the new products and services but also to engage their customers and receive valid feedback. For Boomers, communicating with a Fortune 500 company CEO required passing several gatekeepers following formal procedures. Nowadays, for millennials, communication with the top management is just a tweet away. Social media users understand the power they have in their hands when they can talk directly to a top-level manager or sometimes to a well-known CEO who embraces their feedback and responds in person.

Fierce competition on how people manage to stand out from the crowd characterizes today's social and corporate world (Tarnovskaya, 2017; Brooks & Anumudu, 2015; Dutta, 2010; Shepherd, 2005). Therefore, social media entrepreneurship is becoming a global concept and has taken hold among the Digital Natives. Most of the scholarly literature on self-promotion for entrepreneurial reasons suggests that self-branding is the key to personal and professional success (Gandini, 2016; Khedher, 2015; Gander, 2014, Gehl, 2011; Harris & Rae, 2011; Schawbel, 2011; Rampersad, 2008; Lair et al., 2005).

Today, the notion of humans promoting their skills, creating online content, and using social media as a marketing platform is popular because humans "1) can be strategically managed, and 2) have additional associations and features of a brand" (Khedher, 2015, p. 19). Maintaining one's reputation in social media has become essential and advantageous not only for the top management executives but also for their organization. It further provides a digital footprint to help individuals create and sustain their brand

(Labrecque et al., 2011). Thus, this study aims to explore DNs' entrepreneurial mindset concerning their openness to demonstrate their skills and identity online. Are there only benefits for DNs using social media to promote their business?

There are some drawbacks as well of using social media for personal branding and entrepreneurship. Rampton (2016) argues that overselling oneself, remaining authentic, and dealing with negative publicity and hate comments could impact both people's and an organization's image. Social media overexposure could lead to social media entrepreneurs acting as brands sharing their stories with their followers. Another disadvantage is when millennials manage their business inconsistently due to poor timing and lack of experience. Being unable to remain relevant and authentic could quickly lead to defaming and ignoring others online (Altman, 2017). Such drawbacks could increase the level of anxiety among DNs, who understand that social media overexposure could lead to significant risks of being publicly defamed, offended, and socially embarrassed (France, 2007).

Anxiety and Risk Culture

Professional late modernity involves high risks, uncertainty, and anxiety (France, 2007). Today's fierce global competitive environment requires DNs to be more adaptive and capable of negotiating with alternative and asymmetrical threats (Lehmann, 2004). The rapidly emerging online market; the proliferation of new technologies; the global competition regardless of age, nationality, and background; as well as the recent COVID-19 crisis could increase the levels of anxiety and uncertainty for young entrepreneurs. A privileged individual, such as a millennial living in Kuwait, has opportunities that stem from financial stability for a desirable career. The example of GoldenPay in Azerbaijan shows that individuals from developing economies could also succeed in online entrepreneurship as long as the offered service is valuable and satisfies a genuine global need (Ismayilzada, 2019).

Young individuals want to make their mark without necessarily following the well-known paths determined by their social class, family, gender, or educational background (Papakonstantinidis, 2017). On the contrary, one could argue that it is not sure that millennials are more risk-driven than the previous generations. The lines between late modernity Generation Yers represent and Generation Xers' early modernity blur in online entrepreneurship. DNs and DIs are now competing on a different battlefield aiming for professional success through social media. Risk and uncertainty define the dynamic and competitive societies of the past that Cieslik and Pollock (2002) call "risk society". Generation Xers were ambitious and anxious to find a good job even if they had to travel overseas and leave their country. Generation Yers take different risks of exposing their privacy and letting their life become a commodity. Such decisions could make them famous overnight without having to leave their room.

Uncertainties over social identities and social membership reshape modern families, employment, and communities in today's dynamic and risk-oriented society. Prensky (2001) calls DNs restless minds who want to achieve in life through random professional decisions. In other words, Cieslik and Pollock's "risk society" is Prensky's Digital Natives. A better understanding of how social media transforms the way DNs make their transition from college to the start-up business world is among the objectives of this study.

Scholarly literature offers a comparison between DNs' and DIs' acceptance of technology and social media using an initial adoption, longitudinal model to explain their technology adoption behavior (Kesharwani, 2020). The latter study identifies a relatively stable over time pattern of differences between generations. One of the differences is how DNs approach social media exposure and entrepreneurship. The current research fills the void in the literature about DNs' technology acceptance and entrepreneurial intention with their sense of self-efficacy and anxiety for the future. The current study conceptualizes well-established models in technology acceptance and entrepreneurship to decode the Entrepreneurial Intention (henceforth EI) and Entrepreneurial Capacity (henceforth EC) of the Digital Natives living in Kuwait (henceforth DNs). The next section integrates methodology with results to answer the aforementioned questions and shed light on the DNs by decoding their entrepreneurial mindset.

Methodology and Results

To develop a better understanding of DNs, we rolled out an online survey in May 2020. The survey consisted of 18 questions that covered the constructs from the Technology Acceptance Model (TAM), entrepreneurial intention, and demographic descriptors. We measured EC and EI using the scales adopted from EIQ (Liñán & Chen, 2009). The EC was measured through five items on a seven-point Likert-type scale anchored from "totally disagree" to "totally agree". The EI was measured through four items on an analogous type of scale. The measures of TAM constructs, namely self-efficacy, anxiety, perceived usefulness, ease of use, and attitude toward social media, were adopted from Blut et al. (2016). The constructs were measured through a four-item Likert-type with five-point scales anchored with "strongly disagree" to "strongly agree".

With the disruption brought globally by COVID-19, we embraced snowball convenience sampling and invited participants through social media networks. The survey was opened for ten days and allowed us to gather 225 responses. The data was analyzed in SPSS 24 (IBM Corp. Released, 2016).

Sample Characteristic and Social Media Usage

The sample was narrowed down to 180 millennial participants (i.e., those aged below 35). The millennials' sample consisted of 95 male respondents

Table 3.2 Demographic profile of respondents

Demographic	n	
Gender		
Male	135	60.0
Female	90	40.0
Nationality		
Kuwaiti	100	44.4
Non-Kuwaiti	125	55.6
Age		
18–25	115	51.1
26–35	65	28.9
36–45	20	8.9
46 or more	25	11.1
Education		
Secondary school	5	2.2
Vocational education	10	4.4
Bachelor	180	80
Masters and above	30	13.3
Occupation		
Student	40	17.8
Private sector employee	75	33.3
Self-employed	25	11.1
Government employee	30	13.3
Other	20	8.9
Unemployed	35	15.6

Source: Author's own

(52.8%) and 85 females (47.2%), 65 Kuwaiti nationals (36.1%), and 115 of other nationalities (63.9%). A little over 41% of respondents held an unemployed or student status (Table 3.2).

The millennials use social media extensively, focusing on visual channels, like YouTube and Instagram (combined 50%), followed by Twitter and Facebook. We note a marginal difference between Kuwaiti and non-Kuwaiti groups. The first one leans slightly more toward YouTube and the latter toward Instagram. Most importantly, none of the Kuwaiti respondents indicates Facebook as a favorite platform.

Digital Natives Under the Microscope

In this section, we present DNs in more detail. We begin by discussing the patterns of using social media in terms of scope. Next, we analyze their entrepreneurial intention regarding social media. Since Kuwait is a country with a diverse population, we compare the results across nationality and gender.

The reasons for engaging in social media differ by nationality and gender. Kuwaiti respondents use social media to shop, follow, and exchange information about their favorite brands more than the non-Kuwaiti. On the other hand, non-Kuwaiti respondents use social media more for contacting family and friends and engage with media entertainment (music, books, films, etc.) The comparison between genders provides exciting results. Male respondents use social media to contact family and friends more (M = 2.8) than female respondents (M = 2.0). In contrast, females use social media for entertainment more (M = 3.5) than males (M = 2.8).

Entrepreneurial Intention of Digital Natives

We used previously validated scales to measure the focal constructs. The entrepreneurial constructs are drawn from the EIQ (Liñán & Chen, 2009) that consists of 24 items and four subdimensions (intention, capacity, social valuation, and professional attraction). EIQ adopts a seven-point Likert-type scaling.

We confirm that the reliability threshold is met for EI (α = .87) and EC (α = .93). Both measures of entrepreneurship received high mean scores, with the EI (M = 5.37, SD = 1.39) outscoring the EC (M = 4.13, SD = 1.39). We move on to comparing groups on the basis of gender. Since the Kolmogorov–Smirnoff test performed on EC and EI yielded significant results ($p < 0.01$), we employed a non-parametric Mann–Whitney test for the intergroup comparison. There was no difference between genders concerning self-reported entrepreneurial capacity. However, we found a significant effect of gender on EI (U = 4.075, Z = –2.78, $p < 0.01$, r = .31). The effect size was calculated by dividing the absolute standardized test statistic by the square root of pairs compared. Female respondents reported higher entrepreneurial intention (M = 5.66) than male respondents (M = 5.12).

We also evaluated the entrepreneurial components (capacity and intention) with a nationality split. By adopting the same procedure (U = 3.400, Z = –3.54, $p < 0.01$, r = .26), we conclude that Kuwaiti respondents have higher EC (M = 4.61) than non-Kuwaitis (M = 3.86). An essential component of entrepreneurial intention is searching for external approval/support by young entrepreneurs. We note that though approvals are important for all respondents (over four on a seven-point scale of importance), female respondents tend to look for approval from experts more (M = 5.35) than male respondents (M = 4.42).

The more pronounced pattern can be observed in the split by nationality. Kuwaiti respondents tend to value the approval more than non-Kuwaitis, particularly when it comes from peers (M_K = 5.62; M_{nK} = 4.74).

Components of TAM and Entrepreneurial Intention

The survey uses two models, the Technology Acceptance Model TAM (Davis et al., 1989) and the Unified Theory of Acceptance and Use of Technology

UTAUT (Venkatesh et al., 2012). Both models provide a theoretical framework for how DNs tend to accept and use technology for their entrepreneurial ventures. Whereas TAM postulates that perceived usefulness and ease of use determine the adoption and use of technology (Venkatesh & Bala, 2008), UTAUT proposes that individual differences (e.g., age, gender) influence technology acceptance (Venkatesh et al., 2012). In the original models, TAM/UTAUT, the predictors (usefulness, ease of use) are related to technology usage intention and subsequent usage behavior (Blut et al., 2016). However, this study links the predictors to entrepreneurial capacity (mediator) and entrepreneurial intention (dependent variable). Specifically, we test how anxiety and self-efficacy of digital natives interact with their approach to social media and, in effect, result in entrepreneurial intention (Figure 3.1).

In the millennials' group, the use of social media is prevalent. Hence, the adoption is high per se. However, the adoption and use of social media as a venue for entrepreneurial activity have not been previously studied in this way. In our research, the correlation analysis reveals conclusive patterns. First, the perceived usefulness of social media is positively correlated with the attitude toward entrepreneurial activity on social media ($r = .76$, $p < 0.05$). Second, self-efficacy is correlated with the entrepreneurial intention ($r = .33$, $p < 0.05$) but not with entrepreneurial capacity ($r = -.01$, $p > 0.05$). While self-efficacy is positively correlated with social-media-perceived usefulness ($r = .26$, $p < 0.01$) and the attitude toward social media entrepreneurship ($r = .23$, $p < 0.01$), anxiety does not correlate with perceived usefulness ($r = -.15$, $p > 0.05$). It is negatively correlated with the attitude toward social media ($r = -.19$, $p < 0.05$). Also, as expected, the higher the anxiety, the lower the entrepreneurial capacity ($r = -.35$, $p < 0.01$) and entrepreneurial intention ($r = -.57$, $p < 0.01$). In the following part, we evaluate the model depicted in Figure 3.2.

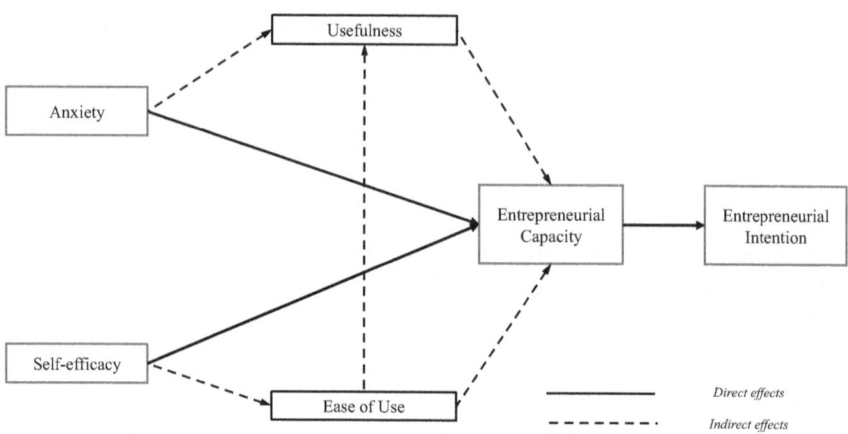

Figure 3.1 Entrepreneurial intention and social media

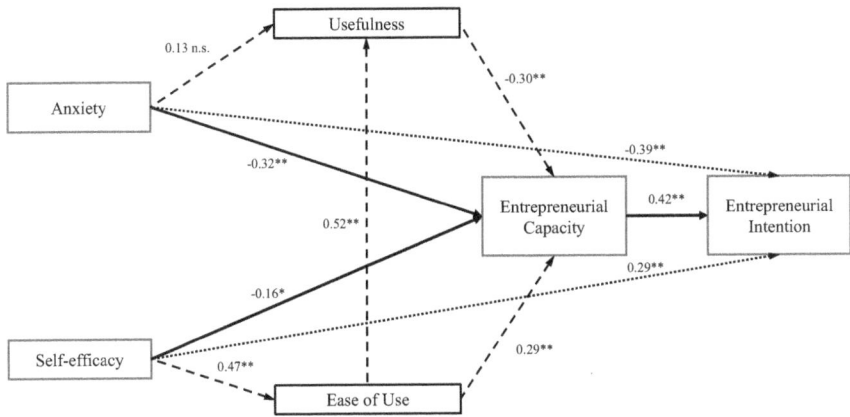

Figure 3.2 Entrepreneurial intention and social media

AVE presents satisfying values above the 0.50 threshold, and composite reliabilities of the constructs above 0.75 thus deem acceptable (Bagozzi & Yi, 1988). Because the dependent variable in the study is based on self-reported data, we controlled for the potential influence of common method variance (CMV) by applying a two-step procedure. First, the anonymity of respondents was emphasized in the survey (Podsakoff et al., 2003). Second, a marker variable technique (Malhorta et al., 2006) was used once the data was collected. Since the questionnaire did not include a separate marker variable, the second-lowest correlation (r_M) was used as CMV proxy (Lindell & Whitney, 2001). The average difference between unadjusted and adjusted correlations was 0.03. Furthermore, the pattern of significance (i.e., significant versus nonsignificant correlations) between unadjusted and adjusted correlations did not change. Thus, it can be concluded that the CMV effect is negligible in this study.

The heterotrait–monotrait ratio of correlation (HTMT) should be verified in order to establish discriminant validity (Henseler et al., 2014). When the HTMT value is below 0.85 (Kline, 2011), discriminant validity is established between constructs. In this study, all HTMT values are between 0.15 and 0.71, well below the demanded threshold. Partial least square structural equation modeling (PLS-SEM) was applied in SmartPLS 3.2.7 (Ringle et al., 2015). The advantage of using PLS is that the modeling does not require normal distributions of data. It accepts the use of smaller samples for the analysis (Kline, 2011). Reinartz et al. (2009) stated that as compared to covariance-based structural equation modeling (CB-SEM), PLS-SEM provides more robust estimations of the structural model.

A common rule of thumb suggests a sample size of at least ten times the largest independent constructs affecting the dependent variable. There were nine independent constructs (including the control variables), so the sample size of 180 satisfies the needed threshold. Additionally, a post hoc power test was performed. The power level of .99 (f^2 = .11, a = .05, N = 180) exceeded the recommended threshold of .80 (Cohen, 1988). The model explains 58.6% of the variance in entrepreneurial intention. We used Stone–Geisser's Q^2 to assess the predictive relevance of the model. The values for both EC (Q^2 = .16) and EI (Q^2 = .41) ascertain good predictive relevance (Chin, 1998) and acceptable accuracy (Hair et al., 2019).

Figure 3.2 provides the estimates for the structural model. We note that EC positively affects EI (β = 0.42, p < 0.05), which confirms previous studies (Jarrahi & Eshraghi, 2019; Ratten et al., 2016). In line with hypothesized relationships, self-efficacy directly and positively affects EI (β = 0.29, p < 0.05), while anxiety has a negative direct effect on EI (β = –0.39, p < 0.05). Interestingly, both anxiety (β = –0.32, p < 0.05) and self-efficacy (β = –0.16, p < 0.05) negatively affect EC. The ease of social media for business (EoU) positively affects EC (β = 0.29, p < 0.05). It is important to note that though the direct effect of self-efficacy on EC was negative, the path through EoU shows a positive effect.

Discussions

The Always-On Lifestyle

The research shows that the Digital Natives living in Kuwait (DNs) have an unparalleled inclination toward technology. DNs use their phones and connect to social media extensively. Primarily, YouTube and Instagram are the dominant platforms for communicating and getting entertained. Our study shows a marginal difference between Kuwaiti and non-Kuwaiti groups as the Kuwaiti nationals slightly prefer YouTube, whereas the non-Kuwaiti respondents lean toward Instagram. As of June 2020, the most globally dominant platform is Facebook, with 74% of the market (StatCounter Global Stats, 2020). Despite the global domination of Facebook, we believe that DNs prefer the less personal social media platforms to maintain a level of anonymity and eliminate the chances for personal identification. For example, the study reveals that no Kuwaiti respondent selected Facebook as his/her favorite platform.

Ubiquitous connectivity characterizes DNs as using social media for shopping, networking, and getting informed and entertained. The Kuwaiti respondents seem to use more social media for commercial use than the non-Kuwaiti. On the contrary, the non-Kuwaiti respondents use social media more for communication and entertainment (music, books, films, etc.).

The language barrier restricts the non-Kuwaiti audience from watching TV or listening to the radio. The study indicates an interesting comparison between the two gender groups of respondents. While the male DNs use social media to contact family and friends, the female DNs show preference in using social media for entertainment. Overall, DNs embrace a fully online and social-media-based lifestyle, allowing technology to filter information.

With the support of high-tech gadgets and top-of-the-line smartphones and wearables, DNs look for convenience, online shopping, and digitally personalized suggestions.

A Technology-Driven Entrepreneurial Intention

The increased reliance on technology and social media seems to impact EI and EC dynamics. Although both measures of entrepreneurship (EI and EC) received high scores, we notice that DNs have a more definite intention than the capacity for entrepreneurship. This finding explains why DNs feel the need to start their business and be financially independent. Still, they do not feel confident enough about their skills and knowledge. In terms of gender and self-evaluated entrepreneurial capacity, we see no difference between men and women DNs. Both genders feel equally ready to start a business considering their equal chances to receive proper education and financial incentives.

Nevertheless, the study shows a significant effect on gender concerning DNs' entrepreneurial intention. Female respondents show a more vital willingness to start their business online than male respondents. This finding can explain some of our observations after living in Kuwait for more than five years. Kuwait's market is female-focused, offering more commercial options to women than men. Hence, women pose a force to reckon with in the market, which reflects in various personal Instagram business pages ranging from women's fashion, accessories, makeup tips, to bakery services.

The study shows that female respondents demonstrate a positive attitude toward using social media for entrepreneurial activities. For male respondents, the correlations are not significant. Women DNs feel less competent, but the females' desire to start a business is high. The focus should be on equipping DNs with the right tools and igniting their passion for self-learning. As the study shows, anxiety is a factor that correlates negatively with women DNs' EI. The opposite stands for the male DNs whose level of anxiety correlates positively with both EI and EC. Another notable finding is that self-efficacy and EI for females correlate positively. At the same time, the study shows no correlation in the male group.

Nationality and social approval are two more factors that affect EI and EC. Kuwaiti respondents evaluate themselves with a higher EC than the non-Kuwaiti respondents. They feel more courageous to start a business. DNs seek external approval and guidance primarily from friends and family. Seeking experts' advice to decide to start a business seems to be the last resort for DNs.

Nevertheless, the study shows that female respondents are more willing to ask for an expert's opinion than men. This aligns with the findings by the Ipsos Group, which highlights a deeply engaged generation with family and friends to trust their opinion on brands, news, and trends (Ipsos, 2019). Overall, the study argues that developing an entrepreneurial culture with practical support on entrepreneurship-oriented education, start-up business infrastructure, and social empowerment would increase DNs' entrepreneurial mindset in Kuwait. The following section offers some practical implications for future consideration.

Implications

The study highlights technology understanding as a driving force for Generation Yers and discusses that social media acceptance and openness to change significantly impact entrepreneurial intention among DNs living in an emerging market such as Kuwait. The chapter increases knowledge on how the Digital Natives living in Kuwait view entrepreneurship and discusses the role of education in cultivating a profound entrepreneurial mindset. The study's results show that the increased reliance on technology and social media seems to impact entrepreneurial intention (EI) and entrepreneurial capacity (EC) dynamics. Although both entrepreneurship dynamics (EI and EC) received high scores, DNs have a more definite intention than the capacity for entrepreneurship. This finding explains why DNs feel the need to start their business and be financially independent. Still, they do not feel confident enough about their skills and knowledge. In terms of gender and self-evaluated entrepreneurial capacity, we see no difference between men and women DNs. Both genders feel equally ready to start a business considering their equal chances to receive proper education and financial incentives.

One implication of the study's findings is the need for improving students' entrepreneurial capacity. Since their intention is more potent than their capacity to start a business, Kuwait's education should offer courses and seminars on entrepreneurship. DNs should feel well equipped to reduce their anxiety about entrepreneurial activities. Residing in a wealthy state such as Kuwait, DNs prefer the safety of a steady publicly funded income than taking risks. The study shows that with the proper education, DNs are willing to start their businesses and help diversify Kuwait's oil-based economy.

Another implication is regarding the empowerment for using social media and technology in Kuwait. This study contributes to scarce literature regarding MENA DNs' beliefs for entrepreneurship, attitude toward accepting technology for business, self-efficacy, and anxiety for the future (Kesharwani, 2020). The State of Kuwait should encourage and incentivize DNs' first entrepreneurial steps. National campaigns and start-up competitions will develop a new business culture among DNs. Also, such publicly and privately funded activities will cultivate DNs' entrepreneurial competencies (Jarrahi & Eshraghi, 2019; Benni et al., 2016).

Conclusion

Technology acceptance and openness to change are two factors that impact entrepreneurship. The more open DNs are with social media, the more willing they are to start their business. This argument is supported by patterns identified in our correlation analysis. DNs believe in themselves to achieve personal goals and perceive social media as a tool to satisfy their aspirations. Social media offers opportunities for starting a business while reaching out to foreign markets. DNs seek social recognition, support, and encouragement in a prosperous economy that aims to further an entrepreneurial culture aligning with the country's 2035 strategic vision (Ministry of Foreign Affairs, 2020). The recent upgrade of Kuwait to an Emerging Market status by the index compiler MSCI Inc. as well as the country's Gross Domestic Product (GDP) worth of $134.76 billion in 2019 (World Bank, 2020) pave the way for a private-led transformation to an attractive financial and trade hub for investors and entrepreneurs.

References

Ahn, Juyeon, and Yoonhyuk Jung. 2014. "The Common Sense of Dependence on Smartphone: A Comparison Between Digital Natives and Digital Immigrants." *New Media & Society* 18 (7): 1236–1256. Doi:10.1177/1461444814554902.

Altman, Ruth. 2017. "The Disadvantages of Personal Branding." *Azcentral.Com.* http://yourbusiness.azcentral.com/disadvantages-personal-branding-14152.html.

Al-Wugayan, Adel, and Turki Alshimmiri. 2010. "Encouragement of Entrepreneurship in Affluent Economies: The Case of Kuwait." *International Business & Economics Research Journal (IBER)* 9 (4). Doi:10.19030/iber.v9i4.560.

Bagozzi, Richard, and Y. Yi. 1988. "On the Evaluation of Structural Equations Models." *Journal of the Academy of Marketing Science* 16 (1): 74–94.

Benni, E., T. Elmasry, J. Patel, and J. aus dem Moore. 2016. "Digital Middle East: Transforming the Region into a Leading Digital Economy." *McKinsey & Compa ny.* www.mckinsey.com/featured-insights/middle-east-and-africa/digital-middle-east-transforming-the-region-into-a-leading-digital-economy.

Bhandari, Krishna Raj, and Sachin Kumar Raut. 2019. "9 Leveraging Tacit." *Advances in Management Research: Innovation and Technology* 1 (1): 127–138.

Blut, Markus, Cheng Wang, and Klaus Schoefer. 2016. "Factors Influencing the Acceptance of Self-Service Technologies." *Journal of Service Research* 19 (4): 396–416. Doi:10.1177/1094670516662352.

Boyd, Danah M., and Nicole B. Ellison. 2007. "Social Network Sites: Definition, History, and Scholarship." *Journal of Computer-Mediated Communication* 13 (1): 210–230. Doi:10.1111/j.1083-6101.2007.00393.x.

Brewer, Laura. 2013. "Enhancing Youth Employability: What? Why? And How? Guide to Core Work Skills 2013." *International Labour Organization.* http://www.ilo.org/wcmsp5/groups/public/@ed_emp/@ifp_skills/documents/publication/wcms_213452.pdf.

British Council. 2017. "The Value of Enterprise and Entrepreneurship Education." *Britishcouncil.Org.* www.britishcouncil.org/education/skills-employability/what-we-do/vocational-education-exchange-online-magazine/october-2017/value-enterprise-entrepreneurship-education.

Brooks, Ann K., and Chinedu Anumudu. 2015. "Identity Development in Personal Branding Instruction." *Adult Learning* 27 (1): 23–29. Doi:10.1177/1045159515616968.

Chin, Wynne W. 1998. "The Partial Least Squares Approach to Structural Equation Modeling." In: Marcoulides, G.A. (Ed.), *Modern Methods for Business Research.* Mahwah, NJ: Lawrence Erlbaum Associates.

Cieslik, Mark, and Gary Pollock. 2002. *Young People in Risk Society: The Restructuring of Youth Identities and Transitions in Late Modernity.* London: Routledge.

Cohen, Jacob. 1988. *Statistical Power Analysis for Behavioral Sciences.* Mahwah, NJ: Lawrence Erlbaum.

Davis, Fred D., Richard P. Bagozzi, and Paul R. Warshaw. 1989. "User Acceptance of Computer Technology: A Comparison of Two Theoretical Models." *Management Science* 35 (8): 982–1003. Doi:10.1287/mnsc.35.8.982.

Dutta, Soumitra. 2010. "Managing Yourself: What's Your Personal Social Media Strategy?" *Harvard Business Review.* November 1. https://hbr.org/2010/11/managing-yourself-whats-your-personal-social-media-strategy.

Engle, Robert L., Nikolay Dimitriadi, Jose V. Gavidia, Christopher Schlaegel, Servane Delanoe, Irene Alvarado, Xiaohong He, Samuel Buame, and Birgitta Wolff. 2010. "Entrepreneurial intention." *International Journal of Entrepreneurial Behavior & Research* 16 (1): 35–57. Doi:10.1108/13552551011020063.

Etemad, Hamid, and Keen, Christian. 2018. Managing rapid change and rapid-growth in emerging industries, *International Journal of Entrepreneurship and Small Business*, 34 (4): 480–499.

France, Alan. 2007. *Understanding Youth in Late Modernity.* Maidenhead, Berkshire, England: Open University.

Gander, Michelle. 2014. "Managing Your Personal Brand." *Perspectives: Policy and Practice in Higher Education* 18 (3): 99–102. Doi:10.1080/13603108.2014.913538.

Gandini, Alessandro. 2016. "Digital Work: Self-Branding and Social Capital in the Freelance Knowledge Economy." *Marketing Theory* 16 (1): 123–141. Doi:10.1177/1470593115607942.

Gehl, Robert W. 2011. "Ladders, Samurai, and Blue Collars: Personal Branding in Web 2.0." *First Monday* 16 (9). Doi:10.5210/fm.v16i9.3579.

Hair, Joseph F., Jeffrey J. Fisher, Marko Sarstedt, and Christian M. Ringle. 2019. "When to Use and How to Report the Results of PLS-SEM." *European Business Review* 31 (1): 2–24.

Harris, Lisa, and Alan Rae. 2011. "Building a Personal Brand Through Social Networking." *Journal of Business Strategy* 32 (5): 14–21. Doi:10.1108/0275666 1111165435.

Henseler, Jörg, Christian M. Ringle, and Marko Sarstedt. 2014. "A New Criterion for Assessing Discriminant Validity in Variance-Based Structural Equation Modeling." *Journal of the Academy of Marketing Science* 43 (1): 115–135.

Herrmann, Heinz, and Rana. Sudhir. 2020. "Which B2B Thinker Are You?" *International Journal of Indian Culture and Business Management* 21 (1): 45–62.

Hoffmann, Christian Pieter, Christoph Lutz, and Miriam Meckel. 2014. "Digital Natives or Digital Immigrants? The Impact of User Characteristics on Online Trust." *Journal of Management Information Systems* 31 (3): 138–171. Doi:10.10 80/07421222.2014.995538.

IBM Corp. Released. 2016. *IBM SPSS Statistics for Windows, Version 24.0.* Armonk, NY: IBM Corp.

Ipsos. 2018. MENA's Millennials Decoded: A Glimpse Into MENA's Most Disruptive Generation. Ipsos News Cent re. https://www.ipsos.com/sites/default/files/ct/publication/documents/2018-09/menas_millennials_decoded.pdf.

Ipsos. 2019. "Spilling the Tea on Gen Z: Understanding MENA's Youth in a Connected World." *Ipsos.C om.* https://www.ipsos.com/sites/default/files/ct/publication/documents/2019-12/spilling-the-tea-on-gen-z-mena.pdf.

Ismayilzada, Farid. 2019. "How Entrepreneurs from Developing Countries Can Succeed in Tech." *Entrepreneur.* June 13. www.entrepreneur.com/article/331979.

Iyer, Radha. 2018. "Understanding the entrepreneurial mind-set of millennial." *ADMIFMS International Management Research Conference*, 33–38. IOSR Journal of Business and Manageme nt. www.iosrjournals.org/iosr-jbm/papers/Conf. ADMIFMS1808-2018/Volume-3/5.%2033-38.pdf.

Jarrahi, Mohammad Hossein, and Ali Eshraghi. 2019. "Digital Natives vs Digital Immigrants: A Multidimensional View on Interaction with Social Technologies in Organizations." *Journal of Enterprise Information Management* 32 (6): 1051–1070. Doi:10.1108/jeim-04-2018-0071.

Kesharwani, Ankit. 2020. "Do (How) Digital Natives Adopt a New Technology Differently Than Digital Immigrants? A Longitudinal Study." *Information & Management* 57 (2): 1–16. Doi:10.1016/j.im.2019.103170.

Khedher, Manel. 2015. "A Brand for Everyone: Guidelines for Personal Brand Managing." *Journal of Global Business Issues* 9 (1): 19–27.

Kiss, Andreea N., Wade M. Danis, and S. Tamer Cavusgil. 2012. "International Entrepreneurship Research in Emerging Economies: A Critical Review and Research Agenda." *Journal of Business Venturing* 27 (2): 266–290. Doi:10.1016/j. jbusvent.2011.09.004.

Kline, Rex, B. 2011. Principles and practice of structural equation modeling. New York: Guilford Press.

Kuwait Times. 2019. "Kuwait Achieves 'Emerging Market' Status." *Kuwait Times,* December 21. https://news.kuwaittimes.net/website/kuwait-achieves-emerging-market-status/.

Kuwait Today. 2020. "Kuwait To Stop Hiring Expats in Oil Sector." *Kuwait Today,* June 10. https://kwttoday.com/kuwait-to-stop-hiring-expats-in-oil-sector/.

Labrecque, Lauren I., Ereni Markos, and George R. Milne. 2011. "Online Personal Branding: Processes, Challenges, and Implications." *Journal of Interactive Marketing* 25 (1): 37–50. Doi:10.1016/j.intmar.2010.09.002.

Lair, Daniel J., Katie Sullivan, and George Cheney. 2005. "Marketization and the Recasting of the Professional Self." *Management Communication Quarterly* 18 (3): 307–343. Doi:10.1177/0893318904270744.

Lee-Ross, Darren. 2017. "An Examination of the Entrepreneurial Intention of MBA Students in Australia Using the Entrepreneurial Intention Questionnaire." *Journal of Management Development* 36 (9): 1180–1190. Doi:10.1108/jmd-10-2016-0200.

Lehmann, Wolfgang. 2004. "'For Some Reason, I Get a Little Scared': Structure, Agency, and Risk in School – Work Transitions." *Journal of Youth Studies* 7 (4): 379–396. Doi:10.1080/1367626042000315185.

Liñán, Francisco, and Chen, Yi-Wen. 2009. "Development and Cross-Cultural Application of a Specific Instrument to Measure Entrepreneurial intentions." *Entrepreneurship Theory and Practice* 33 (3): 593–617. Doi: 10.1111/j.1540-6520.2009.00318.x.

Lindell, Michael, K., and David J. Whitney. 2001. "Accounting for Common Method Variance in Cross-Sectional Research Designs." *Journal of Applied Psychology* 86 (1): 114–121.

Malhorta, Naresh K., Sung, S. Kim, and Ashutosh Patil. 2006. "Common Method Variance in IS Research: A Comparison of Alternative Approaches and a Reanalysis of Past Research." *Management Science* 52 (12): 1865–1883.

Mäntymäki, Matti, and Kai Riemer. 2014. "Digital Natives in Social Virtual Worlds: A Multi-Method Study of Gratifications and Social Influences in Habbo

Hotel." *International Journal of Information Management* 34 (2): 210–220. Doi:10.1016/j.ijinfomgt.2013.12.010.

Metallo, Concetta, and Rocco Agrifoglio. 2015. "The Effects of Generational Differences on Use Continuance of Twitter: An Investigation of Digital Natives and Digital Immigrants." *Behaviour & Information Technology* 34 (9): 869–881. Doi: 10.1080/0144929x.2015.1046928.

Miller, Sharon. 2016. "Small Business Owner Report." *Bank of Ameri ca*. https://about.bankofamerica.com/assets/pdf/Fall-2016-Small-Business-Report-feb17.pdf.

Ministry of Foreign Affairs. 2020. "Kuwait Vision 2035: New Kuwait" *Mofa.Gov.Kw*. www.mofa.gov.kw/en/kuwait-state/kuwait-vision-2035/.

Mueller, Stephen L., and Anisya S. Thomas. 2001. "Culture and Entrepreneurial Potential: A Nine Country Study of Locus of Control and Innovativeness." *Journal of Business Venturing* 16 (1): 51–75. Doi:10.1016/s0883-9026(99)00039-7.

Palfrey, John, and Urs Gasser. 2010. *Born Digital: Understanding the First Generation of Digital Natives*. New York: Basic Books.

Papakonstantinidis, Stavros. (2017). The use of social media in reducing professional uncertainty: An exploratory study, *Nowadays and Future Jobs*, 1 (1): 6–13.

Papakonstantinidis, Stavros. 2014. "Social Recruiting: Exploring the Impact of Social Networking Sites on Digital Natives' Occupational Opportunities." PhD Thesis, University of Leicest er. https://leicester.figshare.com/articles/Social_recruiting_exploring_the_impact_of_social_networking_sites_on_digital_natives_occupational_opportunities/10147610/files/18287888.pdf.

Papakonstantinidis, Stavros. 2019. *Tell Me About Yourself: Personal Branding and Social Media Recruiting in the Brave New Online World*. New York, New York: Business Expert Press.

Podsakoff, Philip, MacKenzie Scott, Lee, Y. Y., and Podsakoff, Nathan. 2003. Common Method Biases in Behavioral Research: A Critical Review of the Literature and Recommended Remedies, Journal of Applied Psychology 88(5):879–903 DOI: 10.1037/0021-9101.88.5.879

Prensky, Marc. 2001. "Digital Natives, Digital Immigrants." *On the Horizon* 9 (5): 1–6. Doi:10.1108/10748120110424816.

Rabaai, Ahmad A., Bashar Zogheib, Abdullah AlShatti, and Enas M. AlJamal. 2015. "Adoption of E-Government in Developing Countries: The e-Case of the State of Kuwait." *Journal of Global Research in Computer Science* 6 (10): 6– 21. www.rroij.com/open-access/adoption-of-egovernment-in-developing-countries-the-case-of-the-state-of-kuwait.pdf.

Rampersad, Hubert K. 2008. "A New Blueprint for Powerful and Authentic Personal Branding." *Performance Improvement* 47 (6): 34–37. Doi:10.1002/pfi.20007.

Rampton, John. 2016. "Six Hidden Risks to Personal Branding." *Fast Company*. November 2. www.fastcompany.com/3065169/six-hidden-risks-to-personal-branding.

Rana, S., Raut, S. K., Prashar, S., and Hamid, A. B. A. 2020. "Promoting through Consumer Nostalgia: A Conceptual Framework and Future Research Agenda." *Journal of Promotion Management* 27 (2): 211–249.

Rana, Sudhir. 2018. "Covering the Gap Between Theories and Practices in Business and Management." *FIIB Business Review* 7 (2): 67–68.

Rana, Sudhir, Prashar, Sanjeev, Barai, Munim, Kumar, and Hamid, Abu Bakar Abdul. 2021. "Determinants of International Marketing Strategy for Emerging Market Multinationals." *International Journal of Emerging Markets* 16(2): 154–178.

Ratten, Vanessa, Joao Ferreira, and Cristina Fernandes. 2016. "Entrepreneurial and Network Knowledge in Emerging Economies." *Review of International Business and Strategy* 26 (3): 392–409. Doi:10.1108/ribs-11-2015-0076.

Ratten, Vanessa. 2014. "Encouraging Collaborative Entrepreneurship in Developing Countries: The Current Challenges and a Research Agenda." *Journal of Entrepreneurship in Emerging Economies* 6 (3): 298–308. Doi:10.1108/jeee-05-2014-0015.

Raut, Sachin Kumar, Sakpal, Subodh, and Soni, Rashmi. 2022. "Understanding the Service Quality Dimensions and Achieving Resilience in Service Retail." In *Handbook of Research on Supply Chain Resiliency, Efficiency, and Visibility in the Post-Pandemic Era*, edited by Ramakrishna Yanamandra (pp. 136–156). IGI Global, UAE. https://doi.org/10.4018/978-1-7998-9506-0.

Reinartz, Werner, Michael Haenlein, and Jorg Henseler. 2009. "An Empirical Comparison of the Efficacy of Covariance-Based and Variance-Based SEM." *International Journal of Research in Marketing* 26 (4): 332–344.

Ringle, Christian M., Stefan Wende, and Jan-Michale Becker. 2015. *SmartPLS 3*. Boenningstedt: SmartPLS GmbH. www.smartpls.com.

Scarborough, Norman M., and Jeffrey R. Cornwall. 2018. *Essentials of Entrepreneurship and Small Business Management*. Upper Saddle River: Pearson.

Schawbel, Dan. 2011. "Branding in a Personal World." *Forbes*. January 31. www.forbes.com/sites/danschawbel/2011/01/31/branding-in-a-personal-world/#5af768a91dbd.

Shepherd, Ifan D. H. 2005. "From Cattle and Coke to Charlie: Meeting the Challenge of Self Marketing and Personal Branding." *Journal of Marketing Management* 21 (5–6): 589–606. Doi:10.1362/0267257054307381.

StatCounter Global Stats. 2020. "Social Media Stats Worldwide". *StatCounter Global Stats*. https://gs.statcounter.com/social-media-stats.

Taipale-Erävala, Kyllikki., Henttonen, Kaisa, and Lampela, Hannele. 2019. Entrepreneurial competencies in successfully innovative SMEs, *International Journal of Entrepreneurship and Small Business*, 38 (3): 251–276.

Tarnovskaya, Veronika. 2017. "Reinventing Personal Branding: Building a Personal Brand Through Content on YouTube." *Journal of International Business Research and Marketing* 3 (1): 29–35. Doi:10.18775/jibrm.1849-8558.2015.31.3005.

Tuqa, Khalid. 2020. "Kuwait Plans to Repatriate 40,000 Citizens on 188 Flights amid Coronavirus: Report." *Al Arabiya English*. April 14. https://english.alarabiya.net/en/coronavirus/2020/04/14/Kuwait-plans-to-repatriate-40-000-citizens-on-188-flights-amid-coronavirus-Report.

United Nations Development Program (UNDP). 2018. "Youth Empowerment in Kuwait. *UNDP in Kuwait*". www.kw.undp.org/content/kuwait/en/home/operations/projects/democratic_governance/youth-empowerment-in-kuwait.html.

Venkatesh, Viswanath, and Hillol Bala. 2008. "Technology Acceptance Model 3 and a Research Agenda on Interventions." *Decision Sciences* 39 (2): 273–315. Doi:10.1111/j.1540-5915.2008.00192.x.

Venkatesh, Viswanath, James Y. L. Thong, and Xin Xu. 2012. "Consumer Acceptance and Use of Information Technology: Extending the Unified Theory of Acceptance and Use of Technology." *MIS Quarterly* 36 (1): 157. Doi:10.2307/41410412.

World Bank. 2020. "World Bank Kuwait Data." 2020. *Data.Worldbank.Org*. https://data.worldbank.org/country/kuwait.

4 Early Bird Catches the Worm

Exploring Promotional Capability of Retailers

Bodh Raj Sharma and Aditi Sharma

Introduction

In the present volatile and competitive marketplace, the survival of retail business has become more challenging due to the technological advancements, innovations, and globalization (Enderwick & Buckley, 2019). The global retail market involves billions of physical and digital retailers, selling several brands through conventional or modern retail formats at different locations (Van de Sanden, Willems, & Brengman, 2019; Rana et al., 2021). Indeed, the study by Forrest and Tallapally (2018) reveals that retailers have been facing difficulty in selling the products and services to the modern customers who are more conscious, rational, and brand loving. However, the endeavours of the whole supply chain network remain unrewarded, if the offered brands are ultimately refuted by the customers. Nevertheless, the marketers often design a suitable promotion strategy keeping in view the resources, either to push the product (trade promotion and personal selling) or make the customers capable to pull the products (advertising, publicity, and public relations). To conceptualize, the word '*promotion*' is derived from the French word '*promocion*' that means to 'move forward' or 'push forward' and is supported by the Latin word, 'promotionem' that means 'moving forward'. Therefore, promotion, in a common sense, signifies uplifting of something while in marketing realm, promotion connotes disseminating the information pertaining to the brands to make the customers aware about the new product arrivals, usage of the product, and persuasion to purchase it (Dearing, Maibach, & Buller, 2006; Raut, Sakpal and Soni, 2022). The study by Khan (2016) affirms that promotion is a very useful strategy to attract and motivate customers for visiting the retail outlet and purchasing the desired products (Yrjölä, Saarijärvi, & Nummela, 2018). The promotional mix (marketing communication mix) includes tools such as advertising, sales promotion, publicity, personal selling, and direct marketing (Zineldin & Philipson, 2007). Each tool of promotional strategy has significant influence on the target audience as advertisement though is costly but covers a large pool of audience in a fraction of a second. Personal selling may be less costly with limited reach; however, it is worthwhile for

DOI: 10.4324/9781003315582-5

demonstrating the product features and usage (Familmaleki, Aghighi, & Hamidi, 2015). In fact, the promotional capability is the most essential capability of retailers that supports other capabilities (Moore & Fairhurst, 2003) for persuading customers and enhancing sales performance (Nour & Almahirah, 2014). In this regard, Nathwani (2017) defined promotion as 'the way or process by which the retailers target potential customers and furnish the information to purchase the product from them' whereas Nangoy and Tumbuan (2018) highlighted the influence of promotion strategy on the customers in their buying decisions. The study by Pitta, Weisgal, and Lynagh (2006) considered promotion strategy as a communication method of retailers by which they present their brands for gaining higher sales and margins. Furthermore, the products and services are valueless, if they are not effectively communicated and purchased by the customers (Liu, 2002). The study by Bulitia, Wanjala, and Mwangi (2018) mentioned three theories pertaining to the promotion mix which are helpful in increasing the short-term sales revenue of a business. The theories are named as *'push theory', 'pull theory', and 'combination theory'*. The *'push theory'* states that marketers offer some incentives or discounts to the distribution channels vis-à-vis wholesalers or retailers to sell more quantity of products for sales maximization. By offering high discounts, the marketers push them to purchase more quantity of products at lower prices. In this strategy, the focus is on maximization of sales through distribution channel rather than communicating with customers about product arrival. However, in *'pull strategy'*, the focus is on customers, and it relies on different communication channels to make customers aware about the product, so that the need for the product can trigger and lure customers to purchase the particular product. At the end, *'combination theory'* is the combination of aforementioned two theories in which first theory is used to deliver more products to the retailers through huge discounts while second theory creates awareness among customers about the existing and new brands.

In the retail sector, promotional capability plays a decisive role to attract the new customers for boosting sales and profitability (Grewal, Levy, & Kumar, 2009). The study by Moore and Fairhurst (2003) stated promotional capability as the strategy through which retailers effectively distinguish their stores from others by using different promotional techniques while Shamout (2016) opined sales promotion as a purposeful attempt to deliver the relevant information about the product along with the extra benefits to get the satisfactory response from the customers. The study by Nathwani (2017) considered sales promotion as the process of persuading the consumer to buy the product or services. Indeed, advertising and sales promotion are mostly used by the retailers, particularly those selling shopping and specialty products such as apparels, footwear, jewellery, and electronic products (Nangoy & Tumbuan, 2018). There is a need to explore the promotional capability of retailers, and, thus, the present chapter empirically explores the promotional capability of retailers and presents the demographic divergence regarding the promotional capability of retailers. The remainder of the chapter is presented as given here.

After the introduction section, the conceptual background is provided followed by the research objectives and hypotheses. The next section provides the details about the methodology adopted for conducting the present study followed by the analysis, results, and discussions. The final section portrays the implications, directions for future research, and conclusion.

Conceptual Background

In today's intensely competitive retail environment, the customer creation and retention are quite challenging for the retailers (Alalwan et al., 2016). Meanwhile, the promotional techniques assist the retailers to inform, convince, and attract the potential customers for shopping (Jeong & Lee, 2017). However, the retailers are required to identify the most efficient and effective promotion method for motivating the customers to purchase their products (Erdem & Jiang, 2016). In the supply chain process, retailers' promotion plays a decisive role in attaining the organizational goals as well as the fulfilment of customers' demands (Waterschoot & Van den Bulte, 1992). Indeed, Chavadi and Kokatnur (2010) suggested four key factors that attract the customers to purchase products from the shopping malls, viz., product mix, services, ambience, and various promotional strategies used by malls such as advertising, personal selling, sales promotion, publicity, and direct marketing. The promotional tools benefit the retailers in terms of attainment of sales, competitive superiority, and market share (Khan, 2016).

The accomplishment and effectiveness of promotion strategy depend on the rigorous search, identification of consumers' needs, and selection of suitable promotional media (Al-Badi, Tarhini, & Al-Sawaei, 2017; Bhandari and Raut, 2019). Similarly, Alananzeh, Tarhini, and Algudah (2018) considered promotional capability as a way to interact with the customers to accomplish the desirable promotional objectives. The promotional capability encourages the customers' purchases that ultimately augment retailers' performance indicators (Berezan, Yoo, & Christodoulidou, 2016). However, sales promotion is usually used to gain quicker as well as higher sales of products or services during a particular season, festival, or special occasion (Fassnacht & Königsfeld, 2015). It is, in fact, titled as an *'aggressive promotion strategy'* to retain existing customers as well as to attract the new customers (Hanaysha, 2016). Furthermore, Grewal, Levy, and Kumar (2009) opined that one of the most important activities of marketing is promotion that supports the retailers to inform their customers and influence their decision to buy products from their store. In the existing literature, several researchers have concentrated on various promotional tools, and for better conceptual understanding, some of the contributions are presented as in the next section.

Advertising

Advertising is the presentation of goods or service to target population in which there is impersonal relationship, and one party pays to the other for the promotion. To support, Bachnik, Nowacki, and Szopiński (2018) regarded advertising as non-personal communication and paid for by the seller of a product or services. Although, in past, advertising messages or commercials were communicated to target population through media like radio, television, newspapers, magazines, and posters displayed outdoors (Wakefield, Loken, & Hornik, 2010), but in the modern scenario, there are a number of other channels, that is social media (Facebook, WhatsApp), web pages, e-mails, and mobile apps that can assist in promoting the product or services (Buted et al., 2014). Thus, the arrival of online platforms has resulted in the vanishing of the chasm between advertised brands and consumers by crafting a dynamic communication platform leading to the development of an innovative way of advertising media (Thornhill, Xie, & Lee, 2017). The definition of advertising is to convey the message of the organisation to the large number of population about the offers or deals given by retailers to customers through mediums like radio, internet, print media, and social networks (Russo & Simeone, 2017). As a result, the modern milieu of advertising media comprises both traditional and new forms of media. In fact, new advertising media sum up large number of benefits, such as rapid customization (Bachnik, Nowacki, & Szopiński, 2018), lower

Figure 4.1 Promotional capability of retailers

cost (Russo & Simeone, 2017), and high amount of flexibility (Whitelock et al., 2013). The success or accomplishment of advertising drive as well as its ability to influence target people is wholly dependent on the choice of making a successful program that goes viral in the market and well defines the objectives of the organization (Alananzeh, Tarhini, & Algudah, 2018).

Publicity

One of the ways to promote the product or service by the retailers is publicity, and from the last decade, publicity has gained much more importance than any other traditional marketing channel (Story & French, 2004). Many dealers are using publicity as a means to spread awareness about the products in the market (Ching, 2016). In fact, publicity is a form of promotion that assists in delivering information about the retail brands to wide range of customers in the news form and is cheaper as well. Publicity means getting editorial column coverage in the media such as newspapers and usually does not require a message sponsor (Eisend & Küster, 2011). Publicity builds the image of retailers in the minds of the customers about the product or retail outlet. In general, publicity is designed by intermediaries who are the reporters or bloggers and provides a broader range of information (Spotts, Weinberger, & Weinberger, 2014; Rana et al., 2020a). This component of promotion edifies the reputation of retailers in the market as well as in the branding process of a company (Eberl & Schwaiger, 2005). Furthermore, Bond and Kirshenbaum (1998) defined publicity as the information obtained from the public, and confidently perceived, from the trusted sources in the market. Information so obtained from public sources can be positive or negative. In fact, wide research on negative publicity has inferred that consumers pay more attention as well as put more weight on publicity which is negative rather than positive, when it comes to decision-making process (Gendel-Guterman & Levy, 2017).

Sales Promotion

According to Shamout (2016), the most effective strategy or component of promotional mix is sales promotion as compared to advertisement, personal selling, publicity, or public relations. Even some researchers stated that sales promotion is a direct incentive or special discounts given on the products or services to attract customers towards the retail establishment (Gardener & Trivedi, 1998). To support, the study by Joncos (1990) defined sales promotion as an effective and efficient way of attracting customers to compete in the market rather than marketing activities. Similarly, Asrinta (2018) defined sales promotion as a procedure through which the retailers attract customers on a temporary basis by giving some special offers or benefits for a particular period. The sales promotion is a mechanism to encourage customers for buying extra quantity of products, which, in turn, enhances the quantum of trade between two parties. The offers are in the form of buy one get one free, coupons on purchase of specific amount, special discounts, and so on. According to Shamout (2016), sales promotion provides information to the buyers and persuades for shopping. Meanwhile, majority of the retailers have been applying sales promotion technique nowadays for the more customers and sales maximization (Satit et al., 2012). Moreover, Shamout (2016) stated that sales promotion is a deliberate effort of a seller to communicate the appropriate information about the product in suitable way in the market to get desirable result like response from the customers or target population. Furthermore, the research contribution of Hughner et al. (2007) regarded sales promotion to be an important part of marketing mix, which is purposely planned to inform, persuade, and remind a particular group of buyers about the product thus influencing their knowledge and beliefs regarding that product. Although Yang et al. (2010) stated that promotion can be classified into value-increasing promotions and value-adding promotions – where price deals, various coupons, and offers related to funds come under value-increasing promotions, and offers like providing gifts, free samples, or schemes related to customer loyalty come under value-adding promotions.

Personal Selling

The selling function plays an important role as the whole process from production to consumption depends upon selling, and this function is under strain from decreased effectiveness and rising costs (Paesbrugghe, 2018). Decreased effectiveness of personal selling may be due to the dearth of research on customer perspective or lack of sufficient attention to personal selling and sales management (Williams & Plouffe, 2007). Personal selling plays a vital job in creating and establishing long-term contact between customers and retailers for improving the efficiency of the business. Furthermore, personal selling is an essential method by which a salesperson meets the potential buyers, gives required information about the products, and persuades them to buy that product. It is personal communication whereby the salespersons contact buyers and promote the product through demonstration. Through this technique, salespeople provide information to their customers about a product with its use and benefits. The customers can interact with and ask queries regarding the product. Personal selling also helps in enlarging sales, margins, and market share by identifying new customers, retaining the existing users, and convincing them to shop more units of a product (Anyadighibe, Awara, & Esu, 2014). The abilities of convincing customer, handling their questions, and satisfying them with arguments and demonstrations are the bases for the success of personal selling (Williams, Michael, & Jill, 1996).

Direct Marketing

Direct marketing is a practice whereby the products and services are sold to the customers directly without any intermediaries. Customers place their orders through e-mail, telephone call/SMS, or other digital platforms, and subsequently the products are delivered. Through different mediums, direct marketing strategy allows businesses to communicate directly with their customers. There are a number of mediums like electronic newsletters, websites, online adverts, fliers, online as well as offline catalogues, mobile messaging apps, promotional letters, television, newspaper and advertisement in magazine as well as outdoor advertising. Direct marketing usually relies on the scheme, offer, communication, choice of channel, and the ultimate target customer. While in advertisements, there is a non-personal communication between two parties, direct marketing seeks to generate relationships, that is one-to-one personal relationships with end users or customers (Camilleri, 2018). This promotional tool is attractive to many businesses due to its effectiveness in getting direct response from the customers without any agent, and its result can be measured directly by the concern. In fact, Morimoto and Chang (2006) stated direct marketing as being like a conventional postal direct mail and telemarketing. However, modifications in the technology like Internet have changed this promotional strategy of marketers. Nowadays, unsolicited commercial mails which usually are known as '*spam*' are trending due to two reasons, that is cost effectiveness as well as having high possibility to get interactive with target customers.

Research Objectives and Hypotheses

The present study is an empirical investigation of the promotional capability of retailers. After conceptualizing the various tools of promotion mix, the research objectives have been formulated. The main objectives of the study are listed as under:

- To explore the promotional capability of retailers
- To highlight the promotional tools used by the retailers
- To identify the demographic differences in the promotional capability of retailers
- To suggest the most effective promotional tool(s) for the retailers

The earlier research in the marketing area has considered the demographic variables as control factors or moderators (Lee, Bai, & Murphy, 2012). In this regard, the study by Kwon and Kwon (2007) found education level to have positively influenced customers' buying behaviours. However, the findings did not provide consistent results as to which segment is more promotion prone. The study by Kuruvilla, Joshi, and Shah (2009) concluded that the female customers have more positive shopping attitude as they generally purchase more products by considering shopping as a more free time activity. To supplement, Harmon and Hill (2003) asserted that female respondents are highly influenced by the promotional appeals as compared to their male counterparts. Similarly, age is regarded as being a significant demographic variable, and increased age brings maturity, exposure, and rationality in shopping. To support the argument, the study by Khare, Achtani, and Khattar (2014) stated that age and income of customers significantly influenced the consumer attitude towards promotion, while Kwon and Kwon (2007) argued that the benefit of sales promotion is mostly taken by high-income consumers. In fact, the study by Preeti (2017) explored the effect of marital status as it is seen that people become more sensible as well as responsible after marriage, and, similarly, the levels of consumers' income also play a vital role in their buying decision. Finally, the study recommended that retailers before framing their promotional policies should consider their consumer demographic variables. Since the findings of various research studies have conflicting outcomes, so there is a need to better understand and explain the related results (Lee, Bai, & Murphy, 2012). Hence, the study is based upon the following hypotheses.

H1: Gender wise, customers do not differ in perceived promotional capability of retailers.

H2: Qualification wise, customers do not differ in perceived promotional capability of retailers.

H3: Marital status wise, customers do not differ in perceived promotional capability of retailers.

H4: Age wise, customers do not differ in perceived promotional capability of retailers.

H5: Occupation wise, customers do not differ in perceived promotional capability of retailers.

As promotion is indispensable for every business concern, and retailers are also largely dependent on promotion endeavours, it is through promotion the retailers persuade the target customers to buy the desired products or services (Huynh, 2016). The study by Adeniran, Egwuonwu, and Egwuonwu (2016) examined the relationship between promotion and sales turnover of a firm and concluded that only proper promotion boosts sales volume (Fam et al., 2019). Although in marketing studies, the demographic variables were considered to be control factors and these are also regarded as very useful predictors of promotion (Hansen, Samuelsen, & Sallis, 2013). The study attempted to know whether more experienced and less experienced retailers use different promotional strategies to attract target customers. Different researchers have explored demographic factor differences in various sectors, but there is a paucity of research on retailers' experience, monthly sales, and number of employees' wise differences in the usage of promotional capability. Hence, the next hypotheses are:

H6: Experience-wise, retailers have the same promotional capability.

H7: Average monthly sales wise, retailers do not differ in promotional capability.

H8: Number of employees' wise, retailers do not differ in promotional capability.

Research Method

The present study empirically explores the promotional capability of retailers from the perspectives of customers as well as retailers. The reason for selecting the retail sector is that retailers apply several promotional tools I advertising, sales promotion, personal selling, and publicity to attract and retain the customers. The justification for fixing Indian Territory as the geographical domain of the research being Indian retail market has both traditional and modern outlets catering the demands of customers belonging to different demographic backgrounds. To the best of the knowledge of authors, India has a dearth of research on promotional capability of retailers. The various aspects of research methodology are described in the next section.

Sampling and Data Collection

The present study is based upon the data obtained from the secondary as well as primary sources. The secondary sources include the publications in the reputed research journals and digital databases. The primary data were obtained from the Indian customers and retailers. Two samples were drawn from a locality in J&K union territory in India. The first sample comprised 50 customers selected through purposive sampling technique keeping in view the research objectives as there is need to contact only those customers shopping from the selected retailers for undertaking a dyadic comparative approach. Another sample of 35 retailers selling the branded products vis-à-vis apparels, footwear, electronic products, etc., operating in same locality were contacted to take the responses regarding the promotional capability. The retailers were selected through the purposive sampling technique keeping in view the objectives and hypotheses of the present study.

Measures

The responses were obtained through a self-administered instrument designed after a thorough literature review and discussions with the subject experts, researchers, and faculty members. The survey instrument comprised demographic variables and items representing the promotional capability measured on a five-point Likert scale ranging from 5 representing 'strongly agree' to 1 representing 'strongly disagree'. The customers' perceived promotional capability construct had ten items while the retailers' promotional capability had 11 items, obtained and modified from the scales developed by Hanaysha (2018) and Shamout (2016). Meanwhile, to ensure accurate response and active involvement of respondents while filling the instrument, some of the items were kept as the internal consistency of marker variables and cross-checking of the data.

Analyses and Results

As the study is based upon two different samples, hence, the analysis for both samples is presented separately – initially for the customers, followed by the retailers.

Customers' Opinion About Promotional Capability of Retailers

The responses obtained from the customers were analysed with SPSS (20 Version) Software. After feeding and coding of the data, the demographic variables were assessed in terms of frequency and percentage. It was found that the proportion of female customers (56%) figured more as compared to the male counterparts, and among the total respondents, about 60% possessed post-graduation and above qualification. About two-thirds of them were in the age group of 25–50 years, while the proportion of unmarried shoppers (64%) emerged to be higher than that of their married counterparts. Last, occupation wise, respondents were segregated as self-employed (34%), service class (26%), and remaining 40% were segregated as students and homemakers (Table 4.1).

Exploratory Factor Analysis

For the data purification, exploratory factor analysis has been applied through Statistical Package for Social Sciences (SPSS, 20 Version) with principal component analysis along with varimax rotation. The factor analysis provided the factor loadings, AVE and KMO, and condensed the total data into two meaningful factors. The items having factor loading less than 0.5 and eigenvalue less than 1 were dropped and not considered for further

Table 4.1 Demographic profile of customers

Category	Variable	Frequency	Percentage
Gender	Male	22	44
	Female	28	56
Qualification	Up to graduation	20	40
	Postgraduate and above	30	60
Age	Below 25	15	30
	25–50	32	64
	Above 50	03	06
Marital status	Married	18	36
	Unmarried	32	64
Occupation	Service	13	26
	Self-employed	17	34
	Others	20	40

Source: Author's own.

analysis and the remaining items were clubbed in two factors that are explained as under:

Sales offers: It represents the offers made by the retailers to maximize the sales volume. This factor has an average value of 3.42 with alpha value ($\alpha = 0.78$) explaining 33.10% of the variance. Sales offers factor consists of five items with the item '*I come to know about product through advertisement*' having the highest factor loading (FL = 0.79), followed by the items '*a coupon enables to buy another brand*' (FL = 0.73), '*retailers provide additional gift with purchase*' (FL = 0.73), '*store offer us coupons for future purchasing*' (FL = 0.70), and last, '*price deals for this store are frequently offered*' having the least factor loading (0.60). The results indicate that advertisements and coupons are widely used by the retailers to persuade the customers for making the purchases from a particular retailer leading to sales maximization. In addition, the customers become aware about the retailers and their brands through the advertisements in the print, electronic, and social media (Rana et al., 2020b). Though advertisements are costly, yet retailers spend huge amounts for designing them so that they can cover a large number of audience. The advertisements are given in the local newspapers, local TV channels, neo-sign boards, radio, Facebook pages, WhatsApp, mobile apps, etc., as most of the people have accessibility to these types of media channels. Another promotional strategy adopted is to give coupons to the customers allowing them to purchase another product at a low price. Sometimes, additional gifts are given to customers like speakers with computers, headphones, and pen drives to convince the customers to shop more and more products.

Sales promotion: The second factor is named as sales promotion, having alpha value of ($\alpha = 0.63$) with overall mean of 3.98 thus explaining 25% of the variance. It consists of three items, and the item '*seasonal promotions in this store is available*' has the highest factor loading (0.83) followed by the variable '*price deals in this store are offered on many items*' (FL = 0.75) and '*store provides special offers in festivals*' (FL = 0.63). This reveals that the retailers make the seasonal sales promotion in the form of discounts, price deals, extra quantity (buy 1 get 1 free) offers, and special offers on different festivals like Diwali, Baisakhi, Holi, Navaratri, Christmas, and New Year. The aim of these promotional campaigns is to attract a large pool of customers in the retail outlet and enhance the sales in the shortest span of time. If a customer wants to purchase a car, jewellery, or other durable products, they wait for the festival offer whereby they get huge discounts, gifts, and extra benefits (Table 4.2).

Hypotheses Testing

To examine the mean differences in the customers' perceived promotional capability on the basis of gender, qualification, and marital status, independent sample t test has been applied. The independent sample t test is

Table 4.2 EFA results of customers' perceived promotional capability

Factor-wise dimension	Mean	SD	FL	VE	Alpha	EV	C
Sales offers	3.42			33.10	0.78	2.65	
I came to know about the product by advertisement.	3.40	1.16	0.79				0.66
A coupon enables to buy another brand.	2.78	1.40	0.73				0.61
Retailers provide additional gifts with purchase.	3.28	1.34	0.73				0.57
Stores offer us coupons for future purchasing.	3.74	1.12	0.70				0.56
Price deals are frequently offered.	3.90	0.95	0.60				0.49
Sales promotion	3.98			24.99	0.63	1.99	
Seasonal promotions in this store are available.	4.26	0.78	0.83				0.69
The price deals are offered on many items.	3.60	1.11	0.75				0.58
Store provides special offers in festivals.	4.08	1.03	0.63				0.50

Note: SD = Standard Deviation, FL = Factor Loadings, VE = Variance Explained, EV = Eigenvalues, C = Commonalities.
Source: Author's own.

Table 4.3 Independent sample t-test results for customers' perceived promotional capability

Variables	Category	N	Mean	SD	t	Sig.
Gender	Male	22	3.586	.837	−.692	.493
	Female	28	3.732	.593		
Qualification	Up to graduation	20	3.565	.786	−.830	.405
	Postgraduation and above	30	3.737	.653		
Marital status	Married	18	3.667	.783	−.010	.992
	Unmarried	32	3.669	.673		

Source: Author's own.

applied when independent variable has two categories like gender with male and female resspondents. The dependent factor in this case is the average mean score of all the items representing customers' perceived promotion capabilities. The results indicate insignificant mean differences in the perceived promotional capability on the basis of gender (Sig.=.493), qualification (Sig.=.405), and marital status (.992) as the p value is > 05 (Table 4.3). Thus, H1, H2 and H3 are supported. The results reveal that all types of customers seek promotion of products through advertising, offering discounts, coupons, gift vouchers etc. by the retailers (Table 4.3) so, that they can be informed about the retailers offerings and additional benefits. Both male as well as female customers seek the promotion of products as indicated by the above average mean score accorded by the respondents. These findings arein contradictionto the earlier studies in the extant literature (Harmon & Hill, 2003; Kuruvilla, Joshi, & Shah, 2009) but the solid reason is that both male and female respondents have needs and wants and they prefer unique quality products at reasonable prices. In this regard, sales promotion supports them to avail the product or service at lower prices or with some additional benefits in terms of extra quantity, gifts, vouchers etc. Similarly, qualification wise respondents perceived promotion of retailers as similar due the reason that both undergraduates and post graduates rush to the store on the occasion of seasonal or festival sales discounts. Eductaion is not the factor that differenciate between the responses of respondents regarding the benefits of promotion. All customers are being benefited by the advertisement, coupons, gifts, and discounts. Meanwhile, the findings are distinct from the results of the study conducted by (Kwon & Kwon, 2007) who found significant differences on the education levels of respondents. Furthermore, both married and single respondents having the same opinion regarding the customers' perceived promotional capability. However, the study by Preeti (2017) provide the opposite results. It is because the consumption pattern and lifestyle aI similar between married and single customers nowadays, as unmarried customers are also brandconscious and consume various products at several occasions. Earlier the branded apparel and jewellery were mostly used by the married customers but presently the unmarried customers are equally consuming the same products.

Moreover, to identify the age and profession-wise differences in the customers' perceived promotional capability of retailers, Univariate Analysis of Variance (ANOVA) was applied. The results portray that there are insignificant mean differences in the responses of customers belonging to different age and occupational groups regarding the customers' perceived promotional capability (Table 4.4). Thus, H4 and H5 are also supported. It is evident that respondents belonging to various age groups do not differ in their perceptions about promotional capability of retailers. The findings

Table 4.4 ANOVA results for customers' perceived promotional capability

Variables	Category	N	Mean	SD	F	Sig.
Age	Below 25	15	3.747	.669	.255	.776
	25–50	32	3.616	.721		
	Above 50	03	3.833	.950		
	Total	50	3.668	.706		
Occupation	Service	13	4.031	.538	2.538	.090
	Self-employed	17	3.588	.834		
	Others	20	3.500	.627		
	Total	50	3.668	.706		

Source: Author's own.

are different from the earlier studies undertaken by Khare, Achtani, and Khattar (2014). The reason is that customers of all age groups take advantage of promotional benefits, viz., discounts, coupons, vouchers, gifts and other offerings in addition to the product. Even the children are so conscious about the product choices developed through advertisements and other tools of promotion. Indeed, the service customers, self employed, homemakers and students have similar perceptions about the promotional compaigns of the retailers as the influence of materialism, social status and prestigehave changed the mindset and consumption pattern of consumers. Indeed, the increased family income of customers have raised the demands and preference for quality products and even those consumers who are dependent on parents never comprise in shopping the branded products the they prefer footwear of Nike, Bata, Adidas, Puma, Liberty, Woodland and garments of Levi's, Wrangler, Numero Uno and Pepe Jeans. Most of the customers in India wait till the discount on these brands is declared and as soon as seasonal sales starts people of all age groups, gender, occupation, qualification rush to these stores for immediate shopping of these available brands.

Retailers' Opinion About the Promotional Capability

The primary data so collected from the retailers have been analysed with SPSS Software. After proper coding of the data, the retail store demographics and characteristics have been presented in terms of frequency and percentage (Table 4.5). The proportion of male respondents was higher (83%) than their female counterparts. About half of the respondents were above 30 years of age, and 57% had studied up to the graduation level. About 46% of the respondents had less than five years of experience as retailers, and approximately one third of them earned an average monthly sale between 10 lakhs to 20 lakhs. Majority of the retailers had less than 10 employees, serving as salespeople to assist the customers in buying decisions, handling the stock, and receiving the payments at the counter in cash or digital payments (Table 4.5).

Exploratory Factor Analysis

The technique of factor analysis provides the descriptive statistics, factor loadings, KMO, and variance explained and summarizes the total data into factors. The variables having factor loadings less than 0.5 and eigenvalues less than 1 were excluded from the subsequent analysis. The factor loadings above 0.50 also support the convergent validity. All the variables compressed to two factors are explained as follows.

Sales offers: The first factor comprises five variables with a factorial mean value of 3.93 and alpha value (α = 0.86), explaining 36.27% variance. The item *'approaching celebrities to promote products'* has the highest factor loading (0.91) followed by the items *'free trails to customers'* (FL = 0.84),

Table 4.5 Demographic profile of retailers

Variables	Category	Frequency	Percentage
Gender	Male	29	83
	Female	06	17
Age (yrs)	Below 30	17	49
	Above 30	18	51
Qualification	Up to graduation	20	57
	Postgraduation	15	43
Experience in the outlet (yrs)	Less than 5	16	46
	5–10	10	29
	10–15	09	25
Average monthly sales (in lakhs)	Below 10	10	29
	10–20	12	34
	20–30	06	17
	Above 30	07	20
Number of employees	Less than 5	15	43
	5–10	14	40
	Above 15	06	17

Source: Author's own.

'*send alerts to customers for new arrivals*' (FL = 0.74), '*free gifts to customers at certain level of purchase*' (FL = 0.72), and at the end, '*special offers on festivals*' (FL = 0.69) has the least loading. It means the advertisements endorsed by celebrities creates more impression on the customers and thus forces the retailers to involve them in promotion.

Promotion Tools: Sales promotion is the second factor with alpha value of (α = 0.88) with overall mean of 4.15, explaining 24.99% of variance explained and consists of six items. The items inform customers about new products (FL = 0.88), focus on seasonal promotions (FL = 0.86), use social media for promotion of product (FL = 81), offer coupons for future purchase (FL = 76), use various types of media for promotion of product (FL = 61), and least value of factor loading is for advertisement of products (FL = 0.56).

Hypotheses testing

For identifying the the mean differences regarding the promotional capability of retailers on grounds of experience of retailers, average monthly sales, and number of employees at the retail outlet, ANOVA has been applied. The results indicate that experience-wise, there is no significant difference in the promotion capabilities which means that all the retailers use the promotional capability irrespective of the level of experience at the retail outlet. In fact, they consider promotion as the influencing factor for attracting the customers, magnifying the sales and profitability. Thus, H6 is accepted. Indeed,

Table 4.6 EFA results of promotional capability of retailers

Factor-wise dimension	Mean	SD	FL	VE	Alpha	EV	C
Sales offers	3.93			36.27	0.86	3.99	
Approach celebrities to promote products.	4.00	1.03	0.91				0.84
Free trials to customers.	3.74	0.95	0.84				0.76
Send alerts to customers for new arrivals.	4.14	0.69	0.74				0.72
Offer free gifts at a certain level of purchase.	3.60	1.17	0.72				0.54
Special offers on festivals.	4.17	1.01	0.69				0.67
Promotional Tools	4.15			34.99	0.88	3.85	
Inform customers about new products.	4.29	0.46	0.88				0.87
Focus on seasonal promotions.	4.31	0.58	0.86				0.82
Use social media for promotion of product.	4.17	0.71	0.81				0.88
Offer coupons for future purchase.	4.23	0.73	0.76				0.82
Use of media for the promotion of product.	4.20	0.41	0.61				0.37
Advertisement of products.	3.71	0.83	0.56				0.50

Note: *SD = Standard Deviation, FL = Factor Loadings, VE = Variance Explained, EV = Eigenvalues, CV = Commonalities.*
Source: Authors own.

on the basis of average monthly sales, all the variables have insignificant differences except two variables, viz., *'we send alerts to customers for new arrivals'* and *'we give special offers on festivals'* however, having significant differences (Table 4.7). Hence, H7 is partially supported.

The post hoc test using LSD method on these two variables portrays that retailers having average monthly sales below 10 lakhs differ significantly with regard to the alerts to customers for new products, while insignificant differences emerge between the retailers earning the average monthly sales of Rs 10 lakhs to 20 lakhs and above 20 lakhs. Similarly, regarding special offers on festivals, the retailers earning less than 10 lakhs of monthly average sales differ from the higher sales categories; however, insignificant differences emerge in the retailers having monthly sales between 10 lakhs to 20 lakhs and above 20 lakhs. The reason for sending new product alerts and giving more festival offers is to attract a large pool of customers by disseminating information through message alerts on mobile phones, e-mails, social media platforms as well as offering high discounts, gifts, coupons particularly on the occasion of festivals. In India, there are several festivals

Table 4.7 ANOVA results of promotional capability of retailers

Promotion capability	Experience		Monthly sales		No. of employees	
	F	Sig.	F	Sig.	F	Sig.
Inform customer about our new products.	2.821	.074	1.264	.304	.043	.958
Use media for the promotion of product.	.020	.980	.359	.783	.520	.600
Use social media for the promotion of our product.	.365	.697	2.395	.087	.335	.718
Offer coupons for future purchasing.	.770	.472	1.731	.181	.632	.538
Focus on seasonal promotions.	1.806	.181	2.159	.113	.546	.585
Do advertisement of products.	2.157	.132	1.142	.348	.619	.545
Offer free trials to customers.	.780	.467	1.652	.198	.161	.852
Send alerts to customers for new arrivals.	.989	.383	3.696	.022	.962	.393
Make special offers on festivals.	.021	.980	4.917	.007	.161	.852
Approach celebrities to promote the products.	.726	.492	1.261	.305	.062	.940
Offer free gifts at a certain level of purchase.	1.740	.192	.564	.643	.282	.756

Source: Authors own.

that are celebrated, and consumers do a lot of shopping on these auspicious occasions such as Navratri, Diwali, Holi, Eid, Christmas, Karva Chauth, and Dhanteras (Table 4.8).

Furthermore, on the basis of number of employees at the retail store, insignificant difference are emerged (p: >.05, Table 4.7). Therefore, H8 is supported. The reason is that irrespective of the number of employees, the customers are influenced by advertisement and sales promotion to shop. In conventional retailing, salespeople make efforts to bring the customers at the store by standing at the entrance of the outlet and call the passers-by to purchase the products, but in modern retailing more effective roles have been played by the promotional tools vi-a-vis sales promotion and advertising.

Discussions

The study presents the perceptions of customers and retailers regarding the promotional capability of retailers. It is evident from the aforementioned analysis that customers are influenced by the retailers' promotional campaigns in terms of the creation of awareness through advertising and attracting them through discounts, coupons, vouchers, free trials, festival sales, etc. Customers appreciate the information sent through the alerts to them that inform them about the latest brands. On the basis of gender, age, qualification, marital status, and occupation, no significant differences emerged in the perceived promotional capability as all types of respondents awaited

Table 4.8 Post hoc analysis

Variables	(I) Average monthly sales	(J) Average monthly sales	Mean difference (I – J)	Std. error	Sig.
We send alerts to customers for new arrivals.	Below 10	10–20	–.73333*	.26634	.010
		20–30	–.90000*	.32122	.009
		Above 30	–.68571*	.30655	.033
	10–20	Below 10	.73333*	.26634	.010
		20–30	–.16667	.31102	.596
		Above 30	.04762	.29584	.873
	20–30	Below 10	.90000*	.32122	.009
		10–20	.16667	.31102	.596
		Above 30	.21429	.34608	.540
	Above 30	Below 10	.68571*	.30655	.033
		10–20	–.04762	.29584	.873
		20–30	–.21429	.34608	.540
We give special offers on festivals.	Below 10	10–20	–1.36667*	.37434	.001
		20–30	–1.20000*	.45148	.012
		Above 30	–.98571*	.43085	.029
	10–20	Below 10	1.36667*	.37434	.001
		20–30	.16667	.43714	.706
		Above 30	.38095	.41580	.367
	20–30	Below 10	1.20000*	.45148	.012
		10–20	–.16667	.43714	.706
		Above 30	.21429	.48640	.663
	Above 30	Below 10	.98571*	.43085	.029
		10–20	–.38095	.41580	.367
		20–30	–.21429	.48640	.663

Source: Authors own.

sales promotion and appreciated the other promotional endeavours of the retailers. The study highlights that retailers focus on advertising and sales promotion to attract and retain the customers for higher retail business performance in terms of sales margins, market share, and diversification. The customers, for satisfying their needs and wants, aspire for the right product at the right time, place, price, and promotion. The retailers use their promotional capability to make the best use of other capabilities such as merchandising, pricing, selling, innovation, and customer relationship management capability. Promotional capability includes the application of various promotional tools such as advertising, sales promotion, publicity, and personal selling to convince the customers and intensify their business performance. However, the results of the present study reveal that retailers prefer advertising and sales promotion as compared to other promotion tools because they are more effective to generate more customers and sales maximisation in a short span of time. It is also evident that retailers involve celebrities in the advertisements to create more influence on customers for shopping from a particular retail outlet. Indeed, retailers inform the existing customers about

Table 4.9 Testing of hypotheses

Gender-wise customers do not differ in perceived promotional capability of retailers.	Supported
Qualification-wise customers do not differ in perceived promotional capability of retailers.	Supported
Marital-status-wise customers do not differ in perceived promotional capability of retailers.	Supported
Age-wise customers do not differ in perceived promotional capability of retailers.	Supported
Occupation-wise customers do not differ in perceived promotional capability of retailers.	Supported
Experience-wise retailers have the same promotional capability.	Supported
Average-monthly sales-wise retailers do not differ in promotional capabilities.	Partially Supported
Numbers of employees-wise retailers do not differ in promotional capabilities.	Supported

Source: Authors own

new products through SMSs, social media, Facebook pages, e-mails, etc. Retailers have been giving out coupons for future purchase with a specified time limit to increase the sales of their products and services. Retailers spend huge amounts of money on designing advertisements as sound advertising copy, suitable media, services of advertising agency, and payment to celebrities involve large sums of funds which are ultimately added to the price of the products. Retailers offer seasonal and festival discounts to increase the sales turnover and profit margins in a particular time span. They also provide free trials to customers to mIthemselves familar with the products in terms of trying out the garments, footwear, or cars before actually buying these products. Another strategy adopted by the retailers is to offer the gifts to customers for buying beyond a certain amount or units of products to maximize the sales turnover. The study also provides robust findings in terms of the insignificant differences in the perceptions of promotional capability on the basis of experience of retailers, number of employees, and average monthly sales (except two variables) with sound reasons.

Implications of the Study

Theoretical Implications

The present study fills the gap in the existing literature by considering various promotional tools in the retail sector, which ultimately amplify the retail business performance. Various promotional tools are explained along with their effect on customers as well as retailers in the short and long run. The present piece of work is unique in the sense that it identifies all the promotional tools which contribute to business performance. In addition, the tools of promotion mix are tested from retailers' as well as customers' perspectives to understand the demographic differences regarding promotional capability. The study also provides robust findings with sound justification in terms of insignificant differences in various demographic factors regarding promotional capability. The academicians, researchers, and students can be benefitted from this piece of research in terms of conceptual understanding and getting insights for further research. This study is an addition to the extant literature on marketing capabilities and retailing as new approaches, relationships, and frameworks can be designed on the basis of the findings and conclusions. The study offers more clarity and portrays comprehensively the extent of promotional capability of retailers dealing in shopping and specialty products.

Managerial Implications

Retailers face huge competition in today's dynamic market, and it is important for a retailer to retain their customers and attract new ones for increasing their market share. It is suggested that retailers should use appropriate promotional mix to sustain their business in the market (Kumar & Patra, 2017) as proper promotional strategies attract new customers in the retail outlets and make them aware about the arrival of a new product in the store. The results of the present study provide managers with a deeper understanding of how different promotional tools can be applied effectively for customer delight and value. Different tools have different benefits for retailers operating in the market, and to explore which tool(s) will be efficiently useful and more convivent for them is the need of the hour. The study highlights that customers are strongly influenced by the promotional compaigns, and the retailers should make it a routine matter for continuous improvement in the retail performance and diversification. Indeed, the retailers should use advertisements as well as sales promotion to attract new customers as personal selling will not be useful for them. So, it is important for retailers to understand these different tools of promotional mix and that the proper implementation of these tools will help them to enhance their profit margins and sales volume (Morimura & Sakagawa, 2018). Moreover, through these tools, retailers can improve their customer satisfaction which is important to compete in the market and to attract new customers as satisfied customers will spread positive word of mouth, and good services will retain the existing ones (Nambiar et al., 2018). The retailers should rethink about and redesign their promotion strategy keeping in view the expectations of customers and the availability of resources.

Agenda for Future Research

The study provides a conceptual understanding of various promotional capabilities of retailers, and further research can design a research framework and examine the relationship of promotional capability with other marketing capabilities. In future, the effect of promotional tools on business performance (finacial and non-financial) can also be tested. The comparative study among various sectors can be one of the research agenda for the upcoming research. At the end, the cross-cultural studies can also be conducted by the prospective researchers.

Conclusion

The present study explores the promotional capability of retailers from the data generated from customers as well as retailers. First, the chapter contributes to the extant literature by defining the various promotional tools in retail sector and explains how by using these tools retailers can improve their survival chances in the market with sound business performance. Second, the study provides the demographic differences in the perceived promotional capability of retailers on the basis of gender, age, qualification, experience, marital status, etc. Third, it emphasizes on the maximum use of advertising and sales promotion tools by the retailers for their sales and profit maximization. The study provides a sound basis for further research on promotional capability in relation to other capabilities and offers sound implications for retailers, customers, researchers, practitioners, and decision-makers.

References

Adeniran, J. A., Egwuonwu, T. K., & Egwuonwu, O. K. (2016). The impact of sales promotion on sales turnover in airlines industry in Nigeria. *International Journal of Marketing Studies*, 8(3), 99–110.

Alalwan, A. A., Rana, N. P., Algharabat, R., & Tarhini, A. (2016). A systematic review of extant literature in social media in the marketing perspective. *Spri nger*, 9844, 79–89. https://doi.org/10.1007/978-3-319-45234-0_8.

Alananzeh, O., Tarhini, A., & Algudah, O. (2018). The effect of promotional mix on hotel performance during the political crisis in the Middle East. *Journal of Hospitality and Tourism Technology*, 9(1), 33–49.

Al-Badi, A., Tarhini, A., & Al-Sawaei, S. (2017). Utilizing social media to encourage domestic tourism in Oman. *International Journal of Business and Management*, 12(4), 84–94.

Anyadighibe, J. A., Awara, N. F., & Esu, B. B. (2014). The impact of personal selling on the productivity of selected banks in Calabar Metropolis. *International Journal of Development and Sustainability*, 3(8), 1697–1708.

Asrinta, P. S. (2018). The influence of sales promotion and store atmosphere towards impulse buying with shopping emotion as intervening variable. *Journal of Research in Management*, 1(2), 23–33.

Bachnik, K., Nowacki, R., & Szopiński, T. S. (2018). Determinants of assessing the quality of advertising services-The perspective of enterprises active and inactive in advertising. *Journal of Business Research*, 88, 474–480.

Berezan, O., Yoo, M., & Christodoulidou, N. (2016). The impact of communication channels on communication style and information quality for hotel loyalty programs. *Journal of Hospitality and Tourism Technology*, 7(1), 100–116.

Bhandari, K. R., & Raut, S. K. (2019). 9 Leveraging Tacit. *Advances in Management Research: Innovation and Technology*, 1(1), 127–138.

Bond, J., & Kirshenbaum, R. (1998). Under the Radar an ADWEEK book. *John Wiley and Sons*, 605, 10158–10012.

Bulitia, G., Wanjala, J. W., & Mwangi, G. W. (2018). Factors affecting the choice of promotional mix by commercial banks in Kenya: A case study of Kenya commercial bank limited. *School of Business & Economics*, 5(3), 168–178.

Buted, D. R., Gillespie, N. S., Conti, J. B., Delgado, B. A., Marasigan, R. M. P., Rubico, S. K. A., & Felicen, S. S. (2014). Effects of social media in the tourism industry of Batangas Province. *Asia Pacific Journal of Multidisciplinary Research*, 2(3), 123–131.

Camilleri, M. A. (2018). Integrated marketing communications. *Travel Marketing, Tourism Economics and The Airline Product*, 5, 85–103. https://doi.org/10.1007/978-3-319-49849-2_5.

Chavadi, C. A., & Kokatnur, S. S. (2010). Driving factors and effectiveness of sales promotion in shopping malls: A consumer perspective. *Indian Journal of Marketing*, 40(4), 18–26.

Ching, A. T., Clark, R., Horstmann, I., & Lim, H. (2016). The effects of publicity on demand: The case of anti-cholesterol drugs. *Marketing Science*, 35(1), 158–181.

Dearing, J. W., Maibach, E. W., & Buller, D. B. (2006). A convergent diffusion and social marketing approach for disseminating proven approaches to physical activity promotion. *American Journal of Preventive Medicine*, 31(4), 11–23.

Eberl, M., & Schwaiger, M. (2005). Corporate reputation: Disentangling the effects on financial performance. *European Journal of Marketing*, 39(7/8), 838–854.

Eisend, M., & Küster, F. (2011). The effectiveness of publicity versus advertising: A meta-analytic investigation of its moderators. *Journal of the Academy of Marketing Science*, 39(6), 906–921.

Enderwick, P., & Buckley, P. J. (2019). Beyond supply and assembly relations: Collaborative innovation in global factory systems. *Journal of Business Research*, 103, 547–556.

Erdem, M., & Jiang, L. (2016). An overview of hotel revenue management research and emerging key patterns in the third millennium. *Journal of Hospitality and Tourism Technology*, 7(3), 300–312.

Fam, K. S., Brito, P. Q., Gadekar, M., Richard, J. E., Jargal, U., & Liu, W. (2019). Consumer attitude towards sales promotion techniques: A multi-country study. *Asia Pacific Journal of Marketing and Logistics*, 31(2), 437–463.

Familmaleki, M., Aghighi, A., & Hamidi, K. (2015). Analyzing the influence of sales promotion on customer purchasing behavior. *International Journal of Economics & Management Sciences*, 4(4), 1–6.

Fassnacht, M., & Königsfeld, J. A. (2015). Sales promotion management in retailing: Tasks, benchmarks, and future trends. *Marketing Review St. Gallen*, 32(3), 67–77.

Forrest, J. Y. L., & Tallapally, P. (2018). Customers are less patient, sustainable advantage becomes transient and the key for firms to succeed in fast changing markets. *Journal of Business, Economics and Technology*, 21(1), 1–14.

Gardener, E., & Trivedi, M. (1998). A communication framework to evaluate sales promotion strategies. *Journal of Advertising Research*, 38(3), 67–71.

Gendel-Guterman, H., & Levy, S. (2017). Consumer response to private label brands' negative publicity: A relational effect on retailer's store image. *Journal of Product & Brand Management*, 26(2), 204–222.

Grewal, D., Levy, M., & Kumar, V. (2009). Customer experience management in retailing: An organizing framework. *Journal of Retailing, 85*(1), 1–14.

Hanaysha, J. R. (2016). The Importance of social media advertisements in enhancing brand equity: A study on fast food restaurant industry in Malaysia. *International Journal of Innovation, Management and Technology, 7*(2), 46–58.

Hanaysha, J. R. (2018). An examination of the factors affecting consumer's purchase decision in the Malaysian retail market. *PSU Research Review, 2*(1), 7–23.

Hansen, H., Samuelsen, B. M., & Sallis, J. E. (2013). The moderating effects of need for cognition on drivers of customer loyalty. *European Journal of Marketing, 47*(8), 1157–1176.

Harmon, S. K., & Hill, C. J. (2003). Gender and coupon use. *The Journal of Product and Brand Management, 12*(2/3), 166–179.

Hughner, R. S., McDonagh, P., Prothero, A., Shultz, C. J., & Stanton, J. (2007). Who are organic food consumers? A compilation and review of why people purchase organic food. *Journal of Consumer Behaviour: An International Research Review, 6*(2–3), 94–110.

Huynh, K. T. (2016). Sales promotion effectiveness: The impact of culture on demographic level. *International Business Research, 9*(4), 123–130.

Jeong, M., & Lee, S. A. (2017). Do customers care about types of hotel service recovery efforts? An example of consumer-generated review sites. *Journal of Hospitality and Tourism Technology, 8*(1), 5–18.

Joncos, L. (1990). A retailer promotion policy model considering promotion signal sensitivity. *Marketing Science, 12*(4), 339–356.

Khan, M. S. (2016). Impact of promotional mix elements on tourist's satisfaction: A case study of Mussoorie. *International Journal of Research in Commerce & Management, 7*(4), 98–101.

Khare, A., Achtani, D., & Khattar, M. (2014). Influence of price perception and shopping motives on Indian consumers' attitude towards retailer promotions in malls. *Asia Pacific Journal of Marketing and Logistics, 26*(2), 272–295.

Kumar, S., & Patra, S. (2017). Does promotion mix really help to enhance brand equity: A literature review. *Asian Journal of Management, 8*(4), 1387–1392.

Kuruvilla, S. J., Joshi, N., & Shah, N. (2009). Do men and women really shop differently? An exploration of gender differences in mall shopping in India. *International Journal of Consumer Studies, 33*(6), 715–723.

Kwon, K.-N., & Kwon, Y. J. (2007). Demographics in sales promotion proneness: A socio-cultural approach. *Advances in Consumer Research, 34*(1), 288–294.

Lee, S. H., Bai, B., & Murphy, K. (2012). The role demographics have on customer involvement in obtaining a hotel discount and implications for hotel revenue management strategy. *Journal of Hospitality Marketing & Management, 21*(5), 569–588.

Liu, C. M. (2002). The effects of promotional activities on brand decision in the cellular telephone industry. *Journal of Product & Brand Management, 11*(1), 42–51.

Moore, M., & Fairhurst, A. (2003). Marketing capabilities and firm performance in fashion retailing. *Journal of Fashion Marketing and Management: An International Journal, 7*(4), 386–397.

Morimoto, M., & Chang, S. (2006). Consumers' attitudes toward unsolicited commercial e-mail and postal direct mail marketing methods: Intrusiveness, perceived loss of control, and irritation. *Journal of Interactive Advertising, 7*(1), 1–11.

Morimura, F., & Sakagawa, Y. (2018). Information technology use in retail chains: Impact on the standardisation of pricing and promotion strategies and performance. *Journal of Retailing and Consumer Services, 45*, 81–91.

Nambiar, B. K., Ramanathan, H. N., Rana, S., & Prashar, S. (2018). Perceived service quality and customer satisfaction: A missing link in Indian banking sector. *Vision, 23*(1), 44–55.

Nangoy, C. L., & Tumbuan, W. A. (2018). The effect of advertising and sales promotion on consumer buying decision of Indovision TV cable provider. *Jurnal EMBA: Jurnal Riset Ekonomi, Manajemen, Bisnis dan Akuntansi, 6*(3), 1228–1237.

Nathwani, D. (2017). Impact of sales promotion on consumer buying behaviour. *Dawn Journal for Contemporary Research in Management, 4*(1), 1–11.

Nour, M. I., & Almahirah, M. S. (2014). The impact of promotional mix elements on consumers purchasing decisions. *International Business and Management, 8*(2), 143–151.

Paesbrugghe, B., Sharma, A., Rangarajan, D., & Syam, N. (2018). Personal selling and the purchasing function: Where do we go from here? *Journal of Personal Selling & Sales Management, 38*(1), 123–143.

Pitta, D. A., Weisgal, M., & Lynagh, P. (2006). Integrating exhibit marketing into integrated marketing communications. *Journal of Consumer Marketing, 23*(3), 156–166.

Preeti, K. N. (2017). Demographic profile of customer: A study on Organized vs. Unorganized retail sector. *International Journal of Engineering Research & Technology, 5*(11), 1–6.

Rana, S., Prashar, S., Barai, M. K., & Hamid, A. B. A. (2021). Determinants of international marketing strategy for emerging market multinationals. *International Journal of Emerging Markets, 16*(2), 154–178.

Rana, S., Raut, S. K., Prashar, S., & Hamid, A. B. A. (2020b). Promoting through consumer nostalgia: A conceptual framework and future research agenda. *Journal of Promotion Management, 27*(2), 211–249.

Rana, S., Raut, S. K., Prashar, S., & Quttainah, M. A. (2020a). The transversal of nostalgia from psychology to marketing: What does it portend for future research? *International Journal of Organizational Analysis*, Vol. ahead-of-print No. ahead-of-print.

Raut, S. K., Sakpal, S., & Soni, R. (2022). Understanding the service quality dimensions and achieving resilience in service retail. In *Handbook of Research on Supply Chain Resiliency, Efficiency, and Visibility in the Post-Pandemic Era*, edited by Ramakrishna Yanamandra (pp. 136–156). IGI Global, UAE. https://doi.org/10.4018/978-1-7998-9506-0

Russo, C., & Simeone, M. (2017). The growing influence of social and digital media: Impact on consumer choice and market equilibrium. *British Food Journal, 119*(8), 1766–1780.

Satit, R. P., Tat, H. H., Rasli, A., Chin, T. A., & Sukati, I. (2012). The relationship between marketing mix and customer decision-making over travel agents: An empirical study. *International Journal of Academic Research in Business and Social Sciences, 2*(6), 522–562.

Shamout, M. D. (2016). The impact of promotional tools on consumer buying behavior in retail market. *International Journal of Business and Social Science, 7*(1), 75–85.

Spotts, H. E., Weinberger, M. G., & Weinberger, M. F. (2014). Publicity and advertising: What matter most for sales? *European Journal of Marketing, 48*(11/12), 1986–2008.

Story, M., & French, S. (2004). Food advertising and marketing directed at children and adolescents in the US. *International Journal of Behavioral Nutrition and Physical Activity*, 1(1), 1–17.

Thornhill, M., Xie, K., & Lee, Y. J. (2017). Social media advertising in a competitive market. *Journal of Hospitality and Tourism Technology*, 8(1), 87–100.

Van de Sanden, S., Willems, K., & Brengman, M. (2019). In-store location-based marketing with beacons: From inflated expectations to smart use in retailing. *Journal of Marketing Management*, 35(15–16), 1514–1541.

Wakefield, M. A., Loken, B., & Hornik, R. C. (2010). Use of mass media campaigns to change health behaviour. *The Lancet*, 376(9748), 1261–1271.

Waterschoot, V., & Van den Bulte, C. (1992). The 4P classification of the marketing mix revisited. *Journal of Marketing*, 56(4), 83–93.

Whitelock, J., Cadogan, J. W., Okazaki, S., & Taylor, C. R. (2013). Social media and international advertising: Theoretical challenges and future directions. *International Marketing Review*, 30(1), 56–71.

Williams, B. C., & Plouffe, C. R. (2007). Assessing the evolution of sales knowledge: A 20-year content analysis. *Industrial Marketing Management*, 36(4), 408–419.

Williams, M. R., & Attaway, J. S. (1996). Exploring salesperson's customer orientation as a mediator of organizational cultures influence on buyer-seller relationships. *Journal of Personal Selling & Sales Management*, 16(4), 33–52.

Yang, L., Cheung, W. L., Henry, J., Guthrie, J., & Fam, K. S. (2010). An examination of sales promotion programs in Hong Kong: What the retailers offer and what the consumers prefer. *Journal of Promotion Management*, 16(4), 467–479.

Yrjölä, M., Saarijärvi, H., & Nummela, H. (2018). The value propositions of multi-, cross-, and omni-channel retailing. *International Journal of Retail & Distribution Management*, 46(11/12), 1133–1152.

Zineldin, M., & Philipson, S. (2007). Kotler and Borden are not dead: Myth of relationship marketing and truth of the 4Ps. *Journal of Consumer Marketing*, 24(4), 229–241.

5 The First is Free

Promoting Facebook in Emerging Markets

Kira Strandby and Søren Askegaard

Introduction

The Janus-faced existence of corporate promotional activities in emerging markets and here in particular among subaltern consumers is demonstrating not only the consequences of corporate control over spending among consumers with only very little to spend but also the dynamics of inclusion and exclusion in global consumer culture. Public attention to the exploitative side of this may first have been created by journalists and filmmakers Michael Moore and Louis Theroux in the mid-1990s in their report about promotional activities of beauty giant Avon while the ambivalence has been pointed out by researchers in, for example, South Africa (Dolan & Scott 2009; Scott et al. 2012) and Brazil (Chelekis 2017). While there's no shortage on research praising the benefits of democratic communication and popular empowerment following from social media on the one hand, the negatives of the ensuing exploitative surveillance capitalism (Zuboff 2019) have also become part of the public debate on the other. The objective of this chapter is to explore the similarly ambivalent implications informational capitalism has for the dynamics of the Ugandan telecommunications industry, particularly regarding the consumption of the social media application Facebook. We choose Facebook as our focal point, as this particular site has established itself to be the dominant social media technology in large parts of the world, with more than two billion users globally.

We are living in an age of increased globalization, accelerated by the rapid spreading of Information and Communications Technologies (ICTs). As connectivity becomes increasingly accessible, with the expansion of network infrastructure and the rise of affordable devices, emerging markets become the new frontier for tech companies looking to expand their businesses. Traditionally, in the industrial era, this would have meant producing and distributing consumer products in new markets (Raut, Sakpal, & Soni 2022). However, in the age of informational capitalism (Castells 1996), the consumer generates data, a process which we shall view as a process of labor, which ultimately becomes the product to be packaged and sold to a third party. Thus, the success of a venture depends on critical mass.

DOI: 10.4324/9781003315582-6

The winner is the company with the most data-generating machines and the most consumers creating content. In order to attract users, companies must offer something to the consumers in return. This chapter examines the processes of exchange occurring when Facebook uses zero-rated services as a promotion tool. In doing so, we also draw on perspectives of immaterial labor (Terranova 2004) in an attempt to offer a critical perspective on the effects of promotion practices in a Sub-Saharan context – a perspective we hope can contribute to a somewhat understudied topic.

The spreading of information technology profoundly influences markets and the marketing institutions in a systemic and mutually generative way, forming and conditioning relationships that constitute what has been termed the infotransformation of markets (Zwick & Dholakia 2008; Rana et al. 2021). In this infotransformation process, consumers also obtain new roles in the market institution. The process through which consumers are mobilized as free labor and as resources has been the focus of a number of studies, also within macromarketing. Arvidsson (2008) suggests that we consider this a new "ethical economy" of social customer co-production that operates on different conditions compared to the standard capitalist production system. While this new economy undoubtedly has enabling and creativity-generating capacities of various kinds among different types of consumers (Kozinets, Hemetsberger, & Schau 2008; Rana et al. 2020a), the engagement of consumer labor has usually been considered through a double lens of as well positive and enabling angles of creativity and autonomy as well as more critical perspectives of exploitation and disempowerment (e.g., Bonsu & Darmody 2008; Fırat & Vicdan 2008; Molesworth & Denegri-Knott 2008; Nambiar et al. 2018). However, these investigations of power relations in the engagement of consumers in the infotransformation of markets are almost exclusively addressing consumers in developed contexts. We will address the exceptions later but underline that the purpose of this chapter is to address the specific conditions and relations experienced by the particularly vulnerable consumers in developing contexts by the rise of informational capitalism.

In this so-called Information Society, technologies such as the Internet enable exchanges of finances, ideologies, and media across distances, as well as facilitate migration, in what Appadurai (1990) conceptualized as different scapes: Ethnoscapes, Technoscapes, Finanscapes, Mediascapes, and Ideoscapes. In developing contexts, such as Sub-Saharan Africa, this apparent bridging across geographical distances carries hopes of inclusion, particularly into the global finanscapes. In a 2013 report, the corporate consulting agency McKinsey (2013) estimates that the Internet has potential to contribute more than $300 billion to Africa's GDP by 2025 through sectors such as agriculture, retail, and financial services. However, scholars such as Castells (1998), Dyer-Witheford (2015), and Terranova (2004) warn us that this form of informational and economic development may merely serve to re-enforce and increase global inequalities, rather than include third-world countries in the global economy.

Informational Capitalism as a New Paradigm

Castells argues that technology and the rise of the Information Society have created a socio-technological paradigm shift toward an informational form of capitalism, where *"the source of productivity lies in the technology of knowledge generation, information processing, and symbol communication"* (1996, p. 17). Thus, informationalism does not replace capitalism, rather it presents as a new form of capitalism, where the *"core processes of knowledge generation, economic productivity, political/military power and media communications are deeply transformed by the informational paradigm"* (1996, p. 20). This paradigm thus is based on the same principles as the ethical economy suggested by Arvidsson (2008). In this paradigm, the control of resources and production power translates from a classical materialist-Marxist focus on industrialism into a neo-Marxist matter of control of the network, control of access to the network, and control of knowledge and skills to operate the network. Access to ICTs and the ability to use and adopt them become critical factors in generating wealth, power, and knowledge (Castells 1998). This becomes particularly evident in Castells' early analysis of the diffusion of ICTs on the African continent, where the African elites make use of technologies to increase their wealth, while the majority of the population lacks access to the infrastructure that makes using computers possible (Castells 1998). Thus, in the network society, the spatial logic of social exclusion no longer determines the boundaries of marginalization, as we shall see in the next section.

Labor

The building and maintenance of online brand communities are largely dependent on the free labor of consumers, who contribute to the value of the brand through value creation practices such as impression management and teaching brand use (Schau, Muñiz, & Arnould 2009). While the company can provide an online or offline framework and infrastructure for the community to grow, it is entirely dependent on free labor to create value within the community. In this context, it is useful to remind ourselves that any major brand, such as Facebook, constitutes a complex social semiotic system (Conejo & Wooliscroft 2014) that is dependent on the 'labor' of the brand users to sustain its place in the social imaginary. Furthermore, this has as a consequence that a brand cannot be 'apolitical' (e.g., Kravets 2012; Bhandari & Raut 2019).

Drawing upon the Hardt and Negri (2000) notion of the social factory, Terranova (2004) frames the labor that makes up the user-generated content of web 2.0 as *"Cultural Work"*. In social media, users generate the content that attracts advertisers at the expense of a previously paid workforce consisting of comics, critics, journalists, etc. (Dyer-Witheford 2015). As such, bloggers now operate as cultural intermediaries (McQuarrie, Miller, &

Phillips 2013), yielding power that was formerly reserved for editorial staff at magazines, newspapers, and television.

Generating personal data, for example, by creating a profile on a social media website like Facebook, is another form of free labor. In this case, the data entered into the database of the website becomes a commodity that the website user can either use for generating profit within their company or sell to a third party (Dyer-Witheford 2015). Dyer-Witheford views these users as being part of a '*Cyberproletariat*', a class in the new informational economy with no control of their work process or the products produced. Furthermore, he interprets their participation as a submissiveness where elements of the users' identity, creativity, and sociality are surrendered for someone else's capital. Failure to do so can result in social exclusion.

A soothing, while not uncritical, voice against this choir of lamenters is David Hesmondhalgh, who in a variety of contexts has underlined the complex constitution of the free labor in the cultural industries. He is equally critical toward a general "underlying but underdeveloped normative position [is] that all the time we spend under capitalism contributes to a vast negative machine called capitalism; nothing escapes this system" and "seeing unpaid labour as a sign of an immanent revolutionary potential among workers" (Hesmondhalgh 2010, p. 280). What these studies lack, he concludes, is a more pragmatic approach to the lived experiences and political struggles involved in the processes of free labor. We would like to contribute such a pragmatic reflection on the lived experiences and the market conditions in the Ugandan context.

Social Exclusion and the Digital Divide

We ended the prior section with some reflections on mechanisms of social exclusion. Within information technology, such mechanisms have been studied and discussed through the notion of the "digital divide". Introduced in the mid-1990s by the National Telecommunications and Information Administration (NTIA), it has been widely used to describe the gap between populations with access to the connectivity and those without. It should be added that technological developments of the "smartphone" have since altered the digital divide to encompass not only computers but also smartphone-based technology (e.g., Stump, Gong, & Li 2008). However, Castells et al. (2007) stress the importance of differentiating between mediums when discussing the divide, noting that a decreasing mobile phone gap does not in and by itself guarantee a lower Internet gap. A somewhat broader interpretation of the digital divide was introduced by Warschauer (2003, p. 6), stating that "the digital divide is marked not only by physical access to computers and connectivity but also by access to additional resources that allow people to use technology well".

Castells argues that the emergence of the informational society has rendered the second and third world denominations obsolete. Instead, we are facing a new reality so stratified that it only makes sense to talk about the first and fourth world (Castells 1998). The fourth world is systematically excluded from participating in the informational society, and its inhabitants do not possess, and most likely will not acquire, the skills needed to use and adapt ICTs, skills which Castells views as being critical in generating and accessing wealth, power, and knowledge in the informational society. Using Sub-Saharan Africa as an example in his analysis, he demonstrates how the disinvestment in the African continent during the informational revolution has contributed to the de-linking of African firms and labor, while reinforcing the power position of the African elite. As such, not all of Africa can be said to be marginalized in the global economy – a small affluent class benefits from connectivity. This also serves to prove another of Castells' points that social inclusion is not limited to a specific geographical area. Elites can have access in areas with low connectivity, while others can be excluded and marginalized due to homelessness, drug use, and functional illiteracy, while living in a highly developed country.

While Castells argues a compelling case against social exclusion in the informational society, it becomes at the same time utopian and fatalistic at times. There can be little doubt that connectivity plays a great part in contemporary development policies; however, it can be argued that Castells overemphasizes this role in his reasoning. While he recognizes the impact and importance of culture in his later work (Castells & Himanen 2014), he proceeds to lump all but one (South Africa) Sub-Saharan countries together in his analysis. Furthermore, while his analysis is quite clear on the consequences of social exclusion, they are less clear on the potential impact of social inclusion on fourth world economies. This will be a focal point for the remainder of this article. At the end, Castells may be overreaching in his argument that social exclusion in the global informational age leads to a rise in the global criminal economy of trafficking, child exploitation, and drug use. It may certainly play a role in a mass-marginalization that enables such activities, but one should be quite wary of inferring causalities of this magnitude.

The Anthropology of Facebook: Division or Union?

Research on Facebook's role in the contemporary circuit of culture has been addressing critical issues pertaining to Facebook in terms of disconnective practices as well (Light & Cassidy 2014), as community-building and social resourcing outcomes of Facebook usage (Ellison et al. 2014), also among various types of vulnerable consumers (Taylor, Falconer, & Snowdon 2014; Rana et al. 2020b). Most obviously linked to our present context, however, are Kumar's (2014) study of Facebook's role for self-empowerment in India and Wyche et al's (2013) study of the use of Facebook in informal settlements in Kenya. While Kumar highlights the specific conditions in terms of balancing vulnerability and search for global inclusion that, as we shall see, is also prevalent in our context, Wyche and colleagues offer insights on how Facebook can be used to generate income at a micro level.

If we turn to anthropology, there is more substantial material about the lived experiences of Facebook usage in developing contexts. One major example of a piece of work that underlines the positive social consequences of Internet usage in a developing context (without disregarding the negative) is Daniel Miller's work on the role of Facebook in Trinidad (Miller 2011). In his concluding chapters, he uses his anthropological insights from this particular context to challenge a number of especially critical notions of how the use of Facebook influences individual and social values, norms, and practices. These influences include the constructive role of Facebook for the self(-representation), as well as for the relations with friends, family, and past and present social connections. Indeed, he presents the thesis that Facebook is a "meta-friend", a metaphorical space for, and representation of, friendship. On a more social level, he argues for Facebook as being a change agent in terms of reversing centuries of degradation of social community. He argues for the significance of Facebook in altering our relationship with space – through its linking value beyond distances – and time through its insistence on the co-presence of the past (my history), the present (my here-and-now), and the future (my legacy in an online reality).

The most momentous contributions of Miller's work for our context, however, are two other discussions that address a more social level of analysis. First is his allegory of Facebook as a contemporary and global version of a particular subsystem of the classical anthropological system of exchange, the *Kula* ring, as analyzed by anthropologist Nancy Munn in her book *The Fame of Gawa*. In this work, it is accentuated how the exchange system is what allows the Gawans to live a life that reaches beyond local subsistence and enter into a system of fame and status-building or, in other words, to become social. Facebook, in Miller's view, does much of the same for the Trinis, which he analyzes. What he writes about the fame in Gawa can be held as being equally true for contemporary Facebookers: *"If there is not a great world out there in which we can do deeds and become known for them, there is no possibility of fame, and much less to live our lives for. Culture provides the platform that allows every person to become a player"* (Miller 2011, p. 207).

This underlines the fundamental importance of being connected, of not being on the wrong side of the digital divide. Consequently, if this analogy has something going for it, this influences profoundly the value of Facebook for its participants, in particular, in developing contexts where other networking and symbolic exchange platforms are not accessible. This is no new insight for research in social media. The Twitter users as discussed by Marwick and Boyd (2010) use this social media platform in a collective generation of imagined audiences. And Kumar (2014) underlines how Facebook is a vehicle for inclusion in a global community for the Indian urban youth. We intend with our study to extend these insights into a context of consumer culture theorizing, investigating not only the negative consequences of informational capitalism but also the benefits of imagined and manifest communities for Facebook users in Uganda.

However, prior to that discussion, we would like to bring forth another significant contribution of Miller's work for our reflections. An often repeated criticism of Facebook – especially since its entering the stock market – is that it is a corporate entity and as such carries a particular kind of power structure and commercial interest. While that is certainly part of the truth of Facebook, Miller argues, it does not follow from that that anything people can do with Facebook can be reduced to enacting that particular power structure. We live in a consumer culture where a great number of activities and symbolic expressions are mediated by markets (Arnould & Thompson 2005), while Gawan culture is "mediated" by history and tradition. However, Miller underlines, this does not make the latter cultural format inherently more benign than the former. In both contexts, ordinary people are subjects to powerful agents' governance, tribal or (and/or) economic, based on tradition or based on market power.

It may well be argued that Miller is too oblivious to the destructive forces and the inequality created through appropriation of immaterial labor. But we should not allow ourselves to extend that blindness to other dimensions of the reality of Facebook. Much like Consumer Culture Theory (Arnould & Thompson 2005) has provided the analysis of contemporary consumer culture with both an updating of classical criticism of mass consumer culture, echoing and extending those of the Frankfurt School, *and* a theoretical and empirical underpinning of the many ways agentic consumers resist and circumvent these forces and also generate genuine fantasies, feelings, and fun through consumption processes, we aim to provide an argument against a too dichotomist and Manichean portrayal of Facebook in the Ugandan context.

Methodology

Context

Uganda was chosen to be the empirical context of this study due to a number of circumstances. While zero-rated Facebook is a contested business practice in several emerging economies, this chapter is part of a study of the Internet in Uganda in general. At the beginning of this study, high-speed mobile Internet was a relatively novel concept in Uganda, replacing slower connections in public spaces such as Internet café and educational institutions. This created an enhanced awareness of the opportunities created with the diffusion of Internet among the consumers interviewed. Rather than being an integrated part of the cultural landscape, the Internet and everything it entails were subject to scrutiny and reflection among the informants. Combined with the pricing structure described later, which plays a part in the perception of the Internet as a consumer good where the consumption of virtually every megabyte is subjected to some degree of decision-making, this made for an interesting context. Studying the same topic in a Western context with flat-rate Internet plans would not have offered the same depth of nuances, as zero-rated Facebook has no value to consumers who do not have to pay every time they follow a link or perform a Google search. Furthermore, the fact that Uganda is a developing country where the average citizen has limited access to sources of informational power allows us to analyze disparities of power in a more extreme setting, allowing us to identify issues that may or may not be visible (albeit still relevant) in contexts characterized by a higher degree of informational equality.

Data Collection

Data was collected during a 5-month field study in the capital of Uganda, Kampala. Twenty-five consumers were interviewed about the role of the Internet in Uganda in general and in their everyday lives in particular. The informant group was heterogenous, varying from informally employed novice users, over university students to bloggers and IT professionals, with monthly incomes ranging between $80 and $2000. The interviews took place at cafés, Internet cafés, informants' homes, and at the compound of the interviewer. The length of the interviews varied from 45 minutes to 3 hours. The informants were not paid to participate but were in some cases compensated for transportation costs.

While informational capitalism and free labor were not a part of the initial interview guide, these issues were uncovered in conversations with IT professionals, who questioned the premise of free Facebook in terms of Internet-neutrality. As the issues of labor and exchange are largely latent and were not brought up by the consumers, the consumer interviews informed the analysis of the relationships between the consumers and Facebook, and the consumers and the Internet Service Providers (ISPs), rather than forming the basis of the problematization of the issue.

In addition to primary data, the field study enabled us to collect secondary data not accessible online, such as salary statistics and editorials published in three local newspapers (*Daily Monitor*, *New Vision*, and *The East African*) and promotion material published locally by telecommunications companies. Combined with netnographic material (Kozinets 2002), primarily from social media such as Twitter and Facebook, this contributed to the creation of an intégraphy (Levy 2015), an integration of multiple sources in the interpretation of a phenomenon.

The Ugandan Context

In this section, we will introduce the Ugandan context and the three institutional agents we have identified as being significant to the subsequent analysis of the exchange processes involved in offering Free Facebook in Uganda: the Ugandan consumers, the Ugandan telecommunications industry, and Facebook.[1]

The Ugandan Consumer

Uganda, an East-African country situated on the equator, has a population of approximately 36,000,000 (2014 est./CIA). At an estimated 5.89 children born per woman (CIA/2015), it has one of the highest fertility rates in the world. Combined with a relatively low life expectancy (47.5 years for people born in 1990, UNICEF), this has resulted in a remarkably young population where close to 70% is below the age of 25.

In trying to estimate Uganda's GDP per capita, one comes across several numbers from established agencies such as UNICEF, the World Bank, and the CIA, ranging from $600 (UN 2012) to $2,000 (CIA 2014 est.). While albeit a bit frustrating from the perspective of a researcher, this discrepancy clearly illuminates the challenges of quantification in developing contexts. Otiso (2006) points toward the large informal economy of barter, petty trade, and small scale production as being one of the main sources of uncertainty when describing the economy of a Sub-Saharan country. Other likely sources of uncertainty could be the relatively unstable currencies, when measured against the US dollar. Either way, the numbers do not reflect the significant income inequality in Uganda, as shown in the first national labor force survey. The survey distinguishes between formal/informal employment, as well as gender, in income. Thus, a formally employed male could expect to earn $133 per month, while an informally employed male could expect to earn $56. For women, the figures were $120 and $31, respectively. Furthermore, the survey revealed large geographical differences, with the urban population out-earning the rural. Furthermore, it is important to note, as mentioned before, that the Ugandan population is young, with 48% being between the ages of 0 and 14, and thus there is bound to be a large degree of dependency on the household income earners.

The African Development Bank (2011) offers a classification system of social class in Sub-Saharan Africa, determining that the middle class is defined by a daily consumption of $2–$20.[2] Within this rather wide scope, consumers who spend $2–$4 are defined as "floating class", consumers who are at the risk of falling back into poverty. Consumers spending $4–$10 are defined to be lower middle class, who are able to save and spend money on non-essential goods, while those spending $10–$20 are defined to be upper middle class. While practical for analytical reasons, this classification does not reflect the nuances of the remittance economy, nor does it take into consideration the significant differences in daily expenses occurring in rural and urban contexts, respectively. Furthermore, recent reports have punctured the myth of the fast-growing African middle class,[3] finding that the latest decade of economic growth has mainly benefited the elite, rather than the lower and middle classes.

Uganda and the Telecommunications Market

The four main actors on the Ugandan telecommunications market are MTN Uganda (8.8 million subscribers), Airtel/Warid (7.2 million subscribers),

Uganda Telecom (2 million subscribers), and Orange (1 million subscribers). However, the total number of subscriptions does not equal the total number of subscribers, as many Ugandan consumers have multiple cellphones or cellphones with multiple SIM slots in order to capitalize on the differences in prices of services across the companies. Similarly, the number of subscribers does not necessarily equate the number of actual users, as cell phones are seen as a social possession with a multitude of potential users, especially in rural areas. As this chapter focuses mainly on the cell phone as being instrumental in the consumption of mobile Internet, we shall delimit ourselves from further analysis of the Ugandan telecommunications market.

In the following, we will spend a little time discussing the pricing structure of the market for mobile network access, since in a developing context like Uganda, the price mechanism operates as a means of access and/or exclusion that is much more significant for many goods and services which in more affluent countries are considered fairly unproblematic parts of "cultural standard packages" of consumption. As of December 2013, the Internet penetration rate was approximately 16.2% (ITU 2014). While there is no recent data available on access points, access to the Internet via cellphone is growing increasingly popular, with MTN Uganda reporting an increase in data revenue of 51.6% in 2013. In comparison, the increase in outgoing voice revenue during the same period of time was 10.9% (MTN Group 2014). The pricing structure is centered around so-called "bundles", while the subscriptions are predominantly prepaid. The pricing structure is quite complex, divided into temporal categories as well as volume, cf. the information provided in Table 5.1. Reading the table, one may also note how the prices do not seem to fluctuate significantly between the different telecommunications companies.

In spite of their apparent complexity, the bundles represent the most popular, and by far the cheapest, way of accessing the Internet via a mobile device. The only alternative presented by the telecommunications companies is a "pay-as-you-go" solution at 0.9 Ugandan Shillings per kilobyte, which translates into a staggering $308 per gigabyte (in comparison, Danish telecommunications companies charge consumers between $7 and $10 per gigabyte). In Uganda, where the median income across formal and informal sectors and gender is approximately $44 a month,[4] the relatively high cost of mobile data emphasizes the role of airtime and Internet as consumer goods and underlines the perceived value and related sacrifice connected to the consumption of mobile data.

Facebook in Uganda – Zero-Rating

According to Google, the most searched website in Uganda in 2013 was Facebook. While there is no updated statistics at the country level (the latest being from December 2012), Facebook announced having reached 100 million African users in September 2014,[5] up from 51 million in December 2013.[6] (While this allegedly represents half of Africa's Internet users, it is

Table 5.1 Mobile network access prices, September 2014

Uganda Mobile Networks Data Package Comparison Chart (USD)

ISP	Orange	MTN	Airtel	UTL
Data		*Daily*		
<50 MB	$0.18 (25 MB)	$0.18 (20 MB)	$0.18 (25 MB)	
50 MB	$0.36	$0.43	$0.36	$0.22
100 MB	$0.72		$0.72	$0.36
		Weekly		
50–150 MB	$0.90 (75 MB)	$0.90 (20 MB)	$0.90 (80 MB)	$0.72 (100 MB)
		$1.09 (100 MB)		
		Monthly		
<500 MB	$1.81 (125 MB)	$1.63 (100 MB)	$1.81 (125 MB)	
	$3.62 (250 MB)	$5.07 (350 MB)	$5.43 (350 MB)	
500 MB	$7.24	$7.24		$5.25
1 GB	$12.67	$13.57		$10.13
1–2 GB	$18.09 (2 GB)		$16.28 (1.5 GB)	
3 GB		$27.14	$27.14	$23.52
5 GB		$36.19		$36.19
10 GB	$45.24	$45.24	$54.28	$41.28
30 GB	$108.57	$103.14		

Source: Author-constructed table, content adapted from www.dignited.com/10242/orange-mtn-airtel-utl-uganda-internet-data-bundles-rates-compared-internet-package-best/

worth taking the divide between North and Southern Africa into considera-tion – thus this statement should be interpreted with reservations.) Eighty percent of these Facebook users access the website through a mobile device.

All of the four main telecommunications actors in Uganda offer free access to Facebook in one or both of the following formats: text-based and zero-rated. Text-based services allow the users to access a limited selection of Facebook services, such as poking, adding friends, and status updates, via SMS. This service functions on any SMS-enabled device, making it easily accessible to any of the 84% of Ugandans with access to a cellphone (insight-safrica.com, 2012). The service is marketed as free; however, the extent to which it is so seems unclear. While *receiving* information like status updates and wall posts is indeed free, *engaging* via SMS (updating your status, add-ing a friend, poking) is charged as regular text messages at $0.05 per text.[7]

Zero-rated Facebook uses the URL zero.facebook.com or 0.facebook. com in determining free access to a text version of Facebook. The service works on any Internet-enabled phone, GPRS, or 3G. The user is presented with a simplified interface devoid of any pictures and can use any text-based service on Facebook free of charge. However, should the user want to see or upload pictures, this is charged either via the users' data account, or if none is available, at a going rate of 0.9 Ugandan shillings per kb ($308/GB). This also applies if the user is re-directed to another website through a link found on Facebook. While the specifics of the agreements between the network carriers and Facebook are unattainable, Vodafone CEO Vittorio Colao is quoted on the topic of turning down Facebook on a similar proposal saying: "it does not make any sense... [there] is no reason why I should give my network capacity for free" (Financial Times, February 2014). Thus, the service is seemingly being sponsored by (other) network carriers.

Zero-Rating as Exchange

In this section, we will consider the phenomenon of zero-rated Facebook as an exchange process, where value is exchanged between three agentic units: the consumer, the Internet service provider, and Facebook. In doing this, we analyze the relationships between each set of actors in pairs in an attempt to determine what exactly is being exchanged.

Internet Service Provider–Consumer

The Internet service provider provides the consumer with a free access to a limited version of Facebook. This free access represents value to the consumer in the event that the consumer would have spent money to buy megabytes had they not received the offer for free. Reversely, this object of exchange has little-to-no value to consumers who would not otherwise have used Facebook, or do not use it, even in its current free form.

> *I think the best thing [about social media] to me is about, because you get to communicate to other people, maybe especially facebook, [. . .] it takes low data, low mbs, so you communicate with your friends, maybe send a message and then you get the reply, and sometimes I use facebook free, there is zero.facebook.mobile, you can access free facebook on your mobile phone, that is if you are using airtel.*
>
> (*Violet, 22*)

The consumer in turn provides the Internet service provider with revenue. As the zero-rated version of Facebook is text-based and limited in scope, the object of this promotional strategy is that consumers are inspired by their access to the partial site to spend megabytes or shillings on access to the full version which includes pictures and allows for more interaction. Thus, it is not uncommon to see comments in Facebook groups asking other users to describe a picture or an item of discussion to them, citing that they are on "Facebook Zero". In this perspective, using emojis and posting pictures become status markers communicating not only your ability to pay for your access to Facebook, but also your possession of a phone that can take pictures.

One could argue, and most brand-relationship literature probably would, that the zero-rating of Facebook could be viewed as a gift from the telecommunications company to the consumer, a gift which, according to classical gift-giving theory (Mauss 1954; Sahlins 1967), would then be imbued with reciprocity and strengthen the relationship between the giver and recipient. However, the brand relationships in the telecommunications sector in Uganda are promiscuous. Availability of cell phones with quadruple SIM card slots enables the consumer to maintain several (consumption) relationships – using just one phone. The Ugandan consumers we met during this fieldwork were technologically literate and capable of identifying and choosing the best possible bargain across all networks, at any time of day. Thus, while offering zero-rated Facebook theoretically offers some competitive advantage, in this context it would have to be supported by megabyte bargains as well.

While the majority of consumers encountered during fieldwork were technologically literate, it would be naive not to acknowledge the implications for another group, that of less technologically literate consumers. There is a significant risk that the relatively loosely defined boundaries between the zero-rated and "regular" Facebook will confuse some consumers, causing them to spend more money than intended on a service they believe to be "free", as marketed by the Internet service providers. Only a closer look at the terms and conditions can reveal the highly significant cost of $300+ per Gigabyte (roughly two to three times the average monthly salary). This issue was underlined by several of our informants who made a clear distinction between their Facebook-usage and Internet-usage, thus perceiving them to be independent features of their mobile phones. A similar perception of separation between the application and the actual Internet was found by Horst and Miller (2006), who experienced in Jamaica that consumers did not believe that the Internet enabled chat function on their cell-phones to be part of the Internet services on their phones.

Consumer–Facebook

Consciously or not, the consumer provides Facebook with personal data when creating a profile. According to Facebook,[8] the social network collects and stores information on a plethora of criteria which, for the purpose of this study, we will divide into the following categories: basic demographic data, explicit (consumer) lifestyle data, and calculated (tacit) consumer lifestyle data. The basic demographic data includes information on the user's age, gender, hometown, education, and work, which is typically entered when signing up for a Facebook profile. Explicit lifestyle data mainly comprises the topics of interest listed by the user (e.g., musicians, sports teams, political parties, brands, causes, applications), status updates, posts and shares, social connections, and check-ins.

The basic demographic data and the explicit lifestyle data are both offered by the user on a voluntary, but not necessarily conscious, basis. While the terms and conditions of Facebook are widely accessible, reading and comprehending them presuppose several forms of literacy, lingual as well as technological. It should also be noted that in the event that a user fails to fill in any demographic and lifestyle data, Facebook will prompt the user to do so by asking questions such as "Tell us where you went to school" whenever the user logs in to their profile.

The third category, calculated consumer lifestyle data, is the result of intricate algorithms applied to the sum of all data for each unique Facebook user. This category includes, among others, advertising keywords based on all of the users' activities, such as likes, posts, shares, friends, and demographic data, as well as detailed information on social media usage, including time spent on Facebook and IP addresses of logins as well as logouts. At the end, this data set also includes facial recognition data based on photos uploaded by the users and their peers.

The data collected in these three categories represent a valuable commodity to Facebook, which they can choose to either use to sell ads on their own website or sell to third-party companies (Dyer-Witheford 2015). The online advertising industry is extremely lucrative, with Facebook alone generating almost $70 billion in revenue from online advertising in 2019,[9] and the data which is built upon requires a minimal effort to harvest for corporations. While this is a market advantage in any cultural and geographic context, this data becomes even more valuable in a Sub-Saharan context where market data is sparse, due in large part to the challenges of infrastructure. Any data collection within rural areas is complicated at best and may easily be deemed unfeasible when taking the buying power of rural Africans into consideration. Thus, with minimal effort, Facebook manages to collect formerly unseen amounts of data through their collaboration with the ISPs.

In exchange for their personal data, what the consumers in this exchange triad receive can best be described as access to the network. We found that connectivity to be a valuable resource, providing access to pools of social, economic, and cultural capitals (Bourdieu 1984).

> *People make groups, and if someone has a problem, they have cancer and they need to do something for them, then there's a charity campaign, then people can raise up some money for people.*
>
> (*Violet, 23*)

> *The best thing [about Facebook]. The best thing I think is all the connections just with friends. Because you may have a friend that you have lost, like there are some friends I competed with them all over, I have never seen them again, but you meet them on Facebook, they send for you the photos, and you have a chance to see how they are, keep communicating. Because at that time you may not have a phone, but now you have again a chance of seeing them.*
>
> (*Charles, 24*)

The two vignettes illustrate two different forms of social capital that the informants feel Facebook grants them access to. Violet's example illustrates how Facebook enables online crowdsourcing of medical expenses, a common offline practice in Uganda as well. Networks are activated in the event of larger expenses, such as weddings, funerals, and tuition. The more number of people you have in your network, the larger amount of cash you are likely to receive upon asking. In that sense, Facebook works as a tool for network expansion and maintenance, as seen in the second quote by Charles. Reconnecting with lost acquaintances is not merely a trip down memory lane, it is an expansion of your pool of social capital.

> *Social media somehow, in my music promotion, mainly in the digital distribution, at least it has made me be recognized. People know what I do, people see what I do, and people love what I do.*
>
> (*Douglas, 23*)

Similarly, Douglas uses Facebook to promote his music promotion business by mobilizing his 10.000 (!) Facebook friends[10] as audience in an attempt to convert social capital into economic capital.

> *Interviewer – Has social media changed anything for you?*
> *Louise – Definitely. Definitely. The way I perceive things, the way I speak with people, the way I get into arguments, it has changed a lot, but it has also made me aware that this world is not safe. There are so many wrong things happening. If you didn't know it happened to someone else, you wouldn't have known it at all. It's better than the news. Cause the news is subject to censorship.*
>
> (*Louise, 31*)

At the end, Louise feels that Facebook contributes to her development as a person by offering her new perspectives on life. Furthermore, she underlines a very significant issue in pointing out that social media does not undergo the same degree of censorship that other forms of media in Uganda are subject to. In this perspective, Facebook offers freedom of expression to users in politically unstable environments.

Summing it all up, Ugandan consumers perceive Facebook to be a gateway to a plethora of individual, social, and economic opportunities. While they could perhaps experience these opportunities elsewhere online, the availability and accessibility of Facebook have made it the social media venue of choice, not only to our informants, or to Ugandans, but also to 1.59 billion monthly users[11] across the globe.

Facebook–Internet Service Provider

The relationship between Facebook and the ISP is not entirely transparent. As mentioned earlier, Vodafone CEO Colao has been quoted objecting to the premise that the ISP should be footing the bill for zero-rated Facebook, which makes it plausible to assume that Facebook is not reimbursing the ISPs for megabytes spent. However, according to ICT specialists interviewed in Uganda, Facebook is providing a caching system, a data infrastructure which greatly reduces the cost of providing Facebook for the ISPs. Furthermore, the ISPs stand to gain revenue on their data services in the event that consumers decide to click either links or pictures on the zero-rated version of Facebook, which transfers them to the regular, paid version. One could also argue that the opportunity to offer zero-rated Facebook comes with a competitive advantage. However, as demonstrated before, Ugandan consumers maintain several brand relationships simultaneously, minimizing the effect of co-branding to a point where zero-rated Facebook becomes an industry standard, rather than a bonus feature.

Facebook, in turn, gains access to new consumers, who wouldn't necessarily be willing or able to pay for the relatively expensive data services, thereby expanding their pool of data as described before. This is demonstrated in the following quote:

Interviewer – And do you use social media? I saw the link you just showed me was from Facebook.
Moses – Yes, I do. I even use Facebook as well because the network I have now, yeah, it encourages us to use Facebook. Free. It is free.
(Moses, 36)

As the focal points of this chapter are zero-rated exchange as a promotion strategy, consumers, and the exchange relationships involving immateriality and free labor they engage in, we will delimit ourselves from further discussing the relationship between Facebook and the Internet service providers in the following sections.

We will also, in large part, delimit ourselves from further reflecting upon the relationship between the consumer and the Internet service provider, as that relationship is polygamous in the Ugandan consumption context, and thus the consequences of this particular exchange can be argued to be more arbitrary and limited in scope. While offering zero-rated Facebook is seemingly mandatory for Ugandan mobile operators in the current marketplace, the competitive advantage evaporates in consumer choice. Speed and quality of connection become the true determinants of increased data revenue instead. Therefore, while a lot could (and should) be said in critique of the current practices and lack of transparency of terms of conditions established by the Ugandan telecommunications sector, it is not the offering of zero-rated Facebook that radically transforms the relationship between the ISP and the consumers – it is merely a condition for any establishment of a relationship to begin with. While we have seen how zero-rated Facebook as a promotion strategy has been instrumental in creating a market for Facebook, we also need to critically examine this relationship in terms of

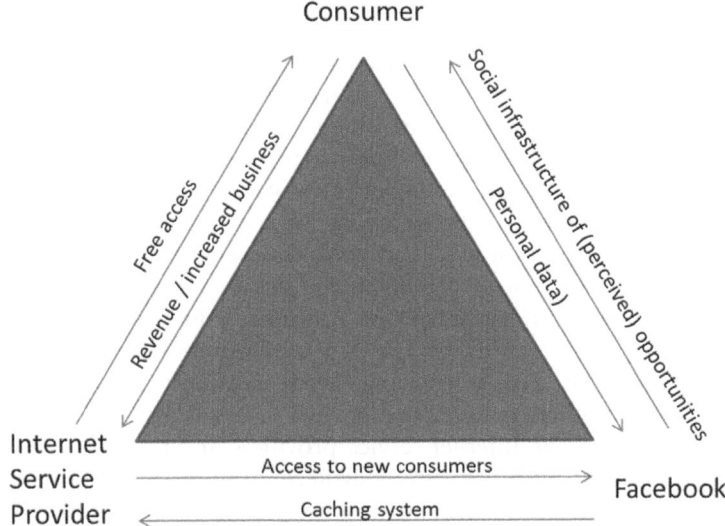

Figure 5.1 Exchange processes in the Ugandan Facebook market

the underlying ethical implications. The relationship between the consumer and Facebook remains as the most outspoken example of how the lack of net-neutrality can shift the power balances through the exchange of zero-rated Facebook. These relationships are summarized in Figure 5.1. In the following section, we offer our reflections toward the potential effects of this particular relationship of exchange.

Discussion – The Valuation of Free Labor/Data

As the saying goes, in the modern world, when you have absolutely no money, being an idealist is difficult. It is obvious from our account of the tripartite exchange processes that the role of "free labor" and "free data" changes into something different, when it is considered that Ugandan consumers get free Internet only as long as they navigate on Facebook. When Internet is sold based on single traffic units rather than on subscription; when, as everywhere else, every byte costs money; and when the consumer is a subaltern with highly limited financial resources, this is not an insignificant detail. It is a condition that fundamentally alters the situation from the "cost-free" utilization of Facebook in the developed world. Internet service providers give up on some income that they might never have gotten in the first place, given the financial (in)capacity of the consumers. They do this in order to attract customers who will subsequently generate other, payable, Internet traffic, very similar to a standard supermarket logic of special offers with little-or-no-profitability margin.

In unpacking these exchanges, we have tried to follow Hesmondhalgh's (2010) call for a pragmatic analysis of what is actually going on in the tripartite relationship between Facebook, the Internet providers, and consumers and tried to isolate what is actually exchanged in this process. It is also obvious that while unequal power relations and exploitation are definitely part of the picture, it is difficult to isolate a highly negative experience of this relationship. This is true even if we find only sparse traces of the playful creativity effects of free labor processes highlighted by the extant literature. Instead, the labor is typically seen as being invested in what we have termed a social infrastructure of opportunities. Facebook does not stop being existential and ludic, but it is definitely also highly utilitarian and critical, to recapture the classic semiotic distinction between consumer valorizations proposed by Floch (1988). In other words, we can view the relationship between the consumer and Facebook to be an exchange where consumers are granted access to an array of resources in exchange for their personal data.

The inclusion of the Internet service providers and the closer look at a developing context with distinctly subaltern consumers – also in general considerably worse off in terms of resources than Kumar's (2014) urban Indian youth – have permitted us to extend the portrayal of free online labor as not only something that goes beyond the cultural industries but also something that illuminates how autonomy is both gained and lost (cf. Hesmondhalgh 2010) in the process. However, we are still to determine whether or not this exchange, which arguably depends on the form of free labor discussed earlier, is simultaneously based on the exploitation of vulnerable 'consumer workers' (Moisander, Könkkölä, & Laine 2013). In other words, how would a critical social 'cost–benefit analysis' fall out in terms of exercise of control over various life situations? In determining this, we need to discuss the value of data; how is data valuated and by whom?

It would be wrong to not acknowledge the seemingly altruistic element of zero-rated Facebook. After all, Facebook is partnering with ISPs globally in an attempt to not only offer zero-rated Facebook, but also offer access to other services through their initiative internet.org.[12] In a similar vein, we could, in the following discussion, assume a neo-liberal position and argue that even vulnerable consumers can be seen as free subjects capable of making their own, informed consumption choices. In doing this, we would be subscribing to the notion of the "Bottom-of-the-pyramid consumer", which Giesler and Veresiu (2014) argue is a subject position created to support the notion that the market is a key component in poverty alleviation. In a similar vein, Bonsu and Polsa (2011) urge us to question who benefits the most from development initiatives implemented by multinational corporations, and it is in this spirit of inquiry we continue.

From the perspective of the individual, Ugandan consumer, personal data has very little value in and of its own. You cannot use your data to buy avocados at the local market, because data as a currency has no value in the struggles of the daily world. Your data only becomes valuable when you encounter a buyer. Granted, this logic applies to any and all commodities. However, in this case, your data is only valuable when you, as the consumer, encounter a *specific* buyer, Facebook, who has monopoly so to speak on this market. Thus, as a consumer, you are not free to shop around and find the bargain of your choice. If you choose not to trade your data for access, it becomes worthless once again. The same logic applies to the notion of labor. In this market, selling your labor to another production facility is simply not an option unless you are able to pay for access.

On the other hand, following the notions of free labor as described by Terranova (2004) and Dyer-Witheford (2015), you can never truly escape working for free. Any interaction online requires a minimum of identification in order to enable interaction. Thus, the only true escape becomes a regulated, de-commoditized Internet or a continuation of the commoditized Internet, where productive laborers can earn a share in the profits they work to create. In this perspective, free access could be interpreted as being a reward for free labor.

At a societal level, the most vocal criticism of zero-rating comes from within the pro-net-neutrality community.[13] Net-neutrality can be described as a network paradigm that dictates that the Internet should be "free from government regulation and commercial distortion" (Ganley & Allgrove 2006, p. 455) through a non-discriminatory data policy which ensures equal prioritization of data packages, regardless of the sender or recipient. In other words, no corporation should be able to buy prioritized access to consumers. They believe that the zero-rating of Facebook undermines other applications that could be more beneficial to the consumer, as Facebook is bound to be the preferred application when offered for free. As stated in an open letter to Mark Zuckerberg, May 2015:

> *Facebook is partnering with ISPs around the world to offer access to certain Internet applications to users at no cost. These agreements endanger freedom of expression and equality of opportunity by letting service providers decide which Internet services will be privileged over others, thus interfering with the free flow of information and people's rights vis-a-vis networks.*[14]

And so it seems that data is at the same time worthless and priceless. To the consumers, it has no value until it is traded, in which event it can be priceless – granting them access to a toolbox of resources for furthering their human, economic, and informational development (Castells & Himanen 2014). At the same time, in the greater societal debate, data has become a commodity so valuable that some believe it should not be traded. That the commodification of it threatens the ideological core of the Internet as the ultimate democratic public sphere. It seems as though there are no personal consequences of parting with data for the individual consumer but great potential consequences for the informational society. However, the consequences of *not* participating as a consumer can be social exclusion – exclusion from the markets, from communications, and from power (Castells 1998).

"Goods are neutral but their uses are social", Douglas and Isherwood (1978, p. 12) asserted in their classic *The World of Goods*. This assertion, which may have seemed legitimate at the time, is no longer as tenable, given that the universe of consumer goods and services is always inscribed in a political economy of production and exchange. And this political economy has profound consequences, also in the field of informational capitalism, where it becomes a political economy of information. So it is not very surprising that we often see a link between arguments concerning the corporate governance of contemporary social media platforms and classical critiques of damaged social life such as the ones promoted by Turkle (2011), who argues that the constant connectivity facilitated by social media develops at the expense of our social relationships and that the preoccupation with technological devices in the public sphere has contributed to a transformation of communal spaces such as cafés and public transportation into mere places of social collection where people gather, but do not interact.

On the other hand, as Miller (2011) has stated, it is unwise to conclude that the Internet in general and Facebook in particular are particularly evil forces in peoples' lives just because they are "corporate". Furthermore, it cannot be assumed that the macro-level consequences of marketing zero-rated Facebook are by definition de-socializing, individualizing, and damaging to some kind of mythologized and 'authentified' social life. The question is not about sociality or no sociality, but which kind of sociality is at stake? Likewise, it is not about empowerment or dis-empowerment, but rather which kinds of empowerment are at stakes for which agents in the system? In this perspective, it is worth nothing the issue pertaining to the risk of the spread of misinformation that has emerged in more recent years, where the global and local political impact of fake information and memes spread on social has proven to be of increasing political significance. The de facto monopoly of particular social media in terms of news dissemination makes it virtually impossible to check the correctness of such memes on the rest of the Internet.[15]

A recent doctoral dissertation underlines the role of Facebook and other social media as a means to navigate and to some extent escape processes of social control among young Muslim women in migrant communities in Denmark (Waltorp 2017). Once again, the fact that Facebook is a corporate institutional agent certainly frames its actions and activities, but to a much lesser extent the activities of its participants, in particular since a too heavy-handed corporate control could easily be the first step toward an unstoppable downwards spiral in terms of popularity. While there most certainly is an element of neo-liberalism in Facebook, and also in this portrayal of the consumer as the dictator over what Facebook can do, Facebook – as we have seen – is *also* an anti-individualistic community building vehicle and as such not reducible to a prolonged arm of neoliberal capitalism, neither in Miller's context of Trinidad, nor in Uganda.

The key question remains whether or not zero-rating is a viable promotional strategy – ethically and legally. Should corporations such as Facebook be allowed to trade data for access with vulnerable consumers? Several countries such as Chile, Brazil,[16] and India[17] have banned zero-rated applications, effectively shutting down Internet access for millions of marginalized consumers. This kind of legislation imposes the consequences of a very particular set of values, developed in the Western world and with a point of departure in a Western understanding of the Internet and its objectives, on impoverished third-world consumers. On the other hand, zero-rating applications such as Facebook seem to be contributing to global inequality and the reinforcement of global class structures, emulating the objectives of traditional, nineteenth-century colonialism: The discovery of new markets. We are left with the question of which is the lesser evil, cultural imperialism or neo-colonialism?

Notes

1 While prices, salaries, and statistics have no doubt been subject to some fluctuation during the years since this data was collected, we are using the original numbers as to not conflict with our data and the context in which it was collected.
2 2005 PPP US Dollars.
3 www.economist.com/news/middle-east-and-africa/21676774-africans-are-mainly-rich-or-poor-not-middle-class-should-worry
4 New Vision, January 24, 2014.
5 http://mashable.com/2014/09/08/facebook-100-million-users-africa/
6 www.internetworldstats.com/africa.htm#ug
7 This applies to one of the two providers offering the service. The other provider offers no information on terms and conditions.
8 www.facebook.com/help/405183566203254
9 www.statista.com/statistics/271258/facebooks-advertising-revenue-worldwide/
10 While Facebook only allows 5.000 friends per profile, Douglas has circumvented this rule by opening several profiles to accommodate his ever-expanding network.
11 http://newsroom.fb.com/company-info/
12 https://info.internet.org/en/
13 http://techcrunch.com/2015/05/04/facebooks-internet-org-project-is-now-a-platform/
14 www.facebook.com/notes/access-now/open-letter-to-mark-zuckerberg-regarding-internetorg-net-neutrality-privacy-and-/935857379791271/
15 www.forbes.com/sites/davidebanis/2019/02/18/how-zero-rating-offers-threaten-net-neutrality-in-the-developing-world/#618898823b41
16 http://europe.newsweek.com/how-net-neutrality-working-countries-have-it-269632?rm=eu
17 http://fortune.com/2016/02/08/facebook-india-regulator/

References

African Development Bank (2011), *The Middle of the Pyramid: Dynamics of the Middle Class in Africa*, afdb.org.
Appadurai, A. (1990), Disjuncture and Difference in the Global Cultural Economy, *Theory, Culture & Society*, 7 (2), 295–310.

Arnould, E.J. and Thompson, C.J. (2005), Consumer Culture Theory (CCT): Twenty Years of Research, *Journal of Consumer Research*, 31 (4), 868–882.

Arvidsson, A. (2008), The Ethical Economy of Customer Coproduction, *Journal of Macromarketing*, 28 (4), 326–338.

Bhandari, K.R. and Raut, S.K. (2019), 9 Leveraging Tacit, *Advances in Management Research: Innovation and Technology*, 1 (1), 127–138.

Bonsu, S.K. and Darmody, A. (2008), Co-Creating Second Life: Market – Consumer Cooperation in Contemporary Economy, *Journal of Macromarketing*, 28 (4), 355–368.

Bonsu, S.K. and Polsa, P. (2011), Governmentality at the Base-of-the-Pyramid, *Journal of Macromarketing*, 31 (3), 236–244.

Bourdieu, P. (1984[1993]) *Sociology in Question*. London: Sage Publications.

Castells, M. (1996), *The Rise of the Network Society*. Chichester: Wiley-Blackwell.

Castells, M. (1998), *End of Millennium*. Chichester: Wiley-Blackwell.

Castells, M., Fernández-Ardèvol, M., Qiu, J.L. & Sey, A. (2007). *Mobile Communication & Society – A Global Perspective*. Cambridge: MIT Press.

Castells, M. and Himanen, P., eds. (2014), *Reconceptualizing Development in the Global Information Age*. Oxford: Oxford University Press.

Chelekis, J. (2017), Risks and Strategies of Amazonian Households: Retail Sales and Mass-Market Consumption Among Caboclo Women. *Economic Anthropology*, 4 (2), 173–185.

Conejo, F. and Wooliscroft, B. (2014), Brands Defined as Semiotic Marketing Systems, *Journal of Macromarketing*, 35 (3), 287–301.

Dolan, C. and Scott, L. (2009), Lipstick Evangelism: Avon Trading Circles and Gender Empowerment in South Africa, *Gender & Development*, 17 (2), 203–218.

Douglas, M. and Isherwood, B. (1978), *The World of Goods. Toward an Anthropology of Consumption*. Harmondsworth: Penguin.

Dyer-Witheford, N. (2015), *Cyber-Proletariat*. London: Pluto Press.

Ellison, N.B., Gray, R., Lampe, C. and Fiore, A.T. (2014), Social Capital and Resource Requests on Facebook, *New Media & Society*, 16 (7), 1104–1121.

Fırat, A.F. and Vicdan, H. (2008), A New World of Literacy, Information Technologies, and the Intercorporeal Selves, *Journal of Macromarketing*, 28 (4), 381–396.

Floch, Jean-Marie (1988), The Contribution of Structural Semiotics to the Design of a Hypermarket, *International Journal of Research in Marketing*, 4 (3), 233–252.

Ganley, P. and Allgrove, B. (2006), Net Neutrality: A User's Guide, *Computer Law & Security Report*, 22, 454–463.

Giesler, M. and Veresiu, E. (2014), Creating the Responsible Consumer: Moralistic Governance Regimes and Consumer Subjectivity, *Journal of Consumer Research*, 41 (3), 840–857.

Hardt, M. and Negri, A. (2000), *Empire*. Cambridge: Harvard University Press.

Hesmondhalgh, D. (2010), User-Generated Content, Free Labour and the Cultural Industries, *Ephemera. Theory and Politics in Organization*, 10 (3/4), 267–284.

Horst, H. & Miller, D. (2006), *The Cellphone, An Anthropology of Communication*. London: Bloomsbury Academic.

ITU. (2014), Measuring the Information Society Report. https://www.itu.int/en/ITU-D/Statistics/Pages/publications/mis2014.aspx

Kozinets, R.V. (2002), The Field Behind the Screen: Using Netnography for Marketing Research in Online Communities, *Journal of Marketing Research*, 39 (1), 61–72.

Kozinets, R.V., Hemetsberger, A. and Schau, H.J. (2008), The Wisdom of Consumer Crowds: Collective Innovation in the Age of Networked Marketing, *Journal of Macromarketing*, 28 (4), 339–354.

Kravets, O. (2012), Russia's "Pure Spirit": Vodka Branding and Its Politics, *Journal of Macromarketing*, 32 (4), 361–376.

Kumar, N. (2014), Facebook for Self-Empowerment? A Study of Facebook Adoption in India, *New Media & Society*, 16 (7), 1122–1137.

Levy, S.J. (2015), Olio and Intègraphy as Method and the Consumption of Death, *Consumption, Markets & Culture*, 18 (2), 133–154.

Light, B. and Cassidy, E. (2014), Strategies for the Suspension and Prevention of Connection: Rendering Disconnection as Socioeconomic Lubricant with Facebook, *New Media & Society*, 16 (7), 1169–1184.

Marwick, A.E. and Boyd, D. (2010), I Tweet Honestly, I Tweet Passionately: Twitter Users, Context Collapse and Imagined Audiences, *New Media & Society*, 13 (1), 114–133.

Mauss, M. (1954), *The Gift: Forms and Functions of Exchange in Archaic Societies*. Glencoe, IL: The Free Press Glencoe.

McQuarrie, E.F., Miller, J. and Phillips, B.J. (2013), The Megaphone Effect: Taste and Audience in Fashion Blogging, *Journal of Consumer Research*, 40 (1), 136–158.

Miller, D. (2011), *Tales from Facebook*. Cambridge: Polity Press.

Moisander, J., Könkkölä, S. and Laine, P-M. (2013), Consumer Workers as Immaterial Labour in the Converging Media Markets: Three Value-Creation Practices, *Journal of Consumer Culture*, 37, 222–226.

Molesworth, M. and Denegri-Knott, J. (2008), The Playfulness of eBay and the Implications for Business as a Game-Maker, *Journal of Macromarketing*, 28 (4), 369–380.

MTN Group. (2014), MTN Grows Subscriber Base 14.4% to 8.8M In 2013; Revenues Increase 17.8%. https://www.redpepper.co.ug/2014/03/mtn-grows-subscriber-base-14-4-to-8-8m-in-2013-revenues-increase-17-8/

Nambiar, B.K., Ramanathan, H.N., Rana, S. and Prashar, S. (2018), Perceived Service Quality and Customer Satisfaction: A Missing Link in Indian Banking Sector, *Vision*, 23 (1), 44–55.

Otiso, K. M. (2006). *Culture and Customs of Uganda*. Westport: Greenwood Press.

Rana, S., Prashar, S., Barai, M.K. and Hamid, A.B.A. (2021), Determinants of International Marketing Strategy for Emerging Market Multinationals, *International Journal of Emerging Markets*, 16 (2), 154–178.

Rana, S., Raut, S.K., Prashar, S. and Hamid, A. B. A. (2020b), Promoting Through Consumer Nostalgia: A Conceptual Framework and Future Research Agenda, *Journal of Promotion Management*, 27 (2), 211–249.

Rana, S., Raut, S.K., Prashar, S. and Quttainah, M.A. (2020a), The Transversal of Nostalgia from Psychology to Marketing: What Does It Portend for Future Research? *International Journal of Organizational Analysis*, Vol. ahead-of-print No. ahead-of-print.

Raut, S. K., Sakpal, S. and Soni, R. (2022), Understanding the Service Quality Dimensions and Achieving Resilience in Service Retail. In *Handbook of Research on Supply Chain Resiliency, Efficiency, and Visibility in the Post-Pandemic Era*, edited by Ramakrishna Yanamandra (pp. 136–156). IGI Global, UAE. https://doi.org/10.4018/978-1-7998-9506-0

Sahlins, Marshall (1967), *Stone Age Economics* [fr]. New York: de Gruyter.

Schau, H.J., Muñiz, A.M. and Arnould, E.J. (2009), How Brand Community Practices Create Value, *Journal of Marketing*, 73 (September), 30–51.

Scott, L., Dolan, C., Johnstone – Louis, M., Sugden, K. and Wu, M. (2012), Enterprise and Inequality: A Study of Avon in South Africa, *Entrepreneurship Theory and Practice*, 36 (3), 543–568.

Stump, R.L., Gong, W. and Li, Z. (2008), Exploring the Digital Divide in Mobile Phone Adoption Levels across Coutnries, *Journal of Macromarketing*, 28 (4), 397–412.

Taylor, Y., Falconer, E. and Snowdon, R. (2014), Queer Youth, Facebook and Faith: Facebook Methodologies and Online Identities, *New Media & Society*, 16 (7), 1138–1153.

Terranova, T. (2004), *Network Culture: Politics for the Information Age*. London: Pluto Press.

Turkle, S. (2011), *Alone Together*. New York: Basic Books.

Waltorp, K. (2017), *Spejlbilleder: Smartphonen som relationelt redskab og virkelig virtualitet blandt unge muslimske kvinder i København*, Doctoral dissertation, Copenhagen: Copenhagen University.

Warschauer, M. (2003), *Technology & Social Inclusion: Rethinking the Digital Divide*. Cambridge: MIT Press.

Wyche, S.P., Forte, A. and Schoenebeck, S.Y. (2013), *Hustling Online: Understanding Consolidated Facebook Use in an Informal Settlement in Nairobi*, CHI'13: Proceedings of the SIGCHI Conference on Human Factors in Computing Systems, 2823–2832.

Zuboff, S. (2019) *The Rise of Surveillance Capitalism*. New York: Public Affairs.

Zwick, D. and Dholakia, N. (2008), Infotransformation of Markets. Introduction to the Special Issue on Marketing and Information Technology, *Journal of Macromarketing*, 28 (4), 318–325.

6 Globalization and Innovation Districts

R+D, Knowledge Exchanges, and Assemblages

Gerardo del Cerro Santamaría

Introduction: Globalization and Innovation

It is well known that globalization is a highly controversial development, with both far-reaching potential benefits and severe drawbacks for millions of people in each case. Among its benefits we find its promotion of productivity-enhancing technology transfer and innovation worldwide. The April 2018 World Economic Outlook by the International Monetary Fund highlights freer trade, increased foreign direct investment, and the international use of patents and copyrights as some of the pillars of the increased transnational exchange in trade, good, services, capital, and information characterizing globalization.

The diffusion of knowledge and technology promoted by the functioning of a global economy operating in real time at a planetary scale accelerates and strengthens incentives to adopt new technologies and to innovate (IMF, 2018). With globalization, new ideas and technologies can quickly spread across the world. Increased exposure to a highly diverse cultural world results in the blending and hybridization of established ideas, a fact which both drives and produces process- and product-innovation.

In emerging-market economies, foreign knowledge accounted for about 0.7 percentage points of annual growth in labor productivity from 2004 to 2014 and a total of 40% of observed sectoral productivity growth. In 1995–2003, that rate was just 0.4 percentage points. These results remain robust even when China is excluded, indicating that the productivity effects associated with globalization and innovation were broad-based (WEF, 2018).

Moreover, the global diffusion of knowledge and technology generates positive network effects through cross-pollination, "as it enables technology-receiving countries to advance their own research and development". Such dynamics are a major reason why "in China, R&D expenditures have skyrocketed, and in South Korea, stocks of international patents are piling up". These countries have joined traditional leaders in sectors such as electrical and optical equipment and (in South Korea's case) machinery (WEF, 2018).

While emerging market economies continue to increase investment in R+D and innovation, advanced economies have experienced a slowdown

DOI: 10.4324/9781003315582-7

since 2000 relative to both prior periods and to other, less advanced economies. Experts tend to agree that the effect of ICTs is fading whereas the effects of newer innovative technologies such as AI, machine learning, and automation are not yet visible. Even if significant advances are hard to sustain over time, persistent technology gaps mean that emerging economies can catch up through adoption and to engage in adaptation and innovation of their own.

Innovation Districts

The high-tech sector has long promoted expert knowledge exchanges by spatially concentrating their activities, first in technopoles and, more recently, in urban innovation districts. In order to meet the challenges of the global economy, many countries have resourced to infrastructure development in the form of industrial corridors (for example in India), and reterritorialization via megaregions (in China), and they are paying increasing attention to the innovation district phenomenon. Cities and regions are witnessing the urban relocation to urban areas of advanced manufacturing and high-tech corporate activity around so-called "innovation districts".

Innovation districts constitute new urban megaprojects that significantly alter the urban fabric and the socioeconomic structure of entire neighbourhoods. In turn, many urban megaprojects concentrate on innovative corporate functions and activities. In so far as these new centers of corporate activity are located in cities, corporate strategies have a direct impact on urban sustainable development. Innovation districts work as a type of urban megaproject in terms of significance and impacts. In this context, innovation districts present formidable challenges for sustainability: they enable it and constrain it in urban areas to an unprecedented scale.

The ongoing socio-spatial transformations in the global economy represent a formidable challenge for business and society in the twenty-first century, particularly for developing countries. The rise and continued expansion of megaprojects worldwide stand out as one of the most significant transformations currently impacting the global economy. Megaprojects, and innovation districts, are multiplying around the world as an urban response to pressures for development, competitiveness, and innovation in a context of globalization and neoliberalism. The narrative of international competitiveness and the rhetoric of economic survival pervade most megaprojects. In this context, innovation districts work by fostering urban transformations that would enhance the city's position in the global economy and within a fluid sociopolitical division of labor. The agenda is to align urban initiatives with the real or perceived requirements of global production, consumption, and a deregulated international neoliberal economic system.

Innovation districts share with most megaprojects the fact that they are "privileged particles in the development process". They are planned to be "trait-making", that is, to significantly modify the structure of society and cities (Hirschman, 1967, 36). However, their promoters and some commentators present innovation districts as a major alternative to megaprojects, property-led urban regeneration, and neoliberal urbanism strategies, an alternative that purportedly enhances economic development, quality of life, and sustainability.

This chapter addresses the spatial ties between globalization and innovation by examining the recent development of innovation districts as a distinct spatial formation aimed simultaneously at economic development and urban regeneration. The chapter focuses on processes of knowledge generation, exchange, and adoption in innovation milieux, and it suggests that the metaphor of "assemblages" can be helpful to understand the highly complex nature of knowledge production processes taking place in innovation districts.

The Coming of Innovation Districts

For the past 50 years, the innovation landscape has been dominated by regions such as Silicon Valley: spatially isolated corporate suburban corridors, accessible only by car, with little emphasis on quality of life or the integration of work, housing, and leisure. However, in recent years, a new complementary urban model has emerged: the so-called "innovation districts". According to the Brookings Institution, these districts are "geographic areas where state-of-the-art institutions and companies are grouped and connected with new businesses, business incubators and accelerators" (Katz & Wagner, 2014, 1).

The compact innovation districts, accessible to traffic and with high-tech infrastructure, encourage open collaboration, promote talent pooling, and offer attractive places to live. With increasing frequency, startups, incubators, and technology accelerators around the world are grouped around these innovation districts. By creating shared value, and promoting "placemaking", this emerging geography of innovation in cities has been attracting the attention of scholars and experts (Katz & Wagner, 2014, 7).

Innovation districts can play an important role in an integrated strategy designed to attract, retain, and cultivate talent; improve networks and communication flows among innovators; and also make the district an attractive destination. Innovation districts have begun to occupy today the preeminent place that culture and tourism have occupied for three decades in urban revitalization strategies.

Thus, the geography of innovation is changing. Google, for example, over the previous ten years has taken Silicon Valley's core R&D and innovation activities to a number of cities and urban cores. The company's presence in the Tech City of London, the Chelsea district of New York City, and Bakery Square of Pittsburgh, displays Google's calculation that being in cities increases the company's accessibility to the growing ecosystems aimed at technology, including quality institutions, top talent and a number of regional economic specialized markets (Katz & Wagner, 2014; Rana, 2018; Rana et al., 2021).

Barcelona, Berlin, Copenhagen, London, Medellin, Montreal, Seoul, Stockholm, and Toronto include emerging or set-up innovation districts.

In the United States, the most iconic districts can be found in the city facilities of Boston, Atlanta, Cambridge, Detroit, Philadelphia, Pittsburgh, and St. Louis. In each of those innovation districts, there is a combination of high-quality research universities, scientific and technological agencies, firms, and complexes that trigger business expansion as well as commercial and residential growth.

Movers to innovative districts include high-value and research-oriented sectors, such as life sciences, and creative fields such as architecture, design, theater production, advertising, and marketing. We even see a return to small-scale and personalized manufacturing activities, made viable by 3D printing and robotics. Much of this activity displays an indispensable rethinking of corporate activities around the concepts of innovation, open innovation, entrepreneurship, sustainability, and the requisites for increased competitiveness (Katz & Wagner, 2014; Herrmann & Rana, 2020).

Barcelona is credited with creating the first innovation district with its Project 22 @ Barcelona, which began in 2000. 22 @ is perceived as a success and has become the pioneer model for other innovation districts, including the Innovation District from Boston.

> Today, 70% of the industrial land in El Poblenou has been remodeled, led by 141 individual plans for this redevelopment. Since 2000, 4,500 companies that employ 56,000 workers have opened or moved to 22 @. Approximately 72% of the total employees in 22 @ have university studies.
>
> (Ajuntament de Barcelona, 2013, 16)

The 22 @ project also requires the continuing education of the community in information-oriented activities, such as coding, product design, and training in IT services. Many universities have also established their presence at 22 @, such as the Pompeu Fabra University, the University of Barcelona, the Polytechnic University of Catalonia, and the Open University of Catalonia.

> Several incubators and accelerators have been created, such as the Biomedical Park, the MediaTic building and Barcelona Activa. The MediaTic Barcelona Growth Center is an innovation center that was built through a public-private partnership. The population of the area has grown by 130,000 people since 2000.
>
> (Ajuntament de Barcelona, 2012, 19)

The Boston Innovation District is the first innovation district officially labeled as such that is created in the United States. In May 2010, former

Boston Mayor Thomas Menino announced plans for the city to develop 400 hectares of land in the South Boston Waterfront.

> The Boston Innovation District is the fastest growing area in Boston today and has stimulated significant economic development in the city. Since the origin of the District, 5,000 new jobs have been created and more than 200 new businesses have been formed. 40% of companies located in the Innovation District share joint work spaces.
>
> (Boston Mayor's Office, 2014, 33)

More than 1,100 housing units have been built, including 300 innovation micro units. The increase in rental prices in the Innovation District has raised concerns that rapid real estate development in the area

> is discouraging entrepreneurs and emerging businesses, organizations and people that the District's own design intended to attract. In just a few years, rents increased by 43% at the seaport, and the trend continues today.
>
> (Ross, 2014, 31)

Innodistricts and Ecodistricts

Masdar represents a failed innovation district. However, innodistricts are becoming widespread in Western cities. Innovation districts (*innodistricts*) are usually embedded in regional and national innovation systems, and include a number of stakeholders from civil society. In some cases, such as Barcelona @22, these districts are based on a government-led planning and investment effort, built on the premise that innovation districts can become both effective urban regeneration and economic development tools. Thus, the creation of an innovation district is usually "an attempt for the city to leverage its strengths and resources to emerge as a hub of innovation in the knowledge economy" (Carnes, 2016, 61).

Innovation districts show a wide typology depending on leadership, cluster-type, and firm-support programs.

> In general, the move towards these innovation hubs reflects the growing importance of the geography of innovation to urban areas, and how developing industry clusters can deliver economic growth, employment and community regeneration. Brookings has called for local decision-makers, global companies and financial institutions, and government "to 'unleash', 'embrace', 'support and accelerate'" innovation districts. The result: a step toward building a stronger, more sustainable and more inclusive economy.
>
> (Cameron, 2016, 53)

In the case of MIT's Kendall Square,

> the revitalization effort was also an attempt to aggregate international and local firms in a more concentrated geographic environment with hopes of fostering increased collaboration. Collaboration amongst the city-government, education institutions, and the private sector has contributed to the success of the district.
>
> (Carnes, 2016, 45)

In the case of Barcelona @22, the most important takeaway

> is the particular validation of innovation districts as a sustainable urban economic regeneration tool. Through strategic programming and a robust planning model that emphasizes the physical, social, and economic aspects, the City of Barcelona has created one of the most successful innovation districts in the world.
>
> (Carnes, 2016, 47)

There are a number of requisites and constraints surrounding the development of innovation districts. Perhaps one of the main barriers to innovation district development is the current structure of incentives for investment privileging finance and property-led urban regeneration. A gradual shift-of-focus is required from built-environment investment to socioeconomic output, and from financial, real estate, property investments into innovation.

As Marginson argues:

> As long as the rewards for investment in financial assets are higher than the rewards for investment in knowledge-intensive industry innovation, the latter will be neglected. . . . This is a serious problem in the UK economy, where finance generating finance often seems to be the main game.
>
> (Marginson, 2016, 21)

Rather than primarily pursuing unrealistic growth targets through major capital-intensive projects (e.g., megaprojects), cities in developing regions should recognize their local context, history, and culture and concentrate on their strengths to address priorities such as affordable housing, accessibility of public services, and education, thus being able to create a resilient, long-term positive exponential impact (Dall'Orso, 2017; Raut et al., 2022).

Among the requisites for successful creation of innovation districts, we find the value of collaboration among stakeholders and investors. Today's most powerful innovation originates from collaboration, sharing of ideas, and mashing up of radically different disciplines and technologies to create new solutions to new problems or to upgrade traditional industries. Effective multidisciplinary, open collaboration requires intellectual density (concentration of skilled actors); diversity; tight proximity; strong networks; and partnerships among citizens, businesses, laboratories, academic institutions, and investors (Dall'Orso, 2019).

All innovation districts include physical, economic, and networking assets. An innovation ecosystem results when these three assets combine in a context and culture, which are prone to risk-taking. Such ecosystem often follows a triple-helix model whereby entrepreneurs tie up with universities and research centers to promote innovative thinking and practices supported by government funding. The role of universities is important because they are the actors that have the potential to increase revenues by fostering opportunities for R&D.

Capital, technology, and the built environment constitute tangible assets in innovation district development. Intellectual density, impact innovation, and social and economic networks are the intangible assets. Physical proximity and density of these key actors can be created in urban environments to foster collaborations. However, creating an entrepreneurial spirit also demands some social, cultural, and behavioral aspects of crucial importance, which have to do with "intangible", long-term societal processes such as quality of education, leadership formation, and business ethics.

R+D and Innovation Districts

Cities as Intercultural Milieux

Cities are contexts in which cultures and societies are produced and transformed; cities themselves are produced and transformed by those cultures and societies. If the global scale is constructed and transformed in specific territories, the local scale also contributes to the intersection of multiple social relations, processes, structures, and representations. Although not every metropolis can be said to be "global" (a main node in the international financial network), most of them participate in transnational cultural flows and produce and experience the specific consequences of such flows, visible at the local level in the presence and influence of companies, workers, tourists, and foreign products. Thus, globalization brings us to the experience of cultural diversity in spatially bounded milieux such as cities (del Cerro Santamaría, 2009).

R+D and innovation need a cosmopolitan attitude, and such an attitude can be found in cities. Contemporary transnationalism has transformed the idea of cosmopolitanism in two ways: (1) it is no longer an elite attitude exclusively (although class distinction mechanisms continue to operate at all levels) and (2) it is possible to develop a cosmopolitan attitude within a certain place in a sufficiently diverse city. Cities are also *civitas*, places of personal cultivation and intellectual and cultural openness, where "complete strangers observe and appreciate each other" (Anderson, 2011, 36).

Scattered throughout the city there are oases of cosmopolitanism, places characterized by "the acceptance of space as belonging to all kinds of people" (Anderson, 2011, 33). In such places, cosmopolitanism is part of what attracts a crowd: people enjoy meeting and observing other people who are different from themselves. It is a relaxation of the emotionally taxing social protection that one must maintain the rest of the time. They are safe, warm, and in intimate spaces thanks to a shared experience: food, shopping, travel, a sports show, etc.

There is also an intangible ingredient: a mood, writes Anderson, of "civility" that allows people to "strive mentally, emotionally and socially" and develop "social sophistication that allows various urban people to get along" (Anderson, 2011, 52). Because they are so difficult to replicate, Anderson argues, all these places should be treasured and protected, and those of us who enjoy them should treat them not as moments outside of normal life but as a model for social relations in increasingly diverse cities.

The civic urbanism to be fostered today is one that nurtures, explores, and learns in such zones of *civic friction* in external environments: spaces that widen the scope of action and, therefore, of thought. They are spaces in which a cosmopolitan attitude can be cultivated. The urban ethic that we can build is the ability of a city to normalize meetings with the other (Sennett, 2018). The many small signs of banal, everyday, vernacular, or low-intensity cosmopolitanism in our daily lives are a civic manifestation of an attitude shaping the preconditions for participatory urbanism, a form of intercultural research.

Consumer Participation

A major feature of the building of innovation in urban settings happens through citizen and consumer participation. In recent years, citizen participation in urban planning processes has become both a demand and a reality (Anciano & Piper, 2018). Collaborations among city planners, architects, social scientists, urban activists, and citizens to analyze and try to solve city problems constitute a form of intercultural research, given the different worldviews and epistemic cultures of each group involved (Knorr-Cetina, 1999). Such intercultural mutualism provides a conducive environment and context for the high-density milieu of expert knowledge exchanges characterizing innovation districts.

This mode of intercultural action research involves issues of decentralization and devolution of powers, building trust, achieving fair representation, enabling resources and support systems, or building transparency through platforms of engagement.

Enabling true and effective citizen participation in an existing administrative set-up is a complex process with challenges such as finding an amicable power and responsibility distribution framework, a building of additional capacity among both government officials and citizens alike, "ensuring fair civil society representation and enabling resources to support it. In many countries, decentralization of power requires institutional, legislative and political support at different levels of governance" (USAID, 2008, 121).

In parallel is the perceived threat of erosion of powers leading to cases where the effectiveness of decision-making and impact of local committees "are significantly hampered by red tape, bureaucracy, and required approval from government agencies. In addition, approaches may lead to prioritization of only those projects that will contribute to increasing revenue of the area, over socially benefitting projects" (Rajesh, 2009, 62).

City governments sometimes look at citizen engagement both through institutionalized structures and others such as citizen-led groups to act as active partners in the co-creation of the policy and planning process. Enabling multiple platforms of engagement enabling active participation helps build transparency by making information readily available.

> While e-governance platforms have proven to be very effective in cities across the world there have been many other technological platforms that have been developed and are being used in the areas of collecting empirical data and allowing participation from different stakeholders.
>
> (CURS, 2008)

Collaborations among different epistemic cultures in processes of expert knowledge exchange yielding innovative processes and products require city governments to make different channels of engagement and participation available. These engagements will also essentially need to tie together into a comprehensive local area development plan and ensure optimal utilization of all available resources.

Circuits: Innovation Policy Travels

Researchers on transnational innovation policy seek to analyze the factors enabling and constraining the formation of transnational circuits of policy adoption and adaptation as well as the social organization and consequences of the complex interconnectivity of cross-border networks in innovation policy. Urban innovation policy and ideas, framed or not as "best practices", travel around the world (Healey, 2013). This process lies at the foundation of a mode of intercultural research whereby transnational policy circuits foster spatially unbounded collaborations and implicit partnerships from policy creators to receptors and adopters.

Urban innovation policy travels can thus be said to underline "the socio-spatial processes by which social actors and their networks forge the *trans-local* connections and create the translocalities that increasingly sustain new modes of being-in-the-world" (Smith, 2005). This complex interconnectivity working at a distance is multidimensional, encompassing social, economic, and political relations as well as cultural and interpersonal networks and technological linkages. It is also a complex process subject to misplaced expectations and failure. The Bilbao Effect and Dubaization are paradigmatic examples of policy travel and information circuit formation that we have described elsewhere (Del Cerro Santamaría, 2020). Both take place in contexts of local–regional distinctive planning cultures which are neverthe-less translocally bounded in complex ways.

Urban Innovation Planning Cultures

Planning culture refers to conceptions, institutions, ethos, attitudes, and practices and has a direct effect on the prospects for intercultural research (Friedmann, 2005). Urban innovation planning practices and cultures are perceived to have converged due to the rapid expansion of information and communication technologies since the mid-1990s. However, empirical research on innovation planning cultures shows that the strategies devel-oped by planners to adapt to change vary widely, and the variation depends on multiple factors. For example, there is a significant degree of variation in the adoption of neoliberal policies and rhetoric and the translation of these to planning practice among nations (Sanyal, 2005, 17).

Transnational interconnectivity has changed local planning cultures, but we cannot speak of a significant move toward homogenization or conver-gence of urban planning practices at a global scale. In fact, the collective ethos and dominant attitude of professional innovation planners in differ-ent nations vary toward the appropriate roles of the state, market forces, and civil society in urban, regional, and national development. "The reality of changing urban planning cultures over time leads to characterize urban planning cultures as not indigenous and immutable, but rather evolving with social, political, and economic changes both within and outside the national territory" (Sanyal, 2005, 21).

The claim by neoclassical economists that cultural differences among peo-ples of the world are not relevant cannot be defended. If economists were right, innovation research and knowledge transfers in innovation districts would simply focus on creating institutions that would facilitate, not hinder, the universal urge among people to maximize their self-interests. Such is not the case. As a result, we face a complex phenomenon. As Sanyal states:

> International flow of planning ideas also affects planning styles, although not to the extent claimed by either its critics or its proponents. How does one develop new insights about such a complex social pro-cess with multiple and interconnected causes and effects?
>
> (Sanyal, 2005, 18)

As cultural anthropologist Richard Shweder recently noted,

> Cultural elements are too hard to define, too easily copied and too long detached from their points of original creation. Contact between cul-tures and processes such as borrowing, appropriation, migration, and diffusion have been ubiquitous for so long that little remains of the authentically indigenous.
>
> (Shweder, 2003, 27)

All of these have direct consequences for the realization of innovation research in urban settings because the existence of a diversity of cultures resembling "a complex traffic of ideas", according to Said, challenges and complicates both alliance formation and the processes of adoption and adaptation of innovation policies and practices, as we have seen in our examples (Sanyal, 2005, 32; Pasquier & Nicolescu, 2019).

Even if the city as an intercultural milieu is conducive to the necessary cosmopolitan attitude that fosters intercultural linkages, the challenges are formidable. The structuring of cities around borders and citadels, virtual and symbolic or cultural walls and ghettos, as well as the challenges to translation, adoption, and adaptation of innovation policies across distinct local planning cultures are obstacles for the transferring of innovation around the world.

Consumer participation shows the way forward as an intercultural practice for researching and analyzing innovation issues. However, issues of decentralization and devolution of powers, building trust, achieving fair representation, enabling resources and support systems, or building transparency through platforms of engagement represent potential limitations to this approach.

In addition, the sheer complexity of alliance formation and circuit efficacy, as well as the predominance of different epistemic cultures (with distinct conceptual sets) among participants in innovation processes, analysis, and practice present substantial challenges to effective intercultural communication. The existence of different values and cultural contexts complicates efforts at interpretation and fair judgment among parties involved in practices of complexity and innovation research.

As Sanyal remarks:

> There is no cultural nucleus or core planning culture, no social gene that can be decoded to reveal the cultural DNA of planning practice. Planning culture, like the larger social culture in which it is embedded, is in constant flux.
>
> (Sanyal, 2005, 22)

Thus, the focus of inquiry for innovation research (which fosters innovative capacity) should be the continuous process of social, political, and technological change, which affects the way planners in different settings conceptualize problems and structure institutional responses to them.

> If planning culture is viewed in this dynamic way, in contrast to traditional notions of culture that are used to evoke a sense of immutability and inheritance, then we can go beyond "cultural essentialism," which, in essence, is exclusionary, parochial, and an inaccurate representation of history.
>
> (Sanyal, 2005, 23)

This implies developing a *mentally mobile attitude* informed by flexibility and creativity, which is able to translate symbolic codes across fields of endeavor and practices. Such disposition to translate can be expressed as "practicing places". For complexity and innovation research, the notions that best capture such mobile disposition are "assemblages" and "hybridization". Research strategies, such as transdisciplinarity, also have the potential to cross over binary oppositions and overcome the challenges of alliances and circuits.

Knowledge Exchanges

Social Learning

One factor that enhances the potential for innovation and complexity is the idea that learning is essentially a social, collective process. Learning and research are cultural practices bounded by values reflected in practices. They are fundamentally collective practices. According to Vygotsky (1962, 33), we learn through our interactions and communications with others. Webs of sometimes complex interactions of students and learners with peers, teachers, and other experts are conducive to enhanced learning. It is therefore possible to create appropriate learning environments that maximize the chances of participants to benefit through discussion, collaboration, and feedback.

We also learn and construct knowledge, according to Vygotsky, within the boundaries of our own cultural frameworks, rules, skills, and abilities. Culture thus becomes the single most significant factor for learning, research, and knowledge creation (Vygotsky, 1962, 45). For Vygotsky, "language is the main tool that promotes thinking, develops reasoning, and supports cultural activities like reading and writing" (Vygotsky, 1978, 45).

In part as an application of Vygotsky's ideas, I conducted a study of communication modes and content used by engineering students in a special project-course, Robotics for Theater, focused on the planning and construction of a robot from scratch to support theatric production as actor and prop (del Cerro Santamaría, 2015). The student projects studied in the pilot program assumed the format of client-based product development and delivery. A preferred scenario would involve industrial partners who sponsor and participate in specific product prototyping projects. In this ideal case, a technical representative of each industrial partner would be the *client* to the student team working on the industrial partner's project. This model was successfully implemented by Prof. Leifer at Stanford University through a graduate-level project course (Leifer, 1997).

Analysis of the case study of the Robotics for Theater project revealed a complex learning process where the social aspects of team dynamics had a significant positive impact on students' knowledge acquisition: 1. Resource mobilization was fostered by the role of the advisor as information facilitator and "weak tie" in the network and also by the frequent informal contacts among the students in the team. 2. Innovation was fostered by intra-team trust. The strong friendship and teaming experience of the group were critical for effective team dynamics. 3. Probably due to time constraints, the field of theater did not become a fundamental reference of the project, contrary to plans. 4. Time constraints and technical difficulties in implementation inhibited progress. 5. Informal meetings were crucial in the progression of design and implementation.

Collective Intelligence and Complexity

From the concept of "social learning", we can logically move toward the idea of "collective intelligence". The Massachusetts Institute of Technology's Center for Collective Intelligence is fully devoted to advancing knowledge on this matter. Collective intelligence has been the goal of visionaries throughout the history of the Internet. As Gruber reports:

> Douglas Engelbart, who invented groupware, the mouse, and a form of hypertext designed for collective knowledge, wrote in 1963 of his career and project objective: 'The grand challenge is to boost the collective IQ of organizations and of society.' His Bootstrap Principle was about a *human-machine system* for simultaneously harvesting the collected knowledge for learning and evolving our technology for collective learning. In human-machine systems, both the human and machine contribute actively to the resulting intelligence, each doing what they do best. Other early pioneers of the human-machine model of collective intelligence include Norbert Wiener, the father of cybernetics, Buckminster Fuller, the consummate inventor and system thinker, and Stewart Brand, creator of the first large virtual community on the Internet. Tim Berners-Lee, the inventor of the World Wide Web, describes his vision of the Semantic Web in these terms: "the Semantic Web is not a separate Web but an extension of the current one, in which information is given well-defined meaning, better *enabling computers and people to work in cooperation*" [emphasis added].
>
> (Gruber, 2008, 3)

Most discussions on collective intelligence or "wisdom of crowds" refer to the Social Web. Here the idea is that the individual contributions by web participants create value for anyone just by being available for reading and usage. To what extent new knowledge emerges by the juxtaposition of high number of data and information sources is clearly a complexity issue. As Gruber argues, emergent knowledge (inherent to complex situations) takes place when "the system enables computation and inference over the collected information, leading to answers, discoveries, or other results that are not found in the human contributions" (Gruber, 2008, 4).

In fact, "emergent knowledge" (i.e., complexity) is one of the potential outcomes of innovation processes. Knowledge emergence in intercultural research would materialize if research participants are able to "bootstrap" their collective intelligence. Intercultural research can be conceived as a complex information repository. It can also be conceived as an active framework where participants actively interact to express their knowledge interests and needs to request specific knowledge and to apply intercultural knowledge to problem-solving and in general to address their collective needs. Some of the examples in this chapter show these possibilities and also some current limitations.

Converging Epistemic Cultures

Another factor or pre-condition that fosters both complexity and the possibility of innovation research in urban districts is the idea of converging epistemic cultures. Scholars in the field of social studies of science and technology are providing examples indicating a certain degree of convergence of research fields under a new techno-scientific paradigm. Mostly, these discussions refer to the macro-scale and adopt a broad understanding of convergence. Kastenhofer introduces a focus on epistemic cultures and raises the question of what convergence might imply on the micro-level of everyday research practices (Kastenhofer, 2007). She distinguishes three forms of scientific change over time (convergence, divergence, and emergence) and three modes of convergence (cooperation, integration, and assimilation).

Further, as Knorr Cetina has argued, "the concepts of knowledge culture and epistemic culture are used here against the background of contemporary transformations in global financial architecture" (Knorr Cetina, 2007, 363). The focus of this chapter is on the construction, within the field of urbanism, of the machineries of knowledge construction, relocating culture in the micropractices of city life as a bounded habitat of intercultural research practice through processes of alliance formation. Not all places of intercultural research in urbanism, however, are bounded spaces, and there is a case to be made for including in the empirical agenda more distributed locations, a typical scenario of complexity. We describe here wider networks and circuits of knowledge generation as processes of innovation in what is often known as transnational space.

Assemblages as Hybridization

Literary critic Homi K. Bhabha introduces the concept of 'hybridity' against the containment of cultural differences and challenges all hegemonies structured through binary antagonism. For him,

> [A]ll forms of culture are continually in a process of hybridity. But the importance of hybridity is not . . . to race two original moments from which the third emerges, rather hybridity is the 'third space' which enables other positions to emerge. This third space displaces the histories

that constitute it, and set up new structures of authority, new political initiatives . . . The process of cultural hybridity gives rise to something different, something new and unrecognizable, a new area of negotiation of meaning and representation.

(Bhabha, 1994, 56)

Bhabha locates the origin of the notion 'cultural difference' and hybridity within colonial discourse itself where it is articulated as resistance to 'colonial authority' – a process by which in the very practice of domination the language of the master becomes hybrid.

The field of signification of colonial cultural differences announces a modality of misappropriations of signs that produces a discursive instability at the level of enunciation; a productive ambivalence which deconstructs the fixity of the boundaries (coloniser/colonised) of colonial discursivity and construct hybrid identities.

(Bhabha, 1994, 73)

The notion of hybridity or third space of Homi Bhabha is a floating metaphor for a critical historical consciousness that privileges spatiality over temporality; but the privileging of spatialization is not ahistorical and timeless, rather he tries creatively to spatialize temporality. This is an envisioning of cultural politics of third space, an effective consolidation that helps to dislodge its entrapment in hegemonic historiography and historicism.

The social articulation of difference, from the minority perspective, is a complex, ongoing negotiation that seeks to authorize cultural hybridities that emerge in moments of historical transformation. The "right" to signify from the periphery of authorized power and privilege does not depend on the persistence of tradition, it is resourced by power. He explains further the notion "going beyond":

Beyond signifies spatial distance, marks progress, promises the future, but our intimations of exceeding the barrier or boundary – the very act of going beyond – are unknowable, unrepresentable, without a return to the "present" which in the process of repetition, becomes disjunct and distance – to live somehow beyond the border of our times – throws into relief the temporal, social differences that interrupt or collusive sense of cultural contemporaneity.

(Bhabha, 1994, 132)

Hence, the going beyond is the spatial act of intervention to revisit and reconstruct subjectivities in order to inhabit multiple positions of subjects as an enunciation of cultural difference. Thus, Homi Bhabha's notion hybridity/third space is akin to the notion of "assemblage" developed by Deleuze and Guattari (1987). Both notions connect spatial concerns with cultural politics to provide multiple identities challenging all the binaries which are part of homogenization and universalization of human existence with singular analytical categories. Innovation processes inherently have the potential to overcome the barriers to alliances and circuits through an ontology and epistemology developing around the complex idea of assemblages or "rhizomatic research cultures" (Guerin, 2013).

Future Research Directions

Socio-Materiality

Socio-materiality reveals the inherent complex nature of empirical reality and the need to account for such complexity in our analyses. Actor–network theory and assemblage materialist approaches propose to overcome what Alfred North Whitehead named "the bifurcation of nature" expressed in the secular dichotomy nature–culture (Whitehead, 1920, 85). A step in this direction can be helpful in efforts at developing meaningful intercultural research on the ecological crisis and sustainability in the Anthropocene (Morton, 2019).

Within urbanism, materiality and assemblage thinking have found friendly ground (Farías & Bender, 2010). After all, the built environment is an inescapable material reality to be grasped from the outside through "the observation of concrete materials, not the workings of the mind in isolation" (Sennett, 1992, 196). Jane Jacobs already observed that buildings, streets, and neighborhoods work as dynamic organisms, changing in response to how people interact with them (Jacobs, 2000).

Materiality aims at knowing not by defining the objects but instead by becoming sensitive to the immanence of vibrant matter itself, its influences, results, and consequences. In this vein, French sinologist François Jullien has stated that "a wise man does not have ideas" that are independent of matter (Jullien, 2001).

We need not produce a conventional, rationalist theory to explain urbanism and, specifically, innovation in urban districts. As Beauregard and Lieto have shown (Beauregard & Lieto, 2016), we need to aim at something different and perhaps more necessary and effective: to give meaning to new materiality by fostering a new sensitivity, orientation, and disposition toward the central role of nonhuman elements in intercultural research within urbanism and urban planning. Urbanists as innovation researchers would need to be both craftsmen of good ideas (by gathering knowledge, people, and material things) and public intellectuals (by forming alliances around matters of concern).

A new focus on materiality in urban innovation research would focus on the role of nonhuman entities (plans, documents, arguments, expertise, buildings, etc.) in how planners envisage the connections among norms, technologies, and lifeworlds through networks of human associations, technologies, natural ecologies and places, sites, and settings (Beauregard, 2015).

In spite of a new focus on matter, innovation research needs to be sympathetic to inclusive epistemologies that affirm ontological realism while giving room for the shaping role of the knowing subject via perception, imagination, memory, and affects. This is important because the pretensions of pure objectivism in some interpretations of ANT, rejecting or downplaying the crucial role of the mind in shaping human understanding and inquiry, are hard to defend. It is crucial to not misrepresent the causal capacities of nonhuman objects while effacing the significance of the capacities of human beings. Human attributes such as intuition, affect, and emotion are the pulse of socio-materiality (Müller, 2015, 36).

A relational approach in urban innovation research is not qualitatively different from conventional sociological or technical applications of network analysis, which are mainly devoted to mapping connections among network members. However, it is possible to suggest that "network" would work in intercultural research as a metaphor conveying the complexity of trying to capture the multiple and changing relational dimensions of always-mobile assemblages.

Socio-materiality is not widely embraced among planning theorists or innovation theorists or practitioners. The reason might have something to do with humanism and post-humanism. It certainly has something to do with the misconception that ANT proposes to make nonhumans into humans, thus ignoring the very precise definition of an actor that ANT deploys – which is, itself, a theoretical extension of the notion of "affordances" (Gibson, 1979). The idea of "affordances" refers to the properties of matter, these properties being what influences how humans interact with things. Affordances, as applied to both things and places, are properties that allow a person to do some things and not others, but are not fully constraining (Lieto & Beauregard, 2016).

Complexity and Holism

The relational thrust in complexity approaches leads to holism and avoids reductionist perspectives. Thus, innovation research can be said to be holistic when a transdisciplinary research strategy is used to account for problems that are global in nature, such as sustainable megaproject development, where megaprojects need to be conceived as complex disruptive innovations. Development processes in the built environment have significant environmental impacts, and thus attaining acceptable levels of environmental sustainability needs to become a priority for planners, developers, and other stakeholders. However, the attainment of environmental sustainability does not in itself ensure megaproject sustainability, a goal that needs to be pursued holistically. One way to do it is to use the notion of "key or multiple success factors" (Grunert & Ellegaard, 1992).

This notion is not new in the field of project management and, in fact, constitutes one of the topics most discussed by specialists. It is increasingly important "to evaluate projects and their impacts at different times and based on multiple criteria in order to fully evaluate their performance. Success is often driven by political and/or power-related factors" (Grunert & Ellegaard, 1992). Due to the strongly political nature of the stakeholders throughout the supply chain and their different underlying objectives, the success factors usually considered no longer seem sufficient. This configuration requires innovative governance solutions that align the interests of the different stakeholders in a complex environment with a large number of key actors (Harris, 2017).

By following the notion of "multiple success factors", we contend that there are a number of requirements that need to be met in order to achieve sustainable megaprojects: environmental sustainability (sustainable infrastructure delivery and sustainable development zones), sustainability in design and planning, sustainability in megaproject management, institutional sustainability, and socioeconomic sustainability.

Thus, a megaproject can be defined to be sustainable if it is planned and executed to account for the capacity, fitness, resilience, diversity, and balance of its urban ecosystem. We take the view of sustainability as an organic process including environment, economy, and community: form and efficiency – environmental factors in design, architecture, engineering, and construction – as well as policy – urban plans and practices that explicitly aim at maintaining and improving the social and economic well-being of citizens (del Cerro Santamaría, 2019).

The notion of "strategic urban planning" has become paramount in efforts to address sustainability challenges in urban environments (Hersperger et al., 2018). This notion involves a holistic approach to problem-solving in the area of sustainability that implies placing the idea of complexity at the forefront of analysis and action. Complex thought, education, and knowledge, in Edgar Morin´s understanding, take into account contextual, global, and multidimensional factors to devise strategy conducive to more fruitful action.

> Pertinent, knowledge must confront complexity. Complexus means that which is woven together. In fact there is complexity whenever the various elements (economic, political, sociological, psychological, emotional, mythological . . .) that compose a whole are inseparable, and there is inter-retroactive, interactive, interdependent tissue between the subject of knowledge and its context, the parts and the whole, the whole and the parts, the parts amongst themselves. Complexity is therefore the bond between unity and multiplicity. Developments proper to our planetary era confront us more frequently, ineluctably with the challenge of complexity.
>
> (Morin, 1999, 36)

Complex knowledge also takes into account the centrality of the knowing subject in analytical endeavors, the uncertainty of the knowledge enterprise itself and the incompleteness and undecidable nature of *homo complexus's* human action. Through complex knowledge, the holistic quality of urban planning naturally leads to a transdisciplinary conception of theory-building and practice development.

Thus, a possibly fruitful way to apply the notion of strategic urban planning would be to propose a transdisciplinary paradigm to address urban challenges related to innovation. A transdisciplinary way of thinking would cross traditional disciplines and would modify the classical notion of science. A new vision fostering innovation principles requires a rethinking of human values and a reconsideration of the integration among the flow of perception, experience, and consciousness. It is impossible to imagine a single solution to the problem of innovation but many complex, interrelated, and evolving solutions (Kagan, 2019).

Transdisciplinarity

The iconography of complex assemblages is akin to transdisciplinarity, which is a particularly well-suited strategy for creating and fostering innovation. The kind of knowledge exchange taking place in transdisciplinary processes, through shifting and integration, creates innovative knowledge. This is related to social constructionism. Since Berger and Luckmann we know that reality is socially constructed (Berger & Luckmann, 1966). People and groups interacting in a social system create, over time, concepts or mental representations of each other's actions and that these concepts eventually become habituated into reciprocal roles played by the actors in relation to each other. When these roles are made available to other members of society to enter into and play out, the reciprocal interactions are said to be institutionalized. In the process, meaning is embedded in society. Knowledge and people's conceptions (and beliefs) of what reality is become embedded in the institutional fabric of society. Reality is therefore said to be socially constructed.

However, the social sciences by themselves cannot adequately come to terms with the ontology of reality, in particular in urban innovation districts. Leading social science researchers such as Manuel Castells, Janet Abu-Lughod, and Saskia Sassen have recognized that the reality of the city cannot be understood from a single disciplinary perspective. Also, in two joint sessions of the British and American Sociological Associations held during the course of 2001, the conclusions pointed toward a necessity for interdisciplinarity and multidisciplinarity to enrich the perspectives within urban sociology (Perry, 2002). Even if it seems appropriate to prescribe interdisciplinarity and multidisciplinarity for urban studies, this strategy would not solve the conceptual and epistemological problems of a field that faces the massive ontological transformations brought about by conditions of planetary urbanization. We are in need of a new perspective that goes beyond disciplines: a transdisciplinary perspective.

Because urbanism engages, both as a discipline and as a profession, with broader societal concerns (e.g., situated knowledge, participatory design, everyday practices), it therefore seems obvious that hybrid modes of inquiry ought to be part of the knowledge landscape. Whereas *inter*disciplinary knowledge is located in scholarly environments, *trans*disciplinary knowledge production entails a fusion of academic and nonacademic knowledge, theory and practice, and discipline and profession.

Several attempts have been made toward less reductive approaches to space and design; approaches that no longer *choose* between theory and practice as the ideal locus for critique but, instead, allow critique to be processed in ways that are more complex and more entangled; approaches that advocate hybrid modes of inquiry and research. These could be used in innovation research.

One can think of the hybridization of nature and technology, engineering and the social, facts and values, human and nonhuman, and the explicit attention to agency in science and technology studies (STS), and ANT, actor-network-theory (Latour, 1987). Such approaches have in common their suggestion to approach issues such as urban innovation not according to predefined ideologies or (critical) theories but to study them as a problem of the outside – as situated, complex gatherings of all sorts of agencies, where the notion of transdisciplinarity can be applied meaningfully.

References

Ajuntament de Barcelona. (2012) @22 Barcelona Plan. A Programme of Urban, Economic and Social Transformation, www.22barcelona.com/documentacio/Dossier22@/Dossier22@English_p.pdf, Retrieved July 2019.

Ajuntament de Barcelona. (2013) 22@Barcelona. Background. Urban Planning Management, www.22barcelona.com/documentacio/Dossier2²@/Dᵒˢsier22@English_p.pdf, Retrieved July 15th, 2019.

Anciano, F. and L. Piper. (2018) *Democracy Disconnected. Participation and Governance in a City of the South*, London and New York: Routledge.

Anderson, E. (2011) *The Cosmopolitan Canopy: Race and Civility in Everyday Life*, New York: W.W. Norton.

Beauregard, R.A. (2015) *Planning Matter. Acting With Things*, Chicago: University of Chicago Press.

Beauregard, R.A. and L. Lieto. (2016) Can Actor Network Theory Provide a Theory of Action? Planning in New York, USA, Chapter 10 in *Actor Networks of Planning: Exploring the Influence of Actor Network Theory*, edited by Y. Rydin and L. Tate, London: Routledge.

Berger, P.L. and T. Luckmann. (1966) *The Social Construction of Reality. A Treatise in the Sociology of Knowledge*, Garden City, NY: Anchor Books.

Bhabha, H. (1994) *The Location of Culture*, New York: Routledge.

Boston Mayor´s Office. (2014) Boston's Innovation District, Boston Mayor's Office, August 1, www.innovationdistrict.org/2010/10/15/.

Cameron, H. (2016) Innovation Districts – The Way Forward for Sustainable Growth? *The Knowledge Exchange Blog*, January 25, https://theknowledgeexchangeblog.com/2016/01/25/innovation-districts-the-way-forward-for-sustainable-growth/.

Carnes, S. (2016) The Case for the Innovation District as a Sustainable Economic Development Tool in the Knowledge Economy, Georgia Tech Center for Urban Innovation, February 1, https://gtcui.wordpress.com/2016/02/01/the-case-for-the-innovation-district-as-a-sustainable-economic-development-tool-in-the-knowledge-economy/.

CURS, Centre for Urban and Regional Studies. (2008) Digital Tools in Participatory Planning, Centre for Urban and Regional Studies Publications, Aalto.

Dall'Orso, M. (2017) What Characterises an Ideal City, and How Do We Get There? *Urbanet*, June 22, www.urbanet.info/ideal-city/.

Dall'Orso, M. (2019) Promoting Sustainable Urban Development Through I mpact Innovation, *Urbanet*, January 10, www.urbanet.info/sustainable-urban-development-through-impact-innovation/.

Del Cerro Santamaría, G. (2009) An Interpretation of Urban Change in New York's SoHo, *Revista Española de Sociología* 11 (1), 33–60.

Del Cerro Santamaría, G. (2015) Transdisciplinary Technological Futures: An Ethnographic Research Dialogue Between Social Scientists and Engineers, in Special Issue on *Technological Futures. New Epistemic Strategies for an Increasingly Techno-scientific World*, Technology in Society journal, guest edited by Gerardo del Cerro Santamaría.

Del Cerro Santamaría, G. (2019) Fulbright Research Proposal, Unpublished Manuscript.

Del Cerro Santamaría, G. (2020) Possibilities and Challenges of Intercultural Research in Global Urbanism, in *Examining Cultural Perspectives in a Globalized World*, edited by Richard Brunet-Thornton, New York: Palgrave Macmillan.

Deleuze, G. and F. Guattari (1987) *A Thousand Plateaus. Capitalism and Schizophrenia*, Minneapolis, MN: University of Minnesota Press.

Farías, I. and T. Bender, eds. (2010) *Urban Assemblages. How Actor-Network Theory Changes Urban Studies*, London: Routledge.

Friedmann, J. (2005) Planning Cultures in Transition, in *Comparative Planning Cultures*, edited by B. Sanyal, New York and London: Routledge, p. 31.

Gibson, J.J. (1979) *The Ecological Approach to Visual Perception*, Boston: Houghton Mifflin.

Gruber, T. (2008) Collective Knowledge Systems: Where the Social Web meets the Semantic Web, *Web Semantics: Science, Services and Agents on the World Wide Web* 6 (1), February.

Grunert, K.G. and C. Ellegaard. (1992) The Concept of Key Success Factors. Theory and Method, MAPP Work ing Paper no. 4, October, ISSN 09072101, https://pure.au.dk/portal/files/32299581/wp04.pdf.

Guerin, C. (2013) Rhizomatic Research Cultures, Writing Groups and Academic Researcher Identities. *International Journal of Doctoral Studies* 8, 137–150.

Harris, M. (2017) Competitive Precinct Projects. The Five Consistent Criticisms of "Global" Mixed-Use Megaprojects, *Project Management Journal* 48 (6), 76–92.

Healey, P. (2013) Circuits of Knowledge and Techniques: The Transnational Flow of Planning Ideas and Practices, *International Journal of Urban and Regional Research* 37 (5), 1510–1526, September.

Herrmann, H. and S. Rana. (2020) Which B2B Thinker Are You? *International Journal of Indian Culture and Business Management* 21 (1), 45–62.

Hersperger, A.M., et al. (2018) Urban Land Use Change: The Role of Strategic Spatial Planning, *Global Environmental Change* 52, 32–42, July.

Hirschman, A.O. (1967) *Development Projects Observed*, Washington, DC: Brookings Institution.

IMF World Economic Outlook. (2018) Cyclical Upswing, Struct ural Change, The IMF, Washington, DC, www.imf.org/en/Publications/WEO/Issues/2018/03/20/world-economic-outlook-april-2018.

Jacobs, J. (2000) *The Nature of Economies*, New York: Modern Library.

Jullien, F. (2001) *Un Sabio No Tiene Ideas* (*A Wise Man Does Not Have Ideas*), Spanish Edition, Madrid: Siruela.

Kagan, S. (2019) Artful Sustainability in Transdisciplinary Spaces of Possibilities, *Transdisciplinary Journal of Engineering and Science* 10, 63–71.

Kastenhofer, K. (2007) Converging Epistemic Cultures? *Innovation: The European Journal of Social Science Research* 20 (4), 359–373.

Katz, B. and J. Wagner. (2014) The Rise of Innovation Districts, Brookings Institution, Metropolitan Policy Program, May.

Knorr Cetina, K. (1999) *Epistemic Cultures. How the Sciences Make Knowledge*, Cambridge, MA: Harvard University Press.

Knorr Cetina, K. (2007) Culture in Global Knowledge Societies: Knowledge Cultures and Epistemic Cultures, *Interdisciplinary Science Reviews* 32 (4), 361–375, DOI: 10.1179/030801807X163571.

Latour, B. (1987) *Science in Action. How to Follow Scientists and Engineers Through Society*, Cambridge, MA: Harvard University Press.

Leifer, L. (1997) Design Team Performance: Metrics and the Impact of Technology, in *Evaluating Corporate Training: Models and Issues (Evaluation in Education in Human Services)*, edited by S. Brown and C. Seidner, Dordrecht: Kluwer Academic Publishing.

Lieto, L. and R. A. Beauregard, eds. (2016) *Planning for a Material World*, London: Routledge.

Marginson, S. (2016) cited in Cameron, H. (2016) Innovation Districts – The Way Forward for Sustainable Growth? *The Knowledge Exchange Blog*, January 25, https://theknowledgeexchangeblog.com/2016/01/25/innovation-districts-the-way-forward-for-sustainable-growth/.

Morin, E. (1999) *Seven Complex Lessons in Education for the Future*, Paris: UNESCO.

Morton, T. (2019) *Being Ecological*, Cambridge, MA: The MIT Press.

Müller, M. (2015) Assemblages and Actor-Networks: Rethinking Socio-Material Power, *Politics and Space, Geography Compass* 9 (1), 27–41.

Pasquier, F. and B. Nicolescu. (2019) To Be or not to Be Transdisciplinary, That Is the New Question. So, How to Be Transdisciplinary? *Transdisciplinary Journal of Engineering and Science* 10, 1–8.

Perry, B. (2002) The Future of Urban Sociology: Report of Joint Sessions of the British and American Sociological Associations, *International Journal of Urban and Regional Research* 26 (4), 844–853, December.

Rajesh, K. (2009) Participatory Institutions and People's Practices in India: An Analysis of Decentralisation Experiences in Kerala State, Institute for Social and Economic Change, Bangalore, June.

Rana, S. (2018) Business Performance: Earlier Stage and Looking Forward, *FIIB Business Review* 7 (3), 153–155.

Rana, S., S. Prashar, M.K. Barai and A.B.A. Hamid. (2021) Determinants of International Marketing Strategy for Emerging Market Multinationals, *International Journal of Emerging Markets* 16 (2), 154–178.

Raut, S. K., S. Sakpal and R. Soni. (2022) Understanding the Service Quality Dimensions and Achieving Resilience in Service Retail, in *Handbook of Research on Supply Chain Resiliency, Efficiency, and Visibility in the Post-Pandemic Era*, edited by Ramakrishna Yanamandra, pp. 136–156. IGI Global, UAE. https://doi.org/10.4018/978-1-7998-9506-0.

Ross, C. (2014) Office Rents Soaring in City's Innovation District, The Boston Globe, January 10, www.bostonglobe.com/business/2014/01/10/rents-soaring-city-innovation-district/nqeKNcRiLJiyjKEEGog8GP/story.html.

Sanyal, B. ed. (2005) *Comparative Planning Cultures*, New York and London: Routledge.

Sennett, R. (2018) *Building and Dwelling: Ethics for the City*, New York: Farrar, Straus and Giroux.

Sennett, R. (1992) *The Conscience of the Eye. The Design and Social Life of Cities*, New York: W. W. Norton.

Shweder, R. (2003) Who Owns Native Culture? The Gatekeepers, *The New York Times*, September 14, 13.

Smith, M.P. (2005) Transnational Urbanism Revisited, *Journal of Ethnic and Migration Studies* 31 (2), March.

USAID. (2008) Preparation of Local Area Plans: Pilot Project for Delhi, India, The Communities Group International (TCGI) in Partnership with AECOM, April.

Vygotsky, L.S. (1962) *Thought and Language*, Cambridge, MA: MIT Press (Original work published in 1934).

Vygotsky, L.S. (1978) *Mind in Society: The Development of Higher Psychological Processes*, Cambridge, MA: Harvard University Press.

Whitehead, A.N. (1920) *The Concept of Nature*, Cambridge: Cambridge University Press, cited in Latour, B. (2016) *Facing Gaia. Eight Lectures on the New Climatic Regime*, London: Polity.

WEF, World Economic Forum. (2018) H ow Globalization Is Changing Innovation, www.weforum.org/agenda/2018/08/globalisation-has-the-potential-to-nurture-innovation-heres-how/.

7 Impact of Creativity in Advertising on Customer's Recall Value

A Perspective from Emerging Markets

Sangeeta Sharma and Arpan Bumb

Introduction

Due to increase in free trade, foreign direct investment, and international patents, globalization has been able to reinforce the spread of knowledge, technology, and skills throughout the globe. The world is transforming into a "global village", with countries and people connected to each other through several platforms. With globalization, there is an increased competition among the companies to establish their position in the market. This pressing competition provides a need for the companies to involve creativity and innovation in their strategies as well as marketing plans to make sure that the products and services offered by the companies are distinct from the competition. The only key to success in this fierce competitive globalized world is to be different and ensure customers remember that difference offered by the products or services of the companies. One such way is to market the product effectively and make sure customers notice the product. Usually, marketers rely on advertising to promote their product or service, but customers remain oblivious of the advertisements as they are presented with multiple advertisements in a day. Hence, to remain relevant, the advertisers should attempt to make their advertisements creative. This book chapter illustrates the use of creativity in emerging markets to boost the recall value of the advertisement.

Globalization

The emergence of a borderless world with uniform standards or a single-world global society is termed as globalization (Albrow, 1990). Owing to globalization, the products, services, and ideas travel globally into different countries. With the advent of faster communications, transportation, digital technologies and Internet access, time and distance among countries are no longer barriers to globalization (Belch & Belch, 2003; Rana et al., 2021). Further, the proliferation of strategies such as joint ventures, franchising, and strategic alliances has led to the spread of brands in different countries. Also, the proliferation of Western ideas due to globalization led to an increased

DOI: 10.4324/9781003315582-8

demand of goods and services of Western countries throughout the world. However, as markets in developed countries such as the United States and Europe became saturated with the existing products and unfavorable marketing environment, companies began to look for opportunities in less developed market in developing countries, which were called as emerging markets.

These emerging marketing in developing countries are considered as the fastest-growing markets for most of the products or services offered by a particular company or organization (Khanna et al., 2005). The developing countries provide huge market to sell the products at lower cost by cutting expenses in manufacturing, labor, and process facilities. Further, policies by developing countries to facilitate large FDI inflows attracts the multinational companies to expand their markets (Sabir et al., 2019).

In order to identify the most profitable countries to expand their venture, companies often use tools like country portfolio analysis and political risk assessment. However, these approaches receive criticism that they fail to consider the nuances particular to a specific country that include culture, language, social norms, labor laws and privileges, behavioral patterns, nonverbal cues, etc. The past studies by (Khanna et al., 2005; Bhandari & Raut, 2019) have incorporated these aspects and have provided a framework for companies to determine their profitability in a particular market which they want to enter.

However, even after effectively determining which market to enter, some companies still are unable to carry or create the brand image that they enjoyed in their domestic market. Main reasons identified for this gap are: companies are unable to align their marketing mix, brand image, and product quality with the customer's expectations (Keller & Moorthi, 2003; Rana et al., 2020b). There are multiple cases of failure of the brands in international ventures just because they were unable to take care of the customer preferences. There are multiple cases for failure of established companies in emerging markets. Examples for such failure in Indian market include Dunkin Donuts, Fiat, Danone, etc.

The presence of several local, small- and medium-sized industries along with multinational companies leads to a fierce competition among the companies in emerging markets. Local brands can provide customers with quality products at a lower cost, which is not possible for multinational companies as they have to deal with international tariffs, brand equity, and quality control procedures. However, the brand value associated with products of multinational companies gives them a clear advantage against local companies. In all, companies present in emerging markets have to make sure that customers know the company and recall their products or services at the point of purchase. This can be accomplished by using advertising campaigns.

Advertising

Advertising is an indispensable element of marketing strategy of any organization; it allows marketers to showcase their product, service, or idea in a convincing manner to the target audience. The main aim of any advertisement is to enhance the sales and therefore increase the profit. The media for the advertising is getting complex, as the new development in technology and shift to digital marketing have provided tools for better analysis. Each activity of the consumer can now be monitored, which leads to targeted marketing hence increasing the competition for the various organizations.

The problems related to marketing mix and brand image are easily countered by effective advertising (Rana et al., 2020a). Effective advertising allows companies to communicate the intended benefits of the product and initiatives taken by company to influence social, environmental, and economical factors. It also allows to make sure that the advertisement breaks the clutter and that advertising message reaches the target audience without any distortions. Research by Till and Baack (2005) has proven that effective advertising leads to higher unaided recall value and purchase intentions that become more necessary in emerging markets owing to the fierce competition.

Role of Creativity in Advertising

Creativity is indispensable for the marketers and remains the central theme for the advertising industry. Several industry competitions such as EFFIE, CLIO, and Cannes Lions International Festival of Creativity are organized to showcase the popularity of effective ad campaigns (Reinartz & Saffert, 2013; West et al., 2019). Creativity in advertisements is necessary to present ideas effectively to make sure that the intended meaning is not lost in between the communication process and also leave an indelible impression on the minds of customers. This creativity is achieved by metaphorical devices, alluring images, jingles, or a combination of all.

Creative advertisements can cut through the clutter and can be retained in the minds of people for a longer duration. There is a general notion about using creativity in advertisements and the positive effect which it creates by connecting with the audience, improving the purchase intent and high attention-capturing ability. From the various models of advertising such as the Hierarchy of Effect (HOE) model and AIDAS model, each of the cognition, affect, and intention stage is significantly influenced enhancing creativity in the advertisement as greater cognition leads to higher affection and intention to buy stage. Using the Attitude-toward-Ad Model (Edell & Burke, 1987), consumers, when coming across any advertising message, think over the content of the ad which is termed as cognition. The outcome of this state exercise produces a certain feeling about the product which is called the affection stage. These lead to an attitude toward advertisement, which in turn generates an attitude toward the brand.

Advertisements from campaigns such as Amazon's Alexa, Walmart's Cars, and Marlboro's Hold My Light created wonders for the brand and even helped in positioning (Raut, Sakpal and Soni, 2022). Past researches by Till and Baack (2005), Ang et al. (2007), and Haberland and Dacin (1992) have also concluded that positive responses result from creative advertisements.

To make advertisement creative, one of the views for the creative processes is to combine the preexisting things in different and unique ways. These advertisements are sometimes very interactive and at the same time make the Unique Selling Proposition (USP) clear to the target audience such as in the print advertisements of Peugeot (air bags), Nivea (Sun Kids campaign), and Ford (smart parking and large storage facilities). Creativity can also be included in an advertisement by using plot twists, poems, metaphors, voice changes, and puffery. The presence of celebrities also makes a big difference which is visible in majority of brands such as Maggie, Lux, Xiaomi, and many others.

Copywriters usually express creativity through language that includes deviations in pronunciation (Phonological Deviation) as evident in the case of Mother Dairy advertisement campaign of "very thundamental funda". Another deviation includes changes in the spelling (Graphological Deviation), which is present in brands such as Krack Foot cream and Xtra Premium, and in grammatical rules of omission or suspension, rule addition or omission as in "Connecting India" and "Your friend for life". Copywriters may often create new expressions for the creative copy, called lexical deviations (Sharma & Singh, 2006). Humor can also work wonders, as it creates a positive mindset. Particularly when it comes from visual and music, the examples can be "Happydent white" and the great "Amul butter" print series with "Amul girl", "Fevicol", "Mentos", Vodafone advertisements involving ZooZoos, etc.

Creativity has various interpretations, some of them are to include new elements, to present preexisting idea in a new form, generating a different idea, putting the old wine in the new bottle, etc. The definitions and interpretations also vary with respect to several areas of studies which make creativity a tricky area to study. There are innate parameters of creativity which, when present, make a particular advertisement alluring, eye catchy, and extremely creative as is identified by past research of Haberland and Dacin (1992), etc.

However, creativity is still at a research crossroad. There is a significant debate about the impact of creativity, and recent studies observe the increasing skepticism among the marketers to use creativity (Rosengren et al., 2020). Although there is a notion in current research that creativity affects the recall value, there is a lack of studies which establish it quantitatively and systematically in emerging markets. This chapter tries to establish the effect of creative parameters on recall value by using Structural Equational Modeling by first establishing the model of creative parameters identified through the past studies and linking them with recall value.

Literature Review

The studies of creativity and its application have started from the times of Guilford (1950). Guilford (1956) tried to develop a model for creativity by linking intelligence with it. There is also clarity that creativity is subjective and varies according to groups (MacKinnon, 1962), which leads to different interpretations of the definition and perception of creativity, making it a complicated area to study.

Some of the researches have based the definition of creativity on the extent to which an advertisement is able to achieve its goal or the targets and expectations of the organization (Duke & Sutherland, 2001; Kover et al., 1995). In advertising field, this definition has been varied in different researches, but most of them focus on two parameters – Divergence and Relevance that are considered to be the key determinants of the creative process (Mumford & Gustafson, 1988).

In past literature, relevance is considered to be the involvement of either the customer or brand to the product being advertised (Greenwald & Leavitt, 1984; Krugman, 1965; Thorson & Zhao, 1997; Petty & Cacioppo, 2012). In all of these researches, originality is perceived as one of the dimensions of creativity, which is explored further in the study by Haberland and Dacin (1992), Wells et al. (1989), and Sobel and Rothenberg (1980). The study by Besemer and Treffinger (1981) has associated novelty, that is, newness with creativity. According to Jackson and Messick (1965), who associated unusualness with creativity, infrequent or unusual factor can act as a divergence parameter and appropriateness, and condensation can act as relevance factor. This was also considered in the study by Tellis (1998).

Past studies by Duke and Sutherland (2001), and Nambiar et al. (2018) have identified imaginativeness as being one of the parameters for divergence. As imaginativeness can lead to several interpretations, it leads to generation of interest about the product or service being advertised and improves the recall value. The collection and combination of these parameters are the ones on which the divergence of the advertisement depends – that is, how significantly the advertisement is different from the others. Similarly, the relevance of the advertisement – either to consumer or through brand to consumer – is the measure of advertisement's relatability to the needs of the consumers. It has been found out that advertisements ridden with creativity grabs more attention, interest, message comprehension, and memorability in relation to curiosity, brand, and other pertinent traits in Hierarchy of Effects (HOE) model, creating positive image for the subsequent stages, which is also confirmed by the research by Smith et al. (2008).

The research by Smith and Yang (2004) has identified these determinants of divergence: fluency, flexibility, originality, elaboration, resistance to premature closure, unusual perspective, synthesis, humor, richness and colorfulness of imagery, fantasy, expression of emotion, empathic perspective, provocative question, and future orientation. The model for depiction of creativity will consist of the parameters as described by these past studies. It is hypothesized in the study that each of the constructs in the model of the creative parameter will have a significant and positive impact on the recall value.

Purpose of the Study

Although there is a notion that creativity affects advertisements in positive manner, little attention is paid to how a particular divergence parameter affects the recall value in emerging markets. The past studies in emerging markets have taken only two or three parameters into consideration while computing the effects of creativity on recall value.

This study considers the effect of 12 parameters that contribute to creativity in advertisements. These parameters are identified through past studies, and their effect on recall value is measured by using Structural Equational Modeling. By applying multivariate technique, the study analyzes the effect of creative parameters when they are present simultaneously in an advertisement, an aspect not included in past studies. Further, the participants in the study are from India, which is one of the emerging markets.

Method

As the divergence (Till & Baack, 2005; Smith & Yang, 2004) is associated with the creativity, this chapter considers some of the parameters which are usually found associated with creativity in the past studies and observes some of the common advertisements appearing in common media such as newspaper, television, and social media. Table 7.1 provides the set of parameters which are considered for this chapter.

Procedure

The procedure can be broadly classified in three stages: Pre-data collection – involves the formulation of a questionnaire, assessing its validity and reliability by appropriate content experts and pilot samples. Data collection – involves the collection of data from the sample participants in a quiet environment as to maintain participants' focus. Post-data collection – involves the analysis of data, developing a model using exploratory and confirmatory factor analysis, and identifying the combination of parameters that are best suited to enhance the recall value.

Pre-Data Collection

After identifying the parameters from the past studies, a questionnaire was developed to identify how the consumers perceive creativity associated with these parameters or, in other words, if included in a particular advertisement, how would these affect the creativity.

The questionnaire was tested by conducting a pilot study with participants who were university students constituting the age group 18–27 years from different metropolitan areas of India.

Table 7.1 Description of various creative parameters

S. No.	Parameter	Description
1.	Generate large number of ideas	Inclusion of large number of ideas with different perspectives in the advertisements.
2.	Unusualness in content	Utilizing ideas not commonly occurring in ad campaigns.
3.	Unexpected switch (Plot twist)	Rapid change of plot or progression in unexpected direction.
4.	Current issues	Involving topical issues or trending topics in order to generate interest.
5.	Imaginativeness	Content or plots that utilize the imaginativeness and based on fantasy or unreal situations.
6.	Attractiveness	Use of scintillating elements such as colors, decorations in the advertisement.
7.	Interesting message	Including messages that generate interest and enable customers relate with the product or service advertised.
8.	Ability to connect with emotions	Ideas presented roil a lot of emotions so there is direct connect with the campaign.
9.	Humor	Message that is found amusing or comical.
10.	Interest-generating details	Resistance to premature closure, allowing interest to be developed in customers' mind about the product or service advertised.
11.	Celebrity endorsement/ public figure	Ratifies the use of the product and service if associated with celebrity.
12.	Connecting unrelated details	Synthesis of ideas and connecting them in an appealing manner.

Source: Author's own

The questionnaire consisted of the following two sections:

1. Creative parameters: In this section, the participants had to rate the effect of identified parameters listed in Table 7.1 in making the advertisement creative on the Likert scale of 1–7: 1 being the least and 7 being the most.
2. Recall value: In this, a particular parameter was presented, and participants had to rate the items on the scale of 1–7: 1 being no details can be recalled and 7 being all details about brand logo, brand name, and advertisement can be recalled. This was based on their previous experiences with creative advertisements – that is, if they found the advertisement creative due to the parameters relevant for the study, how likely they were able to recall the contents of that particular advertisement.

The questions in the questionnaire developed by researcher were in the form: "Based on your previous experience, how likely are you to recall the details of advertisement with a particular creative parameter in it on the scale of 1–7: 1 being no details can be recalled and 7 being all details about brand logo, brand name and advertisement can be recalled". Other sections in the questionnaire measured the age, gender, and types of media where ads are encountered by participants.

To measure the validity of the questionnaire, that is, to make sure that the questionnaire measures the intended, four content experts were asked to rate the scale questions mentioned earlier on an ordinal scale of 1–4 to calculate I-CVI, which is mentioned by Lynn (1986) and Waltz and Bausell (1981). These were the ratings on the ordinal scale: 1 – not relevant/need not be considered, 2 – somewhat relevant/might be considered, 3 – quite relevant/may be considered, and 4 – highly relevant/should be considered. The response was then dichotomized into relevant (3 and 4 response on scale) and non-relevant (1 and 2 response on scale) regions as per the method proposed by Lynn (1986) and Waltz and Bausell (1981).

As all the items mentioned received a rating of either 3 or 4, each item of the questionnaire falls in the relevant zone. Hence, the I-CVI comes out to be 1.00, which was recommended by Lynn (1986), that in a panel constituting at most five experts, each member should have agreed on the questionnaire elements for content validity to hold true, for an effective representation of entire population. To compute the S-CVI, universal agreement among experts (S-CVI/UA) was used, which caters to the quite/very relevant rating from the raters (Waltz & Bausell, 1981). As all the ratings are either 3 or 4, condition of universal agreement holds true, and hence S-CVI also has the value 1.00. Therefore, this questionnaire is valid.

For reliability, that is whether the responses are consistent throughout, the questionnaire was used in a pilot study and was followed by calculating the Cronbach's alpha for the responses, which yielded an overall reliability of 0.821. The observed value is more than the recommended value of 0.7 (Taber, 2018); hence, this questionnaire is reliable too and can be used in further study.

For the data collection stage, the participants were asked to fill out the questionnaire in a quiet environment in order to avoid any distractions. After the data collection, the responses were analyzed by using R language. The pilot study constituted 20 participants within age group of 18 to 27 years. In the main study, the number was 145, and the participants were chosen randomly from the population. The participants were from India, one of the emerging markets. The demographic details of participants in the main study include – Age: 19–48 years and Gender: 44.8% females and 55.2% males. The sample can be considered to be a representative of the population as the gender proportion (1.23 males per 1 female), and the average age of the sample (24.5 years) is in lieu of national averages of gender proportion (1.08 males per 1 female) and average age (26.46 years).

Results

It can be noted from the first section of the questionnaire that majority (88.9%) of the participants in the study encountered advertisements through social media platforms such as Faccbook, Instagram, WhatsApp, WeChat, and Tumblr. These media are followed by other media – newspaper and magazines 83 (57.2%), television 79 (54.4%), online TV shows 74 (51%), mobile applications 75 (51.7%), and radio 25 (17.2%). This gives a clear estimate about the media through which advertisements are seen.

To generate the model, first KMO index was calculated in order to measure the sampling adequacy. The overall KMO index obtained was 0.75, which is more than the recommended value of 0.5; therefore, the parameters can be used to develop a model.

Before running the exploratory factor analysis, the number of latent variables should be identified. In order to determine them, eigenvalue criterion is used, which involves selection of the factors having eigenvalue greater than 1. As Figure 7.1 shows, the number of latent variables is four in this case.

After obtaining the number of latent variables, exploratory factor analysis was used with Varimax rotation. Table 7.2 shows the grouping of the parameters under these latent variables as the results for exploratory factor analysis. The grouped variables under latent variables in columns have been presented in boldface. Table 7.2 also indicates the representative symbol used in Figures 7.2 and 7.3.

The four latent variables were named as:

MR1: Content Hub
MR2: Topical
MR3: Universal Tactics
MR4: Imaginative Realm

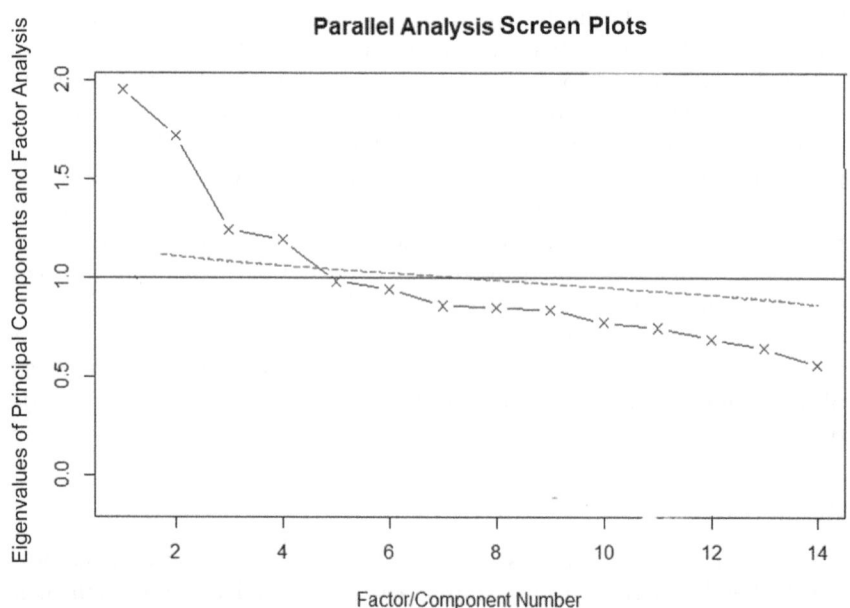

Figure 7.1 Number of latent variables by parallel analysis

Table 7.2 Results for exploratory factor analysis

S. No.	Parameter	MR1	MR2	MR3	MR4
1.	Generating large number of ideas (M)	**0.49**	−0.05	−0.06	0.07
2.	Unusualness in content (UD1)	**0.48**	0.19	0.10	−0.07
3.	Unexpected switch (US)	0.07	0.08	**0.44**	−0.07
4.	Current issues (CI)	−0.01	**0.52**	−0.20	−0.08
5.	Imaginativeness (F)	0.10	−0.14	0.06	**0.49**
6.	Attractiveness (AC)	−0.03	0.04	−0.12	**0.48**
7.	Interesting message (CM)	−0.17	0.24	0.08	**0.44**
8.	Ability to connect with emotions (EC)	−0.03	**0.58**	−0.05	0.06
9.	Humor (H)	0.06	−0.02	**0.61**	0.26
10.	Interest-generating details (IAD)	0.18	0.07	0.06	**0.42**
11.	Celebrity endorsement (CE)	−0.13	−0.09	**0.53**	−0.08
12.	Connecting unrelated details (ACUD)	**0.49**	−0.01	0.03	−0.03

Source: Author's own

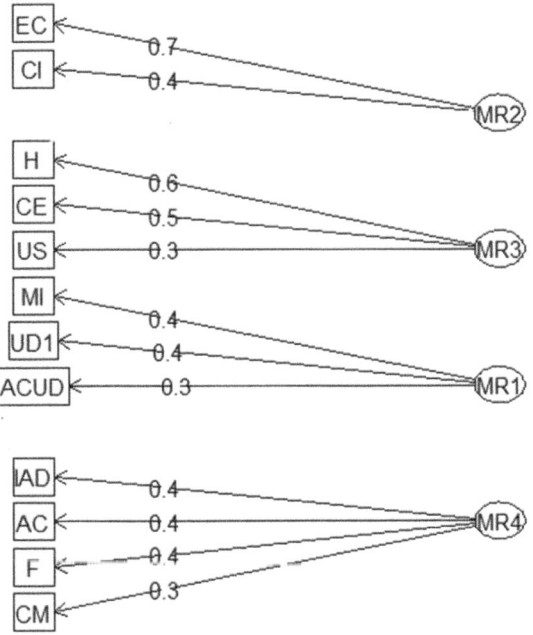

Figure 7.2 EFA results

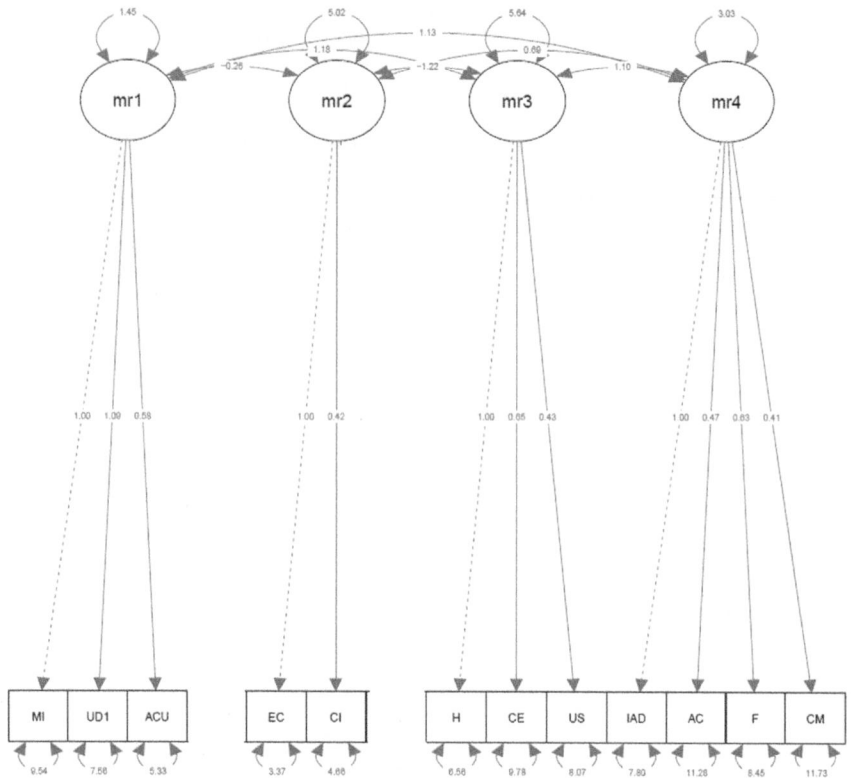

Figure 7.3 Structural model results

The results for the exploratory factor analysis are valid as RMSEA value is 0.038 which is lower than 0.05, and a good fit according to MacCallum et al. (1996). Further, TLI value is 0.89 which is comparable to an ideal fit value of 0.9. Figure 7.2 shows the results of exploratory factor analysis.

To get a further idea that the model is valid, confirmatory factor analysis was also used, with the same model as obtained by exploratory factor analysis. The results obtained were in accordance with the standard values: RMSEA value was 0.058, RMSR was 0.043, and CFI was 0.91.

Hence, the model can be used to determine the impact of creative parameters on recall value. To do this, the data from section 2 of the questionnaire was utilized. Figure 7.3 shows the estimates from the structural equation model, and for simplicity error terms are not shown.

Table 7.3 shows the correlations of recall value with the latent variables observed.

After this, the critical ratio was computed in order to validate the hypothesis proposed in the earlier sections. Table 7.4 shows the critical ratio values and the results of hypothesis as accepted or rejected.

Table 7.3 Correlation values

Correlation between	Value
Recall value – Topical	0.78
Recall value – Content Hub	0.73
Recall value – Universal Tactics	0.68
Recall value – Imaginative Realm	0.64

Source: Author's own

Table 7.4 Hypothesis results

Hypothesis	Critical ratio	Result
Topical variables will have a significant and positive correlation with recall value.	5.66	Accepted
Content Hub variables will have a significant and positive correlation with recall value.	6.75	Accepted
Universal Tactics variables will have a significant and positive correlation with recall value.	7.01	Accepted
Imaginative Realm variables will have a significant and positive correlation with recall value.	5.13	Accepted

Source: Author's own

Discussion and Conclusion

There are four latent variables identified in the study. The organization of latent variable was done on the basis of similarity among the underlying variables. The "content hub" is the first latent variable, which caters to the content of advertisement and includes the parameters generating large number of ideas, connecting unrelated details and unusualness in content. The content hub includes all the details that are loaded with information. The second latent variable is slightly different as it focuses on current issues and emotional connection; resultantly, it is named as "topical". All the contemporary content that is related with news and is situational falls under the category of second latent variable.

The parameters such as humor, unexpected plot twist, and celebrity endorsement were organized and put under the umbrella of the third latent variable called "Universal tactics". The parameters used under this variable are universally accepted and aid the advertisement for creative depiction. The techniques classified under this latent variable have indelible impact as they engross the viewers by binding them emotionally. The fourth latent variable is named as "Imaginative realm" as it explores the imaginative power of the consumer by including parameters such as fantasy, interest-generating details, attractiveness, and interesting message. This is a significant latent variable as its representation is such that the consumers get engaged by doing interpretations as per their understanding.

Tables 7.3 and 7.4 clearly depict that each of the creative parameters positively impacts the viewers; therefore, it can be concluded that these parameters lead to an increase in unaided recall value. Therefore, it is necessary for marketers in emerging markets to use creative parameters in the advertisement to ensure that it gets retained in the minds of the audience. It is also clear from the results that all of the creative parameters lead to an increase in recall value according to the study of Till and Baack (2005), which stated that creativity in advertisements leads to an increase in the unaided recall value. Further, the results of the parameters humor and ability to connect with emotions on recall value are in line with the study of Srivastava (2020). In all, for emerging markets, creativity in advertisements is necessary to increase the recall value of the product/service being advertised.

Implications and Future Scope

Conferring to the ongoing debate about the use of creativity in the advertising for positive results (Rosengren et al., 2020), the study indicates that creativity is necessary to improve the recall value of the advertisements in emerging markets. Results also describe that advertising creativity generates positive responses in terms of recall value that exceeds only being a source of attention. Advertisers can utilize the creative elements mentioned in the study to improve the memorability of the product or service promoted.

Moreover, future research can be aligned to identify the most effective creative element from the identified parameters. A study can be conducted to facilitate understanding of how affect transfer, processing, and signaling contribute to make advertising investments less unpredictable as mentioned in the study by West et al. (2019). The study can also be extended to other measurable traits such as willingness to buy, advertising believability, and aided recall.

References

Albrow, M. (1990). *Globalization, Knowledge and Society*, edited by M. Albrow and E. King. London: Sage.

Ang, S. H., Lee, Y. H., & Leong, S. M. (2007). The ad creativity cube: Conceptualization and initial validation. *Journal of the Academy of Marketing Science*, 35(2), 220–232.

Belch, G. E., & Belch, M. A. (2003). *Advertising and Promotion: An Integrated Marketing Communications Perspective*. Boston: The McGraw–Hill.

Besemer, S. P., & Treffinger, D. J. (1981). Analysis of creative products: Review and synthesis. *The Journal of Creative Behavior*, 15(3), 158–178.

Bhandari, K. R., & Raut, S. K. (2019). 9 Leveraging tacit. *Advances in Management Research: Innovation and Technology*, 1(1), 127–138.

Duke, L., & Sutherland, J. (2001). Toward a confluence model of advertising creative concepts. In *Proceedings of the Conference-American Academy of Advertising* (pp. 231–231). Pullman, WA: American Academy of Advertising, 1999.

Edell, J. A., & Burke, M. C. (1987). The power of feelings in understanding advertising effects. *Journal of Consumer Research*, 14(3), 421–433.

Greenwald, A. G., & Leavitt, C. (1984). Audience involvement in advertising: Four levels. *Journal of Consumer Research*, 11(1), 581–592.

Guilford, J. P. (1950). Creativity research: Past, present and future. *American Psychologist*, 5(1), 444–454.

Guilford, J. P. (1956). The structure of intellect. *Psychological Bulletin*, 53(4), 267.

Haberland, G. S., & Dacin, P. A. (1992). *The Development of a Measure to Assess Viewers' Judgments of the Creativity of an Advertisement: A Preliminary Study*. New York: ACR North American Advances.

Jackson, P. W., & Messick, S. (1965). The person, the product, and the response: Conceptual problems in the assessment of creativity. *Journal of Personality*, 33(3), 309–329.

Keller, K. L., & Moorthi, Y. L. R. (2003). Branding in developing markets. *Business Horizons*, 46(3), 49–49.

Khanna, T., Palepu, K. G., & Sinha, J. (2005). Strategies that fit emerging markets. *Harvard Business Review*, 83(6), 4–19.

Kover, A. J., Goldberg, S. M., & James, W. L. (1995). Creativity vs. effectiveness? An integrating classification for advertising. *Journal of Advertising Research*, 35(6), 29–41.

Krugman, H. E. (1965). The impact of television advertising: Learning without involvement. *Public Opinion Quarterly*, 29(3), 349–356.

Lynn, M. R. (1986). Determination and quantification of content validity. *Nursing Research*, 35(6), 382–385.

MacCallum, R. C., Browne, M. W., & Sugawara, H. M. (1996). Power analysis and determination of sample size for covariance structure modeling. *Psychological Methods*, 1(2), 130.

MacKinnon, D. W. (1962). The nature and nurture of creative talent. *American Psychologist*, 17(7), 484.

Mumford, M. D., & Gustafson, S. B. (1988). Creativity syndrome: Integration, application, and innovation. *Psychological Bulletin*, 103(1), 27.

Nambiar, B. K., Ramanathan, H. N., Rana, S., & Prashar, S. (2018). Perceived service quality and customer satisfaction: A missing link in Indian banking sector. *Vision*, 23(1), 44–55.

Petty, R. E., & Cacioppo, J. T. (2012). *Communication and Persuasion: Central and Peripheral Routes to Attitude Change*. New York: Springer Science & Business Media.

Rana, S., Prashar, S., Barai, M. K., & Hamid, A. B. A. (2021). Determinants of international marketing strategy for emerging market multinationals. *International Journal of Emerging Markets*, 16(2), 154–178.

Rana, S., Raut, S. K., Prashar, S., & Hamid, A. B. A. (2020b). Promoting through consumer nostalgia: A conceptual framework and future research agenda. *Journal of Promotion Management*, 27(2), 211–249.

Rana, S., Raut, S. K., Prashar, S., & Quttainah, M. A. (2020a). The transversal of nostalgia from psychology to marketing: What does it portend for future research? *International Journal of Organizational Analysis*, Vol. ahead-of-print No. ahead-of-print.

Raut, S. K., Sakpal, S., & Soni, R. (2022). Understanding the service quality dimensions and achieving resilience in service retail. In *Handbook of Research* on *Supply Chain Resiliency, Efficiency, and Visibility in the Post-Pandemic Era*, edited by Ramakrishna Yanamandra (pp. 136–156). IGI Global, UAE. https://doi.org/10.4018/978-1-7998-9506-0

Reinartz, W., & Saffert, P. (2013). Creativity in advertising: When it works and when it doesn't. *Harvard Business Review, 91*(6), 106–111.

Rosengren, S., Eisend, M., Koslow, S., & Dahlen, M. (2020). A meta-analysis of when and how advertising creativity works. *Journal of Marketing, 84*(6), 39–56.

Sabir, S., Rafique, A., & Abbas, K. (2019). Institutions and FDI: Evidence from developed and developing countries. *Financial Innovation, 5*(1), 8.

Sharma, S., & Singh, R. (2006). *Advertising: Planning and Implementation.* New Delhi: PHI Learning Private Limited.

Smith, R. E., Chen, J., & Yang, X. (2008). The impact of advertising creativity on the hierarchy of effects. *Journal of Advertising, 37*(4), 47–62.

Smith, R. E., & Yang, X. (2004). Toward a general theory of creativity in advertising: Examining the role of divergence. *Marketing Theory, 4*(1–2), 31–58.

Sobel, R. S., & Rothenberg, A. (1980). Artistic creation as stimulated by superimposed versus separated visual images. *Journal of Personality and Social Psychology, 39*(5), 953.

Srivastava, R. K. (2020). Comparing the three types of approach of advertising in brand building in emerging markets. *Journal of Strategic Marketing*, 1–14.

Taber, K. S. (2018). The use of Cronbach's alpha when developing and reporting research instruments in science education. *Research in Science Education, 48*(6), 1273–1296.

Tellis, G. J. (1998). *Advertising and Sales Promotion Strategy.* Prentice Hall. London.

Thorson, E., & Zhao, X. (1997). Television viewing behavior as an indicator of commercial effectiveness. *Measuring Advertising Effectiveness*, 221–237.

Till, B. D., & Baack, D. W. (2005). Recall and persuasion: Does creative advertising matter? *Journal of Advertising, 34*(3), 47–57.

Waltz, C. F., & Bausell, R. B. (1981). *Nursing Research: Design, Statistics, and Computer Analysis.* Philadelphia: F.A. Davis Co.

West, D., Koslow, S., & Kilgour, M. (2019). Future directions for advertising creativity research. *Journal of Advertising, 48*(1), 102–114.

8 Energy Star Labels in Promoting Energy

Efficient Appliances in India

Gauri Joshi, Pratima Sheorey, Rajesh Panda and Ravi Kulkarni

Introduction and Background of Eco-Labels

Product labels form an important part of a product as they are used to inform the consumers about the product quality and performance, ingredients, and safe use and care (Schwartz, 1980). Product labels enable consumers to take informed decisions with regards to product quality, product price, and safety (Bettman et al., 1986). Labels in the form of trademarks and brand names form a part of a rich ritual of practices which sellers have developed to assure buyers of the genuineness of their products or services. They are often aimed to attend to changing buyer demands and new competitive positions in the market (Boer, 2003; Rana, 2018a; Rana 2018b).

Product labelling is an important tool for facilitating consumer purchases when other forms of quality signalling are inadequate (Bonroy & Constantatos, 2011). It is estimated that the usage and importance of product labels as information-providing vehicles are likely to grow with the increasing scientific evidence (Voon et al., 2013).

Firms propose products containing the desired attributes at many different levels creating varieties with different levels of quality (Bonroy & Constantatos, 2011; Nambiar et al., 2018). In terms of understanding the attributes of a product, the goods whose attributes can be known before purchase are termed as 'search goods', the goods whose attributes can be verified after purchase are 'experience' goods, and the goods whose attributes cannot be verified even after purchase or consumption are 'credence goods'. The credence goods pose a problem as consumers are unable to check the attributes in such kind of goods (Dulleck & Kerschbamer, 2006). Environmental labelling has emerged as one of the 'promising forms' of environmental information policy in terms of providing appropriate and pertinent information to the consumers (Hansen & Kull, 1994) (Energiministeriet, 1995)

Signalling of credence qualities is possible through eco-labelling, which serves as third-party certification process from a reliable certification agent, whom consumers can trust (Bleda & Valente, 2009). Thus, eco-labels can be thought of as being "seals of environmental approval" awarded by public or private organizations (Brau & Carraro, 1999). Producers who apply

DOI: 10.4324/9781003315582-9

for a label and meet the standards are awarded a license for its use on their product. This label informs the consumer about the environmental impact of the product that is otherwise unknown.

The eco-labels are designed to offset this information asymmetry between manufacturers/providers and consumers in various domains (Codagnone et al., 2016). They enable in educating the consumers on the environmental friendliness of a product (Taufique et al., 2014). Eco-labels are defined as *a tool for consumers to enable decision making for select environmentally friendly products and also enable them to know how products are made* (Rex & Baumann, 2007). Eco-labels can also be thought of as being "attractive instruments" informing consumers about the environmental impact of their purchasing decisions (Nik Abdul Rashid, 2009). The presence of an eco-label has positive impact on consumer's knowledge about green product which impacts their purchase intention.

An eco-label commonly known as "environmental certification" is a market-based instrument that awards a label or certification to a company or product in acknowledgment of having met certain environmental impact standards (Washington & Ababouch, 2011). Eco-labels have been produced (Berry et al., 2005) as a result of mandatory labelling schemes or voluntary labelling initiatives. These labels communicate aspects of sustainable consumption to consumers and can potentially influence consumers to make positive choices for the environment (Peattie, 1995). Eco-labels are believed to promote sustainable consumption.

The effectiveness of an eco-label depends not only on the manner in which the information is presented but also on the ability of the consumer to absorb and act upon it (Teisl, 2003). The label becomes truly effective when consumers can differentiate competing products on the basis of key environmental performance attributes (Lee & Geistfeld, 1998). Eco-labels enable to communicate the non-observable product characteristics of environmentally friendly products (Bleda & Valente, 2009). From a business perspective, eco-labels are 'environmental management tools' that guide customers on the product's new green feature in a new way (Thøgersen et al., 2010). Working in parallel, governmental institutions try to guarantee transparency in the markets and encourage responsible consumption of goods and services. This creates a cyclical dynamic between three levels: consumers, firms, and governmental institutions. As compared to the emerging economies, the developed economies have a higher number of eco-labels like the Blue Angel in Germany and the Nordic Swan in Scandinavia, Fairtrade Logo in the United States, the leaping Bunny logo of the Coalition for Consumer Information on (Cosmetics), government agencies, the organic label of the (U.S. Department of Agriculture) (Atkinson & Rosenthal, 2014).

The Energy Star Label as Eco-Label in Indian Context

In the Indian context, first there are few labels and second fewer studies based on the utility of labels to consumers in decision-making. In the case of developing economies like India, the eco-labelling schemes are of two types: one sponsored by the Government and the other by the non-Government organizations (NGOs) (Joshi, 2004). In the Indian context, the presence of Eco mark (an eco-label introduced by the Government of India in 1991) and the energy star labelling by the Bureau of Energy indicate the efficiency of an appliance.

The present study seeks to understand consumers' perception towards the eco-labels on the home appliances. Home appliances are chosen as a category to study the impact of labels due to the following reasons:

- The usage of home appliances is visible to others in the society (other consumers),
- The usage of home appliances is ubiquitous in an emerging economy like India, and, finally,
- The home appliances have an energy label on them.

The energy star label in this case is the eco-label enabling the consumers to take informed decisions by understanding the label. Studies on checking the effectiveness of the energy star on consumer's decision-making while appliance purchase are few in the Indian context (Chunekar A., 2014) (Jain et al., 2018), and hence this study makes an important contribution with regards to it.

The growing concern over the environmental impact and India's energy security led to acknowledging the benefits of having energy efficiency (Singh et al., 2011). The energy star eco-label was an outcome of this concern which led the Government of India to establish the Bureau of Energy Efficiency (BEE) with the primary intention of reducing the energy intensity. The BEE commenced its Standard & Labelling Program (S & L) program in 2006 wherein it just got 14 products under its purview with mandated labelling on 4 products namely the frost-free refrigerators, room air conditioners (ACs), fluorescent tube lights and distribution transformers, and the remaining under the voluntary labelling scheme (Singh et al., 2011). Subsequently, with the increasing demand for home appliances, additional appliances were also mandated by the BEE for Energy star rating. This energy star eco-label was new to the Indian consumer as till date they had been accustomed to unbranded appliances manufactured by local players (Sheth, 2011) with limited or almost no Government control. The aspect of getting the home appliance certified (if it was under mandatory category) was new for the local manufacturers, and it faced some resistance as the manufacturers had to undergo additional checks over the ISI and ISO certifications. An energy label is shown in Figure 8.1.

The program envisaged that the information would reduce the energy usage of the residential consumer as urban households in India contribute to 45% of total energy usage nationally (Ramachandra & Aithal, 2017–18). The labelling programme spanned over 21 products, wherein mandatory disclosure of energy savings potential was applicable for eight appliances. The appliances like fixed-speed room air conditioners, refrigerators (frost

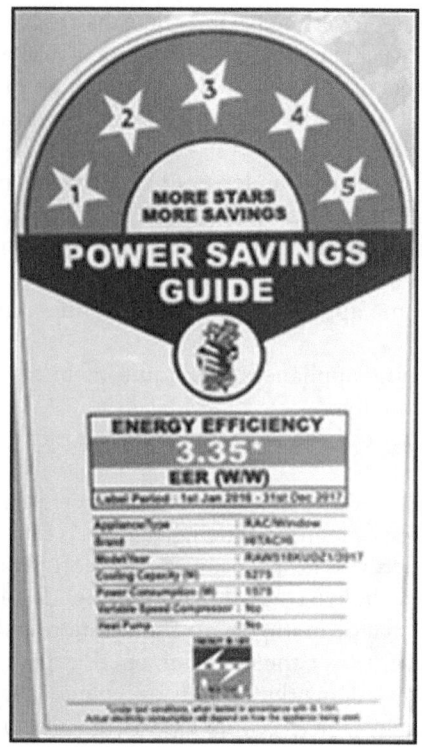

Figure 8.1 Energy star label on appliance
Source: Author

free and direct cool), fluorescent tube lights, distribution transformers, electric water heaters, and TVs were covered under the mandatory labelling program and were classified as being energy efficient. The label was placed on the visible portion of the appliance, and it provided information on the energy-saving potential of some of the most commonly used residential appliances. Despite the presence of information campaigns to increase the consumer awareness in developing countries, studies indicate that increasing awareness and the existence of a positive attitude do not necessarily imply a change in the consumer's purchase and consumption behaviour (Atănăsoaie, 2013).

The objective of this chapter is to check the residential consumer's understanding, awareness, and interpretation of the energy star eco-label on appliances. It checks if the energy labels prompt the consumer's appliance purchase decisions or inhibits their decisions of purchasing an eco-labelled appliance. In the context of an emerging economy, there is compelling reason for the Indian consumers to prefer the eco-labelled appliances as the Government of India is keen on ending the system of cross subsidization of end consumer tariffs (Ranajoy Bhattacharyya, 2017). As the country progresses towards achieving the Sustainable Development Goal 7 of energy access to all, it has accounted for the increased energy-related pollution (International Energy Agency, 2020), and thus assessing the consumer's perceptions towards eco-labelled appliances is vital.

The study is based in a tier 2 city (Pune) in the state of Maharashtra, a state which has the highest domestic tariffs for electricity and which also records the highest number of emissions in the country. The city has second highest growth rate of 40% after Mumbai (the financial capital of India). The city is also chosen to be one of the 'Smart Cities' in India. The study uses a sample of households residing in the city and possessing more than three appliances. The study uses the exploratory sequential sampling technique in which qualitative studies were used to inform the subsequent quantitative phase.

The qualitative study is validated using a structured questionnaire administered to around 600 respondents online (through questionpro.com) living within the Pune city limits to check their understanding, awareness, and interpretation of energy star labels on the appliances. The researchers abided by the ethical guidelines of the research as there was strict confidentiality maintained, and no data was shared with any outsider. The IP addresses were not shared with anybody in cases where data was collected online. The participants were all above the age of consent, and hence no special consent was required. The respondents were not bribed or coerced or incentivized to answer the questionnaire.

The Indian Consumer and Appliance Purchase Behaviour

The studies on the purchase pattern of appliances from emerging countries like India yield interesting findings. The consumers from emerging economy instead of emulating the purchase pattern of the upper class in their country emulated the middle class of the West (Holt et al., 2004). As a result of which the middle class from the low industrialized countries, on possession of discretionary income, spent it in purchasing the items that would elevate their status in the society and signal that they had 'arrived' (Ü STÜNER & Holt, 2009). In the Indian context, this may be the reason for the increase in the microwave and food preparation appliance purchases in India between 2009 and 2014 (Tawichai, 2014). While the influence of cooking Western food is catching up among the Indian middle class consumers, there is also the availability of disposable income among the consumers (Tawichai, 2014). International studies indicate the shift in consumption pattern from necessity to discretionary as the country witnesses economic growth and increase in per capita income (Mukherjee et al., 2012). The demographic profile and the income of the household have changed resulting in a change in the demand perspective (Sinha & Kar, 2007). The increase in the purchase of appliances could also be due to the increase in the educational qualifications of women thus enabling them to enter the workforce and the replacement of joint family system with nuclear families (Mukherjee et al., 2012). This has further increased the propensity of investing in home appliances to ease the work at home. With women joining the workforce, shopping patterns also have changed. The increasing awareness, easier access, and changing lifestyle have been the key growth drivers for the consumer market. The rising incomes and declining prices of appliances have escalated the demand for residential, commercial appliances in India over the last few years (Abhyankar et al., 2017).

The Government of India's policies and regulatory frameworks, such as easing of license rules and consent of 51 per cent Foreign Direct Investment (FDI) in multi-brand and 100 per cent in single-brand retail, are the major growth drivers for the consumer market (Indian Brand Equity Foundation, 2020). This change in the socio-economic structure has also led to a changed socio-economic classification system.

In terms of income and wealth diversity in India, the consumers in the Indian society were classified under various socio-economic categories based on the occupation and the level of education of the chief wage earner. However, with the changes in the economy, this pattern has been altered to classify the consumers on the basis of the educational qualifications of the chief wage earner in the household and the number of assets owned (out of a pre-specified list of 11 assets). Based on these parameters, each household is classified under one of 12 SEC groups. The 11 assets namely electricity connection, ceiling fan, gas stove, fridge, two-wheeler vehicle, washing machine, colour TV, computer, four-wheeler vehicle, air conditioner, and agricultural land (in rural areas) and possessing a postgraduate degree are classified under A1; slightly a smaller number of durables and graduation are classified under A2; and so on. In the context of the existing study, the respondents from SEC A1, A2, and A3 were selected as this category had higher number of durables as compared to the others. The new SEC system is shown in Table 8.1

In terms of preference for branded products, Indian consumer acknowledges the association of brand name with value (Ramachander, 1988). The brand loyalty and preferences for brands are strongly linked in India (Gupta & Singh, 2007). Indian consumers are also price sensitive (Joseph & Soundararajan, 2009; Khare et al., 2014). These studies are done on the conventional products and not on eco-labelled products. In the context of understanding consumer's preference for labels, the Indian market so far has no system to collect consumer's purchase behaviour and store choices (Mukherjee et al., 2012; Rana et al., 2020a).

In the case of eco-labelled products, studies have shown that consumers are unable to interpret the information on the label as they do not understand the terms related to the guarantee of green products (Cervellon & Lindsey, 2011). This study subsequently checks the consumer knowledge in terms of awareness of the label and its intended use with respect to energy star eco-label.

Table 8.1 The new socio-economic classification in India

Number of owned durables	Education of the CWE						
	Illiterate	Literate but no formal school/ School up to 4 yrs.	School: 5 to 9 years	SSC/ HSC	Some College (incl. Diploma) but not Grad	Grad/ PG: General	Grad/PG: Professional
	1	2	3	4	5	6	7
None	E3	E2	E1	E1	D2	D2	D2
1	E3	E1	E2	E2	D2	D2	D2
2	E1	E1	D2	D2	D1	D1	D1
3	D2	D2	D1	D1	C2	C2	C2
4	D1	C2	C2	C1	C1	B2	B2
5	C2	C1	C1	B2	B1	B1	B1
6	C1	B2	B2	B1	A3	A3	A3
7	C1	B1	B1	A3	A3	A2	A2
8	B1	A3	A3	A3	A2	A2	A2
9+	B1	A3	A3	A2	A2	A1	A1

Source: Broadcast Audience Research Council India, September 2015

The Consumer Durables Industry in India

The consumer durables industry is the fastest growing segment in India. Reports indicate the increase in the demand of consumer durables in the urban markets (65%) along with the possibility of increasing the demand in rural India after rural electrification. The consumer durables market was posed to increase by CAGR of 15 percent from Financial Year 2010 to Financial Year 2020 (Statista, 2021). The estimates by the Index of Industrial Production (IIP, India) had projected growth of 8.5% for the consumer durables industry for the year 2018–19. The consumer durables industry in India is categorized in two: Brown goods and White goods as shown in Table 8.2.

The consumer spending in excess of more than 40% is accounted by consumer durables (Kulshreshtha et al., 2017). As the spending evolves, there is a shift in the factors driving the purchase of appliances (PWC, 2018). This would result in a growth of the Indian consumer durables and electronics industry by 9 percent in the next four to five years. Major demand for the appliances (almost 65%) of it is from the urban market, and the remaining is from the rural markets (Sarangi, 2016). In terms of the home appliance enterprises, the emerging markets differ from the developed markets in terms of their large-scale domestic enterprises, which are larger in their domestic market than the largest multinational corporation in the United States, Japan, Europe, South Korea, Canada, and Australia (Sheth, 2011; Rana et al., 2020b). The presence of unbranded products (to the extent of

Table 8.2 Consumer Durables industry in India

Consumer Durables industry in India	
Brown Goods	*White Goods*
Television, DVD Player & CD, Laptops and Electronic accessories Audio Systems, Personal Computers, Digital camera, and Camcorders	Air-conditioners, Washing machines, electric fans, microwave ovens Refrigerator, Sewing machine, cleaning equipment and other domestic appliances

Source: Indian Brand Equity Foundation

more than 60%) due to affordability and lack of regulations to keep such unbranded products in control results in difficulty in regulating the effective and efficient Government standards (Sheth, 2011). In the context of making online purchase of the appliances, the lack of access to the Internet of all strata of population makes the presence of brick-and-mortar stores essential for selling the home appliances in India (Akalamkam & Mitra, 2017). Additionally, in the Indian context, home appliances are also a part of electric and hardware stores in some cases. There is also a surge of company-owned stores in the appliance retail sector (Indian Brand Equity Foundation, 2020). Hence, unlike in the developed countries where appliances are majorly purchased online, in India there is sufficient sale of appliances offline and in-store. The offline purchase provides another opportunity to assess the consumer's understanding along with the retailer's understanding of the importance placed on purchasing an eco-labelled appliance over a conventional one.

There has been vast amount of literature on understanding the consumer's preferences of durables in the emerging markets; however, not much has been studied about Indian consumers (Kulshreshtha et al., 2017). Despite the prominence of energy labelling worldwide, there is limited research on the consumer's perceptions and preference towards these labels (Weil & McMahon, 2003; Ha & Janda, 2012).

Indian Consumer's Label Understanding and Label Preference

This section lays the foundation for the study undertaken by defining the Standards and Labelling and then moving on with the conceptual model for the study. First to define Standard, it is a kind of rule or is made up of a family of rules such as 'principles' and 'criteria' in addition to other kinds of rules. Standards are voluntary rules in contrast to directives (such as law) (Brunsson & Jacobsson, 2000). Standards are explicit, written, and codified, in contrast to norms; and labelling is about steering actors (policy instruments) and informing about buying options (information). Labels are categorical claims. Labellers generally claim that labelled products are better for the environment, health, animal welfare, social justice, and so forth than competing 'conventional' products. Such claims need to be legitimized by reference to authoritative knowledge claims, which are typically provided by scientific studies.

In the Indian context, the Standards and Labelling (S & L) (Ministry of Power, Government of India, 2015) has been a well-known policy instrument used to promote energy efficiency (Chunekar A., 2014). Standards are commonly called minimum energy performance standard (MEPS). Labels rate the appliances on the basis to their energy efficiency and help consumers make informed decisions on their purchases (Chunekar A., 2014). However, from a consumer's perspective, recognizing a label is not same as understanding it (Thøgersen, 2000). Consumer will use the label information in decision making if they trust the information it conveys (Hansen & Kull, 1994). Many studies in the past have found that consumers are sceptical about green product claims (Peattie, 1995). The increasing competition results in companies trying to exaggerate their product attributes by making unconfirmed false claims (Carlson et al., 1993). These repeated false claims result in consumer's backlash towards eco-labelled products as they are constantly misled. Such actions result in consumers doubting the environmental claims on the labels. This has been proved by research from countries like the United States and Peoples Republic of China that consumers are sceptical about environmental claims made by the company (Chan & Lau, 2004).

Studies on graded eco-label by Bleda & Valente (2009) focus on checking the effectiveness of the eco-label through economic models. Studies have also revealed the lack of information on Government-mandated labels that disable consumer's ability to take appropriate decision (Davis & Metcalf, 2014). In the Asian context, studies on checking the impact of eco-labelling electric appliances on consumer's purchase behaviour have been conducted in China, South Korea (Jeong & Kim, 2015), Malaysia, and Indonesia (Hathaway & Zhao, 2011) to name some. Studies also reveal that information provided by public and other independent sources is trusted more than the information provided by the retailer or the producer (Schlegelmilch et al., 1996). In terms of assimilation of information from the eco-labels, the consumer must be aware of the environmental hazards of purchasing the products which are not eco-labelled (Thøgersen, 2000). This indicates that prior to making the purchase, the consumer must be aware of the environmental impacts of the product usage, know about the existence of the eco-labels, trust the authenticity of the labels (Thøgersen, 2000), and must be willing to take extra efforts to search the products which are eco-labelled (Carrington et al., 2014).

Consumer's Green Purchase Behaviour and Purchase Intentions

In the context of this study, to check the consumer's consideration towards eco-labels especially on appliances, one needs to check the consumer's intention to make a green purchase, viz., the purchase of goods which have minimum impact on the environment. Green purchase behaviour or environmentally friendly purchase is the practice in which consumer considers the environmental impact of buying, utilizing, and discarding various products or using various green services. While consumers are enthusiastic on making green purchases, evidence suggesting the increase in sale of environmentally friendly products over a period is little (Bray et al., 2011). This implies that though consumers display positive attitude towards green products, their actions do not reflect their environment-friendly attitude.

Customer's purchase behaviour is assumed to be a consequence of his purchase intention (Ajzen, 1991). Information on consumer's intentions is used by firms in predicting the future sales. However, measuring intentions to predict the behaviour is not always straightforward. It is observed by researchers (Carrington et al., 2014; Auger & Devinney, 2007) that certain kind of intentions do not lead to actual enacting of behaviour especially when the purchase involves ethical goods, environmental-friendly goods, quitting smoking, etc.

Intentions are assumed to be predecessors of actual behaviour (Ajzen, 1991). Intentions control the motivational factors influencing the decision-making process (Ramayah et al., 2010). The intention to purchase is a key factor to calculate consumer behaviour (Fishbein & Ajzen, 1975). In some instances, consumer's intention has been used as a predictor for actual behaviour (Follows & Jobber, 2000). Purchase intention as defined by Fishbein & Ajzen (1975) is the 'willingness or readiness to purchase certain product or service as displayed by an individual'. In context of this research, as the purchase intention indicates purchasing an energy star eco-labelled appliance which can reduce energy consumption and thus emissions, hence the intention is termed as Green Purchase Intention. Thereby these appliances reduce emissions and conserve environment. Hence, the purchase of such appliances can also be termed as green purchase behaviour. The energy star-labelled appliances and energy-efficient appliances are used interchangeably throughout the chapter.

The study adapts the theory of planned behaviour (Ajzen, 1991) to study the impact of intentions on the consumer's purchase behaviour. It also uses the loss aversion aspect of the Prospect theory (Kahneman & Tversky, 1979) to explain caution exercised by consumers to avoid loss which they perceive could be a result of investing in eco-labelled product.

Consumer's Perceptions of Eco-Labelled Appliance Purchase

1   Risk Perceptions

In addition to the issues of affordability and willingness to pay, the consumers perceive energy- star-labelled appliances riskier as compared to conventional ones. Perceived risk towards future energy savings by investing in energy-efficient (EE) appliances has been a barrier to adoption of energy-star-labelled appliances (Christie & Walton, 2011). The effect of risk aversion has received little attention in understanding the barriers to energy-efficient investments. In another study on assessing the risk preferences of individuals, it was noted that individuals not in favour of risk taking were less likely to remodel their homes or purchase energy-efficient appliances (Qiu et al., 2014). The purchase of EE appliances is associated with techno-logical and financial risks (Schleich et al., 2016) has there is an uncertainty over the actual and expected energy savings. Thus, consumer's risk prefer-ences play an important role in the purchase of EE appliances. The uncer-tainty of the price of electricity poses as a risk as consumers are wary to invest in high EE appliances when the prices of energy are low (Thollander et al., 2010). The perception of negative consequences of global warming are thought to be distant and unimaginable and as the consumer cannot cor-relate their purchases in mitigating the global warming.

2   Price Sensitivity

The attitude of risk towards EE appliances creates bias in willingness to pay for such appliances. Price sensitivity is defined as the extent of consciousness and reaction displayed by the consumer when finding differences in prices of products and services (Monroe, 1973). Price sensitivity is the extent to which consumer accepts growth in price for a specific product in terms of economic and psychological gains.

The behavioural factors that pose as barriers in developing economy like China were analysed and high initial price of the equipment along with a dearth of suppliers in the province selected and a lack of standardization of energy efficiency labels were identified as being barriers to purchase EE appliances (Dianshu et al., 2010). The willingness to pay for an eco-labelled appliance reduces as consumer undervalues the savings incurred in future by using these appliances to the upfront purchase price (Fehr-Duda et al., 2011). Research suggests that owing to the limited awareness of EE appli-ances and the complex calculations in estimating the appliance use and the electricity bills paid, consumers tend not to deliberate on the energy star label of the appliance (Yamamoto et al., 2008) but focus on other attributes while purchasing.

3   Perception of Discomfort to Self

In case of environmentally friendly products (EFPs), personal discomfort is the aversion to personal efforts when purchasing the products (Follows & Jobber, 2000, p. 727). On the similar lines, consumers perceive the purchase of EE appliances a stressful activity as it is time consuming and requires extra effort, extra cost, and use of cognitive resources while purchasing (Bray et al., 2011). Consumers perceive lack of availability of EFPs, narrow product range, higher price, and lower quality of EFPs as reasons for lack of

EFPs' purchase (Gleim et al. 2013). Individuals who believe that they lack resources to invest in EFPs are unlikely to form strong behavioural intentions to purchase the same (Carrington et al., 2014).

4   Impact of Social Influence

The influence of social norms on an individual's behaviour is well known in literature (Allcott, 2009). The social comparison theory illustrates that people evaluate themselves by comparing themselves to others especially with those with whom they share similar personal characteristics. People are more likely to follow the behaviour of others with similar features like age (Murray et al., 1984), gender (White et al., 2002), personality attributes (Carli et al., 1991), and attitudes (Suedfeld et al., 1971). The tendency of individuals to identify themselves with a group is based on their relevant social identity (Forehand et al., 2002). The extent to which the individuals consider the social identity personally important to them, individuals will adhere to the norms (Reed, 2004); ; (Terry et al., 1999). While social norms are based on the perceptions of the people about self, descriptive norms are the actual behaviour as displayed by the individual. For this chapter, the authors consider the subjective norms of an individual which refer to the belief that an important person or group of people will approve and support a particular behaviour (Ham et al., 2015). Subjective norms are formed by the social pressure exerted on an individual to behave in a manner desired by others.

5   Scepticism Towards Claims Made on the Energy Label

The environmental claims made by a product can be classified under credence attributes, the characteristics of which cannot be checked reasonably by the consumer (Bleda & Valente, 2009) which makes it difficult for the consumer to evaluate the product (Karl & Orwat, 2000). Credence attributes make it difficult for the consumers to gauge the environmental benefit caused by using the product due to their inability to assign with certainty the amount of benefit purchasing the product would cause on the environment (Akerlof, 1970). 'Dishonest dealings tend drive honest dealings out of the market' (Akerlof, 1970), and this creates distrust in the consumer's mind on the credibility of the energy label on the appliance. Due to increasing competition, some companies try to exaggerate their product attributes; as a result, they make unsubstantiated false claims (Carlson et al., 1993), and such repeated false claims could be attributed to consumer's backlash towards environmentally friendly products as they are constantly misled. Anticipating that companies are highly motivated by the 'bottom line', some consumers have keen cynicism when they profess to do good or be 'environmentally friendly' (Wenbo et al., 2016). The scepticism has also been reinforced by media as commentators have criticized various social efforts as thinly veiled efforts to reap more profits under the pretext of cause-related marketing (Krishna & Rajan, 2009). When consumers observe a company introduce a new green programme or label which also saves the firm some money, they become sceptical about the company's intention to conserve the environment versus increasing the firm's profits (Wenbo et al., 2016).

6   Insufficient Information on the Energy Label

The consumer's decision to purchase EE appliances is also hampered by the insufficient label information. The label information indicates the monetary savings, nudging the consumers to make the purchase as against the reduction in carbon emissions (Newell & Siikamäki, 2013; Bhandari and Raut, 2019). Thus, displaying information to which a consumer cannot assign a direct value forms barrier to purchase. The insufficiency of label information as a barrier in purchasing EE appliances was shown by the use of discrete choice experiments, and this proved that insufficient information on the energy labels deters consumers from purchasing EE appliances and it also decreases consumer's willingness to pay for these appliances (Zhou & Bukenya, 2016). The study analysed Chinese energy labels on air conditioners through three sets of questionnaires which deferred on energy consumption in Nanjing province in China. The study findings showed consumer's willingness to pay higher price for EE air conditioners over the conventional ones if the provision of comparable energy consumption information was made. The provision of additional information on the label was found to increase the willingness to pay. The consumer's unawareness of EE appliances could also be attributed to the lack of information (Gerarden et al., 2015; Raut et al., 2022). Hence, distrust and lack of information can be two aspects which deter consumers from purchasing EE appliances.

7   Demographics and EE Appliance Purchase

While studies on barriers account for economic and technical barriers, the impact of demographic factors cannot be ignored. A study on the demographic variables like sex, marital status, education level, type of dwelling, number of occupants, and residence (rented/own) using modified chi-square test of association indicated a strong association between demographics and barriers. The ownership of the residence influences EE investments (Gillingham et al., 2011) as owner-occupied residences are likely to be insulated as compared to rented dwellings. In a choice experiment conducted in New Zealand, it was observed that homeowners are lesser willing to invest in improving the insulation for the tenants (Phillips, 2012). Homeowners are instead willing to pay for heating option instead of retrofitting while the tenants prefer under floor insulation as compared to heating (Phillips, 2012). Study comparing appliance ownership revealed that the probability

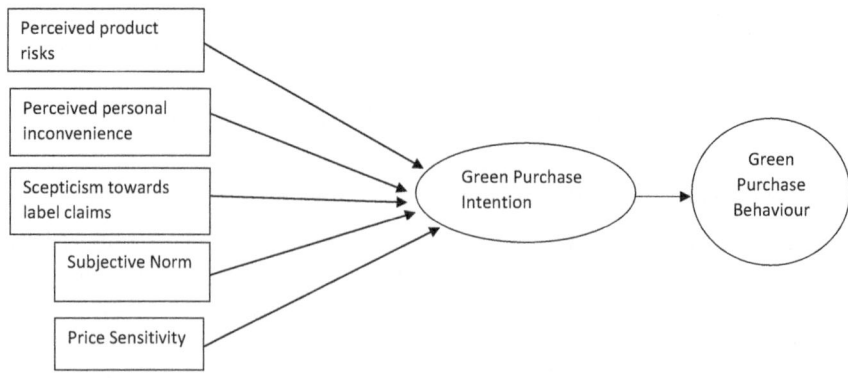

Figure 8.2 Conceptual model

of tenants possessing EE durables like refrigerators, cloth washers, and dish-washers is least. This pattern is apparent irrespective of household income, demographics, energy prices, weather, and other controls.

The study hypotheses were as follows:

H1 – *Consumer's green purchase behaviour is independent of their scepticism towards green claims made on the label.*

H2 – *Consumer's green purchase behaviour is independent of perceived product risks.*

H3 – *Consumer's green purchase behaviour is independent of perceived personal inconvenience.*

H4 – *Consumer's green purchase behaviour is independent of the subjective norm.*

H5 – *Consumer's green purchase behaviour is independent of the price sensitivity.*

H6 – *Consumer's green purchase behaviour is independent of consumer's green purchase intention.*

Methodology and Findings

As mentioned in the introduction section, the study used the mixed method, where the inputs from the qualitative study were used to design the final questionnaire to check the consumer's awareness on the energy-star-labelled appliances. The qualitative study was conducted with the consumers from Pune city possessing white goods like air conditioners, refrigerators, and television. The sample was chosen on the basis of their possession of more than three household appliances. In-depth interviews of 31 respondents were conducted to understand the decision-making process while purchasing EE appliances. The respondents were interviewed at their residences for 30–35 minutes. The interviewer also accounted for other observations in the house like the interiors of the apartment and the possibility of an appliance left switched on. The number of family members and their age groups. The questions asked were open ended, and aneutral stance was maintained by the interviewer while the respondent answered. This to a certain extent enabled in controlling the bias. The interviews were audio recorded and transcribed later. The transcripts were reported verbatim. Interviews were conducted in English. The transcripts were analysed manually by bucketing the answers on the basis of the questions in the discussion guide. The bucketing was done in MS-Excel, and the themes emerged on from there. The three key themes found to influence an individual's decision related to the purchase of EE appliances were price, availability of the appliance in desired aesthetics, and role of family in purchase decision.

The final questionnaire was based on the following themes –

1. Consumer demographics – This checked the consumer's family size and the ownership of the residence,
2. Availability of appliances with the respondents – Either purchased by the respondent himself or provided by the owner.
3. Respondent's preferences – This checked the priority the respondents assigned for various factors like aesthetics, price, energy efficiency, brand name, and the discounts received on the appliances.
4. Respondent's awareness of energy consumed by their household on monthly basis.
5. Respondent's awareness of energy star logo.
6. Response on latent variables like doubt on the label claims and opinion of other members in family or friends while making a purchase.
7. As latent variables could not be measured directly, various scales were chosen to measure them some of which were the price sensitivity scale, the perceived personal inconvenience scale, etc.

The questionnaire was administered to 650 respondents online and offline and 574 responses were obtained which were used for further analysis. The demographic data was analysed in MS-Excel, and it yielded the following results:

- Fifty-seven per cent of the households in the city were nuclear families.
- Eighty-eight per cent of households were aware of the electricity bills paid by them.
- Fifty-six per cent of the respondents owned their residences.
- Fifty-six per cent had purchased at least one appliance in the last one year as their old appliance was not functioning properly (31%).
- Seventy-five per cent purchases were from a brick-and-mortar store.
- Eighty-one per cent salesmen in the store were aware of energy star label.
- Eighty-one per cent residents were aware of the energy star label.
- Sixty-six per cent were able to interpret the label correctly.

Table 8.3 Comparison of goodness-of-fit indices of five-factor, four-factor, and three-factor models

Parameters compared	Five-factor model	Four-factor model	Three-factor model
R Square value (g.p.i.-→g.p.b)	0.85	0.74	0.73
Goodness-of-fit index	0.66	0.68	**0.71**

Source: Author's calculations from PLSPM in R.

Functionality of the appliance was the top-cited attribute (12%) as compared to its other attributes like aesthetics and the energy label.

The research utilized the Partial Least Squares Path Modelling (PLSPM) module in R program. Partial least Squares path model is a variance maximization structural equation modelling technique that does not make any distributional assumptions for data samples. It has greater statistical power than covariance- based structural equation modelling (Hair et al., 2014). The PLS technique has become increasingly popular in tourism and business research more generally in the last decade or so, influenced by its flexibility. In the given study, there were five factors identified as barriers, while all the five factors were considered to develop the conceptual model, the model with goodness-of-fit (GoF) values more than 0.7 was reported. The comparison of goodness-of-fit values of the three-factor, four-factor, and five-factor models resulted in the three-factor model having goodness-of-fit value more than 0.7, and hence the three-factor model was reported as it had a goodness-of- fit value of 0.71, which is more than 0.70. The constructs dropped for the three-factor model were scepticism towards claims made on energy labels and perceived personal inconvenience. Table 8.3 indicates the comparison of GoF values of all models.

Reliability and Validity

As PLSPM was used to analyse the data, the uni-dimensionality and homogeneity of the reflexive multi-item constructs were measured (EspositoVinzi et al., 2010). The value of Dillon–Goldstein's rho (also known as Jöreskog's rho or composite reliability) was used to examine internal consistency (Wertz et al., 1974). Rho is considered a superior measure to other measures of reliability that assume parallelity or tau equivalence of the manifest variables in PLS path modelling (Chin, 1998). The reliability of all composite measures was above the recommended level of 0.7 (EspositoVinzi et al., 2010). Table 8.4 on block dimensionality of three factors indicates the Cronbach alpha and the rho values which are greater than 7. Convergent and discriminant validity were measured using the methods prescribed by (Fornell & Larcker, 1981) and (Chin, 1998). All items loaded on their

Table 8.4 Block uni-dimensionality of three-factor model

	Mode	MVs	C.alpha	DG.rho	eig·1st	eig·2nd
p.risk	A	5	0.9	0.93	3.64	0.49
s.norm	A	4	0.92	0.94	3.23	0.37
p.sens	A	3	0.73	0.85	1.96	0.55
g.p.i	A	3	0.92	0.95	2.59	0.27
g.p.b	A	4	0.90	0.93	3.13	0.55

Source: Author's calculations from PLSPM in R

Table 8.5 Inner plot summary and average variance extracted (AVE)

Type	R^2	Block_ Communality	Mean_ Redundancy	Ave
p.risk	Exogenous	0.00	0.72	0.72
s.norm	Exogeneous	0.00	0.80	0.80
p.sens	Exogenous	0.00	0.63	0.63
g.p.i	Endogenous	0.58	0.86	0.86
g.p.b	Endogenous	0.73	0.78	0.78

Source: Author's calculations from PLSPM in R

Table 8.6 Crossloadings – depicting differences in constructs

Sno	Name	Block	p.risk	s.norm	p.sens	g.p.i	g.p.b
1	Q17Finloss	p.risk	0.75	-0.08	0.05	-0.21	-0.20
2	Q17Infmtrl	p.risk	0.88	-0.15	0.02	-0.27	-0.31
3	Q17Phyharm	p.risk	0.91	-0.25	-0.08	-0.38	-0.42
4	Q17NSelfcon	p.risk	0.79	-0.08	0.075	-0.21	-0.22
5	Q17NegRep	p.risk	0.89	-0.27	-0.10	-0.43	-0.46
6	Q17ShudBuyEE	s.norm	-0.16	0.90	0.46	0.60	0.59
7	Q17Expectbuy	s.norm	-0.12	0.90	0.45	0.56	0.56
8	Q17Approvebuy	s.norm	-0.23	0.88	0.48	0.60	0.62
9	Q17ConsiderBuy	s.norm	-0.27	0.89	0.49	0.69	0.66
10	Q17Efforlowprice	p.sens	-0.14	0.55	0.88	0.55	0.56
11	Q17Planchange	p.sens	0.15	0.24	0.68	0.20	0.24
12	Q17PriceSen	p.sens	0.04	0.36	0.80	0.39	0.42
13	Q17LessEnvtImpact	g.p.i	-0.25	0.60	0.45	0.89	0.71
14	Q17FuturePur	g.p.i	-0.34	0.64	0.50	0.95	0.80
15	Q17Glad	g.p.i	-0.45	0.67	0.51	0.93	0.86
16	Q18BuyEE	g.p.b	-0.39	0.65	0.53	0.83	0.93
17	Q18SwitchBrnd	g.p.b	-0.08	0.48	0.39	0.54	0.72
18	Q18EffBulb	g.p.b	-0.46	0.62	0.51	0.77	0.92
19	Q18lesspolltng	g.p.b	-0.43	0.63	0.52	0.82	

designated theoretical constructs at p < 0.001, with loadings ranging from 0.726 to 0.914. Table 8.5 shows the inner plot summary and average variance extracted.

Table 8.6 further shows cross-loadings among constructs. As we can see, all items loaded clearly on their own constructs, demonstrating discriminant validity (Chin, 1998). Another test of discriminant validity suggested by Fornell & Larcker (1981) compares the average variance extracted (AVE) for a construct with the squared inter-correlations. Applying this test to our data set, we find that in all cases the AVEs for a construct are higher than the squared inter- correlations with other constructs, confirming discriminant validity. In addition, the values of AVE in Table 8.4 range from 0.63 to 0.80, well above the recommended level of 0.5 (Fornell & Larcker, 1981), demonstrating convergent validity. The path analysis values are depicted in Table 8.7.

Table 8.7 Path analysis

	Original	*Mean.Boot*	*Std.Error*	*Perc.025*	*Perc.975*
p.risk -> g.p.i	−0.263	−0.267	0.031	−0.331	−0.208
s.norm -> g.p.i	0.495	0.490	0.040	0.407	0.560
p.sens -> g.p.i	0.262	0.261	0.038	0.197	0.336
g.p.i -> g.p.b	0.856	0.856	0.015	0.825	0.882

Source: Author calculations from PLSPM in R

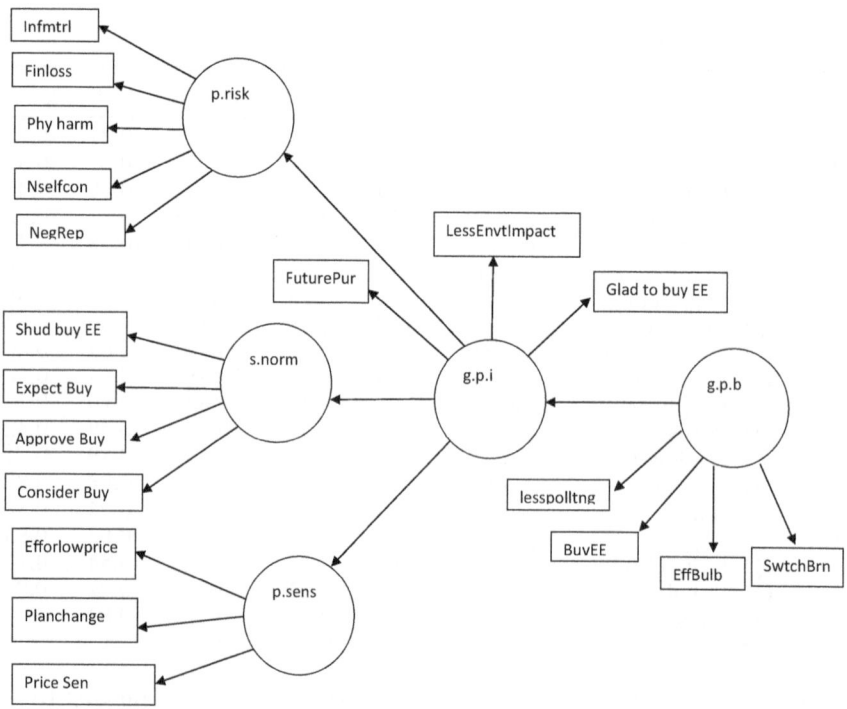

Figure 8.3 The Three-factor model signifying the factors impacting the purchase behaviour

Interpretation of Data Analysed by PLSPM to identify the factors

The study sought to identify the factors that persuaded/dissuaded consumers from purchasing eco-labelled appliances. The impact of various factors identified from the literature and from the qualitative study was validated through a structured questionnaire using the PLSPM technique. The factors perceived product risks and perceived personal inconvenience yielded a negative value to green purchase intention indicating that they were the barriers to green purchase. The construct scepticism towards claims made on energy label was rejected at the onset as the Cronbach alpha's value was less than 0.7. It was also omitted for final model as a better model fit was achieved by omitting this hypothesis along with perceived personal inconvenience.

The remaining two factors, viz., the subjective norm and price sensitivity, yielded positive value to green purchase intention indicating that they were facilitators to green purchase. The emergence of price sensitivity as a facilitator to green purchase intention was counterintuitive finding especially for an emerging economy like India, as majority of studies on investments in EE appliances from China (Dianshu et al., 2010) to Brazil and to the UK (Pelenur & Cruickshank, Closing the energy efficiency gap: a study linking demographics with barriers to adopting energy efficiency measures in the home, 2012) indicate cost as one of the barriers of investing in EE appliances.

Discussions and Managerial Implications

The initial studies on understanding consumer's resistance to purchase energy-star-labelled white goods had assumed the rational perspective of the consumer (Ramayah et al., 2010), and not many studies in the Indian context have adopted the behavioural perspectives. Hence, this study contributes by adopting the Perceived Risk constructs from the Prospect theory (Kahneman & Tversky, 1979). It also uses some constructs from the theory of planned behaviour (Ajzen, 1991).

The study also used the Partial Least Squares Path Modelling (PLSPM) to analyse factors promoting/ demoting consumer's purchase of eco-labelled appliances. To study the factors impacting consumer's preference to eco-labelled appliances, earlier studies have applied the behavioural models (Di Maria et al., 2010), survey data of rural and urban populations (Dianshu et al., 2010), econometric modelling Logit and Probit qualitative interviews, regression analysis, and the AMOS SEM technique; A few studies have used the Partial Least Squares method to explore the factors. This could be considered as methodological contribution to the body of knowledge.

The study also contributes to checking the popularity and knowledge of the energy star label. The energy star label is the GoI's initiation by the Bureau of Energy Efficiency to promote EE appliances to conserve energy. It was observed that majority of the respondents (81%) could recognize energy star

Figure 8.4 Label depicting cost saving
Source: Author

logo, but only 66% could interpret it correctly. This is an important finding as far as the Standards and Labelling policy of India is concerned. Thus, this chapter attempts to connect the current academic studies on research of energy EE appliance with the problem of policy making (de Ayala et al., 2016).

The terms of recommendations for the marketers, the purchase of white goods can be increased by providing incentives to retailers for stocking appliances above three stars. This will nudge consumers to choose only among three-star to five-star appliances. The salesperson could also be incentivized on selling higher star rated appliances. Greater the number of appliances of higher star rating purchased, greater the incentives. Additionally, the companies need to be incentivized by the Government to make large volume sales of energy-star-labelled appliances. There must be policy level changes to ensure that labelled appliances are promoted among manufacturers and the retailers. Manufacturers need to be incentivized for meeting the expectations of higher stars for their durables.

The consumer's tendency to purchase a new appliance was high when their old appliance was no longer functioning or when they shifted to a new house. This could be used as an opportunity to promote energy-star-labelled white goods in the case of purchase due to shifting to a new house; that is the consumers could be incentivized if all the appliances they purchase would be labelled three or more stars.

The study revealed that while many consumers were aware of the star rating pictorially, but only 66% were aware of its interpretation. Hence, a one-liner or a catchy slogan or phrase interpreting the stars could be proposed to Bureau of Energy Efficiency (BEE). A label depicting the cost saved by adopting these appliances could be designed as shown in Figure 8.4. This would directly enable the consumer in linking the monthly savings accrued by installing such appliances.

Limitations and Future Research Direction

Although this research helps in expanding our understanding of the impact of perceived product risk, scepticism towards green claims made on the label, subjective norm, price sensitivity and perceived personal inconvenience on consumer's green purchase intention, and consumer's green purchase behaviour, it still has some limitations.

First, the study uses a homogenous sample as the respondents were pre-tested to possess more than three appliances which indicate that most of the respondents were from economically sound background (mostly from the socio-economic classification with higher incomes the category possessing higher number of durables)

Second, the research examined the usage of white goods only and not any other appliances like fan, tube light, LED bulbs, and table fans. These could be examined in future researches.

Third, the research examined the salesman's knowledge of energy star appliances, and not the retailer's perspective towards EE appliances. The retailer is the one who needs to be aware of and motivated to sell EE appliances. Future research could complete the loop by checking the barriers faced by retailers to push EE appliances. The study is not technical in nature as it blends the concepts of economics, marketing, and energy. Future research could attempt converging the technical aspects of energy usage with behavioural aspects.

References

Abhyankar, N., Shah, N., Letschert1, V., & Phadke, A. (2017). Assessing the cost-effective energy saving potential of top 10 appliances in India. In *9th International conference on energy efficiency in domestic appliances and lighting (EEDAL)* (pp. 13–15). Irvine, CA: University of California.

Ajzen, I. (1991). The theory of planned behaviour. *Organizational Behaviour and Human Decision Processes, 50*(2), 179–211.

Akalamkam, K., & Mitra, J. K. (2017). Consumer pre-purchase search in online shopping: Role of offline and online information sources. *Business Perspectives and Research*, 42–60.

Akerlof, G. A. (1970). The market for lemons: Quality and the market mechanism. *Quarterly. Journal Economics, 84*, 488–500.

Allcott, H. (2009, October). Social norms and energy conservation. *Center for Energy and Environmental Policy Research*, 1–35. https://doi.org/10.1016/j.jpubeco.2011.03.003.

Atănăsoaie, G. S. (2013). Eco-label and its role in the development of organic products market. *Economy Transdisciplinarity Cognition, 16*(1), 122–129.

Atkinson, L., & Rosenthal, S. (2014). Signaling the green sell: The influence of eco-label source, argument specificity, and product involvement on consumer trust. *Journal of Advertising, 43*(1), 33–45.

Auger, P., & Devinney, T. M. (2007). Do what consumers say matter? The misalignment of preferences with unconstrained ethical intentions. *Journal of Business Ethics, 76*(4), 361–383.

Berry, H., McEachern, M., Harrison, R., Newholm, T., & Shaw, D. (2005). *Informing ethical consumers*. London: Sage Publications.

Bettman, J. R., Payne, J., & Staelin, R. (1986). Cognitive considerations in designing effective labels for presenting risk information. *Journal of Public Policy, 5*(1), 1–28.

Bhandari, K. R., & Raut, S. K. (2019). 9 Leveraging tacit. *Advances in Management Research: Innovation and Technology, 1*(1), 127–138.

Bleda, M., & Valente, M. (2009). Graded eco-labels: A demand-oriented approach to reduce pollution. *Technological Forecasting and Social Change, 76*(4), 512–524.

Boer, J. (2003). Sustainability labelling schemes: The logic of their claims and functions for the stakeholders. *Business Strategy and the Environment, 12*(4), 254–264.

Bonroy, O., & Constantatos, C. (2011, December). The economics of labels : A review of literature. *Grenoble Applied Economics Laboratory, Quality Labels in Agrofood Industry, Toulouse, France*, 1–32.

Brau, R., & Carraro, C. (1999). *Voluntary approaches, market structure and competition*. Milan: Note di Lavoro 53.99, Fondazione Eni E. Mattei.

Bray, J., Johns, N., & Kilburn, D. (2011). An exploratory study into the factors impending ethical consumption. *Journal of Business Ethics, 98*(4), 597–608. https://doi.org/10.1007/sl0551-010-0640-9.

Brunsson, N., & Jacobsson, B. (2000). The contemporary expansion of standardization. *A World of Standards, 1*, 1–17.

Carli, L. L., Ganley, R., & Pierce-Otay, A. (1991). Similarity and satisfaction in roommate relationships. *Personality and Social Psychology Bulletin, 17*(4), 419–426.

Carlson, L., Stephen, J., & Kangun, N. (1993). A content analysis of environmental advertising: A matrix approach. *Journal of Advertising, 22*, 27–40.

Carrington, M. J., Neville, B. A., & Whitwell, G. J. (2014). Lost in translation: Exploring the ethical consumer intention-behavior gap. *Journal of Business Research*, 67(1), 2759–2767. https://doi.org/10.1016/j.jbusres.2012.09.022.

Cervellon, M., & Lindsey. (2011). Consumers' perception of green. *Critical Studies in Fashion and Beauty*, 2.

Chan, R., & Lau, L. (2004). The effectiveness of environmental claims among Chinese consumers: Influences of claim type, country disposition and ecocentric orientation. *Journal of Marketing*, 273–319.

Chin, W. (1998). The partial least squares approach for structural equation modeling. In G. M. Marcoulides (Ed.), *Modern methods for business research* (pp. 295–336). Hillsdale, NJ: Lawrence Erlbaum Associates.

Christie, D., & Walton, D. (2011). The apparent disconnect towards adoption of energy efficient technologies. *Building Research and Information* 39(5), 450–458.

Chunekar, A. (2014). Standards and Labeling program for refrigerators: Comparing India with others. *Energy Policy*, 65(1), 626–630.

Davis, A. Y. (2011). *Are Prisons Obsolete?* Seven Stories Press.

de Ayala, A., Galarraga, I., & Spadaro, J. V. (2016). The price of energy efficiency in the Spanish housing market. *Energy Policy*, 94, 16–24.

Dianshu, F., Sovacool, B. K., & Vu, K. (2010). The barriers to energy efficiency in China: Assessing household electricity savings and consumer behavior in Liaoning Province. *Energy Policy*, 38(2), 1202–1209. https://doi.org/10.1016/j.enpol.2009.11.012.

Di Maria, C., Ferreira, S., & Lazarova, E. (2010). Shedding light on the light bulb puzzle: The role of attitudes and perceptions in the adoption of energy efficient light bulbs. *Scottish Journal of Political Economy*, 57(1), 48–67.

Diaz-Rainey, I., & Ashton, J. K. (2015). Investment inefficiency and the adoption of eco-innovations: The case of household energy efficiency technologies. *Energy Policy*, 82,105–117.

Dulleck, U., & Kerschbamer, R. (2006). On doctors, mechanics and computer specialists: The economics of credence goods. *Journal of Economic Literature*, 44(1), 5–42.

Energiministeriet, M. O. (1995). *Natur- og miljøpolitisk redegørelse (Nature and Environment in Denmark)*. Copenhagen: The Ministry of Environment and Energy.

EspositoVinzi, V., Chin, W., Henseler, J., & Wang, H. (2010). PLS path modeling: From foundations to recent developments and open issues for model assessment and improvement. In *Handbook of partial least squares: Concepts, methods and applications* (pp. 47–82). Heidelberg: Springer.

Farsi, M. (2010). Risk aversion and willingness to pay for energy efficient systems in rental apartments. *Energy Policy*, 38(6), 3078–3088.

Fehr-Duda, H., Epper, T., Bruhin, A., & Schubert, R. (2011). Risk and rationality: The effects of mood and decision rules on probability weighting. *Journal of Economic Behavior & Organization*, 78(1–2), 14–24.

Festinger, L. (. (1954). A theory of social comparison processes. *Human relations*, 7(2), 117–140.

Fishbein, M., & Ajzen, I. (1975). *Belief, attitude, intention and behavior: An introduction to theory and research*. Reading, MA: Addison-Wesley.

Follows, S. B., & Jobber, D. (2000). Environmentally responsible purchase behaviour: A test of a consumer. *European Journal Market*, 34, 723–746.

Forehand, M. R., Deshpandé, R., & Reed, I. I. (2002). Identity salience and the influence of differential activation of the social self-schema on advertising response. *Journal of Applied Psychology, 87*(6), 1086.

Fornell, C., & Larcker, F. (1981). Evaluating structural equation models with unobservable variables and measurement error. *Journal of Marketing Research, 18*(1), 39–50.

Gerarden, T., Newell, R. G., & Stavins, R. N. (2015). Deconstructing the energy-efficiency gap: conceptual frameworks and evidence. *American Economic Review, 105*(5), 183–186.

Gillingham, K., Harding, M., & Rapson, D. (2011). Split incentives in residential energy consumption. *Split Incentives in Residential Energy Consumption, 33*(530), 37–62.

Gleim, M. R., Smith, J. S., Andrews, D., & Cronin Jr, J. J. (2013). Against the green: A multi-method examination of the barriers to green consumption. *Journal of Retailing, 89*(1), 44–61.

Ha, H. Y., & Janda, S. (2012). Predicting consumer intentions to purchase energy-efficient products. *Journal of Consumer Marketing*.

Hair Jr, J. F., Sarstedt, M., H. L., & Kuppelwieser, V. G. (2014). Partial least squares structural equation modeling (PLS-SEM): An emerging tool in business research. *European business review*.

Ham, M., Jeger, M., & Frajman Ivković, A. (2015). The role of subjective norms in forming the intention to purchase green food. *Economic research-Ekonomska istraživanja, 28*(1), 738–748.

Hansen, U., & Kull, S. (1994). Öko-label als umweltbezogenes Informationsinstrument: Begründungszusammenhänge und Interessen. *Marketing ZFP*, 265–274.

Hathaway, D., & Zhao, Y. (2011, February 15). *Energy efficiency standards and labeling in Asia*. Retrieved from clasp.ngo/~/media/Files/ . . . /ICF EE SL in Asia.pdf.

Holt, D. B., Quelch, J. A., & Taylor, E. L. (2004). How global brands compete. *Harvard business review, 82*(9), 68–75.

Indian Brand Equity Foundation. (2020, June). *Indian consumer durables industry analysis*. Retrieved from www.ibef.org: www.ibef.org/industry/consumer-durables-presentation.

International Energy Agency. (2020). *World Energy Outlook*. International Energy Agency.

Jain, M., Rao, A. B., & Patwardhan, A. (2018). Consumer preference for labels in the purchase decisions of air conditioners in India. *Energy for Sustainable Development*, 24–31.

Jeong, G., & Kim, Y. (2015). The effects of energy efficiency and environmental labels on appliance choice in South Korea. *Energy Efficiency, 8*(3), 559–576.

Johnson, R. B., & Onwuegbuzie, A. J. (2004). Mixed methods research: A research paradigm whose time has come. *Educational researcher, 33*(7), 14–26.

Joseph, M., & Soundararajan, N. (2009). *Retail in India: A critical assessment*. Academic Foundation.

Joshi, M. (2004). Are eco-labels consistent with world trade organization agreement? *Journal of World Trade*, 69–92.

Kahneman, D., & Tversky, A. (1979). Prospect theory: An analysis of decision under risk. *Econometrica: Journal of the Econometric Society, 47*(3), 263–291. https://doi.org/10.1111/j.1536-7150.2011.00774.x.

Karl, H., & Orwat, C. (2000). Economic aspects of environmental labelling. *The International Yearbook of Environmental and Resource Economics*, 107–170.

Khare, A., Achtani, D., & Khattar, M. (2014). Influence of price perception and shopping motives on Indian consumers' attitude towards retailer promotions in malls. Asia Pacific Journal of Marketing and Logistics.

Koos, S. (2011). Varieties of environmental labelling, market structures, and sustainable consumption across Europe: A comparative analysis of organizational and market supply determinants of environmental-labelled goods. *Journal of Consumer Policy, 34*(1), 127–151.

Krishna, A., & Rajan, U. (2009). Spillover effects of cause-related products in a product portfolio. *Management Science, 55*(9), 1469–1485.

Kulshreshtha, K., Bajpai, N., & Tripathi, V. (2017). Consumer preference for electronic consumer durable goods in India: A conjoint analysis approach. *International Journal of Business Forecasting and Marketing Intelligence, 3*(1), 13–37.

Lee, J., & Geistfeld, L. V. (1998). Enhancing consumer choice: Are we making appropriate recommendations? *Journal of Consumer Affairs, 32*(2), 227–251.

Leiserowitz, A. (2007). Communicating the risks of global warming: American risk perceptions, affective images, and interpretive communities. Creating a climate for change: Communicating climate change and facilitating social change. 44–63.

Mahlia, T. M., & Saidur, R. (2010). A review on test procedure, energy efficiency standards and energy labels for room air conditioners and refrigerator–freezers. *Renewable and Sustainable Energy Reviews, 14(7),* 1888–1900.

Ministry of Power, Government of India. (2015). *Bureau of energy efficiency.* Retrieved from https://beeindia.gov.in/content/standards-labeling.

Monroe, K. (1973). Buyers' subjective perceptions of price. *Journal of Marketing Research 10*(1), 70–80.

Mukherjee, A., Satija, D., Goyal, T., Mantrala, M., & Zou, S. (2012). Are Indian consumers brand conscious? Insights for global retailers. *Asia Pacific Journal of Marketing and Logistics, 24*(3), 482–499.

Nambiar, B. K., Ramanathan, H. N., Rana, S., & Prashar, S. (2018). Perceived service quality and customer satisfaction: A missing link in Indian banking sector. *Vision, 23*(1), 44–55.

Newell, R. G., & Siikamäki, J. (2013, July). Nudging energy efficiency behavior. *Resources for the Future,* 44. https://doi.org/10.3386/w19224.

Nguyen, T. N. (2018). Determinants Which Influence Purchase Behaviour of Energy Efficient Household Appliances in Emerging Markets. In: Crowther, D., Seifi, S., Moyeen, A. (eds) *The Goals of Sustainable Development. Approaches to Global Sustainability, Markets, and Governance.* Springer, Singapore. https://doi.org/10.1007/978-981-10-5047-3_6

Nik Abdul Rashid, N. (2009). Awareness of eco-label in Malaysia's green marketing initiative. *International Journal of Business and Management, 4*(8), 132–141.

Painuly, J. P., & Reddy, B. S. (1996). Electricity conservation programs: Barriers to their implementation. *Energy Sources, 18*(3), 257–267.

Peattie, K. (1995). Environmental marketing management: Meeting the green challenge. *Financial Times.*

Pelenur, M. J., & Cruickshank, H. J. (2012). Closing the energy efficiency gap: A study linking demographics with barriers to adopting energy efficiency measures in the home. *Energy, 47*(1), 348–357.

Phillips, Y. (2012, June). Landlords versus tenants: Information asymmetry and mismatched preferences for home energy efficiency. *Energy Policy, 45,* 112–121. https://doi.org/10.1016/j.enpol.2012.01.067.

PWC. (2018). *Future of consumer durables and electronics in India- The changing landscape*. India: PWC and CEAMA.

Qiu, Y., Colson, G., & Grebitus, C. (2014). Risk preferences and purchase of energy-efficient technologies in the residential sector. *Ecological Economics, 107*, 216–229.

Ramachander, S. (1988). Consumer behaviour and marketing: Towards an Indian approach? *Economic and Political Weekly*, M22–M25.

Ramachandra, T. V., & Aithal, B. (2017–18). Escalating pollution threats in urbanising Indian cities. *Union Budget*.

Ramayah, T., Lee, J. W., & Mohamad, O. (2010). Green product purchase intention: Some insights from a developing country. *Resources, Conservation and Recycling, 54*(12), 1419–1427.

Rana, S. (2018a). Business performance: Earlier stage and looking forward. *FIIB Business Review, 7*(3), 153–155.

Rana, S. (2018b). Managing businesses relevance beyond technology. *FIIB Business Review, 7*(4), 229–231.

Rana, S., Raut, S. K., Prashar, S., & Hamid, A. B. A. (2020b). Promoting through consumer nostalgia: A conceptual framework and future research agenda. *Journal of Promotion Management, 27*(2), 211–249.

Rana, S., Raut, S. K., Prashar, S., & Quttainah, M. A. (2020a). The transversal of nostalgia from psychology to marketing: What does it portend for future research? *International Journal of Organizational Analysis*, Vol. ahead-of-print No. ahead-of-print.

Ranajoy Bhattacharyya, A. G. (2017). Cross subsidy removal in electricity pricing in India. *Energy Policy, 100*(1), 181–190. http://dx.doi.org/10.1016/j.enpol.2016.10.024

Rathi, S. S., & Chunekar, A. (2015). Not to buy or can be 'nudged'to buy? Exploring behavioral interventions for energy policy in India. *Energy Research & Social Science, 7*(1), 78–83.

Raut, S. K., Sakpal, S., & Soni, R. (2022) Understanding the Service Quality Dimensions and Achieving Resilience in Service Retail, in *Handbook of Research on Supply Chain Resiliency, Efficiency, and Visibility in the Post-Pandemic Era*, edited by Ramakrishna Yanamandra, pp. 136–156. IGI Global, UAE. https://doi.org/10.4018/978-1-7998-9506-0.

Reed, A. (2004). Activating the self-importance of consumer selves: Exploring identity salience effects on judgments. *Journal of Consumer Research, 31*(2), 286–295.

Rex, E., & Baumann, H. (2007). Beyond ecolabels: What green marketing can learn from conventional marketing. *Journal of Cleaner Production*, 567–576.

Sarangi. (2016). *The Indian consumer durable market and an analysis of demand pattern*. Retrieved from www.icsi.edu: www.icsi.edu/media/portals/86/Major%20Durables.pdf.

Schlegelmilch, B. B., Bohlen, G. M., & Diamantopoulos, A. (1996). The link between green purchasing decisions and measures of environmental consciousness. *European Journal of Marketing, 30*(5), 35–55.

Schleich, J., Gassmann, X., Faure, C., & Meissner, T. (2016). Making the implicit explicit: A look inside the implicit discount rate. *Energy Policy, 97*, 321–331.

Schwartz, S. P. (1980). Consumer attitudes toward product labeling. In L. A. Morris et al. (Eds.), *Labeling and health risks, banbury report 6* (pp. 89–96). Cold Spring Harbor, NY: Cold Spring Harbor Laboratory.

Shen, J., & Saijo, T. (2009). Does an energy efficiency label alter consumers' purchasing decisions? A latent class approach based on a stated choice experiment in Shanghai. *Journal of environmental management, 90*(11), 3561–3573.

Sheth, J. (2011). Impact of emerging markets on marketing: Rethinking existing perspectives and practices. *Journal of Marketing, 75*(4), 166–182.

Singh, D., Bharvirkar, R., Kumar, S., Sant, G., & Phadke, A. (2011). Using national energy efficiency programs with upstream incentives to accelerate market transformation for super-efficient appliances in India. *Proceedings of the ECEEE 2011 Summer Study.*

Sinha, P., & Kar, S. (2007, March). An insight into the growth of new retail formats in India. *Indian Institute of Management, Ahmedabad.*

Statista. (2021, 04 19). Growth rate of consumer durables industry in India from financial year 2010 to 2015, with estimates till 2020.

Suedfeld, P., Bochner, S., & Matas, C. (1971). Petitioner's attire and petition signing by peace demonstrators: A field experiment. *Journal of Applied Social Psychology, 1*(3), 278–283.

Taufique, K. M. R., Siwar, C., Talib, B., Sarah, F. H., & Chamhuri, N. (2014). Synthesis of constructs for modeling consumers' understanding and perception of eco-labels. *Sustainability (Switzerland), 6*(4), 2176–2200. https://doi.org/10.3390/su6042176.

Tawichai, T. (2014, December 12). *Microwaves and food preparation appliances booming in India.* Retrieved from www.euromonitor.com: https://blog.euromonitor.com/microwaves-and-food-preparation-appliances-booming-in-india/.

Teisl, M. F. (2003). What we may have is a failure to communicate: Labeling environmentally certified forest products. *Forest Science, 49*(5), 668–680.

Terry, D. J., & Hogg, M. A. (1996). Group norms and the attitude-behavior relationship: A role for group identification. *Personality and Social Psychology Bulletin, 22*(8), 776–793.

Terry, D. J., Hogg, M. A., & White, K. M. (1999). The theory of planned behaviour: Self-identity, social identity and group norms. *British Journal of Social Psychology, 38*(3), 225–244.

Thøgersen, J. (2000). Psychological determinants of paying attention to eco-labels in purchase. *Journal of Consumer Policy* (23), 285–313.

Thøgersen, J., Haugaard, P., & Olesen, A. (2010). Consumer responses to ecolabels. *European Journal of Marketing, 44*(11/12), 1787–1810. https://doi.org/10.1108/03090561011079882.

Thollander, P., Palm, J., & Rohdin, P. (2010). Categorizing barriers to energy efficiency: An interdisciplinary perspective. *Energy efficiency,* edited by Jenny Palm, 49–63. ISBN: 978-953-307-137-4, InTech, Available from: http://www.intechopen.com/books/energy-efficiency/categorizing-barriers-to-energy-efficiency-aninterdisciplinary-perspective.

Throne-Holst, H. S., & Stø, E. (2008). Identification of households' barriers to energy saving solutions. *Management of Environmental Quality: An International Journal, 19*(1), 54–66. https://doi.org/10.1108/14777830810840363.

UʺSTUʺNER, T., & Holt, D. (2009). Toward a theory of status consumption in less industrialized country. *Journal of Consumer Research, 37*(1), 37–56.

Voon, T., Mitchell, A., & Gascoigne, C. (2013). Consumer information, consumer preferences and product labels under the TBT Agreement. In *Research handbook on the WTO and technical barriers to trade* (pp. 454–484). Edward Elgar Publishing.

Waechter, S., Sütterlin, B., & Siegrist, M. (2015). The misleading effect of energy efficiency information on perceived energy friendliness of electric goods. *Journal of Cleaner Production*, *93*(1), 1–10.

Washington, S., & Ababouch, L. (2011). Private standards and certification in fisheries and aquaculture: Current practice and emerging issues. *FAO Fisheries and Aquaculture Technical Paper No. 553.*

Weil, W., & McMahon, J. (2003). Governments should implement energy-efficient standards and labels – cautiously. *Energy Policy*, *31*(13), 1403–1415.

Wenbo, W., Krishna, A., & Mcferran, B. (2016). Turning off the lights: Consumers' environmental efforts depend on visible efforts of firms. *Journal of Marketing Research*, *54*(3), 478–494.

Wertz, C., Linn, R., & Joreskog, K. (1974). Intraclass reliability estimates: Testing structural assumptions. *Educational and Psychological Measurement*, *34*(1), 25–33.

White, K. M., Hogg, M. A., & Terry, D. J. (2002). Improving attitude-behavior correspondence through exposure to normative support from a salient ingroup. *Basic and Applied Social Psychology*, *24*(2), 91–103.

Yamamoto, Y., Suzuki, A., Fuwa, Y., & Sato, Y. (2008). Decision making in electrical appliance use in the home. *Energy Policy*, *36*(5), 1679–1686.

Zhou, H., & Bukenya, J. O. (2016). Information inefficiency and willingness-to-pay for energy-efficient technology: A stated preference approach for China energy label. *Energy Policy*, *91*, 12–21. https://doi.org/10.1016/j.enpol.2015.12.040.

9 Cultural Marketing in the Indian Textiles Industry

A Comprehensive Perspective

Kanupriya

Introduction

> Culture does not make people. People make culture.
>
> (Adichie, 2014)

This quote by noted Nigerian author Chimamanda Ngozi Adichie sets the tone of this chapter. In other words, *culture* consists of arrangements, overt and implied, of and for behaviour attained and disseminated by symbols, establishing the unique accomplishment of human groups, incorporating their embodiments in artefacts (Rana, Raut, Prashar, and Quttainah, 2020; Rana, Raut, Prashar, and Hamid, 2020). The vital core of culture consists of traditional (i.e. historically derived and designated) beliefs and especially their attached values; cultural systems may, on one hand, be considered as products of human action and, on the other, as conditioning elements of further action (Kroeber and Kluckhohn as cited in Jahoda, 2012). Clearly, the quote of Adichie must be read in this light, wherein humans make and remake cultures through their acquired and inherited abilities over time. Thus, cultures are never static but constantly evolving (Jahoda, 2012).

Another related concept of this chapter is cultural marketing. The term implies a *specific type of marketing* whose goal is to disseminate an idea, a service or a product to a group of potential customers from a specific culture or demographic (IGI-Global, 2021; Samaha et al., 2014). In other words, cultural marketing caters to the specificities of the cultural variations among populations. It seeks to tap into the cultural differences to enhance sales and profits of customer brands and also create lasting impressions in the minds of purchasers thereby forging long-term relationships with their prospective clients. The core idea is of brand personalization and that the brand in question cares for the needs and desires of the customers and not merely clubs them under a homogeneous group (ibid).

Such is the influence of culture in human life that it impacts almost every aspect of their daily existence. This also includes their purchase decisions and preferences. It is this complex relationship between culture and

DOI: 10.4324/9781003315582-10

consumption that is sought to be explored in this chapter, albeit pertaining only to the textiles sector in India. A deeper study of social psychology reveals that cultural dissimilarities have substantial impact on people's outlook of the world and thereby on their behaviour (Manstead, 1997). Even though there is an agreement in the marketing world on culture greatly influencing the manner consumers perceive and act (Clark, 1990; Hall, 1977; McCracken, 1988; Wellner, 2002), there has to be further research on how culture influences the marketing domain through its impact on customer choices. Such research is especially needed for the Indian textiles sector that is reeling under stagnant domestic and export sales over the past few years and especially so in the COVID-19 era (Madhavan, 2020; Raut, Sakpal and Soni, 2022). An innovative pro-customer choice marketing strategy such as cultural marketing could provide the much needed fillip to the sagging fortunes of the domestic textiles industry both at home and abroad. The fact that as of 2018–2019, the industry employed over 100 million people and contributed about 12 to 13 per cent towards total industrial output, 12 per cent towards total exports and 2 to 2.5 per cent towards the country's gross domestic product (GDP) only seeks to affirm the significance of the same for the Indian economy and society (Kanupriya, 2020).

Notwithstanding the attention paid to the concept of cultural marketing in the marketing domain, the theme is in need of a solid theoretical structure in the context of the Indian textiles sector. In view of the issues raised in the preceding sections, this chapter seeks to answer some of the burning questions pertaining to cultural marketing in the Indian textiles industry. These are mentioned as follows.

1) What are the important issues of cultural marketing in the domain of the Indian textiles sector?
2) What are some of the challenges faced by cultural marketing strategy in the sector?
3) What are the prospects of the cultural marketing approach for the Indian textiles industry?

With the aid of these questions, an attempt is made to synthesize and buttress the findings of existing literature to systematically examine the issues, challenges and prospects in cultural marketing strategy for the Indian textiles sector. An attempt is also made to grasp how marketers could utilize the cultural differences of consumers to boost value for both customers and organizations. The likely outcome of this chapter should advance the development of an apt cultural marketing strategy for the Indian textiles industry.

The chapter is structured as follows. The next section presents a review of literature, including a detailed explanation for studying the theme of cultural marketing within the Indian textiles sector. This is followed by a description of the methodology employed in the chapter. The subsequent section is the discussion segment in which the author provides insights into the major findings of the chapter as well as the uniqueness and limitations of the study. The penultimate section concludes the study. The last segment discusses the future policy implications of the cultural marketing strategy for the Indian textiles sector.

Literature Review

The term cultural marketing can be described as a combination of the two words *cultural* and *marketing*. By coalescing the term *cultural*, meaning the complex set of knowledge, beliefs, arts, laws, customs, morals and any other competencies and conventions acquired by a human being as a member of a society (Taylor as quoted in George and Jones, 1996) with *marketing* or the science of investigating, generating and providing value to gratify the desires of a focus market at a profit, one arrives at unfulfilled needs and desires of a society from a cultural perspective (Kotler as quoted in George and Jones, 1996). Such combinations also aid in identifying the segments the organization is capable of serving while keeping in mind the interests of the customers. In other words, new prospective strategies and focus areas come to light in the wake of this combination of culture and marketing.

George and Jones (1996) came up with the concept of *National Culture* as an explicit acknowledgement of cultural differences among nations. According to them, *national culture* is a specific set of social, economic and political values that exist in a particular nation. And that undeniably impacts the way people therein live and work.

It is Hofstede (1984, 1991) who recognized the five dimensions along which national cultures are placed. They are explained as follows. First is the *Power Distance* or the degree to which people in a society accept the often unequal distribution of power. It refers to the extent to which a nation accedes to the fact that variances in its citizens' intellectual and physical capabilities often give rise to inequities in their well-being. Second is that the *Individualism Versus Collectivism* centre around the relative importance or otherwise of the familial unit. Individualism is a national cultural attribute describing a lax social framework in which people focus only on their own selves and of their immediate family. The self is paramount in the same. Collectivism, on the other hand, is a national cultural attribute describing a snug social framework in which people assume others in their groups to look after and protect them. In other words, the society is a more important constituent of the collective unit. Third, *Quantity of Life Versus Quality of Life* is centred on the concept of materialism or the lack thereof. In the former, that is *Quantity of Life*, societal values are characterized by individual assertiveness, materialism and a general lack of concern for social relationships. *Quality of life*, on the other hand, refers to a national cultural attribute that emphasizes relationships and a concern for others. Fourth, *Uncertainty Avoidance* is a cultural attribute that describes the level to which a society feels threatened by indeterminate and uncertain situations.

It either tries to avoid them or faces them headlong. Fifth, *Long-term Versus Short-term Orientation* is centred on whether the society places emphasis on futuristic or current circumstances. *Long-term orientation* as opposed to its short-term counterpart is mindful of thrift, perseverance and futuristic components of culture. *Short-term orientation* emphasizes the bygone and the contemporary, a respect for traditions and fulfilment of social obligations (Hofstede, 1984, 1991).

It is now prudent to differentiate the Western and Eastern cultural ethos in light of the aforementioned national cultural dimensions. The Western cultures are replete with non-acceptance of *power distance*, greater emphasis *on individualism* as opposed to *collectivism*, *quantity of life/materialism*, a desire to face *uncertainties headlong* and a *long-term societal orientation* with greater importance attached to thrift, perseverance and futuristic components of culture (ibid). The Eastern cultures abound in acceptance of *power distance*, greater emphasis on *collectivism* as opposed to *individualism*, *quality of life/spiritualism*, a desire to avoid *uncertainties* and a *short-term social orientation* with greater importance attached to the respect for traditions and fulfilment of social obligations (ibid). Any subsequent analysis of cultural marketing must ensure that these factors are accounted for (ibid).

The concept has received some attention from researchers and practitioners in the marketing domain. To methodically evaluate the voyage of cultural marketing in the Indian textiles sector, prior literature is appraised. In line with the same, literature review in this analysis is systematized in the sub-sections as follows.

1) Important concerns of cultural marketing;
2) Issues of cultural marketing in the global textiles sector; and
3) Cultural marketing and the Indian textiles sector: Contraventions and prospects.

Important Concerns of Cultural Marketing

As per existing research, cultural values play a central role in shaping consumer behaviour (Carman, 1978; Munson and McIntyre, 1979; Vinson et al., 1977). Dominant local cultures have often found expression in the way a brand product is advertised, keeping in mind the socio-cultural and profit manifestations of the same in the target group. Analyses focusing on Eastern and Western cultures have established a robust local value content in most Eastern advertisements (Belk and Bryce, 1986; Belk et al., 1985; Belk and Pollay, 1985; Lin, 2001; Zhou, Zhou and Xue, 2005) as against their Western counterparts. Some of the leading cultural values more prevalent in the West are enjoyment, individualism, modernity, youth and technology. The Eastern counterparts seem to be more focused on the importance of the family unit and the virtue of parsimony. In other words, cultural marketing targets attaining product likeability among the focus group of customers of a brand (ibid).

An interesting example of the same is the world of Arab clothing advertising. Al-Olayan and Karande (2000) found that Arabic magazine advertisements feature fewer humans/people than their US counterparts. Intriguingly, female depictions in the Arabic magazine advertisements are almost always in long flowing dresses. To several non-Arabs, such depictions may come off as being outright bizarre; yet, they are in perfect consonance with the local Arab sensibilities of less emphasis on human figure, especially the female form. The main reason for such portrayal is the need for the advertisers to be compatible with Islamic sensibilities of the region. Such examples abound for other cultures as well. A study by Singh and Huang (1962) too asserts similar results for India and the United States in the marketing domain. While some marketing strategies and products may be effective in some parts of the world, they may not be so in the other parts, for the simple reason of them being incongruent with local sense and sensibilities.

A careful reading of the section thus far reveals some interesting issues in the domain of cultural marketing. *First*, the strategy of cultural marketing could only be successful if the marketers are fully mindful of the sense and sensibilities of their target market. Any deviation on their part is bound to result in failure and shunning of the brand in question. Cultural misdemeanour is often taken as an unpardonable offence anywhere in the world, but more so in the traditional and developing parts of the world such as in South Asia and Africa (Lin, 1993). *Second*, some of the major cultural marketing blunders that could at best be avoided pertain to the overemphasis on specific product attributes and quality. The second approach of stressing company reputation and aura could be a more effective way of transmitting the proposed *feelings* to consumers than the former. This is because the second approach of stressing only the company brand and aura is not an insult to the customer's intellect. While such nuanced marketing blunders may be hard to notice, yet they could significantly impact the way the brand is perceived in the minds of prospective customers (Lee, 2006). *Third*, treating the target customer group as a single, homogeneous entity may be another marketing pitfall needing correction for even ethnically and culturally homogeneous customers may require a different set of product attributes to fulfil their wants on the basis of differences in their age, lingual, gender and professional structures. For instance, a young Indian medic, regardless of his/her gender, may not differ significantly in terms of his/her clothing preferences. They may both require a set of comfortable yet, chic clothing to suit the demands of their tiresome profession. On the other hand, a woman sports professional may require a different set of clothing than her male counterpart (Lee, 2006; Lin, 1993).

Thus, cultural marketing strategists must keep in mind these nuances while framing appropriate marketing tactics. The next subsection discusses the issues of cultural marketing in the global textiles sector.

Issues of Cultural Marketing in the Global Textiles Sector

Studies indicate that managers in the textiles industry globally score higher on conceptualization than on contextualization. As a result, they perform poorly in international settings. It is, therefore, imperative for the firms to train their managers in local cultural settings of the countries they are to serve. This is bound to result in better value co-creation for both the customers and the textile brands in focus (Arora et al., 2004). It has been comprehended that variances in aesthetic sensitivities, traditional and social values, languages and lifestyles between the product-producer and consumer nations can cause an imported product to feel culturally incongruent to the local consumers, resulting in downgraded product evaluations (Craig et al., 2005; Lee, 2006; Bhandari and Raut, 2019; Ross, 1971).

In addition to greater awareness of local cultures and customs, the firms are expected to possess certain attributes such as the *must be attributes*, the *attractive attributes* and the *performance attributes*. The *must be attributes* define the essential benchmarks expected in a consumer product such as textiles. Non-fulfilment of these tends to leave the customer dissatisfied. However, fulfilment of the same does not entail satisfaction of customer utility in real sense of the term. *Must be attributes* hold more of a symbolic value for the customers. In other words, the customer regards these as pre-requisites for satisfaction of his/her wants, at least psychologically. These are not explicitly demanded by him/her as these are taken for granted by the customer. However, these remain an essential determining factor for the likeability or otherwise of the firm. Non-fulfilment of the same may lead the customer to shun these products altogether (Matzler and Hinterhuber, 1998). For example on e-commerce platforms, punctuality of the delivery schedules might constitute a *must-be attribute*. In other words, customers expect their products to be delivered on time (Irastorza and Perez-Vega, 2017; Matzler and Hinterhuber, 1998).

The other important attributes are the *performance attributes*. As the term itself suggests, *performance attributes* are related to the performance of the company product. These are usually overtly needed by the customers, and performance of the product determines their satisfaction. Customers are gratified with a higher level of product performance than with a lower level. For example the performance attribute in a clothing accessory could be its fitting, washability, wearability, comfortable wear, moisture transmission, thermal resistance, wicking, water proof, flame resistant, fabric durability and value for money features (Wilkie and Pessemier, 1973). Textile products scoring higher on these may end up being the most likeable ones, and those not satisfying these qualities may eventually be relegated in the customers' minds, no matter whatever advertising is undertaken to impress upon their decisions.

Another set of important product attributes are the *attractive attributes*. These qualities surpass customer expectations. These have the greatest impact on customer satisfaction with a given product. These are neither explicitly expressed nor expected by a customer. Their presence, however, leads to a more than proportionate satisfaction in the minds of customers. However, them being absent in a product does not reduce the desirability of the same to any significant extent (Matzler and Hinterhuber, 1998). For example, digitally smart clothing may or may not constitute to be an attribute for a potential customer. It may at best serve a particular class of consumers, that is those who are bent upon purchasing digitally savvy clothing. For the majority of textile users, such attributes may be of little-to-no use (Maiti et al., 2020; Stoppa and Chiolerio, 2014).

Any assessment of cultural marketing in the textiles industry both in global and Indian contexts is centred around the concepts discussed in this subsection. Any textile brand must acclimatize itself to the changing trends, mores and styles in a particular culture to stay relevant (ibid). An example will help explain the point further. *Brand loyalty* has been identified as an important tactic for sellers to obtain a competitive edge in the market (Sirdeshmukh et al., 2002). Consumers develop fidelity to a specific brand in such a way that they intend to buy the brand frequently and do not change their brands often. Furthermore, *brand loyalty* is seen as enduring attachment to a brand (Dick and Basu, 1994; Dillon et al., 2001; Dodds et al., 1991). It is due to *brand loyalty*, thanks to the Asian emphasis on collective as against individual identity, that customers in Asia develop long-term association with the brand. This is in stark contrast to the attitudes of Western customers (ibid). However, with mutable consumption patterns, thanks to the onset of globalization and digitalization, these Asian attributes have come under strain. This calls for developing a dynamic cultural marketing perspective into the issue of brand promotion in the textiles sector.

This is in sharp contrast to the pre-globalization-era Asian consumers (including in India) who were not much familiar with the foreign brands. They tended to become more loyal towards the foreign brands compared to the local brands as they perceived the former to be of a better quality (Lin and Sternquist, 1994). Similarly, Gaedeke (1973) and Yoo et al. (2000) emphasize that developing countries such as India, China and Taiwan prefer brands from the Western or the developed countries and were more loyal towards the same on account of their perceived superior quality. Even though the trend may not continue for long anymore, thanks to the onset of globalization and digitalization-induced customer information overflow, the generic characteristics of the behaviour may remain the same. Building on this section further, the subsequent segment discusses the strategy of cultural marketing in the Indian textiles sector in terms of its contraventions and prospects.

Cultural Marketing and the Indian Textiles Sector: Contraventions and Prospects

Many a times, the firms in their desire to outcompete their rivals end up committing cultural marketing blunders. In other words, they lose sense of the local cultural ethos and thereby witness an erosion in their customer base. Similar downsides have been noticed time and again in the Indian textiles sector as well. A prominent example of the same is the *Jack and Jones* commercial of 2016 featuring a famous Hindi film actor (Ranveer Singh) with a woman on his shoulder. The ad was criticized for its perceptible sexist undertones. The Danish fashion brand's notion of *males not holding back* bombed in an unexpected way. The brand got its brand ambassador actor Ranveer Singh to pose with a woman dangled on his shoulder (apparently, the female model in the ad seemed ecstatic at the idea of a man treating her as his *work*). People across the length and breadth of the country dubbed the ad as being outright indecent and an affront to the dignity of Indian women for the reason that it promoted hyper-sexualization of the female body. Feminists all across the country termed the commercial as unfortunate and a significant step backwards in the fight against the ill-treatment of women in the country (India Today, 2016).

Whatever may have been the motivation behind the said advertisement, it cannot be denied that sexist/gender insensitive and racist ads have all too often been used preposterously to attract greater customer interest. In case of sexist ads such as the one described in the aforementioned paragraph, the supposed intent to attract male customers to the brand can often backfire as was evident by the appreciable male outrage over the said advert. It is somewhat culturally insensitive to assume that all men love to see sexist commercials. While it may be true for a section of men, the same cannot be generalized to their entire ilk. Similarly, the sari (a type of traditional Indian female draping) commercials in India too have had their share of bloopers. A *Myntra* (a prominent e-commerce website for clothing and other accessories) sari commercial in 2016 sought to portray a scene out of the Hindu epic *Mahabharata*, where during Draupadi's *Cheerharan*, Lord Krishna is seen shopping for an 'additionally long sari' on Myntra. The advertisement exposed the lack of religious sensitivity on the part of the e-commerce firm. A fallout of this culturally insensitive marketing strategy was the trending of #BoycottMyntra on Twitter and the site having to take down this outrageous advert after 24 hours (BGR, 2016).

The two examples show the importance of making culturally congruent ads in the target markets so as to strike a genuine and not a superficial cord with the customers. These cultural blunders could at best be avoided if the marketers agree to sensitize themselves of the local customs and cultures and not treat their culture as superior over the target populations. Sensitivity along gender, religious and racial/ethnic lines is a must for any marketing strategy to avoid the challenge of being culturally incongruent (Samaha et al., 2014). A point to be kept in mind at all times is that no culture is inferior or superior to any. Each culture requires its own set of comprehension and understanding. What may be *customary* in a particular culture may be downright outrageous in another setting. This is the message the marketers must remember for all times (ibid).

When it comes to the prospects for the Indian textiles industry in the domain of cultural marketing, several themes come to one's mind. First is the need to practise *ecological marketing* by the culturally thoughtful textile firms or, in other words, to ascertain whether or not their textile product is meeting the required environmental standards. Examples of eco-friendly products are organic cotton fabric, hemp, jute, bamboo and recycled commodities. Such locally available products are a big hit with Indian consumers nowadays who are growing increasingly aware of the need to keep their surroundings free from harmful chemicals. Inorganic textile products often result in the release of unwarranted chemicals (such as colour dyes) into the ecosystem (Dhiman et al., 2020). Also, upon their disuse, these often find their way into stray animals' digestive systems, rendering them vulnerable to ailments and untimely death (Austen, 2000; Craig et al., 2005; Lee, 2006; Ross, 1971).

Another important ethical tactic in the domain of cultural marketing could be *gender-sensitive marketing*. The same refers to not resorting to such marketing tactics that may prove detrimental to the dignity of womenfolk. Categories of *gender insensitive marketing* include sexually explicit/obscene marketing, showing the man of the household as the sole in-charge of the outside world, while the woman is shown toiling with the household chores (in other words, as a glorified household maid), or women preferring only pink-coloured clothing accessories while the men are shown drawn towards neutral colours. Such adverts only seek to reinforce gendered stereotypes prevalent in a developing country like India. The marketers should rather do some justice to the cause of gender equality by portraying the lives of achiever women being assisted by their equally achiever husbands/partners/families. Such ads serve their socio-economic purpose well and would be well received by all and sundry in due course of time, provided the commercial makers have the resolve to go the extra mile and challenge some of the prevalent gender roles/norms. It has been proven time and again that commercials (in both television and print media) have a major impact on the way customers perceive their surroundings. Cultural marketing has a two-way relationship with the target society – they both get influenced and influence the audience they are targeted at. Marketers should try to be *gender ethical* as far as possible with their imagery depictions in the commercials. *Gender neutral* or *unisex clothing* accessories could be the way forward in the direction of gender-sensitive cultural marketing (Austen, 2000; Craig et al., 2005; Lee, 2006; Ross, 1971).

A third prospect for cultural marketers in the Indian textile industry is in the domain of *labour rights*. It would be prudent to expect the textile firms of their degree of adherence to labour laws, International Labour Organization charters and conventions. This could be in terms of indicating whether the firms are adhering to stipulated working hours, wage pays and social security benefits for their workers. The consumers have a right to know these to gauge how *labour ethical* the firms are. Blindly following the tenets of capitalism is only going to result in a vicious cycle of greed, greed and more greed, with no clear winners or losers over the long term. Worker well-being and productivity ensure their active and whole-hearted participation in the textiles production chain. This eventually results in better employment and output prospects for the industry as a whole. A content workforce results in a gratified working atmosphere having a positive ramification for the textiles industrial chain (Austen, 2000; Craig et al., 2005; Lee, 2006; Ross, 1971).

In sum, the Indian textiles industry holds tremendous promise for the strategists of cultural marketing both in the present and future times if they look beyond the traditional norms and focus on emerging areas such as environment, gender and labour sensitivities. In the process, the firms have a moral accountability towards the societies in so far as their influencing power is concerned. They can and should look beyond the horizons to shape popular imagination in more appropriate ways. The subsequent section describes the methodology adopted for this study.

Methodology

Conducting a study using non-empirical approach comes with its own set of issues and challenges. This is owing to a number of factors. The evolving nature of theoretical research design and a methodology study entail recounting a procedure to create another process. Study designs are more often than not constrained by what the researchers already have on their hands, rather than what they could have experienced first-hand in an empirical research (Hulland, 2020; Jakkola, 2020; Rana et al., 2020). In other words, the study is already constrained by the preponderance of other perspectives and not so much by the author's own.

In the absence of the existence of universally acceptable models, thanks to the non-empirical nature of this study, the author followed the method recommended for theoretical papers in the marketing domain by Hulland (2020), Jakkola (2020) and Rana et al. (2020). Taking a cue from the same, the existing study is based on review of literature and theorization. It seeks to study the concept of cultural marketing in the Indian textiles sector from different perspectives and in terms of issues prevalent both globally and in India.

The analysis is implemented in a threefold arrangement of text and its incorporation within a theoretical structure. First, an analysis of important concerns of cultural marketing has been undertaken to explore and understand the theoretical undercurrents of the theme. The second part involves exploring the issues of cultural marketing in the global textiles sector. This part is helpful for the determination of research possibilities and applications of the concept of cultural marketing in the Indian textiles sector. The third related part is concerned with the application of the concept of cultural marketing in the Indian textiles sector, with its concomitant slip-ups and prospects. All in all, the review of literature section forms the backbone of this study. Any subsequent perspective development on the theme is to be formed only along these lines. The next section is on discussion, and it provides insights into the major findings of the chapter as well as the uniqueness and limitations of the study.

Discussion

The real worth of consumer goods lies in their ability to convey and correspond representative meanings and not merely serve utilitarian purposes (McCracken, 1986). The meaning of a marketed product depends more on the cultural elements contained within it (i.e. the idea or goods content), the cultural circumstances that impact customers' information processing and decision-making (i.e. the cultural upbringing of the communication receiver) and some other indicators such as the tactics of the communication sender and the communication generator (ibid).

This study seeks to understand and interpret the interplay of culture, marketing and the Indian textiles sector within the framework of cultural marketing. The same is unique as not many studies have done so for the Indian textiles sector. The theme is still a relatively underexplored area. To study the same, the effects of cultural factors on customers' product appraisals (in this case the textile products of the Indian textiles sector) through their joint effects with the marketing strategy (chiefly, the product advertising strategy) are considered (Carman, 1978; Munson and McIntyre, 1979; Vinson et al., 1977). The study explains the nuances of the relationship between cultural marketing and the Indian textiles sector. It assesses the role customers' cultural outlook plays in its interaction with the firms' cultural marketing strategy to affect customers' evaluations of products filled with cultural substance, herein the textile products of the Indian textiles sector. It also seeks to understand the important issues of cultural marketing both within a globalized and domestic Indian framework, drawing heavily from real-life marketing examples. It also suggests some challenges and prospects of the cultural marketing strategy for the Indian textiles sector.

The key findings of this chapter relate to the effectiveness of the cultural marketing strategy as a marketing tool for the Indian textiles industry and the need to expand the ambit of operation of the strategy to include new concerns such as those pertaining to labour, gender and ecological realms. It also emphasizes the importance of being a *culturally sensitive brand* in order to be able to succeed as a marketer in the focus market. In other words, *cultural congruence* with local customs and traditions must be the motto of any brand seeking to expand its footprint in a market/area/region.

The findings of this study have important consequences for the international marketing strategy related to cultural marketing advertising and new product development for a target destination. The study suggests that in order to be a successful brand in the target market, the brand marketers must resort to an *intelligent cultural marketing strategy* that is *congruent with local cultural sensibilities*. Specifically, the study contributes to the domain of international marketing in the following ways.

First, the research contributes to the marketing theory by implanting culture, marketing and product interactions within its framework and showing how cultural marketing and firms' marketing strategies influence the reception of the culturally loaded product's intended message. The kind of influence such a marketing strategy could have upon the society too is vital for the mutual growth of the customers and the companies.

Second, in terms of the cultural content of a textile product, existing research has shown that products are well received in cultures that are closer to the home country or in cultural environments that approximate with the home country cultural environment (Lee, 2006). National cultural dimensions (individualism/communalism, masculinity/femininity and uncertainty orientation) determine the influence of these interactions and inter-relationships. Studies show that cultural congruence affects product revenues (Lee, 2006; Craig et al., 2005) and that cultural variances in self-construal impact product assessments (Aaker and Lee, 2001). The findings validate the belief that an appropriate cultural marketing strategy is the need of the hour for textile brands to attain greater value co-creation in terms of increased sales and revenues for the textile brands and cultural gratification for the textile brand customers.

At the end, the power distance cultural dimension can influence the effectiveness of cultural advertising spending. Advertising expenditure beckons social status. It is revealed that power distance belief augments this upbeat signalling outcome of advertising spending on product evaluation even further. Beliefs of power distance tend to nurture a demand for esteem among customers, which can only be satisfied by the consumption of culturally heavy advertised products. This study adds to the comprehension of the role of cultural marketing strategy by demonstrating the effect of cultural marketing on customer–brand interactions (Hofstede, 1984, 1991).

Notwithstanding the richness of the research theme, the same suffers from some limitations that may serve as future areas of research. First, even though the study relies on extensive review of literature on the theme, the lack of empirical analysis is a concern. Future researchers could develop the study more as a research paper and less as a perspective piece by trusting the text data mining technique. A potential resolution could be a collection of consumer reviews in multiple languages and applying a text data mining technique for each language separately. Another method could be to examine customer reviews of a textile product in the local language as well as in English to gauge the effectiveness of the cultural marketing strategy (Moon et al., 2016; Moon and Song, 2015). The cultural matter of the advertising message itself could influence the efficacy of cultural advertising strategy for products in foreign countries. While it may be difficult to collect and translate a large number of actual advertising messages, the data so analysed could be beneficial for future research (ibid).

Second, even though the focus of the study is India, a comprehensive analysis on its neighbours in the South Asian region with similar cultures and customs could be another way forward to conduct an exhaustive study (ibid).

Third, future research may investigate the generalizability of the interface between cultural marketing strategy and other industries in a manner akin to the textiles sector (ibid).

Analyses have also unearthed that national cultures affect not only the behaviour of clients but also the business of clients (Hoppner et al., 2015). Future studies must investigate this interaction of cultural factors with marketing strategies in various business-to-business (B2B) markets. The succeeding section concludes this study.

Conclusion

To summarize, the research takes an important step towards revealing how cultural factors interact with marketing strategy in determining customers' product evaluations and, accordingly, how managers' decisions can be shaped by an understanding of national culture in international markets. The study stimulates further research to examine how culture affects the effectiveness of Indian textiles firms' cultural marketing strategy and leads to brand value co-creation in terms of greater brand affinity-induced brand purchases.

All in all, the chapter seeks to locate the issue of cultural marketing in the framework of Indian textiles industry. In the wake of paucity of good research work on the issue, the same would serve as a useful resource material for upcoming generations of research works. After all, the ongoing COVID-19 pandemic only reminds the marketing and industrial fields of the need to come up with innovative solutions to the sagging fortunes of the Indian textiles sector. And what better solution than cultural marketing! In line with the same, the next section elicits some important policy implications of this study.

Future Policy Implications

This study examining the interactions of cultural marketing strategy and the Indian textiles sector has some vital policy implications. It provides useful insights on which marketing strategies are said to be most effectual, *given the cultural characteristics* of the national market. In addition, the findings help marketing managers select appropriate target countries, given their choice of cultural marketing strategies. Even in a globalized economy, customers seek to move to a more individualized and culturally differentiated product environment. Thus, cultures still are the leading force in various types of globalized and glocalized products. Companies around the globe endeavour to achieve the subtle equilibrium between cultural marketing to meet indigenous cultural demands and commercial marketing to benefit from economies of scale and premium acuities (Steenkamp and Jong, 2010; Kjeldgaard and Askegaard, 2006; Ang et al., 2007; Kipnis et al., 2013).

Firms must strive to increase the cultural resemblance of their brand products by tailoring their cultural content to the local cultural needs. Also, paying close attention to cultural congruence between the product content and consumers' cultural background is even more important for textile firms that market products rich in cultural and artistic meanings (ibid). An example could help understand this point further. The Lucknow *Chikankari* clothes must adjust their designs and patterns as per the need of their target markets. A North Indian may prefer *Chikan* kurtas and pyjamas, while a South Indian may prefer *Chikan* saris. Again, numerous such examples abound in the country's customer landscape.

Also, the study implies that textile firms should consider customers' cultural orientation in the power distance belief when allocating marketing funds. They must want and try to increase cultural advertising outlays in locations/regions that exhibit higher levels of power distance belief to take advantage of customers' sensitivity to marketing tactics and ensure a higher return to their advertising policies (Hofstede, 1984, 1991).

Another important policy implication is in the domain of ethical cultural marketing. Such strategies could only help in bringing about benign changes in the socio-economic landscape by promoting salubrious ecological, gender and labour environment through marketing (Carman, 1978; Munson and McIntyre, 1979; Vinson et al., 1977).

All in all, the study succeeds in building a firm ground for cultural marketing within the Indian textiles sector and could also prove to be a useful teaching tool in courses such as consumer behaviour, promotion management, customer relationship management and contemporary practices in international marketing.

References

Aaker, J., & Lee, A. (2001). "I" seek pleasures and "we" avoid pains: The role of self-regulatory goals in information processing and persuasion. *Journal of Consumer Research*, 28, 33–49.

Adichie, C. N. (2014). People make culture. Retrieved from https://cc.bingj.com/cache.aspx?q=culture+does+not+make+people%2c+people+make+culture+meaning&d=4878821060314445&mkt=en-IN&setlang=en-US&w=13Kumf Adh_CqoYOrNGA5C6KokH5rdX1U.

Al-Olayan, F. S., & Karande, K. (2000). A content analysis of magazine advertisements from the United States and the Arab World. *Journal of Advertising*, 29 (3), 69–82.

Ang S., Van Dyne L., Koh C., Ng, K. Y., Templer, K. J., Tay, C., & Chandrasekar, N. A. (2007). Cultural intelligence: Its measurement and effects on cultural judgment and decision making, cultural adaptation and task performance. *Management and Organization Review*, 3, 335–71.

Arora, A., Jaju, A., Kefalas, A. G., Perenich, T. (2004). An exploratory analysis of global managerial mindsets: a case of U.S. textile and apparel industry. *Journal of International Management*, 10 (3), 393–411.

Austen, S. (2000). Culture and the labor market. *Review of Social Economy*, 58 (4), 505–521.

Belk, R. W., & Bryce, W. J. (1986). Materialism and individual determinism in US and Japanese television advertising. *Advances in Consumer Research*, 13, 568–572.

Bhandari, K. R., & Raut, S. K. (2019). 9 Leveraging Tacit. *Advances in Management Research: Innovation and Technology*, 1 (1), 127–138.

Belk, R. W., Bryce, W. J., & Pollay, R. W. (1985). Advertising themes and cultural values: A comparison of US and Japanese advertising. In Mun, K.C. & Chan, T.C. (Eds.), *Proceedings of the Inaugural Meeting of the Southeast Region*. Academy of International Business: Hong Kong.

Belk, R. W., & Pollay, R. W. (1985). Materialism and status appeals in Japanese and US print advertising. *International Marketing Review*, 2 (4), 38–47.

BGR. (2016). Twitter users boycott Myntra for an ad they did not make. Retrieved from www.bgr.in/news/twitter-users-boycott-myntra-for-an-ad-they-did-not-make-416267.

Carman, J. M. (1978). Values and consumption patterns: A closed loop. In Keith Hunt, H. (Ed.), *Advances in Consumer Research*. Association for Consumer Research: Ann Arbor, MI.

Clark, T. (1990). International marketing and national character: A review and proposal for an integrative theory. *Journal of Marketing*, 54 (4), 66–79.

Craig, C. S., Greene, W., & Douglas, S. (2005). Culture matters: Consumer acceptance of U.S. films in foreign markets. *Journal of International Marketing*, 13 (4), 80–103.

Dhiman, R., Kumar, V., & Rana, S. (2020). Why export competitiveness differs within Indian textile industry? Determinants and empirical evidence. *Review of International Business and Strategy*, 30 (3), 375–397.

Dick, A. S., & Basu, K. (1994). Customer loyalty: Toward an integrated conceptual framework. *Journal of the Academy of Marketing Science*, 22, 99–113.

Dillon, W., Madden, T., Kirmani, A., & Mukherjee, S. (2001). Understanding what's in a brand rating: A model for assessing brand and attribute effects and their relationship to brand equity. *Journal of Marketing Research*, 38, 415–429.

Dodds, W. B., Monroe, K., & Grewal, D. (1991). Effect of price and store information on buyer's product evaluations. *Journal of Marketing Research*, 28, 307–319.

Gaedeke, R. (1973). Consumer attitudes toward products "made in" developing countries. *Journal of Retailing*, 49, 13–24.

George, M. J., & Jones, G. R. (1996). *Understanding and Managing Organizational Behaviour*. Addison-Wesley: New York.

Hall, E. T. (1977). *Beyond Culture*. Anchor Press: New York.

Hofstede, G. (1984). *Cultures' Consequences: International Differences in Work-Related Values* (Abridged ed.). Sage Publications: Beverly Hills, CA.

Hofstede, G. (1991). *Cultures and Organizations: Structure of the Mind*. McGraw-Hill: London.

Hoppner, J., Griffith, D., & White, R. (2015). Reciprocity in relationship marketing: A cross- cultural examination of the effects of equivalence and immediacy on relationship quality and satisfaction with performance. *Journal of International Marketing*, 23 (4), 64–83.

Hulland, J. (2020). Conceptual review papers: revisiting existing research to develop and refine theory. *AMS Review*, 10 (1/2), 1–9.

IGI-Global. (2021). The assessment of cultural experience through the measurement of cross cutting skills. Retrieved from www.igi-global.com/dictionary/

the-assessment-of-cultural-experience-through-the-measurement-of-cross-cutting-skills/39240.

India Today. (2016). Jack and Jones India apologizes for sexist ad featuring Ranveer Singh. Will he apologize? Retrieved from www.indiatoday.in/fyi/story/ranveer-singh-sexist-ad-jack-and-jones-apologises-pulls-off-353673-2016-11-24.

Irastorza, M. P., & Perez-Vega, R. (2017). Exploring motivations to engage in online brand communities: A comparative analysis. Retrieved from www.researchgate.net/publication/314154971.

Jahoda, G. (2012). Critical reflections on some recent definitions of "culture". *Culture & Psychology*, 18 (3), 289–303.

Jakkola, E. (2020). Designing conceptual articles: four approaches. *AMS Review*. Retrieved from https://link.springer.com/article/10.1007/s13162-020-00161-0.

Kanupriya (2020). Digitalization and the Indian textiles sector: A critical analysis. *FIIB Business Review*. Retrieved from https://doi.org/10.1177/2319714520961861.

Kipnis, E., Broderick, A., Demangeot, C., Adkins, N., Ferguson, F., Henderson, G., Guillaume J., Mueller, R., Pullig, R., Roy, A., & Zuniga, M. (2013). Branding beyond prejudice: Navigating multicultural marketplaces for consumer well-being. *Journal of Business Research*, 66, 1186–1194.

Kjeldgaard, D., & Askegaard, S. (2006). The glocalization of youth culture: The global youth segment as structures of common difference. *Journal of Consumer Research*, 33 (2), 231–247.

Lee, F. (2006). Cultural discount and cross-culture predictability: Examining the box office performance of American movies in Hong Kong. *Journal of Media Economics*, 19 (4), 259–278.

Lin, C. A. (1993). Cultural differences in message strategies: A comparison between American and Japanese TV Commercials. *Journal of Advertising Research*, 20 (1), 33–45.

Lin, C. A. (2001). Cultural values reflected in Chinese and American television advertising. *International Journal of Advertising*, 21 (4), 83–94.

Lin, L., & Sternquist, B. (1994). Taiwanese consumer's perception of product information cues: Country-of-origin and store prestige. *European Journal of Marketing*, 28, 5–18.

Madhavan, N. (2020). Textile sector needs a vision and mission. Retrieved from www.thehindubusinessline.com/opinion/columns/textile-sector-needs-a-vision-and-mission/article31862988.ece.

Maiti, D., Castellacci, F., & Melchior, A. (2020). Digitalisation and development: Issues for India and beyond. Retrieved from https://10.1007/978-981-13-9996-1_1.

Manstead, A. S. R. (1997). Situations, belongingness, attitudes, and culture: Four lessons learned from social psychology. In McGarty, C. & Haslam, S. A. (Eds.), *Social Psychology*. Blackwell Publishers Ltd.: Cambridge.

Matzler, K., & Hinterhuber, H. H. (1998). How to make product development projects more successful by integrating Kano's model of customer satisfaction into quality function deployment. *Technovation*, 18 (1), 25–38.

McCracken, G. (1986). Culture and consumption: A theoretical account of the structure and movement of the cultural meaning of consumer goods. *Journal of Consumer Research*, 13 (6), 71–84.

McCracken, G. (1988). *Culture and Consumption: New Approaches to the Symbolic Character of Consumer Goods and Activities*. Indiana University Press: Bloomington.

Moon, S., Mishra, A., Mishra, H., & Kang, M. (2016). Cultural and economic factors on global cultural products. *Journal of International Marketing*, 24 (3), 78–97.

Moon, S., & Song, R. (2015). The roles of cultural elements in international retailing of cultural products: An application to the motion picture industry. *Journal of Retailing*, 91 (1), 154–170.

Munson, J. M., & McIntyre, S. H. (1979). Developing practical procedures for the measurement of personal values in cross-cultural marketing. *Journal of Marketing Research*, 16 (1), 48–52.

Rana, S., Raut, S. K., Prashar, S., & Hamid, A. B. A. (2020). Promoting through consumer nostalgia: A conceptual framework and future research agenda. *Journal of Promotion Management*, 27(2), 211–249.

Rana, S., Raut, S. K., Prashar, S., & Quttainah, M. A. (2020). The transversal of nostalgia from psychology to marketing: what does it portend for future research? *International Journal of Organizational Analysis*. Retrieved from https://doi.org/10.1108/IJOA-03-2020-2097/.

Raut, S. K., Sakpal, S., & Soni, R. (2022). Understanding the Service Quality Dimensions and Achieving Resilience in Service Retail. In *Handbook of Research on Supply Chain Resiliency, Efficiency, and Visibility in the Post-Pandemic Era*, edited by Ramakrishna Yanamandra (pp. 136–156). IGI Global, UAE. https://doi.org/10.4018/978-1-7998-9506-0

Ross, I. (1971). Self-concept and brand preference. *Journal of Business*, 44 (1), 38–50.

Samaha, S. A., Beck, J., & Palmatier, W. (2014). The role of culture in international relationship marketing. *Journal of Marketing*, 78 (5), 78–98.

Singh, P.N., & Huang, S.C. (1962). Some socio-cultural and psychological determinants of advertising in India: A comparative study. *The Journal of Social Psychology*, 57 (3), 113–21.

Sirdeshmukh, D., Singh, J., & Sabol, B. (2002). Consumer trust, value, and loyalty in relational exchanges. *Journal of Marketing*, 56, 15–37.

Steenkamp, J-B., & Jong, M. (2010). A global investigation into the constellation of consumer attitudes toward global and local products. *Journal of Marketing*, 74 (11), 18–40.

Stoppa, M., & Chiolerio, A. (2014). Wearable electronics and smart textiles: A critical review. *Sensors*, 14, 11957–11992. Retrieved from www.ncbi.nlm.nih.gov/pmc/articles/PMC4168435/.

Vinson, D. E., Scott, J. E., & Lamont, L. M. (1977). The role of personal values in marketing and consumer behaviour. *Journal of Marketing*, 41 (2), 44–50.

Wellner, A. S. (2002). *The Teen Scene*. Forecast: London.

Wilkie, W. L., & Pessemier, E. A. (1973). Issues in marketing's use of multi-attribute models. *Journal of Marketing Research*, 10 (4), 428–445.

Yoo, B., Donthu, N., & Lee, S. (2000). An examination of selected marketing mix elements and brand equity. *Journal of the Academy of Marketing Science*, 28, 195–211.

Zhou, S., Zhou, P., & Xue, F. (2005). Visual differences in US and Chinese television commercials. *Journal of Advertising*, 34 (1), 111–119.

10 Religion and Strategic Marketing Communication

Perspectivizing Key Facets of Consumption

Manpreet Arora and Roshan Lal Sharma

Introduction

We live in a world where commercialization and commoditization of everything is possible. Every day we use plenty of products that are branded, nicely packaged and smartly circulated in the market, and we get attracted towards them. Companies, while marketing their products, devise various strategies and explore numerous possibilities to reach larger number of people to sell their product/s successfully. In recent years, we have been observing how important religion, media, and culture have become in the field of marketing (Lynchet et al., 2012; Rana, Raut, Prashar, & Quttainah, 2020; Rana, Raut, Prashar, & Hamid, 2020). In fact, the role of media has always been arguable in the field of marketing even though its importance cannot be denied. Media has not just remained there as an instrument for delivery of information; it has rather become a new paradigm which contributes towards influencing perception, beliefs as well as faith of the consumers (Copley, 2007). These days, companies employ a variety of methods to build on the belief and faith of the consumers, which eventually culminates in manufacturing of various kinds of products that are carefully marketed and made available in the market.

Marketing a product involves communicating various aspects of the product or a service to the consumer (Rowley, 1998; Herrmann & Rana, 2020). In today's globalized world where companies operate internationally to sell their products, it becomes imperative for them to understand the social, cultural, and religious beliefs of people to be able to market and sell their products successfully. It implies that to sell a brand globally nowadays requires an understanding of the religion as well as its associated aspects that affect the demand of the product (Gauthier, 2016). If we take the case of India, we can find the mark of religion in every aspect of life as it is hard to identify any socio-cultural arena remaining unaffected by religion. It thus becomes important for the companies to understand various aspects of culture including religion to sell their products in the market (Banerjee, 2008). Broadly, this is an area of cultural studies, but if we look at the inclination of the people towards their religious beliefs, we can say

DOI: 10.4324/9781003315582-11

that religion becomes the very heart of culture in some of the economies like India (Iyer, 1999).

There are not only the products that are influenced by religion in India, but it can be arguably claimed that even services especially in tourism sector are also affected considerably by religion (Bandyopadhyayet et al., 2008). India is known for religious tourism and it is not restricted only to some religious places, but there are certain events as well which are known worldwide (Blackwell, 2007) associated with various religious activities. Tourists from all over the world visit India every year and make sure to visit markets flooded with products which they buy as souvenirs as they know that these are markers of religious affiliation of the people of India. They also get to know gradually how religion forms the core of Indian psyche. At this juncture, it would be in order to explore the notion of religion, its marketization, and consumption based on a survey of available literature.

Religion and Consumption: Literature Survey

The term 'religion' signifies 'belief in and worship of a superhuman controlling power, especially a personal God or gods' and also 'a particular system of faith and worship' (www.lexico.com/definition/religion). It is also understood as a fundamental set of beliefs and practices which people tend to follow/perform by choice. When people practice certain religions and perform rituals and ceremonies, they in turn influence the demand of goods and services in the market. The field of consumer behaviour clearly establishes the notion that the buying behaviour of a consumer is affected by faith (Durmaz, 2014) and her/his connection with particular sets of values and beliefs which s/he practices (Bailey & Sood, 1993). Religion and marketing have been an interest area for many especially in the field of marketing communication. In today's world, religion is consumed just like any other commodity (Belk, 1987). Likewise, religious beliefs too not only affect the choice of products but also the buying decision of a family in terms of colours and other parameters (Singh, 2006, Mansori, 2012).

Studies show how consumers in a particular socio-cultural setup tend to develop a liking for the attributes of a particular product and usually end up forming a brand image. Amidst such a scenario, religion – an integral part of the culture – has a strong bearing on the decision of the customers (Beyer & Beaman, 2007). Culture is considered to be an important source of gaining competitive advantage according to many marketers across the world (Fiol, 1991). These days, the most tedious job for business concerns is to create sense of loyalty in their consumers. Even the globalized firms cannot afford to ignore the impact of cultural factors on their strategic decisions (Hassard & Sharifi, 1989, Thornton et al., 2011; Bhandari and Raut, 2019).

The complexity of relationship among culture, religion, and the strategic business decisions is such that it requires a deeper examination. An appropriate and critical analysis of this relationship may help us decisively devise globally workable strategies for the success of a business. In global businesses, cultural factors are not only crucial but critical as well for decision-making. While reviewing literature, one comes across studies that indicate that even political movements have a deep relationship with religions in several parts of the world (Ellis & TerHaar, 2004, TerHaar & Ellis, 2006, Demerath & Demerath, 2003). Religious influence on global business decisions is a significant problem for the strategic leaders, and it affects their decision-making directly (McFarlane, 2010). Moreover, there are several elements of religion that govern the public sentiments (Siala, 2013) and foremost among them is faith.

Most of the people believe that there are certain forces around us be that the supreme power or the energy. We may name it anything, but it holds so much relevance in our lives that any kind of practice of various rituals/ceremonies along with even politics is governed/regulated by it. At times, it is concerned with gods or the spirit behind everything existent, and at other it is related to some myths and symbolic figures (Butt et al., 2017). Different religions have certain traditions, ceremonies, or rituals, performance of which gives rise to the demand of various products/goods, and many a time these become our necessity (Mathras et al., 2016; Raut, Sakpal and Soni, 2022). The demand in turn creates an opportunity for the producers to create products/manufacture goods and provide services to make religion consumable through performance of rituals. There are several rituals/ceremonies in certain religions that are considered to be sacred. These, at times, are performed secretly but still have the ability to push certain demand factors and thus pave way for the creation and consumption of products. There are religions wherein certain festivals are celebrated, and rituals are performed with great pomp and show. Interestingly, such festivals become events of huge spending and thus create demand for a diverse range of products and services (Patel, 2012). Such festivities and celebrations may be seen in most of the religions in the different parts of the world (Sood & Nasu, 1995) despite the writers' bias towards one particular religion, caste, creed, or community (Choi, 2010, Parameshwaran & Srivastava, 2010) as literature suggests.

People have always been in the quest of defining and redefining life, power, and the transformation processes in the phase of life supported by religion, culture, and their faith. In modern societies, all such things have become materialistically driven, and certain symbols of identity have emerged in the society in tangible manners be it infrastructure, buildings, monuments, flags, signs, accessory, jewellery, or any other consumable products in the form of divine eatables and water. Every culture has got its identity in the form of food, dress, and consumption of various products and also the way people belonging to a particular culture lead their lives. Societies and cultures do live and decline, but consumption of religion goes on in one way or the other.

Hanegraaff (2020) focused on the reconstruction of the study of the religion as a whole and stated that it is very important to understand the importance of religion not only for the society but also for the general human race. He talks about the new narratives and focuses on various key terms such as 'experience', 'consciousness', 'imagination', and 'spirituality'. According to him, the need of the general human race is to focus on spirituality which can help develop new ways of handling the studies on religion. He is of the belief that now the concept of religion is being overshadowed by the concept of spirituality.

On the other hand, Gauthier and Martikainen (2018) try to focus on the concept of marketization and religion in their study. Mitra (2016) talks about the religious consciousness of the Indians who were born in the United States and has tried to analyse the need of the Indians living in the United States to retain and transmit their tradition as well as culture to younger generation. This, after a point, becomes equal to developing the understanding of their religion as the way of expressing tradition and culture is through rituals and festivals which they try to observe and celebrate while living in the United States. She is convinced about the fact that one way of exhibiting the religious affiliation is through the observance of various festivals which ultimately develops an intimate connection with commerce and fashion, festival and celebration, and consumption and religion. She propounds the fact that in the world of mass media, the advertisements and mass production of the products in the United States were confirming the demands of the Hindu community to a large extent in order to satisfy their festival demands associated with their religious affiliations. By narrating a personal incidence, the author tries to establish the fact that in Hindu religion, gods and goddesses are being merchandised and commoditized. Peifer et al. (2016) try to study how the religious beliefs as well as traditions are associated with environmental consumption. The paper states that environmental consumption is a behavioural outcome which ultimately has the potential to yield various greater benefits for the environment. They also highlight an interesting fact that people who have strong belief in god take great care of the environment as there is a fear of change when they believe in god and that inactive god is ready to intervene if anything goes astray.

Consumption of religion thus has two aspects. On the one hand, there are religious institutions that sell faith; on the other, there are multinationals who aim at benefiting substantially from our faith and that is why they make their products and services indispensable for us, which eventually become our way of life. Whatever we consume ultimately is profoundly influenced by our religious faith. We can also say that we use only those products more that are steeped in our culture and influenced by our religion and faith. Viewed thus, the consumption of religion is germane to our sociocultural way of life in the form of production and circulation of various products involving capital in a big way.

Research Questions and Methodology

Based on the aforementioned literature review, it becomes evident that there are multiple facets of consumption of religion. It is being marketized and merchandized as a product and also as products used in religious and ritualistic practices across cultures. Strategic communication thus assumes relevance as religion as a product is envisioned, advertised and marketed very carefully particularly because it involves big money. With each passing day, we may observe an increase in the consumption of religion and related products. The production, circulation and consumption of products concerning religion have been increasing exponentially and that is why this phenomenon needs to be examined thoroughly. This chapter is qualitative in nature and focuses on how our religious beliefs and practices are directly linked with generating business and how big companies catering to a whole range of products related to different religions eventually get benefited. This chapter seeks to explore the following research questions theoretically:

a)   What are the different dimensions of consumption of religion?
b)   How is religion being used in marketing through communicating strategically?
c)   What is the scope of consumption of religion in future marketing practices?

The outcome of the present manuscript can help in the advancement of theoretical aspects concerning consumption and commodification of religion, thereby adding newer communicative dimensions in the field of marketing and advertising. It can also serve as a guide to managerial decision-making while strategizing about marketing communication techniques for positioning and promotion of products which can appeal to the religious sentiments of the consumers.

Diverse Dimensions of Consumption of Religion in Indian Context

We live in an age wherein the most saleable brand/commodity happens to be religion. It is arguably true vis-à-vis most of the religions of the world be that Christianity, Hinduism, Islam, Buddhism, Sikhism, etc. Conventionally, religion has been viewed to be a regulating force in a person's life. It would be well-neigh impossible to attach material aspect to religion due to our understanding of it from the viewpoint of the idea of purifying one's soul and thus attain self-realization through salvation. Ever since the advent of enlightenment modernity, the perception of religion has undergone a tremendous change. Consequent upon industrialization and the resultant thrust on materiality, every single aspect of human life started to be perceived in material terms. The debate between spirituality and materiality over a period of time came to an end with materiality gaining considerable ground and spirituality losing in the battle for supremacy. There have been several other factors responsible for the rise of materialism across diverse cultures of the world, globalization being one of them.

When we think of religion, we seldom allow the thought of wealth and money to take root in our minds. But it will be erroneous to assume that the notion of religion as life-regulating force has nothing to do with money. When we think of religion today, and this has been in vogue for quite some time now, there is much that comes to mind having money involved in it. Viewed simply, this may be related to the ritualistic/ceremonial dimension of religion. For instance, in Hinduism, when we organize community *puja*, *pauranik katha, sundarkand path* (or recitation), different kinds of *jaaps* (chants), *bhajans* (hymns) and ritual performances of various *samskaras* (rites) such as birth *samskaras*, *upnayan samskaras*, marriage *samskaras* and death *samskaras*, we at once become mindful of the expenditure involved therein. At one point in history, every aforementioned ritual used to have negligible capital involved in it. But now the scenario has changed completely as a lot of money is siphoned off in the name of religious ceremonies that require a number of products which are being produced, distributed through marketing chains, and sold commercially in the market. Just to cite an example, cow dung is regarded to be auspicious in various religious ceremonies of Hinduism, and dried cow dung cakes are now available on Amazon for sale.

In addition to that, there may be community performances of certain rituals in the form of *katha*s (recitation of ancient narratives concerning various gods/deities) such as *Bhagvadpuraankatha, Shivpuraan katha,* and *Devibhagvadkatha.* Not everyone today can afford to organize these *kathas* simply because it involves a lot of expenditure as a community event. During ancient times, a *katha vachaka*would be a *rishi* (sage) or an enlightened *guru* (teacher/master) who would simply sit under a tree and narrate incidents and events mentioned in a particular *puraan* and also bringing his own experience to bear upon his discourse. The truth seekers would form a limited audience comprising disciples called *shishyas* and such enlightening sessions would at times take the form of an interaction with disciples asking questions and *gurus* answering them.

Very recently, an interesting trend has gained popularity particularly in electronic media channels about live telecasts of religious discourses and ceremonies. Other religion-specific programmes have also mushroomed catering to the demand of Asian religions specifically. TV channels like Aastha and Sanskar in India are solely dedicated to the propagation of Hinduism religion and its values. However, their marketing through lucrative packaging and advertising impels us to view them as brands and commodities. Every single religion as it is propagated through social media and various religious channels completely fulfils the criterion to be viewed and termed as brands and commodities in the market of diverse range of faiths. The question that one may ask at this juncture is: Can we look at today's religions as carefully packaged brands and commodities to be sold in the market flooded by believers of one religion or the other? The answer would be in the affirmative due to the fact that religion as a packaged brand or commodity is nowadays, packaged, advertised and marketized in a way that it generates as much profit as one can imagine. Therefore, interestingly though, the matter concerning one's faith stands or not only showcased but also sold as a product in the market which has a global character today.

For instance, brand Hinduism is packaged, branded and marketized in a way that it can cater to the demand of immigrant Hindu population dispersed across the globe. The packaging and presentation of religion as a product is so fascinating and easily purchasable that just by shelling out petty cash you can gain access to divine *prasadam* in the form of blessings straight from heaven. Interestingly, it is sold and delivered at your door steps having the capacity of curing any disease in the world. Several TV channels are selling such products online associated with certain *gurus*, philosophers or guides. Likewise, religious ceremonies are interminably intertwined with markets offering various things/items/objects/goods/products required for the performance or observance of certain rituals and ceremonies. As an instance, one may think of *Deepawali* which is a festival of lights as it is celebrated in the memory of Lord Rama's return to Ayodhya after 14 years in exile. And it was to honour Lord Rama that people in Ayodhya lighted *diyas* (lamps) to dispel the darkness of Amavasya. If we analyse this mythological narrative, we can easily understand the symbolic significance of *diyas* (lamps). We can also imagine how simple the celebrations must be if we analyse from the viewpoint of material things involved in that welcome celebration. In a flash forward, if we examine the contemporary times and think in terms of the capital investment to cater to this market supplying material goods/products concerning Deepawali, the humblest estimates will go up to thousands of crores of rupees. This is just a single instance of how diverse kinds of religious ceremonies get commercialized and commoditized.

Marketizing Religion through Strategic Marketing Communication

This chapter mainly deals with religion as a brand/commodity particularly in view of how a religious community acts as consumers without being conscious of it. This culture of branding, packaging and marketizing religion has placed this supposedly or otherwise sacred activity in the market as a product to be bought and sold. Moreover, there cannot be an iota of doubt about the fact that the practice of religion as opposed to theoretical postulations about it, is through and through capital-driven and profit-centric from the marketing perspective. Earning maximum possible money is the sole aim of propagation as well as selling of religion through means such as electronic media and social media.

YouTube has emerged as a powerful platform of popularizing more or less every brand. In India, a popular YouTube channel can easily have few million views of videos propagating religion, ancient texts, mantras, spiritual awakening, chanting, etc. Likewise, we have got Facebook Live as yet another platform which is catching up fast with viewers as consumers. COVID-19 pandemic has opened up the possibility of a whole range of platforms such as Zoom, Webex, Google Meet and Microsoft Teams, where we can easily conduct meetings of several hundred people. In other words, there are innumerable media outlets where brand religion can be popularized and made available to the viewer-consumers. When such observations are made, these may sound very simplistic, but if one analyses the viewership and the screen space and screen time consumption by the consumers across the globe, it may not just surprise but also flabbergast us.

Moreover, a considerable percentage of mobile users consume religion on day-to-day basis. Another material aspect of the propagation of religion is the sale of printed material concerning variety of religions. Despite the fact that we are living in a digitalized world, printed literature about religion is fast becoming extinct. However, in India, still, a sizable chunk of population remains hooked to the printed word. Another area where religion is consumed by community becomes evident when *kathas* (public narration of ancient Indian texts) are organized through week-long and month-long events. It involves a lot of expenditure on the part of the organizers of such events. Even the *kathavachakas* (those who recite ancient texts) along with the *paathis* (who silently chant the name of god and also sing *bhajans* now a days) have started charging hefty amounts of money. In addition to that, the devotees also offer money (howsoever small the amount may be) as they come to listen to *kathas*. Despite the fact that all this is devotion-driven, the hardcore fact of it being capital-driven cannot be denied. Thus, it can be arguably claimed that religion besides being a matter of pure faith which eludes merchandizing of any sort, also remains capital-based as a commodity to be consumed, bought and even sold as and when required.

When we analyse religion and its marketing as strategic communication, we need to keep in mind the fact that any kind of religious discourse, be that through electronic media channels or social media, is through language. It is also, in a way, messaging of a sort communicated through language that is thought through and articulated in a careful and strategic manner. The message may be steeped in genuine sense of religiosity but the manner in which it is conveyed and the way it is made available to people/viewers is interesting and thought-provoking. This is because the communicator has to be well-versed in the art of tale-telling, which means that the first and the most important qualification of the tale-teller is proficiency in the idiom of his story-telling. If he cannot hold the attention of the listener, the entire purpose of marketizing religion would be defeated. Therefore, more diverse and varied the idiom of the taleteller, larger would be the number of his listener-consumers/audience. To view religious discourse as strategic communication aimed at promoting/advertising it as a brand enables us to delve deeper into the layers of marketing strategies.

Marketing strategies that are in consonance with the religious sentiments of the people generally tend to deeply impact the society through communication and advertising techniques adopted by the marketers to mould people and win them over as consumers. Many firms in India act as religious tourist service providers and cater to the need of various socio-economic groups of population. As stated earlier, the entertainment industry is also affected considerably by various religious activities in Indian scenario. Mega episodes of various serials and TV shows can be seen based on mythology and related to the great epics namely the *Ramayana* and the *Mahabharata*. This industry is growing at a great pace with every god and deity having the potential to be showcased in terms of a mega TV serial. The TRP of these serials is much more than the regular TV shows as people watch them religiously with tremendous devotion.

Not only entertainment but music industry as well has been largely dependent on religious activities. It has given birth even to the caller ringtones influenced by devotional songs and *shlokas* (verses). Celebrations of religious festivals in India are not only becoming bigger with the passage of time but have now started affecting whole world as well. These international festivals attract people from all over the world who are passionate about taking part in them. Another aspect of religion which has been influencing our life the most these days is *Vastu Shastra*, which tells us how to build a house and also as to what type of the building can offer us peace of mind, what type of colour/shade of walls can bring us happiness, and so on. *Vastu*guidelines were used only in Indian temples but now this industry is also growing at a rapid pace as people want to build their houses according to the prescriptions in the ancient texts/scriptures to find peace, harmony and prosperity in life.

The fact about any religion is that all rituals/ceremonies associated with it (be that sacrifice, prayers, birth/death ceremony) entail consumption of various products/goods/materials. Every religion is socio-culturally embedded and directly or obliquely becomes instrumental in the use of goods and services. People from affluent class follow certain philosophers/*guru*sas they want to attain salvation, peace of mind or spiritual solace through meditation and yoga. And hence, thousands of healers, *gurus*, meditators and philosophers and even motivational speakers have burgeoned with their YouTube channels having millions of followers. They hold mega-events and, gatherings, wearing and hence commercializing brands and thus become brand ambassadors of their own religious organizations or multinational brands that sell across the globe. People worship them along with their gods and deities. Interestingly, such living gods do not spend their lives like yogis; they have rather built empires, products, and brands either in their names or in the name of their organizations. Quite a few of them have even created their own product lines.

Scope of Consumption of Religion in Future Marketing Practices

The foregoing analysis points towards increasing consumption of innumerable products related to religion. Here, it will be pertinent to examine

Table 10.1 that shows the projected growth of major religious groups in Asia-Pacific (2010–2050), and will help us think through the scope of consumption of religion in future marketing practices.

This table shows the size and projected growth of major religious groups in Asia Pacific and the projections are done by PEW Research Center up to 2050. The percentage increase in some of the religions around the world shows a drastic increase in years to come. Proportionately, the market potential of the products/goods used in religious practices/ceremonies is going to be very high. The figures in the table clearly depict that religions like Hinduism, Islam and Christianity along with others are going to enhance the marketing potential significantly. For instance, the percentage increase in Hinduism is projected to be 33.7% with the highest increase of Islam to 47.8%. The projection also shows high growth rate in Christians which is 32.8%. Therefore, the number of people practicing various religions is going to increase manifold in the years to come all over the world, which ultimately will affect demand of various products and services required to practice a particular religion. In other words, religious practices by people believing in different religions will majorly determine the consumption of the products/goods.

There is yet another study done by the same organization called Pew Research Centre which highlights the percentage of the people who say whether religion is important for them or not. Have a look at Table 10.2 to know how important/unimportant religion is to the people living in Europe, East Asia, Indian subcontinent, Middle Eastern, African and Latin American countries.

The table shows as to how some people in Europe in East Asia say that religion is not very important to them, but there is a sizeable chunk of people from several other countries of the world which shows a reverse trend. A study on various countries done by Pew Research Centre covering the time period from 2008 to 2017 shows that whereas in India, 80% of the people say that religion is important to them, in a country like Brazil there are only 72% people for whom religion is important. In Egypt, 88% people accept that religion is important to them, whereas 72% in Turkey, 68% in Iran, and 98% in Ethiopia acknowledge that religion is crucial in their lives. Likewise, in South Africa also 75% of the people accept the importance of religion in their life. In Uganda, this percentage is 86% and in Indonesia this percentage is as high as 93%. In Pakistan, 94% of the people in the survey accepted the fact that religion is most important to them. On the other hand, we have countries like China, Russia, Japan, Canada, Norway, the UK, Germany, and France wherein religion is not all that important in people's lives. If we go by the percentage, then obviously the consumption of various products is going to be affected by such choices.

Despite a sizeable number of people for whom religion is not important in several European and East Asian countries, there are too large a number of believers/practitioners of various religions who eventually will determine

Table 10.1 Size, Projected Growth of Major Religious Groups in Asia-Pacific, 2010–2050

	2010 Estimated Population	% in 2010	2050 Projected Population	% in 2050	Population Growth 2010–2050	% Increase 2010–2050	Compound Annual Growth Rate (%)
Hindus	1,024,630,000	25.3%	1,369,600,000	27.7%	344,970,000	33.7%	0.7%
Muslims	986,420,000	24.3%	1,457,720,000	29.5%	471,290,000	47.8%	1.0%
Unaffiliated	858,490,000	21.2%	837,790,000	17.0%	−20,700,000	−2.4%	0.1
Buddhists	481,480,000	11.9%	475,840,000	9.6%	−5,640,000	−1.2%	0.0
Folk Religions	364,690,000	9.0%	366,860,000	7.4%	2,170,000	0.6	0.0
Christians	287,100,000	7.1%	381,200,000	7.7%	94,100,000	32.8	0.7
Other Religions	51,920,000	1.3%	48,650,000	1.0%	−3,280,000	−6.3	0.2
Jews	200,000	<0.1	240,000	<0.1	40,000	21.2	0.5
Regional total	4,054,940,000	100.0	4,937,900,000	100.0	882,960,000	21.8	0.5

Source: PEW RESEARCH CENTER, The Future of World Religions: Population Growth Projections, 2010–2050, Population estimates are rounded to the nearest 10,000. Percentages are calculated from unrounded numbers. Figures may not add to 100% because of rounding. www.pewforum.org/2015/04/02/asiapacific/www.pewforum.org/?attachment_id=30112

Table 10.2 Country wise percentage of religious commitment

Country	% who say religion is very important in their lives
Pakistan	94%
Ethiopia	98%
Indonesia	93%
Honduras	90%
Nigeria	88%
Uganda	86%
India	80%
Iran	78%
South Africa	75%
Egypt	72%
Brazil	72%
Turkey	68%
Greece	56%
The United States	53%
Mexico	45%
Chile	41%
Israel	36%
Uruguay	29%
Canada	27%
Spain	22%
Norway	19%
Australia	18%
Russia	16%
France	11%
Japan	10%
Sweden	10%
The United Kingdom	10%
Germany	10%
China	3%

Source: Pew Research Centre Surveys, 2008 to 2017. "The Age Gap in Religion Around the World" www.pewforum.org/2018/06/13/how-religious-commitment-varies-by-country-among-people-of-all-ages/

the extent of the consumption of goods. No business firm can ignore the fact that religion will still be strategically important around which marketing communication is going to revolve. No strategic moves in terms of marketing/production of the product can be decided without taking into account people's religious affiliation/s simply because religion plays a pivotal role in their lives. This undoubtedly points towards a huge market potential of products/goods used/consumed in religious ceremonies/rituals.

In a country like India where alternative medicine systems such as *Ayurveda* are practiced, location of the business is yet another important aspect of marketing. As an instance, Patanjali Ayurved Limited is an Indian consumer goods company which is situated near Haridwar, a holy city of India. This company is run by Ramdev and was going to have a turnover of up to Rs. 25,000 crores during the financial year 2019–20 (*Online Financial Express*, 24 January2020). Currently, the company is in the race of becoming the largest FMCG company which can surpass the giant like Hindustan Unilever. The company has been propagating about manufacturing and marketing Ayurvedic products since its inception and these are based on the teachings of ancient scriptures in India about leading a healthy life. The owner of the company, Aacharya Balkrishna, has been included in the Forbes list of billionaires 2020 and stands at 1851st (as on 30 September 2020) place in the world at the age of just 48. He holds 97th position in the list of India's richest people and the source of his wealth is consumer goods. It is worth mentioning here that most of the products of this company are publicized during religious discourses dovetailed with yogic exercises based on Patanjali's *Yogsutras* and ancient Indian wisdom.

To cite one more example from India, let us take the case of Sri Sri Ravi Shankar, a spiritual guru from India who deals in consumer goods as well as wellness products. His own brand namely 'Sri Sri Tattva' is becoming immensely popular in the retail sector. The company has been targeting the revenue of Rs 5,500 crores from this very sector only. The company owns franchise stores at more than a thousand locations across the world, and, interestingly again, the products are marketed only with the demonstration of physical and breathing exercises along with discourses on religion and culture.

Summative Assessment

To sum up, it would be naive to assume that religion is concerned only with spiritual or non-material pursuits. In fact, it can blend well with business in a way that investors, planners, and marketers can have sure as well as rich returns. The consumption pattern of the people and their consumer behaviour are significant determinants of demand. Since the value-register, behaviour, and actions of the consumers are deeply influenced by religion, it doubtlessly affects the choices and predilections of people. The effect of religions on the consumption of certain products/goods can be positive as most of them strictly prohibit consumption of products like tobacco and liquor. Religious faith and beliefs regulate performance of rituals and practices on certain occasions thereby impacting consumerist behaviour. In fact, such practices help consumers determine what to buy and what not to.

Spending habits of Indians to a considerable extent remain dependent on festivals celebrated by various religious groups. During these festivals, people tend to spend a lot with a wish to buy new items/products/gifts. Religion surely influences the choices of the people. For instance in Christianity, various religious occasions like Easter and Christmas have significant impact on people's buying and spending habits. Likewise, Eid-ul-Fitr and Ramzan in Islam directly affect the consumption of various food items as well as other FMCG products. During festive season, companies like Asian Paints, LG, Cadbury, and Patanjali come up with different marketing strategies to convince customers to use/buy their products manufactured/produced particularly to cater to demands based on their religious affiliations. The seasonality of the products is influenced more by the festive seasons celebrated by religious groups belonging to Christianity, Islam, Hinduism, Buddhism, Sikhism, etc. The consumers' choice has to conform to religious practices in these religions, which determine seasonal variation in the demand of products/goods.

In the Western world, giving a Christmas gift is a mask to celebrate Christmas, and, therefore, every person can be seen trying to buy a present for her/his loved ones. Such a tendency affects the consumption of food, drinks, electronics as well as outfits. Nowadays, MNCs have started to come up with certain personalized items for special festive seasons. In India, electronic items are heavily purchased and traded during Diwali celebrations. With the growing market of technology, mobile phones have become essential, and that is the reason that people love to gift mobile phones as well as other electronic gadgets to their friends from younger generation in particular. Product sale is at its height during the festive season. The fourth quarter starting from October and ending in December has various kinds of festivals celebrated by people affiliated with different religions in India. That is why the demand for consumer goods spikes during this season, and the companies come up with competitive lucrative offers via offering heavy discount/schemes that supposedly benefit consumers substantially.

Thus, based on the discussion, one may conclude that religion has diverse facets and the performance of various rituals and ceremonies is one of them. Ritualistic/ceremonial dimension of religion has always been there, but in today's materialistic world it has become very popular. During ritualistic performances and festivals, there is a whole range of products/goods/items/ commodities that are in demand. The market for such items/ products being global, the dimension of marketizing religion becomes extremely important as it caters to people's *aastha* (devotion). To sell the products and goods in demand, strategic marketing communication is employed in the process of planning, branding, advertising, and marketizing a product as it involves huge capital investment. At times it is done through religious discourses and at others through teaching of yoga or *pranayama* (breathing exercises) through electronic media channels or social media. In view of possibility of tremendous growth in the production and consumption of goods consumed in religious ceremonies/festivals; religion will emerge as a major business arena globally in a decade or two. The demand for the goods and services will rise and the business firms/companies need to gear up accordingly.

References

Bailey, J. M., & Sood, J. (1993). The effects of religious affiliation on consumer behavior: A preliminary investigation. *Journal of Managerial Issues*, 5(3), 328–352.

Bandyopadhyay, R., Morais, D. B., & Chick, G. (2008). Religion and identity in India's heritage tourism. *Annals of Tourism Research*, 35(3), 790–808.

Banerjee, S. (2008). Dimensions of Indian culture, core cultural values and marketing implications: An analysis. *Cross Cultural Management: An International Journal*, 15 (4), 367–378.

Belk, R. W. (1987). A child's Christmas in America: Santa Claus as deity, consumption as religion. *Journal of American culture*, 10(1), 87–100.

Beyer, P., & Beaman, L. (Eds.). (2007). *Religion, globalization, and culture*. Brill.

Bhandari, K. R., & Raut, S. K. (2019). 9 Leveraging tacit. *Advances in Management Research: Innovation and Technology*, 1(1), 127–138.

Blackwell, R. (2007). Motivations for religious tourism, pilgrimage, festivals and events. In *Religious tourism and pilgrimage festivals management: An international perspective* (pp. 35–47). CAB International.

Butt, M. M., Rose, S., Wilkins, S., & Haq, J. U. (2017). MNCs and religious influences in global markets: Drivers of consumer-based halal brand equity. *International Marketing Review*, 34(6), 885–908. https://doi.org/10.1108/IMR-12-2015-0277

Choi, Y. (2010). Religion, religiosity, and South Korean consumer switching behaviors. *Journal of Consumer Behaviour*, 9(3), 157–171.

Copley, P. (2007). *Marketing communications management*. Routledge.

Demerath, N. J., & Demerath, N. J. (2003). *Crossing the gods: World religions and worldly politics*. Rutgers University Press.

Durmaz, Y. (2014). *The impact of psychological factors on consumer buying behavior and an empirical application in Turkey*. Canadian Center of Science and Education

Ellis, S., & TerHaar, G. (2004). *Worlds of power: Religious thought and political practice in Africa* (Vol. 1). Oxford University Press on Demand.

Fiol, C. M. (1991). Managing culture as a competitive resource: An identity-based view of sustainable competitive advantage. *Journal of Management*, 17(1), 191–211.

Gauthier, F. (2016). *Religion in consumer society: Brands, consumers and markets*. Routledge.

Gauthier, F., & Martikainen, T. (2018). Introduction: The marketization of religion. *Religion*, 48(3), 361–366. 10.1080/0048721X.2018.1482614

Hanegraaff, W. J. (2020). Imagining the future study of religion and spirituality. *Religion*, 50(1), 72–82.

Hassard, J., & Sharifi, S. (1989). Corporate culture and strategic change. *Journal of General Management*, 15(2), 4–19.

Herrmann, H., & Rana, S. (2020). Which B2B thinker are you?*International Journal of Indian Culture and Business Management*, 21(1), 45–62.

Iyer, G. R. (1999). The impact of religion and reputation in the organization of Indian merchant communities. *Journal of Business & Industrial Marketing*, 14(2), 102–121. https://doi.org/10.1108/08858629910258982

Lynch, G., Mitchell, J., & Strhan, A. (Eds.). (2012). *Religion, media and culture: A reader*. Routledge.

Mansori, S. (2012). Impact of religion affiliation and religiosity on consumer innovativeness; the evidence of Malaysia. *World Applied Sciences Journal*, 7(3), 301–307.

Mathras, D., Cohen, A. B., Mandel, N., & Mick, D. G. (2016). The effects of religion on consumer behavior: A conceptual framework and research agenda. *Journal of Consumer Psychology*, 26(2), 298–311.

McFarlane, D. A. (2010). Religion and business: Identifying relationship gaps and influences. *Conflict Resolution & Negotiation Journal*, 4.

Mitra, S. (2016). Merchandizing the sacred: Commodifying Hindu religion, gods/goddesses, and festivals in the United States. *Journal of Media and Religion*, 15(2), 113–121.

Online, P. (2020, January 24). *Patanjali group eyes to be Rs 40,000-crore Company in 2020–21, aims to be largest FMCG firm.* Retrieved September 30, 2020, from www.financialexpress.com/industry/patanjali-group-eyes-to-be-rs-40000-crore-company-in-2020–21-aims-to-be-largest-fmcg-firm/1834333/.

Parameshwaran, M. G., & Srivastava, R. K. (2010). A conceptual paper: Should marketers consider religiosity in understanding consumer purchase behavior? *SIES Journal of Management*, 7(1).

Patel, M. (2012). Influence of religion on shopping behaviour of consumers-an exploratory study. *Abhinav National Monthly Refereed Journal of Research in Commerce & Management*, 1(5), 68–78.

Peifer, J. L., Khalsa, S., & Ecklund, E. H. (2016). Political conservatism, religion, and environmental consumption in the United States. *Environmental Politics*,25(4), 661–689.

Rana, S., Raut, S. K., Prashar, S., & Hamid, A. B. A. (2020). Promoting through consumer nostalgia: A conceptual framework and future research agenda. *Journal of Promotion Management*, 27(2), 211–249.

Rana, S., Raut, S. K., Prashar, S., & Quttainah, M. A. (2020). The transversal of nostalgia from psychology to marketing: what does it portend for future research?*International Journal of Organizational Analysis*, Vol. ahead-of-print No. ahead-of-print.

Raut, S. K., Sakpal, S., & Soni, R. (2022). Understanding the Service Quality Dimensions and Achieving Resilience in Service Retail. In *Handbook of Research on Supply Chain Resiliency, Efficiency, and Visibility in the Post-Pandemic Era*, edited by Ramakrishna Yanamandra (pp. 136–156). IGI Global, UAE. https://doi.org/10.4018/978-1-7998-9506-0

Rowley, J. (1998). Promotion and marketing communications in the information marketplace. *Library Review*, 47 (8), 383–387. https://doi.org/10.1108/0024253 9810239543

Siala, H. (2013). Religious influences on consumers' high-involvement purchasing decisions. *Journal of Services Marketing*, 27 (7), 579–589. https://doi.org/10.1108/ JSM-02-2012-0046

Singh, S. (2006). Impact of color on marketing. *Management Decision*, 44 (6), 783–789. https://doi.org/10.1108/00251740610673332

Sood, J., & Nasu, Y. (1995). Religiosity and nationality: An exploratory study of their effect on consumer behavior in Japan and the United States. *Journal of Business Research*, 34(1), 1–9.

TerHaar, G., & Ellis, S. (2006). The role of religion in development: Towards a new relationship between the European Union and Africa. *The European Journal of Development Research*, 18(3), 351–367.

Thornton, P. H., Ribeiro-Soriano, D., & Urbano, D. (2011). Socio-cultural factors and entrepreneurial activity: An overview. *International Small Business Journal*, 29(2), 105–118.

11 Design, Execute, and Manage Promotions

Study on Social Media Platforms

Bikramjit Rishi and Junaid Mohammed

Introduction

It is a widely accepted fact that the Internet has revolutionized the way people consume and share information (Kaul, 2012; Taira, 2021). What earlier used to be considered an alternative to other means of viewing information, such as the television and the radio, is now a place with billions of users (Kietzmann et al., 2011; Quesenberry, 2020; Rana, Raut, Prashar, & Quttainah, 2020; Rana, Raut, Prashar, & Hamid, 2020). Discussions on social media's effectiveness often comprise auxiliary pointers on the Internet (Olotewo, 2015). It stems from how consumers are increasingly using the Internet to stay informed on a spectrum of things that later dictate their purchase decisions (Goodrich & de Mooij, 2014). Social media has evolved as an important place for companies and corporations to establish their presence ("Contemporary Issues in Social Media Marketing – 1st Edition – Bikramjit", 2017).

Further to this, social media has fundamentally altered the nature and logistics of social media plans, thereby opening doors to better reachability to consumers' various segments (Devereux et al., 2020; Veil et al., 2011; Rana, 2018a). While corporations have embraced this changing landscape for the last decade, different ventures have started to enter into the business of designing applications and platforms that have further increased the number of places consumers may be active in. This golden age of marketing and media has also seen large amounts of money invested in such innovations and ventures (Culnan et al., 2010).

Besides being a vital tool to reach consumers, social media has also served as an agent that increased the degree of accountability and transparency among corporations, making them more invested in subscribing to better business practices (Kristensen & From, 2015; Rana, 2018b). Instances such as United Airlines breaking Dave Carroll's guitar only further reinforce how the media can quickly spread content (*United Breaks Guitars – Harvard Business School Working Knowledge*, n.d.). It has also led to companies strengthening their public relations and outreach initiatives to contain negative attention in the global community (Edosomwan et al., 2011). Platforms

DOI: 10.4324/9781003315582-12

like Twitter and Facebook have continued to scout for ways to process and analyse user information and data in a monetizable way to help businesses make informed decisions (Purdam & Elliot, 2015). Social media has served as a driving force across organizations' value chain by deriving from learnings afforded in disciplines like data science and machine learning.

Through the increasing levels of Internet penetration brought about by decreasing costs of access, social media has come up as a less expensive option to reach consumers than other conventional channels of media (van der Graaf et al., 2016). It has helped smaller organizations and ventures to be able to participate on its platform and represent their brand. All these go on to showing how the applications of social media have branched out in vibrant ways over the past half-decade and continue to provide new avenues to explore (Dwivedi et al., 2020).

This chapter addresses how the growing popularity of the social media can act as a useful tool for achieving marketing objectives. Based on the existing literature, the chapter establishes social media's popularity as an essential promotion tool. The chapter also explains the guidelines that can be applied to use the social media platforms for achieving the promotion objectives. At the end, the readers will know about some frameworks that can be used for social media promotion, helping the marketers understand their consumers effectively and design the content to engage the followers. The chapter also highlights a few real examples that can act as a reference point for the marketers to use social media promotion.

Literature Review

The age of the Internet and the subsequent rise of marketing on social media have bought about a different set of opportunities for organizations of all sizes (Farshid et al., 2011). Brands are always trying to delve deeper into these opportunities by exploring different ways to harness social media. This eagerness and interest in social media and subsequent execution of ideas have shown that the tools and thought processes applied to websites and applications may not be the best fit when tackling performance and activity on social media (Mills & Plangger, 2015; Raut et al., 2022).

Social media, which predominantly acts as an avenue for customer engagement, should remain independent of offline activity and extant strategies used to engineer branding and communication activities ("Contemporary Issues in Social Media Marketing – 1st Edition – Bikramjit", 2017; Mills & Plangger, 2015). Social media has seen branching out and shifting of marketing and communication strategies tailored to enable a two-way "customer-to-brand-to-customer" and "customer-to-customer" engagement (Mills et al., 2015).

Social media performance, and more immediately, social media strategy can alter the way businesses are perceived. A proper formulation of a social media strategy equips businesses with personal goals, professional goals, clarity on the audience, company resources, and relevant risks (Tuten et al., 2020). A large number of connections on a platform or a large and active presence on a forum can be a powerful tool that may be channelled, not necessarily always, to one's advantage. The proximity to current and prospective consumers renders the strategic formulation of social media plans and ideas quintessential (Dutta, 2010).

Literature indicates the use of a framework that proposes three levels of social media maturity: "initiation", "diffusion", "maturity" that studied elements such as "target audience and channel choice", "goals, resources, and policies", and "monitoring and content activities", respectively (Tuten et al., 2020). Their evaluation (Effing & Spil, 2016) finds that only three of the nine organizations studied may be placed in the maturity scale on the maturity matrix proposed (Effing & Spil, 2016; Bhandari & Raut, 2019).

Brands need to be active as a part of a robust social media strategy that focuses its attention on social media, as a "core part" of market strategy. Ashley and Tuten (2015) in their quantitative study of "channel and creative strategy usage" and "social media engagement" find a positive correlation between both, thereby reasserting the results of effective strategy implementation. Further to this, Tussyadiah and Zach (2013) also find social media to affect co-creation and channel consumers as assets. Nobre and Silva (2014) study this with particular reference to small or medium-sized firms and their activity on the platform Facebook to find that a "thoughtfully designed strategy" may help small and medium-sized firms benefit from social media. Due to the large audiences and opportunities on social media, opinions are continuously evolving which, requires dynamic marketing strategies to manage the social media presence (Durgam, 2018). Organizations need to divorce social media strategy from any version of a mass advertisement strategy, and it should focus upon identifying, listening, and targeting particular groups. Different social media strategies and other marketing and promotional activities often lead to potential customers' loss (Lindsey-Mullikin & Borin, 2017; Tuten et al., 2020). When combined, website and application strategy and social media strategy, instead of being synchronized, lead to customers not enjoying the process and leaving the website.

All in all, the literature points to the direction that the usage of social media for marketing requires businesses to recognize the need for a dedicated strategy that incorporates particular understanding issues like purchase patterns and branding (Felix et al., 2017).

Designing a Social Media Strategy

Social media platforms have been instrumental in fostering a sense of competition leading to enhanced business outcomes (Lashgari et al., 2018). These platforms continue to serve as a public ground for companies to showcase their prowess in a dynamic market. More and more organizational goals are being met by adopting and implementing a social media strategy. The far-reaching impacts of social media extend to building a robust corporate reputation aided by tools ranging from channel integration to user-generated content (Floreddu & Cabiddu, 2016). Social media has also been found to have impacted dynamics within the "network, relations and culture" (Kwayu et al., 2018).

Despite the demonstrated importance of social media, businesses have not fully ingrained in designing a competitive social media strategy that could influence how they are perceived (Rishi & Kuthuru, 2021). However, to remain competitive, companies stay active on the relevant platform, but with no structured processes, procedures, defined scope, and monitoring mechanisms that render their presence essentially moot in practice (Baptista et al., 2017).

Formulating a strategy has time and again presented itself as a somewhat troublesome hurdle for organizations to pass successfully. Companies functioning in different industries encounter different socioeconomic conditions, behaviours, and consumption patterns, which call for tailored strategies to be sewn into the company's social media marketing practices and goals. Social media applications have branched out to benefit different organizational ways by drawing insights from even grassroots-level data mined through state-of-the-art ethnographic and social listening algorithms (Goh et al., 2013; Li et al., 2020). Constantly evolving, with numerous avenues for change and the potential to enable the leverage of data extant beyond the visible horizon, social media needs to be used in a way that can harness these voluminous boons it endows upon organizations.

The emphasis on a structured and organized social media strategy is justified to benefit both companies and consumers mutually.

An Overview to Steps Involved in Designing a Social Media Strategy

Social media's strategic planning entails identifying organizational goals that would then be addressed through objectives and tactics. The designing of a social media strategy is three-fold, originating at the corporate level, followed by the business level, and ending with the organization's operational and on-ground levels, where the actual impact of these strategies is studied.

A social media strategy starts with a detailed analysis of the business landscape, using appropriate and relevant benchmarks. Understanding of this analysis helps in designing specific goals are formulated, to achieve the social media objectives. Any strategy or plan is only useful when executed on a target audience, fully aware of their preferences and behaviours. An evaluation of the audience gives a rounded idea of the expectations, how they are to be met, and where they are to be met. It enables the selection of appropriate channels and the creation of content creation and engagement plan.

Each of these steps needs to be fully synchronized and played in perfect limbo to ensure that the end product of one stage enables the feeding of insights to make the next one effective. Hence, synergy within steps and the overall strategies, goals, and brand is essential. The social media strategy culminates with a structured approach to measuring the strategy's output and effectiveness through metrics that may excavate information that can better accent subsequent social media strategies. Figure 11.1 lists all the steps to design a social media strategy.

Understanding the Business

Like other strategic plans, social media planning is initiated by studying the landscape and business environment in which it is to be implemented.

Figure 11.1 Designing social media strategy

Source: Authors own

This stage may involve an in-depth evaluation starting from the industry, to the competitors, to the company, its products, previous marketing campaigns, market preferences, and more. This situational analysis helps understand the opportunities and avenues for improvement (Zhang et al., 2020).

With specificity to social media platforms, this understanding usually includes a social media audit, which is an account of the brand's and its competitors' social media presence and performance patterns. A social media strategy may further inform the brand's SWOT (Strengths, Weaknesses, Opportunities, and Threats). These steps also help companies gauge the nature of expectations prospective consumers may have by studying the user engagement on the platform.

Setting Goals and Objectives

Having understood the business, the environment, and the avenues of improvement/desired effect areas, a preliminary list of all expectations from a social media campaign may be created. These may be inspired by different resource constraints ranging from availability of personnel, budgeting, and financial considerations to available time-frames (Abd et al., 2020).

The objective's composition may be S.M.A.R.T. (Specific, Measurable, Attainable, Realistic, Timely) in nature. The setting of objectives should be done to directly address and facilitate what the goal intends to do within the boundaries presented by different constraints realized in this process's first few phases.

Identifying and Understanding the Target Audience

Targeting the relevant audience is as crucial as how organized a social media strategy is, as it helps in achieving the social media objectives. Profiling target audiences can come in handy to understand the target audience's characteristics. The target audience may have been defined by the brand and subsequent product teams, which can be utilized to understand the target audience's demographic, socio-economic, psychographic aspects (Popli & Rishi, 2021b).

Profiling the audience helps in a deeper understanding of social media participation, the rates, and patterns of activity, the perceptions. Different segments may require the usage of different tactics to reach them. The planning process must strategically identify and answer questions as to who the core target might be, how they may be described, how they may be reached out to, how they may be motivated to engage on-platform, what their general social media usage is like, what devices they use, and more (Rishi & Popli, 2021).

Understanding this scale helps form a comprehensive profile of the prospective audience and helps tailor the campaigns to drive engagement and interaction across platforms.

Choosing Relevant Social Media Platforms

The next step following the target audiences' identification is to ascertain the most attractive social media platform or a set of social media platforms available to reach them. The platform's selection may be done based on the composition of users the platform boasts, its applicability for the identified target audience, and the nature of the content being marketed. Usually, the selection is made based on the core idea behind reaching out to the target audience. It may be to foster relationships in communities, publish, or entertain, or perform social commerce (Yang et al., 2020).

For instance, a target audience that includes college-going students predominantly may be best suited to the core ideas of networking and publishing, for which platforms such as Instagram or Snapchat might be most appropriate. This stage also comprises planning and forecasting the volume of content being generated, the volume of content being paid for and promoted, and how these two may move hand-in-hand to resonate with the audience.

Creating an Experience

The content and the ethos manifested through the platform should be in accordance with the brand to create a synchronization between the brand personality, the products, and how they are represented on the platform. Furthermore, all platforms on which the brand establishes a presence should encapsulate the brand's message strategy, which outlines the campaign's creative aspect (s)consistently (Popli & Rishi, 2021a). It will accent the campaign effort in terms of coherence and enable a good experience for the audience following the platform.

The content strategy would benefit from being visually attractive, engaging the visual senses, and creating a hook that interests the user further. The content may also evoke emotions, curiosity, or feelings of closure. Brands should recognise and engineer their content in a manner that the content put on a social media platform serves more than just the goal it intends to address – it serves as a carrier of what a brand stands for and serves as a legacy for other campaigns to gather from (Castro, n.d.).

Apple, Inc.'s launch events and advertisements follow this process. Apple manages to bring together the best of the brand's engineering, technological, design, and sustainability prowess effortlessly. While other giants may make similar efforts, what sets Apple apart is the level of understanding they hold of their target audience and the level of granularity they go into while orchestrating their events and advertisements to create an oasis of a viewing experience. The colours used, the background music, the transitions, and the narration speed are balanced to translate into a perfect interplay that pushes viewers into liking it and sharing it further (Nudd, 2018; Rayport, 2011; Warren, 2018).

For instance, Cadbury's 2007 gorilla advertisement, with no dialogues and no hovering content, features a gorilla, who plays the drums to the iconic drum solo by Phil Collins – "In the Air Tonight", after having been influenced by the smell of Cadbury. This advertisement was a "sweet success", experienced an "overwhelmingly positive" response, and won the top prize at the 2008 Cannes Lions, a big celebration of the advertising industry (Caird, 2016).

Metrics and Analysis

To evaluate social media effectiveness, marketers can use specific metrics to reveal the achievement of goals. Analysis of these metrics may reveal insightful observations of how the plan may have been tweaked to observe different retrospection results (Poecze et al., 2018).

A few metrics that may be used to evaluate the results of a strategy are:

1. Volume – the total volume of content on the social media platform(s) must be considered. These may be the number of posts, the number of likes, shares, reactions, etc. Furthermore, the seasonality of the posting should also be taken into consideration to identify if there are any unusual patterns in the later observed results.
2. Popularity – the number of views, shares, bookmarks, Click to Conversation (CTC) assets observed on posts across the platform.
3. The ratio of earned media to paid media – to understand what percentage of total media is being paid for and what percentage is generated through users, and this may be resourceful in understanding the campaign's actual drivers.
4. Reach – to understand how far and how viral the campaign has been.
5. Influence and engagement – observe how much participation was observed throughout the campaign in what way and pattern – comments, reactions, subscriptions, time spent, clicks, bounce rates, views, etc.
6. Value – the translation of the campaigns into business value in terms of sales, changes in customer lifetime value, acquisition cost, retention rates, and such.

Challenges in Managing and Executing Social Media Strategy

Challenges in Social Media Integration

Despite companies adopting social media, a lack of integration and a lack of efforts to integrate the brand with the platforms thereof are noted. The need to integrate a social media strategy as a part of a brand's more extensive marketing campaign and other media channels is apparent. It offers better clarity of how social media goals and other marketing goals cascade under one other (Shalender, 2021).

The most common challenges in social media integration are:

1.   Measuring ROI (Return on Investment)
2.   Lack of consistency
3.   Falling engagement rate over time
4.   A disconnect between the brand and audience
5.   The content becoming boring/repetitive
6.   Difficulty in responding to consumer queries
7.   Lack of resources for carrying out campaigns

Possible Solutions

The possible solutions to integrate social media for an effective marketing campaign are shown in Figure 11.2. The detailed analysis of each solution is provided in the next sections.

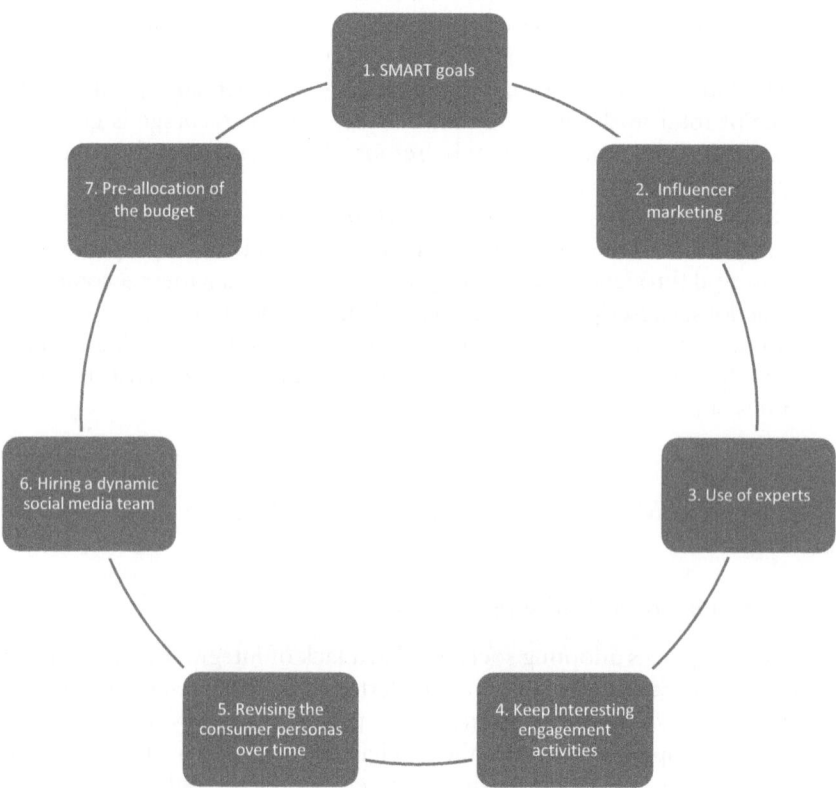

Figure 11.2 Solutions for social media integration

Source: Authors own

S.M.A.R.T. Goals

Defined SMART goals provide a sense of direction and purpose to brands' social media strategy by analysing the performance and keeping track of the progress to achieve the desired results. The goals should be specific so that there is no ambiguity about what the brand is trying to gain from the campaign. The goals should have definitive criteria to measure the progress towards the desired outcome. The goals should be achievable so that the brand can attain the goals. Goals should be realistic so that they can be achieved considering the available time and resources. Goals should be timely so that there is an end date, which would motivate and create a sense of urgency to complete the tasks at hand and achieve the goals (CFI, 2015; O'Connor, 2018).

Influencer Marketing

Influencer marketing uses collaborations and partnerships with famous social media personalities or bloggers to promote the brand. Influencer marketing is on the rise with the increasing use of social media. Since these influencers already have a large following, their credibility and bond with their audience can be leveraged by brands to create brand awareness, attract new customers, and generate leads. However, brands should ensure that they collaborate with the right kind of influencer, appropriate for their products/ services (Patel, 2021; Single Grain Team, n.d.).

Use of Influencers

Brands should try to bring influencers from the industry on board as people trust them. Some experts already use social media such as Instagram or You-Tube to connect with their audience and discuss products and services. Having them on board would help brands promote their offerings as it would increase brand visibility and even brand mentions while creating awareness and attracting new customers (Ouvrein et al., 2021).

Keeping Interesting Engagement Activities

Brands need to stay in touch with their audiences to feel like the audiences have a constant connection with the brand in one way or another, even when they are not buying their products or availing of their services.

The following are some ways to keep your audience engaged:

i.   Contests

When done correctly, contests can engage the audience and help brands expand their customer base by inviting likes, shares, comments, retweets, and pins. Photo or video competitions can be arranged, resulting in a lot of user-generated content (UGC) and promotion that the brand can then use to engage with its audience. Additionally, contests can also act as rich data sources if some information is collected as a part of the entry process to help brands learn more about their customers (American Express, 2011).

ii. Giveaways

Based on the products or services offered by brands, giveaways can be handy in customer engagement. This tactic that requires the customers to perform specific tasks and stand a chance to win some prize also helps increase brand visibility and followers. Depending on the need and the target audience, brands can decide which social media sites would work best for their giveaway (Carufel, 2019).

iii. Discounts/offers

People are always looking for discounts and offers and prefer brands that help them save some money. Discounts and offers not only attract more customers and increase sales, but they also boost brand awareness, repeat purchases, and even followers.

iv. Polls and surveys

Polls and surveys keep the audience engaged as they are required to click and answer quirky and straightforward questions. It also helps build a community as people see how similar they are to others. For the brand, these help them understand customer preferences and routines that could be used later to customize offerings according to the information recorded.

v. Inviting conversations

Inviting conversations are a great way to make customers feel like brands care about their thoughts and opinions. These conversations also provide new insights about the customers, which can then be used to make informed decisions.

For instance, Maybelline, a L'Oreal Group company, faced a fierce competition in the Indian digital space and formulated an idea to reach their customers in a fun and engaging way and drive them to use their products. Inviting conversations being the core of this idea, Maybelline provided a space where men shared their frustrations and more against women in a jovial, comical, and quirk-filled way, and women could revert with similar quirk and excitement levels.

vi. Having branded hashtags

Having branded hashtags is crucial to connect people and the brand to a specific theme or conversation. Branded hashtags help create awareness about the brand and its offerings and create a community around the brand (Chacon, 2016).

In their campaign promoting the Bright Benefit (BB) cream, Maybelline used hashtags inspired by conversations on men sharing their frustrations on women taking "forever" to get dressed and ready. The hashtag #BeforeWomenGetReady, a part of the "WTF – Women Take Forever" campaign, faired exceptionally well, with sales of over 75,000 units of the BB Cream, an increase of 1,00,000+ fans, 2 million blogger reach, digital and PR reach of 13 and 4 million, respectively, and 50 press exposures on different platforms.

vii. Experimenting with technology

The constant advancements in technology result in new features very frequently, which gives brands the chance to experiment with these features and look for new ways to engage with their audience, find out the ones that work best, and use them to their advantage.

Using technology in tandem with a campaign often finds an advantage in greater engagement, as it did in Maybelline's Bright Benefit (BB) cream campaign, where a A pixel application was used where 2,000 girls revealed the pixel by clicking on them, one at a time.

Revising the Consumer Personas over Time

Business and technology are both very dynamic areas, and, along with these, consumers are also continually evolving, which means the needs and preferences are rapidly changing. So there is a need to monitor these changes and revise the consumer personas overtime to ensure that they appropriately reflect the consumer base (Salazar, 2016).

Hiring a Dynamic Social Media Team

With the rising use of social media, it is crucial to have a dynamic social media team for a brand to make its presence felt.

i. Focus on voices that consumers relate to

People on social media are always looking for and sharing relatable content, so there is a need to find a voice to relate to the brand.

Maybelline tapped into the vein of the consumer's mind with conversations on topics dearly to their users. Turning the traditional "Friends Day Band" to the modern "LET'S NAIL IT", where girls were asked to substitute this ceremonial tying of the band with a party that celebrated their friendship. It saw the emergence of a new trend in which over 11,000 Maybelline girls participated. Yet another example of this could be found in their "WTF – Women Take Forever" campaign, where men's voices were heard on how women took forever to get dressed. A topic of discussion quite prevalent saw vast rates of engagement reaching about 38,000 men in a matter of 15 days since it was created.

ii.   Creative and original content

Creative and original content generates brand recognition, engagement for the audience, and even new leads. Customers are interested in seeing how brands keep up with the trends and content that their consumers are consuming.

With no brand ambassador, Maybelline promoted their Colossal Kajal, making their consumers their ambassadors, putting them at the centre of the product. Maybelline drove every woman to bring out the hero in her with the Colossal Kajal, a bold, smudge-free product. One liners like "Old may be gold, but I am young and bold" were used to inform and induce the audience to purchase the product. Facebook interactions were noted to have increased by over 200%, with 98% positive review rate and 1.2 lakh content pegs. Fans shared content in the form of pictures, etc., of their make-ups, etc., on Facebook. Namrata Soni, an expert make-up artist, too, recommended the Colossal Kajal in her tutorials. A similar strategy was followed in Maybelline's welcoming of their lip balm, Baby Lips, where girls used pictures from when they were babies to go with the product name "Baby Lips", which protected and restored their lips within a week of use.

iii.   Relevant platforms with changing times

As times change, different social media platforms' relevance also fluctuates as other sections of people use various sites based on their experience and ease of use. Brands need to ensure that they are present on relevant platforms and reach out to the right audience through the most appropriate platforms.

iv.   Having them on top of all consumer queries

Responding to consumer queries is one of the easiest and most effective ways to engage with customers. Timely replies and acknowledging customer queries show that brands care about their customers, generating loyalty and reputation through positive word of mouth.

Have a Pre-Allocated Sufficient Budget for SMM

Having a pre-allocated sufficient budget for social media marketing (SMM) is essential as social media is rising. As more and more people use social media, brands should be present there as their customers are being exposed to so many different brands and companies selling similar products and services, and there is a need to stand out. The pre-allocated budget would ensure that the online marketing objectives do not interfere with the offline marketing goals and instead complement them to achieve the brand's overall marketing goals.

Discussion

Many studies have identified the advantages of social media and the ways social media can be used for a wide range of marketing needs. The Internet and social media era being foreign and esoteric has passed and now is a stronghold of opinions. Therefore, it has become an imperative space for brands to show their presence on social media.

We elaborated on how the social media landscape is changing and will continue to keep changing. Social media, being a place with a large number of users hailing from different backgrounds, experiences, preferences, and usage patterns, is prone to be influenced by a wide range of factors, thereby requiring companies to implement social media listening to set trends and brand goals accordingly (Godey et al., 2016; Paquette, 2013).

Companies that use the social media space without a defined strategy are often found not to be optimized and convey ideas not coherently. Social media is a tool that allows brands to reach consumers and facilitates a spectrum of avenues such as building loyalty and brand image; separating social media strategy and making it more tailored based on platforms are vital.

With clearly defined goals and objectives, brands can enhance campaign outcomes, synchronize online and offline efforts, congregate brand communications, and more (Appel et al., 2020; Chang et al., 2015). Companies are also required to identify appropriate target audiences to ensure the right fit of platform based on the nature and the aspired effectiveness from the campaign (Vinerean, 2017). It enhances customer relationship building and brings users closer to the brand, setting the stage for brands to orchestrate a superior experience, aided by different metrics collected through platform engagement analytics.

The chapter lists out the challenges while implementing social media strategy. These challenges are primarily centred around ensuring that the users stay connected with the brand on a platform and around brands coming up with requisite ideas, funds, and content to keep the forum lively and valuable.

Implications

Companies can leverage the rising use of social media for product purchase decisions, given its two-way communication between customers themselves and that of customers with brands/organizations. It reduces costs, direct advertising, with sales yields prompting reactions, and favorably sways buyer behaviour (Ramsaran-Fowdar, 2013). Due to the substantial progress in the evolution of interactive social media for marketing and advertising in the past decade, it has been found adaptable to the volatile demographic and economic conditions, especially among the younger consumers (Duffett, 2017). Although it was believed that loyal customers use social media to stay updated about brands/organizations, brand loyalty and the likelihood of purchasing a product are determined by how brands engage with their customers (Ramsaran-Fowdar, 2013). Thus, companies must appropriately communicate with their target audience and interact with them to enable the desired response from current and potential consumers, which would require an effective social media strategy as is established in this chapter.

The social media strategy seems to be a critical determinant of the market value of any company because of word-of-mouth referrals that play a crucial role in altering the buying decisions and attitudinal changes in customers. It is not only to have a social media presence but also to draw out strong emotions and opinions from the users through outlining successful social media strategies (Alves et al., 2016). Rewarding social media strategies should consider both the individual characteristics of customers and the product characteristics to optimize the use of social media to promote brands (Alves et al., 2016). Attention needs to be paid to align the strategies for social media presence across platforms to cater to millions of social media users (Zhu & Chen, 2015). Apart from the common sites such as Twitter and Facebook, online communities and virtual worlds can be analysed to understand customer behaviour and preferences. These would eventually multiply sales and profits and promote positive word of mouth (Alves et al., 2016). Social media marketing needs to strike the right balance between providing brand information to customers and understanding customer perceptions and feelings by designing strategies that help maintain and improve long-term relationships with the customers (Ramsaran-Fowdar, 2013). Social media platforms need to disseminate information, act as communities, foster communication between different customer groups, and complement the existing marketing mix of the company. With social media marketing, the opportunities are immense, but without effective and efficient social media strategies, the outcome would be futile.

Conclusion

Having identified social media as an essential place for brands to be active and how social media has transformed how companies interact with their prospective consumers, this chapter has discussed the need to have a structured social media strategy.

We have determined that being creative and fostering engagement on social media can have many positive outcomes, provided a proper social media strategy guides the execution. An appropriate social media strategy with a clear set of goals and objectives is derived from a detailed social media audit and understanding of the business landscape. Furthermore, we have shown the importance of deciding an appropriate target audience that helps guide the campaign's choice of platform to assess the ways content will be disseminated using the platforms' advertising facilities and tactics.

We have presented the importance of creating an experience for those visiting social media platform pages and subsequently using the website or applications. Maintaining consistency between all these features and complications would lead to superior experience and positive response. It has been reiterated with the examples of Cadbury's 2009 Phil Collins' "Container Experience" and Apple, Inc.'s synchronization of platforms that reflect the best of the brands.

Brands also need to use social media to study trends and patterns with platform-specific features that monitor campaign performance. Brands can use custom-built social listening applications that use state-of-the-art algorithms that provide real-time information on the campaign's effectiveness. It may be done through metrics specific to different goals that meet the campaign's aims, be it sales, image building, followers, etc.

Therefore, social media has opened up a world of possibilities and has since emerged as a discipline that has attracted industry practitioners, marketers, researchers, and entrepreneurs. Organizations continue to embrace, innovate, and utilize social media to persuade consumers to use a spectrum of layers sewn into platform features.

References

Abd, M., Youssef Mahmoud, A., Nemir, Y., Ead, A., Noor, M., & Al Adwan, S. (2020). A proposed paradigm for employing social media in achieving the objectives of sustainable development. *Asian Journal of Economics and Business 1.* www.amf.org.ae/sites/all/libraries/pdf.js/web/viewer.html?file.

Alves, H., Fernandes, C., & Raposo, M. (2016). Social media marketing: A literature review and implications. *Psychology and Marketing*, *33*(12), 1029–1038. https://doi.org/10.1002/mar.20936.

American Express. (2011, July 14). 4 Reasons why contests should be part of your marketing strategy. *American Express*. www.americanexpress.com/en-us/business/trends-and-insights/articles/4-reasons-why-contests-should-be-part-of-your-marketing-strategy/.

Appel, G., Grewal, L., Hadi, R., & Stephen, A. T. (2020). The future of social media in marketing. *Journal of the Academy of Marketing Science*, *48*(1), 79–95. https://doi.org/10.1007/s11747-019-00695-1.

Ashley, C., & Tuten, T. (2015). Creative strategies in social media marketing: An exploratory study of branded social content and consumer engagement. *Psychology & Marketing*, *32*(1), 15–27. https://doi.org/10.1002/mar.20761.

Baptista, J., Wilson, A. D., Galliers, R. D., & Bynghall, S. (2017). Social media and the emergence of reflexiveness as a new capability for open strategy. *Long Range Planning*, *50*(3), 322–336. https://doi.org/10.1016/j.lrp.2016.07.005.

Bhandari, K. R., & Raut, S. K. (2019). 9 Leveraging tacit. *Advances in Management Research: Innovation and Technology*, *1*(1), 127–138.

Caird, J. (2016, January 7). "I was basically told: You are never showing this" – how we made Cadbury's Gorilla ad. *The Guardian*. www.theguardian.com/media network/2016/jan/07/how-we-made-cadburys-gorilla-ad.

Carufel, R. (2019, January 24). How brands use social media giveaway and the key benefits. *Agility PR Solutions*. www.agilitypr.com/pr-news/public-relations/how-brands-use-social-media-giveaways-and-the-key-benefits/.

Castro, D. (n.d.). 6 lessons from Apple Events. *The Storytellers*. Retrieved January 24, 2021, from https://thestorytellers.com/6-lessons-apple events/.

CFI. (2015). *SMART Goal – Definition, Guide, and Importance of Goal Setting*. CFI. https://corporatefinanceinstitute.com/resources/knowledge/other/smart-goal/.

Chacon, B. (2016, October 28). 5 Ways to rock a branded Instagram hashtag. *Later Blog*. https://later.com/blog/branded-instagram-hashtag-guide/.

Chang, Y. T., Yu, H., & Lu, H. P. (2015). Persuasive messages, popularity cohesion, and message diffusion in social media marketing. *Journal of Business Research*, 68(4), 777–782. https://doi.org/10.1016/j.jbusres.2014.11.027.

Contemporary Issues in Social Media Marketing – 1st Edition – Bikramji. (2017). In B. Rishi & S. Bandyopadhyay (Eds.), *Routledge – Taylor and Francis Publishers* (1st ed.). Routledge and Taylor & Francis. www.routledge.com/Contemporary-Issues-in-Social-Media-Marketing/Rishi-Bandyopadhyay/p/book/9781138679184.

Culnan, M. J., Mchugh, P. J., Zubillaga, J. I., Uarterly, M. Q., & Xecutive, E. (2010). How Large U.S. CompanieS Can USe TwiTTer and oTHer SoCiaL media To gain BUSineSS VaLUe 1,2 the need for a new approach to implementing social media. In *MIS Quarterly Executive* (Vol. 9, Issue 4). http://syncapse.com/media/syncapse-value-of-a-facebook-.

Devereux, E., Grimmer, L., & Grimmer, M. (2020). Consumer engagement on social media: Evidence from small retailers. *Journal of Consumer Behaviour*, 19(2), 151–159. https://doi.org/10.1002/cb.1800.

Duffett, R. G. (2017). Influence of social media marketing communications on young consumers' attitudes. *Young Consumers*, 18(1), 19–39. https://doi.org/10.1108/YC-07-2016-00622.

Durgam, V. (2018). Social Media and its Role in Marketing. *International Journal of Advanced Research in Management*, 9(2), 1–10.

Dutta, S. (2010). What's your personal social media strategy? *Harvard Business Review*, 88(11), 127–130, 151. https://europepmc.org/article/med/21049685.

Dwivedi, Y. K., Ismagilova, E., Hughes, D. L., Carlson, J., Filieri, R., Jacobson, J., Jain, V., Karjaluoto, H., Kefi, H., Krishen, A. S., Kumar, V., Rahman, M. M., Raman, R., Rauschnabel, P. A., Rowley, J., Salo, J., Tran, G. A., & Wang, Y. (2020). Setting the future of digital and social media marketing research: Perspectives and research propositions. *International Journal of Information Management*, 102168. https://doi.org/10.1016/j.ijinfomgt.2020.102168.

Edosomwan, S., Sitalaskshmi, K. P., Kouame, D., Watson, J., & Seymour, T. (2011). The history of social media and its impact on business. *The Journal of Applied Management and Entrepreneurship*, 16(3).

Effing, R., & Spil, T. A. M. (2016). The social strategy cone: Towards a framework for evaluating social media strategies. *International Journal of Information Management*, 36(1), 1–8. https://doi.org/10.1016/j.ijinfomgt.2015.07.009.

Farshid, M., Plangger, K., & Nel, D. (2011). The social media faces of major global financial service brands. *Journal of Financial Services Marketing*, 16(3–4), 220–229. https://doi.org/10.1057/fsm.2011.19.

Felix, R., Rauschnabel, P. A., & Hinsch, C. (2017). Elements of strategic social media marketing: A holistic framework. *Journal of Business Research*, 70, 118–126. https://doi.org/10.1016/j.jbusres.2016.05.001.

Floreddu, P. B., & Cabiddu, F. (2016). Social media communication strategies. *Journal of Services Marketing*, 30(5), 490–503. https://doi.org/10.1108/JSM-01-2015-0036.

Godey, B., Manthiou, A., Pederzoli, D., Rokka, J., Aiello, G., Donvito, R., & Singh, R. (2016). Social media marketing efforts of luxury brands: Influence on brand equity and consumer behavior. *Journal of Business Research*, 69(12), 5833–5841. https://doi.org/10.1016/j.jbusres.2016.04.181.

Goh, K. Y., Heng, C. S., & Lin, Z. (2013). Social media brand community and consumer behavior: Quantifying the relative impact of user- and marketer-generated content. *Information Systems Research*, 24(1), 88–107. https://doi.org/10.1287/isre.1120.0469.

Goodrich, K., & de Mooij, M. (2014). How 'social' are social media? A cross-cultural comparison of online and offline purchase decision influences. *Journal of Marketing Communications*, 20(1–2), 103–116. https://doi.org/10.1080/135272 66.2013.797773.

Kaul, V. (2012). Citation: Kaul V (2012) Changing paradigms of media landscape in the digital age. *Journal of Mass Communicat Journalism*, 2012(2), 110. https://doi.org/10.4172/2165-7912.1000110.

Kietzmann, J. H., Hermkens, K., McCarthy, I. P., & Silvestre, B. S. (2011). Social media? Get serious! Understanding the functional building blocks of social media. *Business Horizons*, 54(3), 241–251. https://doi.org/10.1016/j.bushor.2011.01.005.

Kristensen, N. N., & From, U. (2015). Cultural journalism and cultural critique in a changing media landscape. *Journalism Practice*, 9(6), 760–772. https://doi.org/10.1080/17512786.2015.1051357.

Kwayu, S., Lal, B., & Abubakre, M. (2018). Enhancing organisational competitiveness via social media – a strategy as practice perspective. *Information Systems Frontiers*, 20(3), 439–456. https://doi.org/10.1007/s10796-017-9816-5.

Lashgari, M., Sutton-Brady, C., Solberg Søilen, K., & Ulfvengren, P. (2018). Adoption strategies of social media in B2B firms: A multiple case study approach. *Journal of Business and Industrial Marketing*, 33(5), 730–743. https://doi.org/10.1108/JBIM-10-2016-0242.

Li, F., Larimo, J., & Leonidou, L. C. (2020). Social media marketing strategy: Definition, conceptualization, taxonomy, validation, and future agenda. *Journal of the Academy of Marketing Science*, 49(1), 51–70. https://doi.org/10.1007/s11747-020-00733-3.

Lindsey-Mullikin, J., & Borin, N. (2017). Why strategy is key for successful social media sales. *Business Horizons*, 60(4), 473–482. https://doi.org/10.1016/j.bushor.2017.03.005.

Mills, A. J., Botha, E., & Campbell, C. (2015). Managing the new media: Tools for brand management in social media. In *The Sustainable Global Marketplace* (pp. 397–397). Springer International Publishing. https://doi.org/10.1007/978-3-319-10873-5_240.

Mills, A. J., & Plangger, K. (2015). Social media strategy for online service brands. *The Service Industries Journal (Routledge – Taylor and Francis)*, 35(10), 521–536. www.tandfonline.com/doi/pdf/10.1080/02642069.2015.1043277?needAccess=true.

Nobre, H., & Silva, D. (2014). Social network marketing strategy and SME strategy benefits. *Journal of Transnational Management*, 19(2), 138–151. https://doi.org/10.1080/15475778.2014.904658.

Nudd, T. (2018, March 22). This look inside Spike Jonze's apple ad is as fascinating as the film itself. *Ad Week*. www.adweek.com/creativity/this-look-inside-spike-jonzes-apple-ad-is-as-fascinating-as-the-film-itself/.

O'Connor, M. E. (2018, January 18). *How to set SMART social media marketing goals for your business*. https://marieennisoconnor.medium.com/how-to-set-smart-social-media-marketing-goals-for-2018–862d1002a172.

Olotewo, J. (2015). International journal of online marketing research, volume 1, issue 1 pp. 1–9 2015. *International Journal of Online Marketing Research*, 2(2). https://doi.org/10.5455/IJOMR.2016254411.

Ouvrein, G., Pabian, S., Giles, D., Hudders, L., & De Backer, C. (2021). The web of influencers. A marketing-audience classification of (potential) social media influencers. *Journal of Marketing Management*. https://doi.org/10.1080/02672 57X.2021.1912142.

Paquette, H. (2013). *Social media as a marketing tool: A literature review.* http:// digitalcommons.uri.edu/tmd_major_papers/2.

Patel, S. (2021). How you can build a powerful influencer marketing strategy in 2021. *Big Commerce.* www.bigcommerce.com/blog/influencer-marketing/#what-is-influencer-marketing.

Poecze, F., Ebster, C., & Strauss, C. (2018). Social media metrics and sentiment analysis to evaluate the effectiveness of social media posts. *Procedia Computer Science, 130,* 660–666. https://doi.org/10.1016/j.procs.2018.04.117.

Popli, S., & Rishi, B. (2021a). *Crafting Customer Experience Strategy.* Emerald Publishing Limited. https://books.emeraldinsight.com/page/detail/Crafting-Customer-Experience-Strategy/?k=9781839097119.

Popli, S., & Rishi, B. (2021b). The what, why and how of customer experience. In *Crafting Customer Experience Strategy* (pp. 1–20). Emerald Publishing Limited. https://doi.org/10.1108/978-1-83909-710-220211001.

Purdam, K., & Elliot, M. (2015). The changing social science data landscape. In *Innovations in Digital Research Methods* (pp. 25–58). SAGE Publications Ltd. https://doi.org/10.4135/9781473920651.n2.

Quesenberry, K. A. (2020). *Social Media Strategy: Marketing, Advertising, and Public Relations in the Consumer Revolution* (3rd ed.). Rowman & Littlefield Publishers. https://rowman.com/ISBN/9781538138175/Social-Media-Strategy-Marketing-Advertising-and-Public-Relations-in-the-Consumer-Revolution-Third-Edition.

Ramsaran-Fowdar, R. R. (2013). The implications of facebook marketing for organizations. *Contemporary Management Research*, 9(1), 73–84. https://doi.org/10.7903/cmr.9710.

Rana, S. (2018a). Business performance: Earlier stage and looking forward. *FIIB Business Review*, 7(3), 153–155.

Rana, S. (2018b). Managing businesses relevance beyond technology. *FIIB Business Review*, 7(4), 229–231.

Rana, S., Raut, S. K., Prashar, S., & Hamid, A. B. A. (2020). Promoting through consumer nostalgia: A conceptual framework and future research agenda. *Journal of Promotion Management*, 27(2), 211–249.

Rana, S., Raut, S. K., Prashar, S., & Quttainah, M. A. (2020). The transversal of nostalgia from psychology to marketing: what does it portend for future research? *International Journal of Organizational Analysis*, Vol. ahead-of-print No. ahead-of-print.

Raut, S. K., Sakpal, S., & Soni, R. (2022). Understanding the Service Quality Dimensions and Achieving Resilience in Service Retail. In *Handbook of Research on Supply Chain Resiliency, Efficiency, and Visibility in the Post-Pandemic Era*, edited by Ramakrishna Yanamandra (pp. 136–156). IGI Global, UAE. https://doi.org/10.4018/978-1-7998-9506-0

Rayport, J. F. (2011, July 25). Build brands apple's way. *Harvard Business Review*. https://hbr.org/2011/07/build-your-brand-apples-way.

Rishi, B., & Kuthuru, N. R. (2021). A review for managerial guidelines for social media integration of IMC in digital era. In *Digital Entertainment* (pp. 187–212). Springer Singapore. https://doi.org/10.1007/978-981-15-9724-4_10.

Rishi, B., & Popli, S. (2021). Getting into the customers, shoes: Customer journey management. In *Crafting Customer Experience Strategy* (pp. 21–45). Emerald Publishing Limited. https://doi.org/10.1108/978-1-83909-710-220211002.

Salazar, K. (2016, February 14). Are your personas outdated? Know when it's right to revise. *Nielsen Norman Group*. www.nngroup.com/articles/revising-personas/.

Shalender, K. (2021). Building effective social media strategy: Case-based learning and recommendations. In *Digital Entertainment* (pp. 233–244). Springer Singapore. https://doi.org/10.1007/978-981-15-9724-4_12.

Single Grain Team. (n.d.). *Ultimate guide to growing your business with influencer marketing*. Retrieved January 24, 2021, from www.singlegrain.com/content-marketing-strategy-2/guide-influencer-marketing/.

Taira, T. (2021). *The Internet and the Social Media Revolution – University of Helsinki*. Cambridge University Press. https://researchportal.helsinki.fi/en/publications/the-internet-and-the-social-media-revolution.

Tussyadiah, I., & Zach, F. (2013). Social media strategy and capacity for consumer co-creation among destination marketing organizations. In *Information and Communication Technologies in Tourism 2013* (pp. 242–253). Springer Berlin Heidelberg. https://doi.org/10.1007/978-3-642-36309-2_21.

Tuten, T. L., Solomon, M. R., & Rishi, B. (2020). *Social Media Marketing*. Sage. https://study.sagepub.in/tuten_smm3e.

United Breaks Guitars – Harvard Business School Working Knowledge. (n.d.). Retrieved January 18, 2021, from https://hbswk.hbs.edu/item/united-breaks-guitars.

van der Graaf, A., Otjes, S., & Rasmussen, A. (2016). Weapon of the weak? The social media landscape of interest groups. *European Journal of Communication*, *31*(2), 120–135. https://doi.org/10.1177/0267323115612210.

Veil, S. R., Buehner, T., & Palenchar, M. J. (2011). A work-in-process literature review: Incorporating social media in risk and crisis communication. *Journal of Contingencies and Crisis Management*, *19*(2), 110–122. https://doi.org/10.1111/j.1468-5973.2011.00639.x.

Vinerean, S. (2017). Importance of strategic social media marketing. *Expert Journal of Marketing*, *5*(1), 28–35.

Warren, T. (2018, March 7). I can't stop playing Apple's clever new HomePod ad. *The Verge*. www.theverge.com/2018/3/7/17089920/apple-homepod-ad-fka-twigs-spike-jonze-anderson-paak.

Yang, J., Basile, K., & Letourneau, O. (2020). The impact of social media platform selection on effectively communicating about corporate social responsibility. *Journal of Marketing Communications*, *26*(1), 65–87. https://doi.org/10.1080/13527266.2018.1500932.

Zhang, H., Gupta, S., Sun, W., & Zou, Y. (2020). How social-media-enabled co-creation between customers and the firm drives business value? The perspective of organizational learning and social Capital. *Information and Management*, *57*(3), 103200. https://doi.org/10.1016/j.im.2019.103200.

Zhu, Y. Q., & Chen, H. G. (2015). Social media and human need satisfaction: Implications for social media marketing. *Business Horizons*, *58*(3), 335–345. https://doi.org/10.1016/j.bushor.2015.01.006.

12 Prosocial Behaviour and Impact of Influencers During Crisis

A Study Based on Sentiment Analysis

Julie Vardhan and Madhuri Mahato

Introduction

The social media has been a significant contributor on the communication front especially during crisis. Each crisis has a different message which takes the form of warnings, general alerts, evacuations, notifications, etc. However, the various types of crises pose a different kind and intensity of threat (Rana, Raut, Prashar, & Hamid, 2020). Each exigency thus adopts different communication styles. Timely recommendations; instructions; floating of helpline numbers; information regarding food, shelter, or any other requisites form an essential part of crisis communication (Pauchant & Mitroff, 1992; Seeger et al., 2003).

During crisis, it has been found that the social media influencers can play a significant role in mitigating the crisis. The social media influencers are the "third-party actors that have established a significant number of relevant relationships with a specific quality to influence on organizational stakeholders through content production, content distribution, interaction, and personal appearance on the social web" (Enke & Borchers, 2019).

In this chapter, the authors explore the role of social media with special reference to the context of crisis and the effective management strategies thereby adopted. The recent case of lockdown due to spread of COVID-19 pandemic in India has seen many issues that needed to be tackled right from transportation of migrant workers, making availability of essential goods and medicines, and meeting other unforeseen and pressing requirements. While we realize the importance of communication that is faster, cheaper and has a wider outreach especially during situations like natural calamities or public health crisis, this area has been relatively underexplored in research studies. The COVID-19 pandemic has obligated a rethink in this direction.

Among the social media platforms, Twitter is a networking platform designed to communicate with short messages of 140 characters with followers. Twitter is used extensively by individuals, organizations, groups, leaders, and influencers to communicate concise and current viewpoints, ideas, and information on a range of topics. Studies have found that Twitter

DOI: 10.4324/9781003315582-13

is used by mainly the younger age group suggesting a large population base that uses this platform. The outbreak of the pandemic in March 2020 led to several governments taking various measures to contain its spread. The Indian government issued a notification of lockdown in the economy in various phases. Although a measure required to contain the spread of the virus, it resulted in severe repercussions on the economy. For the helpless individuals and many who had been badly affected due to the pandemic effect, help came forth from few individuals. These individuals through their intent and initiative used the social media platform of Twitter to reach out to those in need of help.

The next section of the chapter is a review of literature on social media and crisis communication and influencer's role during crisis and prosocial behaviour. Through an analysis of the sentiments during the period of the study, the next section would provide an insight into the prevalent feelings among the affected and the role of influencers in bringing about the prosocial behaviours and care-giving attitudes through the social media usage. The section is followed by discussion to understand the implications of the result regarding the influencer's communication strategy. The final section is conclusion which summarizes the study and highlights the scope for future research.

Social Media and Crisis Communication

During crisis situations, due to the rise in public expectations, many Government agencies and authorities have started relying on social media channels to release out information or to warn and disseminate safety measures to the public during natural calamities. The study by Jang and Paek (2019) stated that social media plays a significant role during infectious disease outbreaks. Social media offers real time, first-hand information to the general public, which can be easily accessed and shared with the family and friends. In other similar studies, it was found that H1N1 flu, Zika, and Ebola outbreaks were all first reported via the social media (Ding & Zhang, 2010; Chan et al., 2018; Lazard et al., 2015). Even for other public health emergencies like the case of Anthrax, SARS, and West Nile virus outbreak, there were reasonable expectations from the healthcare professionals to provide with effective and coherent communication (Reynolds & Seeger, 2005).

Some research studies have highlighted the dependence on media or social media in the contemporary world, especially in situations like the pandemic that can readily influence the risk perceptions of the public or their ability to access information related to health precautions and hazards (Snyder & Rouse, 1995; Oh et al., 2015; Fung et al., 2011; Paek et al., 2016; Oh et al., 2020). Looking beyond perceiving the new-age media as a tool for awareness and information-seeking platform, there is also the need for more research in the area of crisis communication. While traditionally the crisis communication strategies have been viewed as negative and a cause for establishing blame, alternatively the crisis narratives can create a host of behavioural responses in people (Ma & Zhan, 2016; Coombs, 2016).

Seeger and Sellnow (2016) have categorized the crisis narratives into blame, renewal, victim, hero, and memorial types. The blame narratives seek to identify the responsible ones in a crisis and call for stricter punishments while the renewal narratives focus on growth and restoration through positive changes so as to overcome the crisis. The victim narratives tend to personify the harm caused to a person or group and are used to sell the crisis stories by the media while the memorial narratives celebrate the human resilience and are etched in the public memory (Rana, Raut, Prashar, & Quttainah, 2020). The last and most significant narrative is the hero narrative. This narrative brings forth protagonists who are citizen heroes, first responders, or leader heroes who through their charisma, skill, intelligence, or wisdom can accomplish victories during crisis. Research in the area of hero narratives has been scanty (Liu et al., 2020), and this is where our study will add value.

Some studies have linked effectiveness in crisis management with the emotions experienced by individuals. The ranges of emotions that are experienced from anger to anxiety tend to impact as to how individuals process the crisis information and exhibit their behavioural intentions. Lesser negative emotions enable a positive engagement and a positive post-crisis perception (Jin & Hong, 2010; Jin et al., 2016; Choi & Lin, 2009; Coombs & Holladay, 2009; Kim & Niederdeppe, 2016; Brummette & Sisco, 2015; Yang et al., 2010).

Risk communication patterns during public health emergencies, crisis, or any other exigencies have been a parallel area of interest to the researchers (Rana, 2019). Risk communication has long been viewed as an essential and interactive process during emergencies and fundamentally deals with all the elements, people, or parties involved. Risk communication aims at adopting effective control measures so as to avoid damage (Covello, 1992; Heath, 1995). A study conducted by McGuire et al. (2020) for the pandemic as recent as COVID-19 has linked crisis communication with effective leadership. They have researched the case of New Zealand that has managed to effectively put out clear, consistent messages and narratives to the public that inspired confidence and trust among the people. The study also clearly ascertains the importance of social media communication during crisis as it combines authenticity and informal humanity (Kulkarni, 2019). Jin and Spence (2020) highlighted the communication patterns that emerged throughout the phases of Hurricane Maria according to the crisis and emergency risk communication model.

By combining the risk communication patterns during public health emergencies with the crisis narratives that are duly adopted in such situations, it can be understood that hero narratives play a major role in helping to sail through the crisis. The hero can be any common citizen who comes forward to offer his/her services during the hour of angst and pain. Likewise, the hero can be any person holding an authoritative position in the society or can be anyone like a celebrity wielding adequate influence to see through relief work in such emergencies.

Influencer's Role During Crisis

The protagonists in the hero narratives are the micro-celebrities or the social media influencers. One of the earliest researches on weblogs by Blood (2002) found the presence of social media influencers. Originally, the term "social media influencers" was coined by John Barger in 1997. Senft (2013) in a later study used the term "micro-celebrity" that characterizes a "commitment to deploying and maintaining one's online identity as if it were a branded good, with the expectation that others do the same". Micro-celebrities constantly engage on social media and try to establish strong connections. Posting opinions, responding to queries, engaging in friendly banters are all part of the engagement activities which the micro-celebrities undertake on social media. More visibility and proximity to the followers are what create self-branding to them unlike the traditional or mainstream celebrities who rely on distancing strategies that elevates their celebrity status (Jerslev, 2016; Senft, 2008).

The social media influencers are individuals having a direct impact on the consumers or followers in the social media context (Rana, 2018). Their role in creating and translating the marketing communication by companies has been considered in a number of studies (Kozinets, et al., 2010; Ge & Gretzel, 2018). Most of the research on influencers relates to the impact they have on products, brands, or services affecting the purchase decisions of a large audience who are following them (Schouten et al., 2020), but the influencers are also reliable information sources for the followers in a number of related areas. Numerous studies have found that influencers are perceived as being more credible than the traditional celebrities in creating awareness and intent to purchase. This seems to be particularly true for luxury products, fashion, health, and nutrition. In fact, in these categories of products and services, the influencers are considered to be more relatable as well as approachable than the traditional celebrity endorsers.

One of the reasons for the perceived familiarity with the influencers is due to the fact that the influencers directly address their followers in their posts, and followers can communicate in the post as if they are communicating with their friends, expressing themselves even emotionally. This perceived familiarity also leads to the followers considering the influencers to be one among them.

Crisis communication offers a host of inputs for decision-making. People not only draw in necessary inputs from the official updates, they also learn from varied experiences. In newer and uncertain situations, where there is a possibility of overestimating the looming threat, the narratives can become complex, remain incomplete, or even present conflicting aspects of a particular situation (Seeger & Sellnow, 2016; Sellnow et al., 2018; Bhandari and Raut, 2019). This is when the role of influencers makes way for positive narratives. The social media influencers are those whose credibility and self-efficacy help to mitigate the risk during emergencies. The credibility of such micro-celebrities remains unquestionable, and hence the messages are circulated clearly, widely, and effectively to the intended parties, which are then strategically matched to the needs and situation for the audience involved. Such messages are filled with appeal, logic, and emotion and positively add to the cultural stories (Zhang & Zhang, 2017; Freimuth et al., 2000; Borchers, 2019). The dependence on either the influencers or the need to reach out to wider audiences for advice or more information is a common practice in newer and uncertain situations. This will help in making better and informed choices on the future course of action. A study by Sutton et al. (2014) was an attempt in this direction, which analysed the tweets put up through official government accounts for a 48-hour period during the Waldo Canyon wildfire in Colorado. More informative tweets that involved guidance on protective action were found to be more useful than the regular situational updates.

Influencers and Prosocial Behaviour

The digitalization world has seen a paradigm shift in the socio-psychological mechanisms adopted by individuals. The resultant behaviours reflect on both the positive and negative gamuts. To be precise, the consumption and usage of social media result in both care and non-care behaviours. Earlier studies (Tierney et al., 2006; Tierney, 2007; Gotham, 2007; Recuber, 2013) have documented the role of media in generating the "disaster mythology", but there has been a colossal gap in identifying and bringing forth the role of social media's ability to influence and nurture the prosocial and caring behaviours of individuals (Boulianne et al., 2018).

Apart from the personality and other social influences, the non-digital identities also shape the digital identities of individuals as propounded by the co-construction theory (Wright & Li, 2011; Raut, Sakpal and Soni, 2022). One of the earliest researches to explore the construct of online prosocial behaviours suggested that people may outspread their altruistic gaming behaviours to extend help (Wang & Wang, 2008). In tune with the co-construction theory, the face-to-face prosocial dispositions get extended into the digital world which goes beyond the gaming environment into other electronic mediums and platforms. This was also empirically proven by Wright and Li (2011) that prosocial behaviours adopted during a face-to-face interaction can significantly predict the online prosocial behaviours that get manifested through the various social networking sites.

One of the earliest definitions of prosocial behaviours define them as overt actions taken for the benefit of others. They include actions on resource sharing and donating, cooperation, volunteering activities, engaging in comforting, and the like (Eisenberg, 2006). The socialization patterns of young adults in both the digital and non-digital worlds remain more or less the same (Subrahmanyam & Greenfield, 2008; Subrahmanyam et al., 2006, 2008). What is to be noted here is that as and when the duration of technological usage increases, the prosocial behaviours also increase which is in tandem with the negative behaviours of cyber aggression that show a similar pattern based on the usage. This denotes that the span of technological engagement determines the extent of transferability of non-digital dispositions onto the digital sphere, be it the aggressive behaviours or the prosocial behaviours. However, previous studies have shown a modest relationship between the prosocial and aggressive behaviours. Being low on one dimension does not reflect an inevitable high on the other dimension. Neither can these prosocial behaviours be regarded as akin to socially competent behaviours nor social interaction and communication skills but can be considered as just one dimension of it (Killen & Smetana, 2014).

Previous researches have argued that the traditional media reporting on disasters creates panic; and reports largely on anti-social behaviours like loot, violence, and rioting may or may not be an exaggeration of the undesirable behaviours but certainly delay the response and recovery (Tierney et al., 2006; Gotham, 2007). On the contrary, Boulianne et al. (2018) analysed tweets related to the wildfire that threatened Fort McMurray, Alberta, in the year 2016. In their study, they found that the social media, on the contrary to the traditional media, encourages more care and concern and invites to help thus leading to prosocial behaviours. One of the reasons for the care-giving attitudes to manifest on social media is because the victims themselves share their personal stories through personal accounts rather than mediated accounts (Houston et al., 2015; Murthy & Longwell, 2013).

Methodology

In this study, we have specifically chosen to do a textual analysis of the various messages that were posted on Twitter as a cry for help, that is the narratives during the lockdown period. Around a total of 5,000 messages and appeals were taken from the Twitter platform for further textual scrutiny during the period of April to September 2020. A similar methodology was adopted by Das and Dutta (2021) to understand the sentiments during COVID in India.

The messages and appeals were accessed using the various hashtags like 'please'/ 'request' /'urgent help', 'emergency', 'patient', 'stuck', 'problem', and 'lockdown'. The messages and appeals were initially scrutinized for redundancy, and the duplicity was eliminated.

A total of 5,000 tweets during the given period were analysed. Among these tweets, all the tweets that broadly comprised issues related to lockdown, pandemic, crisis, and help were further sorted, and 1,200 tweets that were relevant to the Indian context and which came under these broad categories were selected. Based on a textual analysis, a sample of 347 tweets was taken that dealt with the issues that were related to food, health, education, and income that also found responses from the influencers. Sentiment analysis was further applied. Sentiment analysis is the process of understanding the feelings of the person who has written a text about the entity/concept. For our study, sentiment analysis API from Meaning Cloud (software for semantic analysis) was used. Based on the methodology adopted by Martínez-Cámara et al. (2012; Lauran et al., 2020; László & Attila, 2021) on sentiment analysis, this study used the polarity classification of the tweets. The API yields results as P+ (highly positive), P (positive), N+ (highly negative), N (negative), and Neu (Neutral).

Results and Discussion

To understand the various texts of the tweets, the first level of analysis was regarding the text classification. The broad classification of tweets chosen initially was from the themes of "pandemic", "lockdown", and "help". Based on the number of tweets and followers an individual had, along with their level of involvement on the crisis incidents, we found that these individuals had taken up the role of influencers. Unlike the traditional role of influencers in encouraging the followers to subscribe for a particular product or service, these influencers and their communication with followers were more engaging and related to searching for a solution.

A number of retweets and hashtags based on the communication with the influencers were subsequently analysed through the meaning cloud. Although a large number of tweets were classified based on the communication of issues among the influencers and followers, the other issues that were found to be most occurring among the people happened to revolve around the basic concerns and after-effects of pandemic, namely food and drink, health and medical fitness, education and career, and business (Figure 12.1).

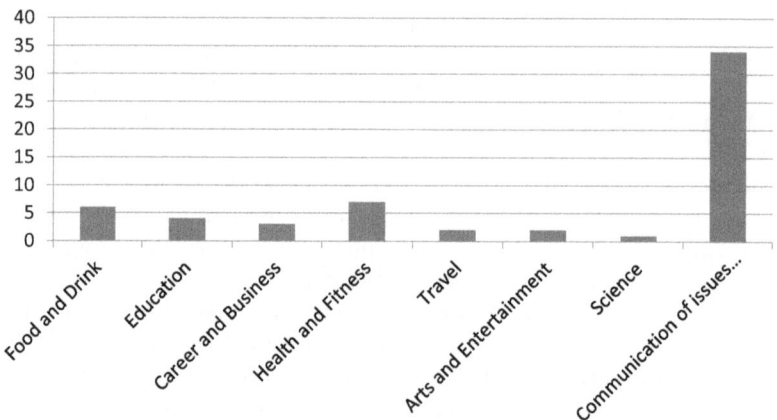

Figure 12.1 Text classification

Source: Authors' analysis

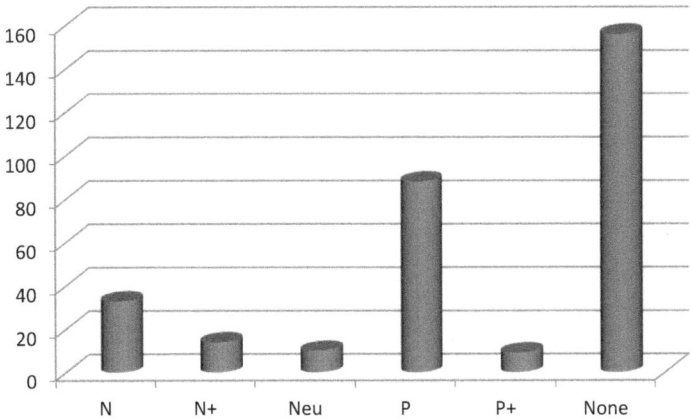

Figure 12.2 Polarity levels

Source: Authors' analysis

As also corroborated through the various news during the lockdown period, a large number of people were affected due to the pandemic crisis, with many suffering due to the shortage of food or lack of medicine. The condition was further aggravated during the lockdown as a large number of people lost their jobs, and there was no means to travel to their home state.

The next level of analysis was to check the polarity level of tweets during the crisis period. The polarity levels are usually measured as P+ (highly positive), P (positive), N+ (highly negative), N (negative), and Neu (Neutral). The pandemic crisis would bring out the negative sentiments among the people affected. However, through the communication exchange with the influencers, it has been found that the percentage of positive and very positive sentiment combined is 97, which represents that even in a distressful situation, the social media influencers were able to bring about the prosocial behaviour and the feelings of care and humanity among the followers (Figure 12.2).

From the data set which was analysed, it was also noticed that 156 tweets were classified as having no polarity as these were either statements with general issue details or inconclusive statements, for example '*Spoken to the doctor and getting the MRI done today. Then doctor will decide the further treatment*'. P+ and P denote positive feelings like thanks, appreciation, love, and blessings. These are also affirmations of success or issues being resolved. Thus, statements like '*Another successful surgery/This Sunday is special/ Thank u for everything*' represent P+. In addition, any arrangements for food, shelter, travel, and fee payment for education move the end result in the positive direction. The negative tweets like the issues which are creating panic or distress among the followers, like the tweets about hunger, certain disease, death, financial hardship, and loss of job, were compiled into the negative side of the polarity. Despite the prevalent negative sentiment due to the crisis, what is noteworthy is that the positive manifestations continued to dominate in the period.

Table 12.1 reveals that there have several exchanges between the influencers and their followers and that the sentiments can be further classified into conversation about concepts or regarding entities. Based on the categorization of tweets of 15 and a total of 347 tweets, the polarity of each tweet in its relationship with the concept or entity was measured. So for the first category out of the total 30 positive tweets (P), 20 were related to the concept and 10 were about the entity.

While the concept was similar to what has already been undertaken in the text classification process, the entity reveals the influencers who have taken the lead in resolving the crisis or engaging in prosocial behaviour during the crisis period. As examples, the influencers like Sonu Sood and Arun Bothra came up quite frequently among the entities in the tweets analysed.

In the present study, an analysis of the tweets during the period of pandemic crisis in India the feelings related to the key factors during the crisis. As indicated in the results, there seems to be a negative concern in the areas of food, health and medical fitness, education and career, travel, and availability of essential items. This arises due to the uncertainty and risk associated during crisis situations. While government initiated several schemes for helping out those in need, the social media influencers seemed to have garnered a huge follower base, turning the negative sentiments into positive sentiments through their initiatives and attitude of help and care.

The results are also indicative of the fact that if communication is fast and two-way and the goals clear, solution can be created for every public issue. The factors that are perceived as being positive are those related to right actions initiated at the behest of the influencers who have been able to connect and reconnect to people who are in need. This is in line with the suggestion by Eriksson (2018) where the study aggregated the recommendations from a number of studies that effective crisis communication is about using the social media's potential to be able to create the right message and the right impact.

While research studies have tried to link social media usage to prosocial behaviours, at the heart of all this lies the basic foundation of felt emotions of gratitude (McCullough et al., 2002; Bakker et al., 2019). Feelings of gratitude can essentially create a sense of satisfaction and happiness with one's life invigorating an individual to extend a helping hand to the needy. The analysis reveals the positive emotion generated by the influencers, whose communications were found to be authentic by the followers. A review of the earlier studies also reflects that the disaster stories or the pleas for help being posted from personal, first-hand accounts/handles come across as trustworthy, while the others do raise apprehensions as they either re-circulate, post solicitation requests of charities and other bodies through mediated accounts. The personal storytelling helps people to easily connect and raises feelings of empathy and a willingness to offer support (Houston et al.,

Table 12.1 Polarity and its relation with concept/entity

Count of P	Column Labels							
Row Labels	N	N+	Neu	None	P	P+	(Blank)	Grand Total
1	13	2	6	44	30	3		98
concept	6	1	3	19	20	3		52
entity	7	1	3	25	10			46
	7	3	1	35	27	1		74
concept	4	3		14	16			37
entity	3		1	21	11	1		37
3	4	2	2	27	13	1		49
concept	2	1	1	7	9			20
entity	2	1	1	20	4	1		29
4	4	2	1	17	11	2		37
concept	2	2	1	5	5			15
entity	2			12	6	2		22
5	2	1		15	6	1		25
concept	2	1		4	3			10
entity				11	3	1		15
6		2		12	4			18
concept		2		4	3			9
entity				8	1			9
7	1	1		9	3	1		15
concept	1	1		4	2			8
entity				5	1	1		7
8	1	1		3	6	1		12
concept	1	1		1	3			6
entity				2	3	1		6
9				4	2			6
concept				1	2			3
entity				3				3
10				3	1			4
concept				1				1
entity				2	1			3
11				1	1			2
concept					1			1
entity				1				1
12	1			1				2
concept	1							1
entity				1				1
13				2				2
concept				1				1
entity				1				1
14				2				2
concept				1				1
entity				1				1
15				1				1
entity				1				1
(blank)								
(blank)								
Grand Total	33	14	10	176	104	10		347

Source: Authors' analysis

2015; Murthy & Longwell, 2013). Further on, research into the domain of philanthropy has also identified the primary role of values and altruism resulting in empathetic concern and principles of care. While empathetic concern triggers the emotions of sympathy and compassion, principles of care echo the moral duties (Bekkers & Dursun, 2013). In lines with the results of this study, a meta-analytic study by Boulianne et al. (2018) also found a positive relationship between social media and civic engagement.

Conclusion

The influencers are the heroes who do the impossible especially during crises. They are backed by millions of people whose compassion and concern go viral on new-age comm, especially during crisesunication media, that is the social media. This research is an attempt to capture the prosocial behaviours and care-giving attitudes that arise from the socio-psychological mechanisms through the social media usage and engagement. Social media has become an indispensable channel of communication during crisis to express opinions, raise issues, and share solutions. The study highlights that although in the prevailing negative sentiment during crisis, the initiative by social media influencers can help in ameliorating the situation and changing it into a positive sentiment.

One of the other insights is that the social media platform has an important role in the crisis recovery. The analysis shows that the social media users not only benefitted individually if they were in need during the crisis, but they spread the awareness of the concerned influencers to others in need as well by retweeting their issues and the solutions.

Although the study highlights the role of influencers in reaching to a wider public during crisis, one of the limitations of the study is that while identifying polarity, there might be inbuilt challenges with the method in not recognizing colloquial terms or usage of local dialect to emphasize a particular point. The analysis is also limited since sentiments can be available on various other platforms apart from Twitter.

The results of the study can be used by institutions and governments to develop or improve their reach to the public during the times of crisis. In future, research could be undertaken to understand the reach and viability of more number of influencers, influencer organizations, and the communities created on the social media platforms during crisis.

References

Bakker, M. H., Kerstholt, J. H., van Bommel, M., & Giebels, E. (2019). Decision-making during a crisis: the interplay of narratives and statistical information before and after crisis communication. *Journal of Risk Research*, 22(11), 1409–1424.

Bekkers, R., & Dursun, E. (2013). A brief history of research on philanthropy. Retrieved from https://understandingphilanthropy.files.wordpress.com/2012/01/13_03_22_development_research.pdf.

Blood, R. (2002). Weblogs: A history and perspective. In J. Rodzvilla (Ed.), *We've got blog: How weblogs are changing our culture* (pp. 7–16). Perseus.

Borchers Nils, S. (2019). Social media influencers in strategic communication. *International Journal of Strategic Communication*, 13(4), 255–260. doi:10.1080/1553118X.2019.1634075.

Bhandari, K. R., & Raut, S. K. (2019). 9 Leveraging tacit. *Advances in Management Research: Innovation and Technology*, 1(1), 127–138.

Boulianne, S., Minaker, J., & Haney, T. J. (2018). Does compassion go viral? Social media, caring, and the Fort McMurray wildfire. *Information, Communication & Society*, 21(5), 697–711.

Brummette, J., & Sisco, H. F. (2015). Using Twitter as a means of coping with emotions and uncontrollable crises. *Public Relations Review*, 41(1), 89–96.

Chan, M. S., Winneg, K., Hawkins, L., Farhadloo, M., Jamieson, K. H., & Albarrabcin, D. (2018). Legacy and social media respectively influence risk perceptions and protective behaviors during emerging health threats: A multi-wave analysis of communications on Zika virus cases. *Social Science & Medicine*, 212, 50–59. doi:10.1016/j.socscimed.2018.07.007.

Choi, Y., & Lin, Y. H. (2009). Consumer response to crisis: Exploring the concept of involvement in Mattel product recalls. *Public Relations Review*, 35(1), 18–22.

Coombs, W. T. (2016). Reflections on a meta-analysis: Crystallizing thinking about SCCT. *Journal of Public Relations Research*, 28(2), 120–122. https://doi.org/10.1080/1062726X.2016.1167479.

Coombs, W. T., & Holladay, S. J. (2009). Further explorations of post-crisis communication: Effects of media and response strategies on perceptions and intentions. *Public Relations Review*, 35(1), 1–6.

Covello, V. T. (1992). Risk communication: An emerging area of health communication research. *Annals of the International Communication Association*, 15(1), 359–373.

Das, S., & Dutta, A. (2021). Characterizing public emotions and sentiments in COVID-19 environment: A case study of India. *Journal of Human Behavior in the Social Environment*, 31(1–4), 154–167. doi:10.1080/10911359.2020.1781015.

Ding, H., & Zhang, J. (2010). Social media and participatory risk communication during the H1N1 flu epidemic: A comparative study of the United States and China. *China Media Research*, 6(4), 80–91.

Eisenberg, N. (2006, October). Empathy-related responding and prosocial behaviour. In *Novartis Foundation Symposium* (Vol. 278, p. 71). John Wiley, 1999.

Enke, N., & Borchers, N. S. (2019). Social media influencers in strategic communication: A conceptual framework for strategic social media influencer communication. *International Journal of Strategic Communication*, 13(4), 261–277.

Eriksson, M. (2018). Lessons for crisis communication on social media: A systematic review of what research tells the practice. *International Journal of Strategic Communication*, 12(5), 526–551. doi:10.1080/1553118X.2018.1510405.

Freimuth, V., Linnan, H. W., & Potter, P. (2000). Communicating the threat of emerging infections to the public. *Emerging Infectious Diseases*, 6(4), 337.

Fung, T. K., Namkoong, K., & Brossard, D. (2011). Media, social proximity, and risk: A comparative analysis of newspaper coverage of avian flu in Hong Kong and in the United States. *Journal of Health Communication*, 16(8), 889–907. doi: 10.1080/10810730.2011.561913.

Ge, J., & Gretzel, U. (2018). Emoji rhetoric: A social media influencer perspective. *Journal of Marketing Management*, 34(15–16), 1272–1295.

Gotham, K. F. (2007). Critical theory and Katrina: Disaster, spectacle and immanent critique. *City*, 11(1), 81–99.

Heath, R. L. (1995). Corporate environmental risk communication: Cases and practices along the Texas Gulf Coast. *Annals of the International Communication Association*, 18(1), 255–277.

Houston, J. B., Hawthorne, J., Perreault, M. F., Park, E. H., Goldstein Hode, M., Halliwell, M. R., . . . & Griffith, S. A. (2015). Social media and disasters: A functional framework for social media use in disaster planning, response, and research. *Disasters*, 39(1), 1–22.

Jang, K., & Paek, Y. M. (2019). When information from public health officials in untrustworthy: The use of online news, interpersonal networks, and social media during the MERS outbreak in South Korea. *Health Communication*, 34(9), 991–998. doi:10.1080/10410236.2018.1449552.

Jerslev, A. (2016). Media times| in the time of the microcelebrity: Celebrification and the YouTuber Zoella. *International Journal of Communication*, 10, 19.

Jin, X., & Spence, P. R. (2020). Understanding crisis communication on social media with CERC: Topic model analysis of tweets about Hurricane Maria. *Journal of Risk Research*. doi:10.1080/13669877.2020.1848901.

Jin, Y., Fraustino, J. D., & Liu, B. F. (2016). The scared, the outraged, and the anxious: How crisis emotions, involvement, and demographics predict publics' conative coping. *International Journal of Strategic Communication*, 10(4), 289–308.

Jin, Y., & Hong, S. Y. (2010). Explicating crisis coping in crisis communication. *Public Relations Review*, 36(4), 352–360.

Killen, M., & Smetana, J. (Eds.). (2014). *Handbook of moral development* (2nd ed.). Psychology Press.

Kim, H. K., & Niederdeppe, J. (2016). Effects of self-affirmation, narratives, and informational messages in reducing unrealistic optimism about alcohol-related problems among college students. *Human Communication Research*, 42(2), 246–268.

Kozinets, R. V., De Valck, K., Wojnicki, A. C., & Wilner, S. J. (2010). Networked narratives: Understanding word-of-mouth marketing in online communities. *Journal of Marketing*, 74(2), 71–89.

Kulkarni, V. 2019. Is it the message or the medium? Relational management during crisis through blogs, Facebook and corporate websites. *Global Business Review*, 20(3), 743–756. doi:10.1177/0972150918761986.

László, N., & Attila, K. (2021). Social media sentiment analysis based on COVID-19. *Journal of Information and Telecommunication*, 5(1), 1–15. doi: 10.1080/24751839.2020.1790793.

Lauran, N., Kunneman, F., & Van de Wijngaert, L. (2020). Connecting social media data and crisis communication theory: A case study on the chicken and the egg. *Journal of Risk Research*, 23(10), 1259–1277. doi:10.1080/13669877.2019.1628097.

Lazard, A. J., Scheinfeld, E., Bernhardt, J. M., Wilcox, G. B., & Suran, M. (2015). Detecting themes of public concern: A text mining analysis of the centers for disease control and prevention's Ebola live twitter chat. *American Journal of Infection Control*, 43(10), 1109–1111. doi:10.1016/j.ajic.2015.05.025.

Liu, B. F., Austin, L., Lee, Y. I., Jin, Y., & Kim, S. (2020). Telling the tale: the role of narratives in helping people respond to crises. *Journal of Applied Communication Research*, 1–22.

Ma, L., & Zhan, M. (2016). Effects of attributed responsibility and response strategies on organizational reputation: A meta-analysis of situational crisis communication theory research. *Journal of Public Relations Research*, 28(2), 102–119.

Martínez-Cámara, E., M. Martínvaldivia, T., Ureñalópez, L. A., & Montejoráez, A. R. (2012). Sentiment analysis in Twitter. *Natural Language Engineering*, 1, 1–28. doi:10.1017/S1351324912000332.

McCullough, M. E., Emmons, R. A., & Tsang, J. A. (2002). The grateful disposition: A conceptual and empirical topography. *Journal of Personality and Social Psychology*, 82(1), 112.

McGuire, D., Cunningham, J. E., Reynolds, K., & Matthews-Smith, G. (2020). Beating the virus: An examination of the crisis communication approach taken by New Zealand Prime Minister Jacinda Ardern during the Covid-19 pandemic. *Human Resource Development International*, 23(4), 361–379.

Murthy, D., & Longwell, S. A. (2013). Twitter and disasters: The uses of Twitter during the 2010 Pakistan floods. *Information, Communication & Society*, 16(6), 837–855.

Oh, S. H., Lee, S. Y., & Han, C. (2020). The effects of social media use on preventive behaviors during infectious disease outbreaks: The mediating role of self-relevant emotions and public risk perception. *Health Communication*, 1–10.

Oh, S.-H., Paek, H.-J., & Hove, T. (2015). Cognitive and emotional dimensions of perceived risk characteristics, genre-specific media effects, and risk perceptions: The case of H1N1 influenza in South Korea. *Asian Journal of Communication*, 25, 14–32. doi:10.1080/01292986.2014.989240.

Ong, W. J. (2002). *Orality and literacy*. Orality and Literacy: The Technologizing of the Word, Routledge, NY.

S.-H., & Hove, T. (2016). How fear-arousing news messages affect risk perceptions and intention to talk about risk. *Health Communication*, 31(9), 1051–1062. doi: 10.1080/10410236.2015.1037419.

Pauchant, T. C., & Mitroff, I. I. (1992). *Transforming the crisis-prone organization: Preventing individual, organizational, and environmental tragedies*. Jossey-Bass, San Francisco, CA, p. 227.

Rana, S. (2018). Business performance: Earlier stage and looking forward. *FIIB Business Review*, 7(3), 153–155.

Rana, S. (2019). Moving in the realm of big data: Using analytics in management research and practices. *FIIB Business Review*, 8(1), 7–8.

Rana, S., Raut, S. K., Prashar, S., & Hamid, A. B. A. (2020). Promoting through consumer nostalgia: A conceptual framework and future research agenda. *Journal of Promotion Management*, 27(2), 211–249.

Rana, S., Raut, S. K., Prashar, S., & Quttainah, M. A. (2020). The transversal of nostalgia from psychology to marketing: What does it portend for future research? *International Journal of Organizational Analysis*. https://doi.org/10.1108/IJOA-03-2020-2097.

Raut, S. K., Sakpal, S., & Soni, R. (2022). Understanding the Service Quality Dimensions and Achieving Resilience in Service Retail. In *Handbook of Research on Supply Chain Resiliency, Efficiency, and Visibility in the Post-Pandemic Era* (pp. 136–156). IGI Global. https://doi.org/10.4018/978-1-7998-9506-0

Recuber, T. (2013). Disaster porn! *Contexts*, 12(2), 28–33.

Reynolds, B., & Seeger, M. W. (2005). Crisis and emergency risk communication as an integrative model. *Journal of Health Communication*, 10(1), 43–55. doi:10.1080/10810730590904571.

Schouten, A. P., Janssen, L., & Verspaget, M. (2020). Celebrity vs. Influencer endorsements in advertising: The role of identification, credibility, and Product-Endorser fit. *International Journal of Advertising*, 39(2), 258–281.

Seeger, M. W., & Sellnow, T. L. (2016). *Narratives of crisis: Telling stories of ruin and renewal*. Stanford University.

Seeger, M. W., Sellnow, T. L., & Ulmer, R. R. (2003). *Communication and organizational crisis*. Greenwood Publishing Group.

Sellnow-Richmond, D. D., George, A. M., & Sellnow, D. D. (2018). An IDEA model analysis of instructional risk communication in the time of Ebola. *Journal of International Crisis and Risk Communication Research*, 1(1), 7.

Senft, T. M. (2008). *Camgirls: Celebrity and community in the age of social networks* (Vol. 4). Peter Lang.

Senft, T. M. (2013). Microcelebrity and the branded self. *A Companion to New Media Dynamics*, 346–354.

Snyder, L. B., & Rouse, R. A. (1995). The media can have more than an impersonal impact: The case of AIDS risk perceptions and behavior. *Health Communication*, 7(2), 125–145.

Subrahmanyam, K., & Greenfield, P. M. (2008). Communicating online: Adolescent relationships and the media. *The Future of Children*, 18(1), 1–27.

Subrahmanyam, K., Reich, S. M., Waechter, N., & Espinoza, G. (2008). Online and offline social networks: Use of social networking sites by emerging adults. *Journal of Applied Developmental Psychology*, 29(6), 420–433.

Subrahmanyam, K., Smahel, D., & Greenfield, P. (2006). Connecting developmental constructions to the Internet: Identity presentation and sexual exploration in online teen chat rooms. *Developmental Psychology*, 42(3), 395.

Sutton, J., Spiro, E. S., Johnson, B., Fitzhugh, S., Gibson, B., & Butts, C. T. (2014). Warning tweets: Serial transmission of messages during the warning phase of a disaster event. *Information, Communication & Society*, 17(6), 765–787.

Tierney, K. J. (2007). From the margins to the mainstream? Disaster research at the crossroads. *Annual Review of Sociology*, 33, 503–525.

Tierney, K. J., Bevc, C., & Kuligowski, E. (2006). Metaphors matter: Disaster myths, media frames, and their consequences in Hurricane Katrina. *The Annals of the American Academy of Political and Social Science*, 604(1), 57–81.

Wang, C. C., & Wang, C. H. (2008). Helping others in online games: Prosocial behavior in cyberspace. *CyberPsychology & Behavior*, 11(3), 344–346.

Wright, M. F., & Li, Y. (2011). The associations between young adults' face-to-face prosocial behaviors and their online prosocial behaviors. *Computers in Human Behavior*, 27(5), 1959–1962.

Yang, S. U., Kang, M., & Johnson, P. (2010). Effects of narratives, openness to dialogic communication, and credibility on engagement in crisis communication through organizational blogs. *Communication Research*, 37(4), 473–497.

Zhang, L., Xu, L., & Zhang, W. (2017). Social media as amplification station: Factors that influence the speed of online public response to health emergencies. *Asian Journal of Communication*, 27(3), 322–338.

Index

Note: Page numbers in *italics* indicates figures and page numbers in **bold** indicates tables on the corresponding page.